JUST ASSASSINS

Just Assassins

The Culture of Terrorism in Russia

Edited and with an introduction by

Anthony Anemone

NORTHWESTERN UNIVERSITY PRESS
EVANSTON, ILLINOIS

Northwestern University Press
www.nupress.northwestern.edu

Printed in the United States of America

ISBN 978-0-8101-3443-0

The Library of Congress has cataloged the original, hardcover edition as follows:
Just assassins : the culture of terrorism in Russia / edited and with an introduction by Anthony Anemone.
p. cm.
Includes bibliographical references.
ISBN 978-0-8101-2692-3 (cloth : alk. paper)
1. Terrorism—Russia (Federation)—History. 2. Terrorism in literature. 3. Terrorism and mass media—Russia (Federation)—History. 4. Russian literature—History and criticism. 5. Russia (Federation)—Social conditions. 6. Russia (Federation)—Politics and government. I. Anemone, Anthony.
HV6433.R9J87 2010
363.3250947—dc22

2010008958

Contents

Acknowledgments

An earlier version of Sally A. Boniece's article appeared in *Kritika: Explorations in Russian and Eurasian History* ("The Spiridonova Case, 1906: Terror, Myth and Martyrdom," 4, no. 3 (2003): 571–606) and appears here by gracious permission of the publisher. An earlier version of Stephen Hutchings's essay, "Russia's 9/11: Performativity and Discursive Instability in Television Coverage of the Beslan Atrocity," was published in *Television and Culture in Putin's Russia: Remote Control,* ed. Stephen Hutchings and Natalia Rulyova (London: Routledge, 2009), 74–89. The editor is grateful to the publishers for their permission to reprint.

I would like to thank the editorial team at Northwestern University Press for their help in making this volume a reality. I am also grateful to the anonymous readers of the manuscript, whose suggestions challenged all of the contributors to make the most of their topics and, in the end, resulted in a stronger, tighter collection. I would especially like to thank my colleagues and collaborators in this venture for their hard work, talent, and patience. Thanks are also due to Amy for some crucial last-minute computer help. And most of all, to Vivian.

Editor's Note

Because this volume is intended both for general readers and specialists, we are using a hybrid form of transliteration. To make the text more readable, we have adapted and simplified the standard scholarly transliteration system. Personal names are usually given in their standard English form, if such exists: thus, Alexander instead of Aleksandr, Dostoevsky instead of Dostoevskii. In addition, we have simplified spellings when the "correct" transliteration would have resulted in unfamiliar or outlandish spellings: hence, Alyosha instead of Alesha and Yulia instead of Iuliia. For the same reason, we have avoided soft signs in the text. All references in the endnotes, however, are given in the standard Library of Congress transliteration system used by scholars.

TsGIAM (Tsentral'nyi gosudarstvennyi istoricheskii arkhiv v Moskve, Central State Historical Archive in Moscow)

TsGVIA (Tsentral'nyi gosudarstvennyi voenno-istoricheskii arkhiv, Central State Military Historical Archive), Moscow

GARF (Gosudarstvennyi arkhiv Rossiiskoi federatsii, State Archive of the Russian Federation), Moscow

TsGALI (Tsentral'nyi gosudarstvennyi arkhiv literatury i iskusstva, Central State Archive for Literature and Culture), St. Petersburg

GATO (Gosudarstvennyi arkhiv Tverskoi oblasti, State Archive for Tver' Region), Tver'

JUST ASSASSINS

Introduction: Just Assassins?

Anthony Anemone

Even in the best, most peaceful and secure of circumstances, the subject of terrorism is remarkably resistant to rational discourse. In the aftermath of major terrorist attacks on the American homeland, and in the midst of an ongoing "global war on terrorism" with no end in sight, devising a generally acceptable definition of terrorism would seem to be a hopeless task. As Charles Townshend has recently written, "When societies feel under threat, attempts at rational analysis are often openly resisted as giving aid and comfort to, or even sympathizing with, the enemy."[1] And yet it is precisely at such times that the effort to understand terrorism takes on an importance that transcends the merely historical or academic. For if terrorism represents the central threat facing early twenty-first-century America,[2] the challenges it presents cannot be met without thoroughly understanding its history, including how other societies have responded to the calamity of political violence. For these reasons, understanding Russia's historical experience of terror and terrorism is crucial for a contemporary American audience.

Indeed, Russia's tragic destiny has been to experience all the varieties of violence used to terrorize individuals or groups for political purposes:[3] palace coups and revolutionary conspiracies, targeted attacks on government officials and random attacks on civilians, "propaganda of the deed," state terror directed against entire classes and ethnic nationalities, double agents and agents provocateurs, "enhanced interrogation," public surveillance, and extrajudicial measures, including preventive detention, "extraordinary rendition," and assassination. While many specialized studies of political violence, revolutionary movements, and especially state terror in tsarist and Soviet history exist,[4] only very recently have scholars started looking at the many and complex ways in which terrorism has been represented in Russian culture.[5] The present collection of essays by leading American and British specialists in Russian history, literature, and media intends, at least in part, to fill this gap. By analyzing a wide range of responses to almost two hundred years of political violence in Russia by poets, novelists, filmmakers, dramatists, and journalists, as well as political thinkers, revolutionaries, soldiers, and terrorists, the contributors to *Just Assassins* hope to add to our understanding of the historical and cultural contexts in which modern terrorism evolved.

While the genealogies of complex phenomena like terrorism will always be contested and open to revision, the notion of terror as a political system was coined in late eighteenth-century France, where it referred to the revolutionary government's policy of "preemptive self-defense" against enemies, real, potential, or imagined: what was then called a "reign of terror" and today simply "state terror."[6] Of course, states have always claimed the right to use violence against internal enemies as a corollary to their power to make war against external enemies and by analogy with the right of an individual to self-defense. Indeed, Weber's notion of the state possessing "a legitimate monopoly of the use of physical force (i.e., violence) within a given territory" is one of the pillars of Western political theory.[7] And yet, when state violence goes unchecked or is used to deny a significant part of the population their human or civil rights, and when peaceful forms of protest and opposition are outlawed, the question inevitably arises: Do individuals or groups have the right to use violence to oppose or even overthrow the tyrannical government? And what kinds of violence are justifiable in the struggle for political rights and social justice?

Traditionally, the main restraint on tyranny was the ancient tradition that justified armed opposition against, and even assassination of, a ruler who, in behaving like a tyrant, lost all claim to legitimacy.[8] Palace coups and acts of regicide carried out and justified, or at least rationalized, in terms of the right to oppose a tyrannical and hence illegitimate tsar were a staple of the Russian monarchy between the reigns of Peter the Great and Alexander I.[9] But palace revolts, coups d'état, and assassinations were mostly about dynastic competition, succession struggles, the privileges of elite groups, and pure lust for political power and, despite the rhetoric of public welfare, were decidedly not ideological in nature.[10]

Terrorism, on the other hand, was born in very different soil in the 1860s in Russia. Frustrated by the slow pace of reform, government incompetence, police brutality, and the impossibility of legal political opposition, increasing numbers of young Russians, espousing ideological positions from nihilist to populist and socialist, convinced themselves that violence was the only way to achieve their political goals.[11] But nineteenth-century Russian terrorism, it must be stressed, was nothing like the random attacks against the noncombatant public and soft civilian targets of opportunity that have become so horribly familiar today. With the exception of a few figures such as Sergei Nechaev, Mikhail Bakunin, and Peter Tkachev,[12] most nineteenth-century Russian advocates of political violence construed legitimate targets quite narrowly and insisted that morality and justice were on their side. Terrorist attacks were intended to punish, intimidate, or eliminate particularly dangerous figures, including spies and double agents, to attract the attention of the people and raise their revolutionary spirit, to destabilize the government, and to destroy the illusion of an omnipotent and permanent monarchy. Those who took up guns and bombs against the tsarist government always insisted that violence was a tragic but necessary choice forced upon them by a tyrannical government that claimed a monopoly not only on physical force but on political activity as well. More than simply a tactic or part of a revolutionary ideology, Russian terrorism was based on a fanatical concern with social justice that demanded the ultimate self-sacrifice. Far from the contemporary image of the terrorist as *hostis humani generis* (enemy of mankind), Russian terrorists saw themselves as martyrs in the cause of freedom and justice:[13] "The terrorist is noble, terrible, irresistibly fascinating, for he combines in himself the two sublimities of human grandeur: the martyr and the hero. From the day he swears in the depths of his heart to free the people and the country, he knows he is consecrated to death. He goes forth to meet it fearlessly, and can die without flinching, not like a Christian of old, but like a warrior accustomed to look death in the face."[14] While an act of terrorism was always intended to provoke a revolutionary spark, it is sometimes unclear whose death was to supply the flame: the victim's or the terrorist's? Indeed, the spectacle of young, idealistic men and women sacrificing themselves in an unequal struggle with the vast resources of the tsarist police state won the terrorists of Narodnaia volia (the People's Will) and the Socialist Revolutionaries (SRs) a degree of sympathy and support in Russia and the West that is hard to credit today. Books describing Russian terrorists as heroes and martyrs were published to great popular acclaim in America, Europe, and Asia, and terrorists such as Vera Zasulich, Sergei Stepniak-Kravchinsky, Maria Spiridonova, and Boris Savinkov were received as heroes in Russian, European, and English drawing rooms.[15] As late as the 1950s, Albert Camus described the history of Russian terrorism as "the struggle of a handful of intellectuals to abolish tyranny, against a background of a silent populace. Their debilitated victory was finally betrayed. But by their sacrifice and even by their most extreme negations they gave substance to a new standard of values, a new virtue, which even today has not ceased to oppose tyranny and to give aid to the cause of true liberation."[16]

In recent decades, academic research on Russian terrorism has tended to downplay the idealism and to emphasize the criminality and even pathology of many participants in the terrorist movement.[17] This reevaluation of nineteenth-century Russian terrorism reflects a changed political atmosphere and, especially, contemporary revulsion at the use of violence for ideological purposes.[18] Nevertheless, to reduce the fifty-year struggle with tsarist despotism to nothing more than a misguided and criminal enterprise is to misuse historical hindsight and to distort the complex historical, political, and ethical issues that were at stake at the time. In rejecting the facile and predictable interpretations of the Right and the Left, the authors of the essays collected in this volume strive to recover the unique cultural and historical contexts in which different acts of the terrorist tragedy were performed in Russia, never losing sight of the question implied in the volume's title, *Just Assassins.*

If the first stirrings of individual terrorism in Russia date to the 1860s,[19] the intellectual roots of terrorism can be traced back to the effects on Russia of the French Revolution and the Napoleonic Wars. Disillusioned with Russia's backwardness and isolation from contemporary Europe, a group of young, highly educated, and aristocratic veterans of the victory over Napoleon organized several secret societies that eventually turned into the first recognizably modern conspiratorial movement to justify murder as part of a revolutionary plan to liberate Russian society. When Tsar Alexander I died suddenly on December 1, 1825, conspirators in St. Petersburg tried to take control of the brief interregnum by rallying their troops at the seat of government in Senate Square and demanding a constitution. This hastily arranged and poorly coordinated attempt at a coup d'état was, not surprisingly, easily put down by troops loyal to the new tsar Nicholas I, and the leaders of the rebellion were quickly arrested, interrogated by the tsar himself, tried, and sentenced. Five leaders of the Decembrists were sentenced to death, while 121 others were condemned to hard labor and exile in Siberia.[20]

When the wives of several leading Decembrists chose to share their husbands' fate in Siberian exile, a tragically botched revolt was transformed into myth.[21] Russian and Western writers and historians enshrined the affecting story of heroic young patriots selflessly sacrificing themselves in a doomed effort to liberate the Russian people as a foundational myth of the revolutionary struggle for democracy in Russia. Like most such ennobling myths, this version of the Decembrists omits some facts that, if they do not contradict the official version, certainly complicate it, notably the willingness of the more radical republicans among the Decembrists to execute "the Emperor and the whole imperial family to introduce a republican form of government."[22] Martin Miller has called the planned execution of the royal family "a combination of traditional regicidal theory and more contemporary revolutionary tactics rooted in the French experience of the 1790s."[23] Although regicide might not satisfy most modern definitions of terrorism, the Decembrists are critical to the birth of a terrorist ideology in Russia: the issues, techniques, and intellectual rationales (and rationalizations) that fueled their revolt were largely adopted by future revolutionaries whose struggle against Russian autocracy would eventually culminate in the revolution of 1917.[24] In "Historical Models of Terror in Decembrist Literature," literary historian Ludmilla A. Trigos examines the roots of the Decembrists' willingness to kill in the name of a political revolution. She locates the intellectual and cultural sources of regicide in the Decembrists' fascination with the heroic and self-sacrificing regicides of ancient Rome whom they knew from works by Cicero, Livy, Tacitus, Plutarch, Shakespeare, and Voltaire. Trigos's conclusion, that the classics of Western culture provided a rationale for the first Russian proponents of political violence, throws a provocative light on current debates on the origins of modern terrorism and its supposed incompatibility with democratic ideals. It also suggests the possibility that the willingness of at least some of the Decembrists to execute the tsar and the royal family in 1825 provided a model for the Bolsheviks' decision to kill Nicholas II and his family in the summer of 1918.[25]

In the years following the disaster of the Decembrist revolt, the slightest hint of political opposition was savagely repressed and forced underground, as Russia entered a deep freeze of reaction, stagnation, and isolation that ended only with the death of Nicholas I in 1855.[26] Nicholas's fanatical opposition not only to revolution but to all versions of political liberalism and his willingness to use Russian troops to repress unwelcome political trends in Europe earned him the sobriquet of "the gendarme of Europe." Despite the best efforts of Nicholas's secret police, the Third Department,[27] opposition to the status quo simmered beneath the surface of Russian society, mostly among young intellectuals and writers in Moscow and Petersburg. The placid surface of Russian life during Nicholas's long reign was periodically upset by the arrests of individuals and groups implicated in "subversive" activities such as reading, writing, or discussing books and poems forbidden by the government. In 1826, for example, the poet Alexander Polezhaev was sent into the army as punishment for writing a poem in sympathy with the Decembrists; in 1827, several Moscow University students were arrested and sent to prison or the army for distributing banned poems by Alexander Pushkin, Kondraty Ryleev, and Polezhaev; and in 1834, Alexander Herzen's friend Ogarev was arrested and exiled for singing the French revolutionary anthem "La Marseillaise" while drunk. Herzen himself was arrested and exiled at the same time when letters in which he wrote approvingly of French utopian socialism were found by the police in a search of Ogarev's belongings.[28]

From the perspective of Russian culture, the most significant of these episodes was the 1849 arrest of members of the Petrashevsky group, including the young Dostoevsky.[29] The criminal penalties meted out to the Petrashevtsy illustrate the fanatical harshness with which the government of Nicholas I treated the slightest divergence from orthodox thought. For circulating the banned text of the critic Belinsky's "Letter to Gogol," in which the great critic took the author of *Selected Passages from Correspondence with My Friends* to task for betraying the progressive and humanitarian ideals of his youth, Dostoevsky was originally sentenced to death by firing squad. Happily, his sentence was commuted to eight, and then to four, years of penal servitude in Siberia, to be followed by five years of army service. The irony is that the authorities never learned that Dostoevsky was actually involved with a secret cell within the Petrashevsky group that was considering using violence against the government.[30] Dostoevsky's abortive flirtation with revolutionary terrorism, his close brush with the firing squad, and his long years of Siberian punishment led him to a spiritual conversion that supplied him with the central theme of his mature novels, the conflict between means and ends in the lives of the Russian progressive intelligentsia in the second half of the nineteenth century.

The St. Petersburg that Dostoevsky returned to in the winter of 1859, after an absence of ten years, was a very different place, largely owing to Nicholas's successor on the throne, Alexander II. Convinced that Russia's isolation and backwardness had caused the humiliation of the Crimean War, the new tsar quickly committed himself to a policy of liberal modernization and reform that included relaxing censorship, reforming the military and police, creating new penal and judicial codes, establishing local self-government (*zemstva*), and, most important, emancipating the serfs.[31] But Alexander's liberal reform policies failed to satisfy an outspoken and increasingly intransigent opposition, which dreamed of the complete transformation of the Russian government, economy, and society. Inspired by radical literary critics such as Nikolai Chernyshevsky (1829–89), the nihilists, as Ivan Turgenev dubbed the young radicals of the 1860s in *Fathers and Sons* (1862), rejected all reform programs as "too little, too late" and supported a social revolution that would put real political and economic power in the hands of the people. They understood that, if successful, Alexander's reforms would result in a stronger monarchy, thereby diminishing the prospects of a social revolution. Similarly, they opposed the liberal dream of transforming Russia into a European-style democracy because they believed such a development would simply shift political power from the tsar to the educated and propertied classes.[32]

Historians of terrorism have often noted that liberalizing states often face a greater threat from terrorism than do repressive dictatorships.[33] The rapid radicalization of the political opposition during the early, liberal years of Alexander's reign bears out this apparent paradox: in the space of just five years, the opposition moved from direct appeals to the tsar to redress social wrongs (e.g., the 1858 appeal of the first Land and Freedom group to the tsar) to calls for an armed uprising of the people (e.g., the 1862 manifesto "Young Russia"). By 1864, the so-called Ishutin Organization was organizing the first plot against the life of the tsar, while the first actual attempt on the tsar's life occurred in 1866.[34] Although the shots fired at the tsar by Dmitry Karakozov on April 4, 1866, represented a desperate attempt by a disturbed and possibly suicidal young man and not the culmination of a real conspiracy,[35] they profoundly shocked the Russian government and, indeed, all of Russian society and signaled the beginning of a new, more violent period in Russian history.[36] The direct results of this act of political terror were the precise opposite of what both sides desired: Karakozov's shots simultaneously horrified liberals,[37] weakened the position of reformers within the government, and precipitated the White Terror, a vigorous police campaign against not only revolutionaries but also a much broader circle of the intelligentsia that, it was supposed, was the source of the ideas and rationale for opponents of the monarchy.[38] Within two years of Karakozov's ill-conceived assassination attempt, the police had succeeded in driving all political opposition underground, where, as had happened in the aftermath of the abortive Decembrist uprising, it gathered strength and grew more dangerous, violent, and intransigent.

Like Freud's return of the repressed, terrorism resurfaced in 1869 in the astonishing figure of Sergei Nechaev. A fantasist of revolution, a tireless conspirator, and a master manipulator, Nechaev was the most polarizing figure of the Russian revolutionary movement before Lenin. The author of the most notorious and extreme justification for terrorism ever written, *The Catechism of a Revolutionary*,[39] and an inspiration to violent revolutionaries ever since,[40] Nechaev was responsible for one of the greatest scandals of nineteenth-century Russian society, the murder in cold blood of a member of his own revolutionary conspiracy. Having organized a small group of young extremists into cells, Nechaev convinced his fellow conspirators that one of their group, the student Ivan Ivanov, was actually a police informant. Although Nechaev's motives are still in dispute today,[41] it is probable that the murder was intended, at least in part, to cement the loyalty of the conspirators to Nechaev. Although the police quickly solved the crime and arrested more than sixty members of the group, Nechaev himself escaped to Europe, where he continued his conspiracies until arrested by the Swiss police in the summer of 1872 and extradited to Russia to stand trial for murder. Duly convicted and sentenced to twenty years of hard labor in Siberia, Nechaev was considered so dangerous that the tsar secretly ordered, in violation of Russian law, that he be kept in solitary confinement in the dungeons of the Peter-Paul Fortress until his death.[42]

The facts of the Ivanov murder revealed during the public trial illustrated how the cold fanaticism, Machiavellian tactics, and complete amorality of *The Catechism of a Revolutionary* could be applied in revolutionary practice. Not only the government and liberal society but also much of the revolutionary-minded younger generation were shocked by Nechaev.[43] Despite the sympathy garnered by his impressive self-defense at his trial, Nechaev's immediate legacy was to discredit terror as a revolutionary tactic and to refocus, at least temporarily, the revolutionary movement on propaganda and education. Nechaev's importance to Russian culture derives from Dostoevsky's use of the Ivanov murder in his antiterrorist novel *Demons* (1873). Dostoevsky's treatment of terrorism in *Demons* supplies the subject of Val Vinokur's essay, "All of a Sudden: Dostoevsky's Demonologies of Terror." Vinokur challenges the facile assumption that literature contains the key to understanding terrorism and criticizes politically partisan readings of *Demons* as an antiterrorist novel *tout court*. In his view, the novel is not only a warning of the dangers of "any kind of political earnestness" but, like all great art, is more concerned with expanding our vision of the irreducible complexity of human experience than with making a narrow political point.

By the time *Demons* appeared in print, the mainstream of youthful opposition to the monarchy had already rejected violence and turned with religious intensity and dedication to propagandizing and educating the peasants and workers. At the height of this so-called "going to the people" movement (*khozhdenie v narod*), thousands of young Russians from the educated middle and upper classes went to live in peasant villages and workers' settlements, where they took menial jobs, taught in schools, provided basic medical care, and tried to serve the people's needs in whatever ways they could. Motivated by a desire to learn about the lives of the people and to exculpate their guilt as members of the privileged classes, they were also trying to overcome the centuries-old division in Russian society between the people and the intelligentsia. At the same time, their ultimate goal was to transform the people's indignation at the injustice and poverty of their lives into revolutionary consciousness. While some of these youthful idealists won over the local peasants by their obvious dedication and generosity, most were greeted with incomprehension or even outright hostility. Hearing the strangers' criticisms of the local landowner, priest, or tsar, the peasants often informed the local authorities about the shocking ideas of the newcomers, and sometimes delivered them into the hands of the police.[44] When word reached St. Petersburg about an inundation of revolutionaries in the countryside, the authorities panicked and responded in the precise way guaranteed to exacerbate the problem: mass arrests of thousands of idealistic young men and women.[45]

Disillusioned by the common people's hostility and the government's brutality, and buoyed by the growing sense of sympathy in educated society for their plight, the revolutionary movement convinced itself that conspiracy and terror against the tsar's government offered the only possible path to social change.[46] Once again, in other words, action taken by one side of the conflict led to the opposite of the intended reaction: the revolutionaries' turn from violence to education and propaganda resulted in more arrests, while the government's repression of nonviolent opposition created both a new generation of bolder, better organized, and more violent terrorists and more sympathy for them in liberal society.[47] Thus began a new campaign of terror, conducted, for the most part, by veterans of the disastrous "going to the people" movement. Beginning in 1878 with the shooting of the governor-general of St. Petersburg by Vera Zasulich and continuing with the assassination of the head of the secret police by Sergei Stepniak-Kravchinsky, this campaign would claim the lives of thousands on both sides of the conflict and come to its logical conclusion with the assassination of Tsar Alexander II on March 1, 1881, by terrorists of the People's Will. The dramatic and bloody events of these years are the focus of the essays by Donna Oliver, Peter Scotto, and James Frank Goodwin. In "Fool or Saint? Writers Reading the Zasulich Case," Donna Oliver describes the complex responses of Turgenev, Dostoevsky, and Tolstoy to the sensational trial of Vera Zasulich. Although there was no question of her guilt, the twenty-eight-year-old Zasulich so impressed the jury with her moral rectitude and tales of police brutality toward political prisoners that she was acquitted of shooting Governor-General Trepov in the most famous act of jury nullification until the O. J. Simpson trial. In "The Terrorist as Novelist," literary historian Peter Scotto brings to life the astonishing career of the notorious terrorist and best-selling author, Stepniak-Kravchinsky. Following the example of Zasulich, Stepniak-Kravchinsky killed General Mezentsev, the head of the Russian secret police, with a dagger in broad daylight in the center of downtown St. Petersburg. Stepniak-Kravchinsky escaped and spent the rest of his life in Europe, where he became a prolific and popular propagandist of the Russian revolutionaries' struggle against the tsar to foreign readers from Europe to America and Asia. In "The Afterlife of Terrorists," James Frank Goodwin explores the paradoxical legacy of the assassins of Alexander II in the early Soviet period. Goodwin shows how the turn to state terrorism in the Stalinist 1930s was accompanied by the transformation of the terrorists of the People's Will from "heroic martyrs" to enemies of Marxism and the Bolshevik Party.

In reaction to the extraordinary wave of terrorist activity of 1878–81, the tsar's government declared martial law, authorized the exile of suspected revolutionaries without a trial, and used courts-martial and summary executions against thousands of suspected revolutionaries. One of the great ironies of Russian history is that at the precise moment when the government of Alexander II was driven to consider a constitution that might have won it the support of mainstream Russian society and perhaps even ended the terror campaign, members of the People's Will finally succeeded in killing the "Tsar Liberator." Compounding the tragedy, the new tsar, under the influence of the ultra-reactionary supreme procurator of the Holy Synod Pobedonostsev, would scuttle the constitutional proposals of Interior Minister Loris-Melikov that had been approved by his father on the very day he was assassinated.[48] Within days of the assassination, the Executive Committee of the People's Will made their final political gesture by publishing *A Letter from the Executive Committee to Alexander III.* In this remarkable document, they described the revolutionary movement as the expression of "the general discontent of the people, the desire of Russia to bring it towards a new social system." Violence was the only way to struggle with a government that did not express the will of the people and had outlawed all normal political processes. In such a situation, the document went on, one of only two outcomes was possible, either revolution or "the voluntary transference [*obrashchenie*] of supreme power to the people." The letter concluded by listing the conditions under which they would disband their organization and renounce terrorism: a general amnesty for all political prisoners and free and universal elections for a national assembly that would work out a new system of government "in accordance with the desires of the people."[49]

Alexander III refused, of course, to negotiate with the terrorists who had murdered his father, and within a matter of weeks the networks of the People's Will were completely disrupted and almost the entire Executive Committee was in police custody. Subsequent attempts to reconstitute these networks were foiled by the police and, while the threat of terrorism persisted, the police were able to avert high-level assassinations for the rest of Alexander III's reign. The most significant plot against the emperor was foiled when the police arrested five young members of the People's Will on March 1, 1887, the sixth anniversary of the assassination of his father. One of those arrested and subsequently executed was the twenty-one-year-old Alexander Ulianov, older brother of Vladimir Ulianov, whose transformation into V. I. Lenin is often traced to the execution of his brother. One cannot doubt that Lenin was aware of the historical irony when, some thirty-one years later, it was his turn to order the execution of the eldest son of Alexander III, the former tsar Nicholas II, and his immediate family.[50]

In historical hindsight, it seems clear that the destruction of the People's Will was a Pyrrhic victory for the Russian government that only postponed its day of reckoning: although massive repression succeeded in driving the opposition underground, the government's brutality and failure to win its self-declared war on terrorism would eventually cost it the support of a significant part of educated society. This would prove especially debilitating in the years to come and would ultimately play a critical role in the fall of the monarchy in 1917. Meanwhile, beneath the placid surface of Russian life in the reign of Alexander III, opposition to the monarchy was growing, and violence would erupt once again during the reign of his successor, Nicholas II. In the years leading up to the revolution of 1905, the SR Combat Organization (Boevaia organizatsiia) played the leading role in a massive terror campaign against the government. Under the leadership of Grigory Gershuni, the double agent Evno Azef, and Boris Savinkov, terrorism grew to levels never before seen in Russia, and the government responded in kind. Thousands were killed on both sides, and many more wounded, maimed, jailed, and exiled. The essays by Lynn Ellen Patyk, Sally A. Boniece, and Tim Langen document the various ways that the unprecedented wave of terrorism in the first decade of the twentieth century was experienced and described by contemporaries. Historian Sally A. Boniece analyzes the creation of the Russian myth of female revolutionary martyrdom in a fascinating case study of Maria Spiridonova. Having shot and killed a government official responsible for the violent suppression of a peasant uprising, the twenty-one-year-old Spiridonova, like Vera Zasulich twenty-eight years earlier, became a veritable heroine to much of Russian society, eventually becoming known as the SR Blessed Virgin. Boniece's research is particularly important for the striking image it draws of educated Russian society's alienation from the government more than a decade before the fall of the monarchy in 1917. In "The Byronic Terrorist," literary historian Lynn Ellen Patyk tells the fascinating story of another mythical SR terrorist, Boris Savinkov. Like Stepniak-Kravchinsky, Savinkov was the author of several spectacular acts of terror against government ministers and members of the royal family, as well as of important memoirs and novels about the terrorist struggles. But while Savinkov's memoir contributed to the canonical image of the terrorist as a heroic and selfless champion of the people,[51] his novels, published under a pseudonym, represented the terrorist as an egotistical and cynical Nietzschean superman, devoid of any political or humanitarian values. Patyk explores how Savinkov's radically different presentations of the terrorist make sense in the context of the changing literary and cultural values of Russia's Silver Age. Finally, in "Andrei Bely's *Petersburg* and the Dynamics of Political Response," Timothy Langen reads a central text of Russian modernism as a critique of all sociopolitical accounts of the epidemic of revolutionary terrorism that plagued Russian society in the decade before 1917. Langen's conclusion that the attention to detail, openness to the unexpected, and willingness to listen that *Petersburg* demands of its readers represent the key to reconciliation in the political sphere is as relevant today as when Bely was writing.

In the years following the revolution of 1917, acts of terror by both opponents and supporters of the Bolshevik regime continued to play a critical role in Russian history. The assassination of Moisei Uritsky, head of the Petrograd secret police, and the attempted assassination of Lenin by a member of the SR Party in August 1918 set in motion the so-called Red Terror, in which thousands of real and potential political opponents of the Bolsheviks were arrested, tried by revolutionary tribunals, and executed.[52] But the Red Terror provoked an equally brutal White Terror during the civil war, whose end in 1921 marked the consolidation of Bolshevik rule. With Stalin's rise to power, terror was firmly established as a standard weapon to defend the regime from all enemies, real and imagined, as well as to manipulate, coerce, and control the civilian population. In "Exile's Vengeance: Trotsky and the Morality of Terrorism," historian Martin A. Miller uses Trotsky's writings to track the evolving position of the Bolsheviks on terrorism. Already the author of an influential Marxist critique of terrorism as a misguided and counterproductive revolutionary strategy, Trotsky returned to the question of terrorism in 1920, when he defended the Red Terror as a necessary policy of self-defense for the infant Soviet state. Years later, however, writing from his Mexican exile, Trotsky became one of the harshest critics of state terrorism as practiced by Stalin. More than simple hypocrisy, Trotsky's writings on terrorism suggest the extent to which views of legitimate and illegitimate violence are determined by one's historical and political perspective.

One of the unanticipated consequences of the dissolution of the Soviet Union in 1991 has been a rebirth of terrorism in Russia. Although often described by Russian government sources as another front in the global war on terrorism, the result of a global jihad of extremists intent on establishing an Islamic caliphate in the Greater Middle East, terrorism in Russia today has also been explained as a continuation of the historical struggle of the Chechen people for independence.[53] Although the proximate origins of the present conflict date to 1991, when Chechen separatists seized power from the communist government, its roots must be sought in long-standing Russian imperial policy in the Caucasus. Seeking to secure its southern border, Russian, Soviet, and post-Soviet governments have faced fierce resistance, religious revolts, and guerrilla warfare from the fiercely independence-minded Chechens.[54] The story of the Chechens' armed struggle against Russian imperialism is also documented both in classical and contemporary Russian literature[55] and, more recently, in the cinema.[56]

While Yeltsin fought the First Chechen War (1994–96) to keep Chechnya part of the Russian Federation, his successor, Vladimir Putin, presented the Second Chechen War (1999–2000) as part of the global war on terrorism. Indeed, the Second Chechen War was provoked by two mysterious acts of terrorism on Russian territory in late 1999. When explosions in two Moscow apartment buildings resulting in more than three hundred dead were blamed on Chechen terrorists, Putin was able to invade Chechnya with massive popular support. Astonishingly, these bombings have never been conclusively linked to any Chechen separatist groups, nor has any Chechen group ever claimed responsibility for them. In fact, many people in Russia and the West believe that the Russian intelligence service, the FSB (Federal Security Service), successor to the KGB, planted the bombs in order to create a *causus belli.* Unlike in the First Chechen War, when Chechens fought the Russian army to a bloody standstill, this time Russian forces were able to defeat organized resistance, although at great loss of Russian and Chechen lives, and to place local allies in power. Since the end of large-scale hostilities in 2000, the Putin government has been engaged in a low-intensity struggle with Chechen separatists and shadowy Islamic jihadists whose main weapon consists of acts of terror against civilians and security forces. In addition to the hundreds of thousands of Chechens and ten to fifteen thousand Russian soldiers killed during the two Chechen wars, more than one thousand civilians have been killed in terrorist operations on the territory of Russia and the Northern Caucasus in recent years.[57]

Four contributions to *Just Assassins* deal with representations of terrorism and the war on terrorism in post-9/11 Russian culture and media. British media critics Birgit Beumers and Stephen Hutchings analyze the responses to the two most horrific terrorist acts in post-Soviet history: the October 2002 attack on the Dubrovka Theater Center in Moscow, when more than

120 hostages and all the hostage-takers were killed in a botched rescue operation, and the September 2004 Beslan school tragedy, in which more than 300 hostages, including 186 children, and 31 terrorists were killed. Stephen Hutchings analyzes Russian television coverage of Beslan, "Russia's 9/11," in terms of the Russian government and media's struggle to create a new national identity to fill the vacuum left by the fall of Soviet communism. Hutchings locates a characteristic irony of contemporary Russian society and politics: while Beslan allowed postcommunist Russia to claim common cause with the West in a global crusade against Islamic terrorism, it could do so only by reverting to Soviet methods of press manipulation. In "Stage(d) Terrorism," Birgit Beumers provides a thorough account of the cultural significance of the terror attack on the Dubrovka Theater. By focusing on fictional "reenactments" of terrorist atrocities in contemporary Russian theater, film, and popular music, she contrasts fictional depictions that attempt to uncover the complex roots of terrorism and those that try to allay viewers' anxieties by assuring them the authorities can protect them from future acts of terror.

At the same time that many Russians feel under siege from an Islamic jihad, the Russian army has been accused of brutal war crimes and systematic violations of the human rights of Chechen civilians.[58] Since September 11, 2001, the Russian government has tried to gain international support and deflect criticism for human rights violations by arguing that the Chechen conflict is both an internal Russian affair and a critical front in the global war on terrorism. By analyzing interviews with soldiers, soldiers' songs, court cases, and popular movies, Anna Brodsky in "'Everyone Here Was Carrying Out Orders'" shows how the two Chechen wars have been experienced and described by foot soldiers and society at large.[59] She argues that contemporary Russian culture and society have shown a consistent and disturbing refusal to demand accountability and ascribe responsibility for what can only be called war crimes and atrocities committed against Chechen civilians. Even when they admit to atrocities committed against civilians, soldiers tend to see themselves—and to be seen by Russian civil society—as the real victims of a brutal and pointless war. Brian James Baer's article on Valery Todorovsky's 2004 feature film, *My Stepbrother Frankenstein,* is also concerned with the effects of the Chechen wars on the soldiers fighting them. Todorovsky's film tells the story of a wounded and traumatized veteran of the Chechen wars who terrorizes his family in order to protect them from the "ghosts" of Chechens he has killed. Baer reads *My Stepbrother Frankenstein* as a parable of one of the most disturbing and far-reaching psychological aspects of life in the post-9/11 world: the breakdown of the familiar dichotomies between war and peace, us and them, front and rear, civilian and soldier, hero and terrorist, soldier and war criminal. In rejecting the clichéd and simplistic visions of the global war on terrorism as a struggle between good ("us") and evil ("them"), Todorovsky and Baer invite us to consider how easily "we" can turn into "they."

Modern Russia's experience of all the possible varieties of political violence is relevant to every aspect of today's so-called global war on terrorism. A student of Russian history and culture cannot but be struck by the parallels and correspondences between Russia's past and the present that have been taking shape before our collective eyes since 9/11. Anyone interested in the intellectual origins of violent ideologies, the dangers of refusing to negotiate with one's enemies, the unanticipated consequences of political violence (whether undertaken by a government or a terrorist group), the deep historical roots of Islamic opposition to Western dominance in the Greater Middle East, the complex interplay between educated, "moderate" society and violent extremists, the problematic morality of political violence, the power of myths to influence and manipulate a society's understanding of history, or the reciprocal relationship between terror and repression will find much to consider in Russia's tragic and violent history over the past two hundred years. Perhaps the central message of *Just Assassins* is to remind us of the necessity of keeping our eyes and minds open to the irreducible complexity of the human experience, including the uses of violence for political purposes by states, individuals, and groups. Studying the representation of terrorism in Russian novels, films, poems, songs, plays, and television news coverage allows us to transcend the simplifications that increasingly have come to dominate the political and media discourse about terrorism in our world. While the authors of the essays collected here will disagree on many specific points of interpretation, their work illustrates the critical influence of culture and history on the development of terrorism in Russia. The lesson that terrorism always springs from a specific cultural and historical context is one that analysts of terrorism today ignore at their, and our, peril.

Notes

1. Charles Townshend, *Terrorism: A Very Short Introduction* (Oxford: Oxford University Press, 2002), 1–2.

2. Although there is no denying terrorism's dominance over the post-9/11 political landscape, many would argue that global climate change represents more of an existential threat to America's future than terrorism. See Albert Gore, *An Inconvenient Truth: The Crisis of Global Warming* (New York: Viking, 2007), and the 2006 Paramount Pictures film of the same name by Davis Guggenheim and Albert Gore.

3. One historian has gone so far as to write a history of Russia in terms of political violence; see Hélène Carrère d'Encausse, *The Russian Syndrome: One Thousand Years of Political Murder* (New York: Holmes and Meier, 1992).

4. Because terror and terrorism have played such a critical role in the nation's past, no history of Russia or the Soviet Union can be written without devoting considerable space to political violence. The essential starting point for the history of Russian terrorism is still Franco Venturi's magisterial *Roots of Revolution: A History of the Populist and Socialist Movements in Nineteenth-Century Russia* (New York: Knopf, 1960). Equally magisterial but less dispassionate politically, Adam Ulam's *In the Name of the People: Prophets and Conspirators in Prerevolutionary Russia* (New York: Viking, 1977) focuses on the 1860s and 1870s. Norman Naimark's *Terrorists and Social Democrats: The Russian Revolutionary Movement Under Alexander III* (Cambridge, Mass.: Harvard University Press, 1983) and Anna Geifman's *Thou Shalt Kill: Revolutionary Terrorism in Russia, 1894–1917* (Princeton: Princeton University Press, 1993) take up where Venturi leaves off. While the bibliography, scholarly and popular, on state terror in the Soviet period is enormous, the classic studies are by Roy Medvedev, *Let History Judge: The Origins and Consequences of Stalinism* (New York: Columbia University Press, 1989), Robert Conquest, *The Great Terror: A Reassessment* (New York: Oxford University Press, 1990), and, of course, the three volumes of Alexander Solzhenitsyn, *The Gulag Archipelago, 1918–1956: An Experiment in Literary Investigation* (New York: Harper and Row, 1974–78). On extrajudicial methods of the tsarist and Soviet secret police, see Richard Pipes, *The Degayev Affair: Terror and Treason in Tsarist Russia* (New Haven: Yale University Press, 2003), Charles Rudd and Sergei Stepanov, *Fontanka 16: The Tsars' Secret Police* (Montreal: McGill-Queen's University Press, 1999), George Leggett, *The Cheka: Lenin's Political Police* (Oxford: Oxford University Press, 1981), and Amy Knight, *The KGB: Police and Politics in the Soviet Union* (Boston: Unwin Hyman, 1990). For a sophisticated comparative history of the French reign of terror and state terror in the Soviet Union by one of the deans of modern European history, see Arno J. Mayer, *The Furies: Violence and Terror in the French and Russian Revolutions* (Princeton: Princeton University Press, 2000).

5. Two recent collections deserve mention here. *Times of Trouble: Violence in Russian Literature and Culture,* ed. Marcus C. Levitt and Tatyana Novikov (Madison: University of Wisconsin Press, 2007), includes essays on real and metaphorical violence in Russian history and literature from the Mongol invasion to the present day. The task of the editors and authors of *The Imprints of Terror: The Rhetoric of Violence and the Violence of Rhetoric in Modern Russian Culture,* ed. Anna Brodsky, Mark Lipovetsky, and Sven Spieker (Vienna: Wiener Slawistischer Almanach, 2006), was to illustrate how twentieth-century Russian writers such as Babel, Zoshchenko, Platonov, Kharms, Nabokov, Solzhenitsyn, and Shalamov and filmmakers such as Sokurov "deconstruct" the violence of the Soviet utopia and its official literature.

6. According to the *Oxford English Dictionary,* the first use in English of "terrorism" in the meaning of "government by intimidation" can be dated to 1795, while the phrase "reign of terror" occurred for the first time in 1801. Martin Miller, however, points out that the term "reign of terror" is actually used in Tacitus's *Annals.* See Miller, "The Intellectual Origins of Modern Terrorism in Europe," in *Terrorism in Context,* ed. Martha Crenshaw (University Park: Pennsylvania State University Press, 1995), 29.

7. Max Weber, *The Vocation Lectures: Science as a Vocation, Politics as a Vocation* (Indianapolis: Hackett, 2004), 33.

8. See Miller, "Intellectual Origins," 28–32, and Greg Woolf, *Et Tu, Brute? A Short History of Political Murder* (Cambridge, Mass.: Harvard University Press, 2007).

9. Cynthia Hyla Whittaker, *Russian Monarchy: Eighteenth-Century Rulers and Writers in Political Dialogue* (DeKalb: Northern Illinois University Press, 2003).

10. Brian Taylor, *Politics and the Russian Army: Civil-Military Relations, 1689–2000* (Cambridge: Cambridge University Press, 2003).

11. "Hundreds and hundreds of these men, themselves the offspring of privilege, go 'among the people,' carrying with them the Gospel of Socialism, the very object of which is the destruction of privileges, the privileges of the class from which they have sprung. Every fresh trial only displays more clearly their heroism and their historical mission. The Russian Government has recourse to extreme measures of repression. It places all Russia under a state of siege, and covers it with gibbets. It almost forces harmless agitators to take up deadly weapons and commence the Terrorist struggle." Peter Lavrov, preface to Sergei Stepniak (S. M. Kravchinsky), *Underground Russia: Revolutionary Profiles and Sketches from Life* (New York: Charles Scribner's Sons, 1892), xi.

12. Venturi deals with all three in *Roots of Revolution,* 354–468. On Bakunin, see Aileen Kelly, *Mikhail Bakunin: A Study in the Psychology and Politics of Utopianism* (New Haven: Yale University Press, 1987). The best sources in English on Nechaev and Tkachev are still Philip Pomper's *Sergei Nechaev* (New Brunswick, N.J.: Rutgers University Press, 1979) and Deborah Hardy's *Peter Tkachev: The Critic as Jacobin* (Seattle: University of Washington Press, 1977).

13. Daniel Brower analyzes the process by which self-sacrifice and martyrdom came to define the mentality of Russian terrorists, who increasingly saw themselves as warrior-crusaders bent on vengeance for the violence done to their comrades by the government. See Brower, "Nihilists and Terrorists," in Levitt and Novikov, *Times of Trouble,* 91–102. See also the essays by Sally A. Boniece, Donna Oliver, and Martin A. Miller in the present volume.

14. Stepniak (S. M. Kravchinsky), *Underground Russia,* 39–40.

15. For more on the terrorist as celebrity, see the essays by Peter Scotto, Sally A. Boniece, James Frank Goodwin, and Donna Oliver in the present volume, and Stephen Marks, *How Russia Shaped the World: From Art to Anti-Semitism, Ballet to Bolshevism* (Princeton: Princeton University Press, 2003).

16. Albert Camus, *The Rebel: An Essay on Man in Revolt* (New York: Vintage, 1992), 149–50. It was not only French philosophers who were caught up in the spell of the Russian terrorists, even decades after their heyday. Robert Payne, the American author of popular books on revolutionaries, for example, compared them to "the Puritans of New England with their strict codes, their icy belief in Messianic revelations and their determination to put the witches and unbelievers, 'those enemies of the Most High God,' out of existence." *The Terrorists: The Story of the Forerunners of Stalin* (New York: Funk and Wagnalls, 1957), xvi.

17. See, for example, Pipes, *Degayev;* Ulam, *Name;* and Geifman's *Thou Shalt Kill* and *Entangled in Terror: The Azef Affair and the Russian Revolution* (Wilmington, Del.: SR Books, 2000).

18. To expect that revolutionary groups such as the People's Will and the Socialist Revolutionary Combat Organization, or indeed the tsarist secret police, would not include both idealists and cynics, dreamers and criminals, would be naive and unrealistic. Pomper's point that "revolutionary leaders do not have the luxury of choosing exclusively high-minded types for the tasks ahead of the organization" is equally true for governmental leaders, police chiefs, and heads of national security services. Philip Pomper, "Russian Revolutionary Terrorism," in *Terrorism in Context,* 63–101, 74.

19. Venturi, *Roots of Revolution,* 285–302, 331–53.

20. For a standard account of the Decembrist revolt, see Anatole Mazour, *The First Russian Revolution, 1825* (Stanford: Stanford University Press, 1937). For a standard Soviet treatment of the Decembrists, see M. V. Nechkina, *Dvizhenie dekabristov* (Moscow: Akademiia Nauk, 1955).

21. See Christine Sutherland, *The Princess of Siberia: The Story of Maria Volkonsky and the Decembrist Exiles* (New York: Farrar, Straus and Giroux, 1984), and Anatole Mazour, *Women in Exile: Wives of the Decembrists* (Tallahassee, Fla.: Diplomatic Press, 1975).

22. *Vosstanie dekabristov: Materialy i dokumenty. Dela verkhovnogo suda i sledstvennoi komissii,* ed. A. A. Pokrovskii, M. N. Pokrovski, et al., 19 vols. (Moscow, 1925–2001), 10:243. For an excellent account of the planned regicide, see Patrick O'Meara, *The Decembrist Pavel Pestel: Russia's First Republican* (New York: Palgrave/Macmillan, 2003), 141–60. O'Meara describes the suicide squad (*cohorte perdue*) that was to carry out the killings as "an intriguingly modern terrorist tactic" and the plot as "ingeniously cynical and utterly callous, a scheme worthy indeed of the Stalin era" (144–47).

23. Miller, "Intellectual Origins," 34. Other writers about the Decembrists have also made the connection between the Decembrists and Russian terrorists of the late nineteenth century. See, for example, Peter Lavrov's introduction to the second edition of his *Historical Letters* (Berkeley and Los Angeles: University of California Press, 1967), 69.

24. In the Decembrists, "one can discern prefigurations of the later attitudes and conflicts of the revolutionary intelligentsia. Pestel, in particular, evokes comparison with later figures in what is often described as the Jacobin tradition, Lenin being the heir." Pomper, *Revolutionary Intelligentsia,* 22.

25. "What made Pestel's proposal so shocking to his peers and judges was the cold, premeditated murder of the entire imperial house, only the second dynasty in the history of Russia. The scale of the intended carnage was without precedent and would be finally inflicted on Alexander I's descendants in an act of unparalleled barbarity by the Bolsheviks in July 1918." O'Meara, *The Decembrist Pavel Pestel,* 142.

26. See W. Bruce Lincoln, *Nicholas I: Emperor and Autocrat of All the Russias* (Bloomington: Indiana University Press, 1978).

27. The standard works on the secret police in the reign of Nicholas I are Sidney Monas, *The Third Section: Police and Society in Russia Under Nicholas I* (Cambridge, Mass.: Harvard University Press, 1961), and I. M. Trotskii, *Tret'e otdelenie pri Nikolae I* (Leningrad: Lenizdat, 1930). For the most detailed study of the secret police's attempt to stifle opposition among writers and the intelligentsia, see M. K. Lemke, *Nikolaevskie zhandarmy i literatura 1826–1855* (St. Petersburg, 1908; rpt, The Hague, 1966). For a recent Russian history of the Third Department reflecting the very different values of Putin's post-Soviet Russia, see Igor' Simirtsev, *Tret'e otdelenie: Pervyi opyt sozdaniia professional'noi spetssluzhby v Rossiiskoi imperii, 1826–1880* (Moscow: Tsentropoligrad, 2006).

28. Martin Malia, *Alexander Herzen and the Birth of Russian Socialism* (New York: Grosset and Dunlap, 1965), 134–50.

29. Joseph Frank, *Dostoevsky: The Seeds of Revolt, 1821–1849* (Princeton: Princeton University Press, 1976), 239–91, and *Dostoevsky: The Years of Ordeal, 1850–1859* (Princeton: Princeton University Press, 1983), 6–17.

30. Frank, *Dostoevsky: The Years of Ordeal,* 8–9.

31. For an excellent study of the period of the Great Reforms, see W. Bruce Lincoln, *In the Vanguard of Reform: Russia's Enlightened Bureaucrats, 1825–1861* (Dekalb: Northern Illinois University Press, 1982).

32. Venturi, *Roots of Revolution,* 145–86; Ulam, *Name,* 53–138.

33. This apparent paradox reflects not only the fact that ruthless dictatorships are better equipped to eliminate enemies of the state but also the powerful and unpredictable effect of rising expectations of change in democracies, especially in times of reforms. See Paul Wilkinson, *Terrorism Versus Democracy: The Liberal State Response* (London: Frank Cass, 2001).

34. See Venturi, *Roots of Revolution,* 253–353, and Ulam, *Name,* 95–168.

35. Claudia Verhoeven, *The Odd Man Karakozov: Imperial Russia, Modernity and the Birth of Terrorism* (Ithaca, N.Y.: Cornell University Press, 2009).

36. A first sign of the increasing violence can be observed in the interrogation of the would-be assassin. As described in Herzen's *Kolokol,* Karakozov was interrogated around the clock and subjected to sleep deprivation, beatings, forced feeding to combat a hunger strike, and electrical shock. Cited in Pomper, *Nechaev,* 45.

37. Herzen's famous response, "Only among savage and decadent nations is history made by assassinations," is quoted in Ulam, *Name,* 359.

38. For more on the reaction of the secret police to the increasing threat from terrorists in the 1860s, see Rudd and Stepanov, *Fontanka,* 16–37.

39. A. Shilov, "Katekhizis revoliutsionera (K istorii nechaevskogo dela)," *Borba klassov,* no. 1–2 (1924): 268–72. A partial English translation can be found in Basil Dmytryshyn, ed., *Imperial Russia: A Source Book, 1700–1917* (Hinsdale, Ill.: Dryden Press, 1974), 303–8. A complete translation can be found online at http://www.spunk.org/library/places/russia/sp000116.txt (accessed June 10, 2007).

40. Eldridge Cleaver, the Black Panther minister of information, famously wrote, "I fell in love with Bakunin and Nechaev's *Catechism of the Revolutionist*—the principles of which, along with some of Machiavelli's advice, I sought to incorporate into my own behavior. I took the *Catechism* for my bible." Eldridge Cleaver, *Soul on Ice* (New York: Dell, 1992), 25.

41. For a convincing psychological portrait of the man and explanation of Nechaevism in terms of the politics of revenge, see Pomper, *Nechaev.* In a recent detailed biographical study, a Russian historian explains Nechaev as a reaction to the extreme social injustice of Russian society in the second half of the nineteenth century. See F. M. Lur'e, *Nechaev: Sozidatel' razrusheniia* (Moscow: Molodaia gvardiia, 2001).

42. For a dramatic account of Nechaev's arrest in Switzerland, extradition to Russia, trial, conviction, imprisonment, and death in the Peter-Paul Fortress, see Pomper, *Nechaev,* 167–215.

43. "Later Russian revolutionaries almost universally condemned Nechaev's methods, an attitude they expressed in typical Russian fashion by adding to his name the suffix '*shchina.*' '*Nechaevshchina*' signified primitivism and unscrupulousness in revolutionary politics." Pomper, *Nechaev,* 216.

44. See Derek Offord, *The Russian Revolutionary Movement in the 1880s* (Cambridge: Cambridge University Press, 1986), 1–35.

45. Venturi, *Roots of Revolution,* 469–506.

46. "Everyone in Russia who is alive, everyone who is filled with the determination to fight intellectual corruption, social indifferentism, the archaic institutions of Russian absolutism, and capitalist exploitation in the entire civilized world—everyone

who had preserved the great ideological tradition of the Russian intelligentsia and who has come to understand the still more mighty practical tasks of scientific socialism—is forced to return to the cautious, conspiratorial work of underground groups." Lavrov, *Historical Letters,* 70.

47. Among the many firsthand accounts of the turn from propaganda to terrorism, see Vera Figner, *Memoirs of a Revolutionist* (Dekalb: Northern Illinois University Press, 1991), and Vera Broido, *Apostles into Terrorists: Women and the Revolutionary Movement in the Russia of Alexander II* (New York: Viking, 1977).

48. For a detailed account of the government's panicked response to the terrorist threat and the complicated struggle between progressive and reactionary advisers to the new tsar, see two books by Peter A. Zaionchkovsky, *The Russian Autocracy Under Alexander III,* ed. and trans. David R. Jones (Gulf Breeze, Fla.: Academic International Press, 1976), and *The Russian Autocracy in Crisis: 1878–1882,* ed. and trans. Gary M. Hamburg (Gulf Breeze, Fla.: Academic International Press, 1979), esp. 190–240.

49. Dmytryshyn, *Imperial Russia,* 309–16.

50. Dmitry Volkogonov conjectures that, when he was considering the fate of Nicholas II, Lenin was thinking not only of his brother but also of Nechaev, who had supported the idea of executing the entire Romanov family in the event of a successful revolution. *Lenin: A New Biography* (New York: Free Press, 1994), 206–10. It is possible, of course, that he was also thinking of the Decembrist Pestel's plan to execute the royal family.

51. Boris Savinkov, *Memoirs of a Terrorist* (New York: Albert and Charles Boni, 1931).

52. S. P. Mel'gunov, *Krasnyi terror v Rossii, 1918–1923* (New York: Izd. Brandy, 1979). Originally published in Berlin in 1923, this first historical account of the Red Terror has not lost its value in the years since.

53. "In truth, Imam Shamyl's war never really ended. It was merely stifled by Russian power. Whenever that power weakened—in 1877, 1905, 1917 and 1990—the peoples of the Eastern Caucasus became restive. Dzohar Dudayev, president of the self-proclaimed Chechen republic in the early 1990s, spoke of continuing the 'three hundred years of struggle with Russia.'" Philip Marsden, foreword to Lesley Blanch, *The Sabres of Paradise: Conquest and Vengeance in the Caucasus* (London: Tauris Parke, 2004), ix–x.

54. For the historical background to this conflict, see Ben Fowkes, ed., *Russia and Chechnia: Essays on Russo-Chechen Relations* (London: Macmillan, 1998), and Robert Seely, *Russo-Chechen Conflict, 1800–2000: A Deadly Embrace* (London: Frank Cass, 2001).

55. For two very different studies of Russian literature on the Caucasus, see Susan Layton, *Russian Literature and Empire: The Conquest of the Caucasus from Pushkin to Tolstoy* (Cambridge: Cambridge University Press, 1994), and Harsha Ram, *The Imperial Sublime: A Russian Poetics of Empire* (Madison: University of Wisconsin Press, 2003).

56. In addition to Valerii Todorovskii's 2004 film, *My Stepbrother Frankenstein,* analyzed in this volume by Brian James Baer, the best recent films about Chechnya include Sergei Bodrov's *Prisoner of the Caucasus* (1996), Aleksandr Rogozhin's *Checkpoint* (1998), Vladimir Khotinenko's *The Muslim* (2000), and Aleksei Balabanov's *War* (2002).

57. For an up-to-date account of the ongoing struggle, see James Hughes, *Chech-*

nya: From Nationalism to Jihad (Philadelphia: University of Pennsylvania Press, 2008). For diametrically opposed visions of the ultimate meaning of the Chechen conflict, see Tony Wood, *Chechnya: The Case for Independence* (London: Verso, 2007), and Jossef Bodansky, *Chechen Jihad: Al-Qaeda's Training Ground and the Next Wave of Terror* (New York: Harper, 2008).

58. For an invaluable journalistic record of the human cost of the struggle, see Anna Politkovskaya, *The Dirty War* (London: Harvill, 2004), and *A Small Corner of Hell: Dispatches from Chechnya* (Chicago: University of Chicago Press, 2007).

59. For a firsthand account of the Chechen struggle by a veteran of both wars, see Arkady Babchenko, *One Soldier's War in Chechnya,* trans. Nick Allen (London: Portobello Books, 2007).

Historical Models of Terror in Decembrist Literature

Ludmilla A. Trigos

> Every attempt to solve the social question with political means leads into terror.
>
> —HANNAH ARENDT

On December 14, 1825, a small group of noblemen and elite officers led their troops into Senate Square in St. Petersburg in an attempt to overthrow the autocracy and abolish serfdom.[1] Taking advantage of the confusion resulting during the interregnum after the death of Alexander I, who left no offspring to inherit the throne, the rebels played on the troops' sympathy for Tsarevich Constantine, Alexander's younger brother and the assumed heir, and demanded his purportedly rightful ascension, in opposition to the claim of Nicholas, third brother in line to the throne. They rallied the troops behind the slogan "Constantine and a Constitution," though they had bigger plans for a change in power. Later known as the Decembrists, this group consisted of a Northern Society, with its members located in St. Petersburg, and a Southern Society, based in regiments in Tulchin, Poltava, and Chernigov, Ukraine. The northern group for the most part advocated for a constitutional monarchy and gradual political reform, while the southern group demanded more rapid and radical change and wanted to establish a republican form of government. The revolt in Petersburg was quashed in relatively short order after the new tsar, Nicholas, commanded his troops to fire on their rebel comrades. Ten days later the southern group learned of the uprising in the north; after their leaders were arrested, they gathered forces to free them, and then rebelled against the authorities. By January 3, 1826, this revolt too had been subdued, as it had little support among locals or the military. The perpetrators were sent to the Peter-Paul Fortress and joined their Northern Society colleagues, who were already incarcerated and undergoing questioning by the tsar to determine the extent of the sedition and treason against the state. After a lengthy investigative process lasting into May 1826, the participants were assigned different levels of guilt, with 121 sentenced to penal servitude or exile, or both. The lower-ranking rebels had to run the gauntlet and, if they survived, were demoted and sent to serve in the war in the Caucasus. The five considered most guilty because of their leadership and espousal of regicide—Kondraty Ryleev (1795–1826), Colonel Pavel Pestel (1799–1826), Lieutenant Colonel Sergei Muraviev-Apostol (1795–1826), Lieutenant Mikhail Bestuzhev-Riumin (1801–26), and Petr Kakhovsky (1799–1826)—were sentenced to death by hanging and executed on July 13, 1826.[2]

The Decembrists' conspiracy arose out of a combination of traditions: the native Russian tradition of palace coups supported by military force and the classical tradition of Greco-Roman tyrants dethroned according to the doctrine of *melior pars,* founded on the principle that small elite groups (such as noblemen at the court, highly placed military officers, or senators) "would recognize an obligation to act on behalf of the community as a whole" and would oppose, depose, or assassinate a ruler if necessary.[3] As the Decembrist Mikhail Lunin (1787–1845) pointed out during his testimony to the Investigating Commission, "the idea of regicide is not new in Russia; there are some quite recent examples of it."[4] Lunin obviously recalled the eighteenth-century palace coups led by guards' officers to secure the crown for a different ruler, but he was actually hinting at more recent examples: the overthrow and murder of Paul I in 1801, in which two members of the Investigating Commission had participated and which put Alexander I on the throne, and the coup d'état and subsequent regicide of Peter III, Alexander I's grandfather, which brought his grandmother, Catherine the Great, to the throne in 1762. In both cases the change in power was justified as the replacement of a tyrannical, unfit tsar by a more appropriate and better-equipped ruler, as Cynthia Whittaker has amply demonstrated. Whittaker suggests that in the post-Petrine era, the legitimacy of each successor to the throne became a hotly contested issue, and points out that between 1725 and 1801 four coups d'état took place, two of which involved assassination. In each case the deed was justified as the replacement of an unfit ruler. Although a coup was considered acceptable under certain conditions, palace revolutions were not free-for-alls but instead had specific rules that needed to be followed. When those rules were abrogated, Whittaker says, problems resulted, which usually led to yet another change in power.[5]

The demise of Alexander I and the subsequent interregnum laid the groundwork for another succession crisis. The Decembrists were well aware of the history of pretenders, palace coups, and peasant uprisings that frequently accompanied uncertainties in the order of succession. In planning their own action the Decembrists also exploited the uncertainty during the interregnum to attempt a change in power. Drawing the contrast between earlier participants in palace coups and his colleagues, Lunin claimed that the Decembrists' "aim was nobler and higher."[6] Though the Investigating Commission wrongly sought to portray the group as a whole as regicides to deflect public disapproval of their harsh sentence (as Decembrist A. N. Muraviev [1792–1863] insisted), the Decembrists' ultimate goal was the greater good of Russia through eradication of the autocracy and the elimination of serfdom. Throughout their enterprise, incarceration, and exile, the Decembrists continually emphasized their loyalty to country over loyalty to the tsar. The Decembrists thus mark a turning point in the evolution of Russian traditions of revolution and of terrorism; they sit between the court assassins executing a palace coup to substitute a preferred ruler for a disliked one without the goal of broad political change and latter-day terrorists targeting the tsar and other imperial officials to bring down the entire autocratic system. That the Decembrists attempted to put together a plan for the government that would come after their revolution and sought to prevent mass revolt and bloodshed distinguishes them as well. Here we see a paradigm shift in ways of looking at regicide and revolution, patriotism and civic duty that would influence generations to come.

The Decembrists have been posited as forefathers of the Russian revolutionary movement by Russian and Western scholars alike. The conceptualization of their ancestral role began with the writings of Alexander Herzen, who thought of himself as assuming the Decembrists' standard, and continued with Lenin's statements in 1912, thus becoming a hallmark of Soviet scholarship throughout the twentieth century. Lenin dictated the general outlines of what became the canonical interpretation of the Decembrists' legacy in Russian history: the Decembrists were the most progressive members of society of the time, but they were limited by their class outlook and interests and so could not gain the support of the people to overthrow the monarchy and abolish serfdom. Because of that lack of mass support, they did not have the ability to carry out a successful revolution. However, according to Lenin, since they were the first to take up arms against the government to change the ruling order, they were to be honored as the progenitors of the Bolsheviks, the only ones who could inherit their mantle.[7] The writings of Militsa Nechkina, the reigning Soviet historian who studied the Decembrists, further elaborated and preserved that interpretation.[8] Given the Decembrists' primary place in Russian revolutionary history during the Soviet period, much effort has been spent perusing the Decembrists' writings and personal papers to find proto-Bolshevik ideas that could then be traced through the revolutionary genealogy to their rightful and accepted heirs. This mode of thinking justified the historical process that culminated in the victory of the Bolsheviks in October 1917. One of the keystones of this trend was the radical agrarian program favored by the military officer and Decembrist leader Pavel Ivanovich Pestel that would have redistributed land to emancipated serfs immediately after the eradication of serfdom. The other was that several Decembrists proposed regicide, though they never acted on their plans.

The Decembrists did not espouse or practice terrorism per se, though they did employ elements of the terrorist arsenal, such as conspiring to bring down the current form of government and discussing the assassination of the tsar and his family. As Walter Laqueur suggests, there are several problems inherent in the study of terrorism, ranging from the lack of an agreed-upon comprehensive definition to recognition that the methods, aims, and character of terrorism have altered and evolved, especially over the past century. In addition, he notes that terrorism is not a philosophy but an "insurrectional strategy" that can be used by widely different groups for various ends.[9] In the Decembrists' case, then, we can consider them proto-terrorists in their "insurrectional strategy," which favored certain terroristic methods. The history of terrorism and its use in the Russian revolutionary tradition frequently engenders an anachronistic treatment whereby some scholars look to the practice of terrorism by revolutionaries in the latter half of the nineteenth century and early part of the twentieth century, then cast their glance backward to earlier generations of revolutionaries. Rather than taking a retroactive look at the Decembrists and their thoughts on terror through the prism of Russian terrorism of the latter half of the nineteenth century, I ground my discussion of the Decembrists in their own historical context to illuminate the historical models that influenced them in their thinking about terrorism and its components. My work both draws from and expands upon the work of M. P. Odessky, D. M. Feldman, and Yury Lotman, who have written about the variety of historical sources available to the Decembrists within larger discussions, respectively, of the poetics of terror and nineteenth-century culture.[10]

As Odessky and Feldman point out, though theories of terror came into being during antiquity, the word *terror* "entered into the political lexicon" only during the French Revolution.[11] E. V. Walter, however, rightly stresses that the classical tradition, especially the works of Cicero, Livy, and Plutarch, provided the men of the French Revolution with a "history of the concept of terror."[12] In addition to their knowledge of Russian history, the study of antiquity similarly provided the Decembrists with examples of tyrants dethroned and assassinated, instances in which tyranny's elimination was portrayed as a noble and just cause and the rule of despotic kings was excoriated as tyranny.[13] French Enlightenment thinkers drew on ancient sources for their own conceptualization of political organization and terror. Indeed, the Comte de Volney, who lived through the French Revolution and analyzed it in his *Leçons d'histoire* (1795), insisted that the excesses of the Terror could be attributed to the Jacobins' readings of classical authors, specifically Livy, Sallust, and Plutarch.[14]

Taking their inspiration from ancient Rome and the French Revolution, the Decembrists cast themselves as fighters against tyranny in their use of force against the autocratic state. As Lotman has argued, the Decembrists conducted themselves differently from the typical nineteenth-century Russian nobleman, patterning their gestures and deeds on those of characters in heroic texts. Though a sense of the individual's historical significance was common among the Russian elite during the nineteenth century, the Decembrists took this mode of thinking into a new sphere of action and extracted their models from a different set of texts than before, distinguishing themselves by their seriousness as manifested in "Roman" or "Spartan" linguistic behavior and shunning frivolous societal pursuits such as cards, dancing, and patronizing bordellos. Their unwillingness to occupy themselves with the empty trivialities of the usual elite lifestyle gave them time to concentrate on important political questions, even though their ideas would not be enacted because of the Russian monarchy's antipathy to questioning of its authority or actions. As Lotman puts it,

> Viewing real life as a performance not only offered a person the possibility of choosing his type of individual behavior, but also filled it with the expectation that things were going to happen. Eventfulness [*siuzhetnost'*], that is, the possibility that unexpected phenomena and turns of events would happen, became the norm. It was precisely the awareness that any political turn of events was possible that shaped the sense of life that young people had in the early nineteenth century. The revolutionary consciousness of the younger generation of the nobility had many sources. Psychologically it was prepared in part by the habit of looking at life "theatrically." It was precisely the model of theatrical behavior that, by turning a person into a character in a play, liberated him from the automatic sway of group behavior and of custom.[15]

Lotman's discussion of the duality of behavior seen among those of the Decembrists' generation is especially appropriate here. The interpenetration of poetry and life, of literary texts and new real-life contexts, provided an entire generation with productive sources for their self-fashioning. So, even though the nobleman could indulge in a type of "aesthetic game-playing" and take on the role of "a Cato, a Brutus, a Pozharsky, a Demon and a Melmoth," all the same he "never stopped being simultaneously a Russian nobleman of his time, no more and no less."[16]

The Decembrists' self-conceptualization greatly influenced both their aesthetic production and their thinking about violence, power, and revolution. Laqueur may well have been the first to suggest that literature gives greater insight into the terrorist mentality and terrorism than political science.[17] This suggestion is especially applicable to the romantic era, when intergeneric dialogue, to use Andrew Wachtel's term, so strongly wove together the lives of writers with their literary representations and their writing of history.[18] That the Decembrists saw themselves as historical actors on the world stage, as Lotman persuasively argues, is evident in their writing about past historical events. Moreover, they could try on various stances of political resistance as they explored Russian and ancient history for appropriate models. Thus, the act of writing, or narrative plotting, became intimately tied to a different kind of plotting, such as the plotting of a conspiracy. In examining how this self-fashioning played out in the complex interrelationship between the Decembrists' art and their actions, I refer mainly to the poetry of the Decembrist Kondraty Ryleev, whose work was especially influential among his contemporaries, and to the trial testimony of Pavel Pestel, considered the de facto leader of the Southern Society and the Decembrists' primary theoretician.[19] More than any other participant in the Decembrist revolt, Pestel attempted to develop a program for the future course of the Russian state after the autocracy's overthrow. His in-depth study of political theory, his military service in Western Europe, and his observations of the Greek uprising of 1821 (as adjutant to Generals Kiselev and Wittgenstein) convinced him that a republican form of government was the most suitable guarantee of personal freedom and economic stability in Russia and that the autocracy had to be eradicated by the most radical means possible.[20]

Exploring the Russian Past: Pretenders, Tyrants, and Karamzin's *History of the Russian State*

The Decembrists as a group were very interested in history and counted among their number both professional and amateur historians. Until his arrest, A. O. Kornilovich (1800–34) edited *Russian Past* (*Russkaia starina*), a journal that published archival documents; Nikolai Bestuzhev wrote *The History of the Russian Fleet;* and Nikita Muraviev (1795–43) and Lunin, among others, undertook serious study of the ancient Russian chronicles.

In their testimony, numerous Decembrists mentioned that reading history greatly influenced the development of their revolutionary convictions. History was a prominent subject at several of the institutions that educated future Decembrists, including the lycée at Tsarskoe Selo (where Pushchin and Kiukhelbeker studied), the Horse Guards' school (which educated twenty Decembrists), and the *pension* at Moscow University.[21] For many, historical examples served as programmatic models of behavior: "History is the collection of examples worthy of directing us in our societal life [*obshestvennoi zhizni*],"[22] an opinion with which Lunin agreed. "History is necessary . . . to conduct us to a higher level of politics," he stated.[23]

The Decembrists cited both ancient and modern history as inspirational models. Among their sources was Nikolai Karamzin's *History of the Russian State* (*Istoriia gosudarstva Rossiiskogo*), the first eight volumes of which were published in 1818 to much acclaim. Others have already commented on the Decembrists' criticisms of Karamzin's *History* for its focus on the tsars' actions alone rather than on the people's experiences and acts. Suffice it to say that for the Decembrist poets and belletrists, it provided rich material for their creative expression all the same. Indeed, after reading Karamzin's depiction of Ivan the Terrible, Ryleev expressed his admiration, despite earlier qualms about the work's orientation: "I do not know which to marvel at more, the tyranny of Ivan or the talent of our Tacitus."[24] Given their study of Karamzin and original sources, the Decembrists had thorough knowledge of Russian historical examples of tyranny, opposition to despotism, and experiences of self-government and political expression, such as the *veche* in ancient Novgorod and the *velikie sobory* of Tsar Aleksei Mikhailovich.[25] Ryleev himself began composing his *Meditations* (*Dumy*), a collection of narrative poems to teach and inspire his readers about the patriotic acts of their forebears, under the direct influence of Karamzin, perhaps even to polemicize with him, and referred to his first poem on Prince Kurbsky, the archetypal critic of tsarist tyranny, as "the fruit of my reading of the ninth volume."[26] Here we see an obvious intergeneric dialogue between history and literary creation in Ryleev's oeuvre. These influences extended from literature into life when the Decembrists also became vocal critics of the autocracy, first by rising up against the tsarist government and later by renewing the tradition of epistolary critique of the autocracy in their letters to Nicholas I after their incarceration.[27]

Brutus: Conspiracy, Assassination, and Tyrannicide

As M. K. Azadovsky has noted, among the Decembrists there was a "cult of antiquity."[28] The Decembrist I. D. Yakushkin (1793–1857), for example, remarked, "We passionately loved antiquity—Plutarch, Livy, Cicero, Tacitus and others were for each of us almost in constant reference," and Plutarch's *Lives* was an especially popular book among the future Decembrists.[29] Most Decembrists knew Latin as part of their classical education, and some also knew Greek; Nikita Muraviev was considered a "fluent Latinist," as were A. F. Briggen (1792–1859) and Kornilovich. Those who had not mastered Greek and Latin had translations (into French, German, or Russian). The book *Plutarch for Youngsters, or The Lives of Great Men of All Nations from the Most Ancient to Our Own Times* was translated from French into Russian in 1808; it then underwent two more republications (in 1814 and again in 1819–23), both of which included biographies of worthy Russian men as well. Under the influence of these models, the Decembrists cast themselves as *tiranobortsy* (fighters against tyranny), in the tradition of the heroic figures of Greco-Roman history. For them Brutus was the ideal, a noble and virtuous man who risked all for the good of his country. They were well aware of Brutus from a variety of sources, ranging from Plutarch to Shakespeare to Voltaire, but it appears that Plutarch held sway for them, whether they read him in the original, in translation, or through the filter of Rousseau, who popularized Plutarch in Russia during the eighteenth century.[30]

Plutarch portrays Brutus as a model citizen and conspirator who is motivated by hatred of tyranny to murder his benefactor, Julius Caesar. Plutarch's portrayal of Brutus must have been compelling to the Decembrists in their contemplation of means to effect change in the Russian Empire. Here was a true patriot, a noble man who despite his personal relationship with Caesar desired to return the land to republican rule and correct the wrongs done by an authoritarian ruler. Brutus's action was lauded by future generations of republican-minded thinkers and resurfaced in literary works, the most famous of which was Shakespeare's depiction in *Julius Caesar*. The Decembrists knew both Plutarch's and Shakespeare's versions of Brutus and referred to them in their literary works through the 1830s.[31]

Kondraty Ryleev, one of the central figures in the Decembrist movement for his de facto leadership of the Northern Society, propagandized the fight against tyranny for the benefit of one's country, frequently mentioning Brutus as a revered hero. In "To the Favorite" ("*K vremennshchiku,*" 1820), the poem that established his reputation as a freedom-loving poet, Ryleev predicts the rebirth of a republican hero to free Russia from tyranny:

> Tremble tyrant! He may be born,
> Either a Cassius or Brutus or Cato, enemy of Caesars!

Oh, how I will sing with my lyre, glorifying
The one who saves my fatherland![32]

In the ode "Civic Courage" ("*Grazhdanskoe muzhestvo,*" 1823), Ryleev paints Rome as the ideal political landscape:

Only Rome, the universal ruler,
That country of freedom and laws
Could produce
Two Brutuses and two Catos. (92:71–74)

However, in *Voinarovsky* (1823–24), Ryleev shows some ambivalence toward Brutus, whom his hero, Voinarovsky, was "accustomed to revere since childhood":

Noble defender of Rome,
Truly free in his spirit,
Truly great according to his deeds. (217:1004–6)[33]

Yet within almost the same breath, Voinarovsky radically changes his assessment:

However, he is worthy of reproach:
He himself ruined freedom—
And confirmed the victory of his country's enemies
With his suicide. (217:1007–10)

Ambivalence toward Brutus as a model may stem from two sources: his suicide, since for Russian Orthodox believers suicide is one of the worst sins, or the fact that Brutus took his own life before he ascertained that he was defeated. (As history tells us, the triumph of Augustus and Mark Antony occurred only after Brutus's death.)[34] In Ryleev's worldview, this inability in the final hour to do whatever must be done, even if it means living ignominiously and bearing shame, makes Brutus appear less ideal than in other portrayals. Or perhaps while writing *Voinarovsky* Ryleev had to be careful not to valorize his hero's treachery against the Russian state for the benefit of his Ukrainian motherland.

Although most of the heroes of Ryleev's poems suffer an ignominious end, they embrace self-sacrifice with enthusiasm for the greater good of their country. Most of all, these heroes are unwilling to sacrifice their honor, though they willingly offer up their lives and families: "For the one who is cast off in distant snows for the sake of his honor and his homeland, reproach is more tolerable than his enemy's pity" (199:282–85). Ryleev's unfinished poem, "Nalivaiko's Confession" ("*Ispoved' Nalivaiko,*" 1824), closes:

> I know that ruin awaits
> The one who first rises up
> Against the people's oppressor—
> Fate has already condemned me.
> But tell me, where has freedom been
> Bought without sacrifice?
> I will perish for my native land—
> I sense this, I know . . .
> And happily, Holy Father,
> I bless my lot! (233–34)

These poems were frequently discussed in the questioning of the Decembrists by the Investigating Commission, which undoubtedly recognized the resonance of their motifs among the conspirators.[35]

The casting off of all important ties and the valorization of self-sacrifice lead to extremes, as can be seen in another later poem, "To N. N." ("*K N. N.,*" 1824–25). Here Ryleev provides the blueprint for the future terrorist personality:

> I do not need your love,
> I have other occupations.
> Only war and military alarms gratify me.
> Love never enters my mind: Alas, my homeland suffers,
> —My soul in the agitation of deep thoughts
> Now thirsts only for freedom. (100)[36]

Isolated from the basic emotions of humanity, this figure can only think and act with the knowledge that his country suffers and must be freed. Ryleev subverts the traditional love lyric, transforming it into a programmatic credo appropriate to the terrorists of the latter half of the nineteenth century, akin to the radical Rakhmetev in N. G. Chernyshevsky's novel *What Is to Be Done?* (1863) or the ideal revolutionary figure described in Sergei Nechaev's *Catechism of a Revolutionary* (1869).[37] Ryleev's heroes become increasingly radicalized in parallel with his own political convictions as he moves from supporting a constitutional monarchy to advocating, under the influence of Pestel, regicide and republicanism.

Inspired by the mythic figure of Brutus, Ryleev's colleagues styled him as a model freedom fighter and romantic-era hero who placed civic duty above all else. In his "Memoirs of Ryleev" ("*Vospominaniia o Ryleeve*"), N. A. Bestuzhev (1791–1855) writes that Ryleev told his mother of his involvement in a secret society, declaring, "If I fall in the battle between law and power, even if my contemporaries will not understand or value me, you will know the purity and sanctity of my intentions; perhaps posterity will justify me, and history will write my name together with the names of great people who perished for humanity. In it [i.e., history] Brutus stands higher than Caesar!"[38] Bestuzhev cites the closing lines of Ryleev's poem, little known at the time but often repeated later, "Will I be at that fateful time?" ("*Ia l' budu v rokovoe vremia,*" 1825): "And, in stormy rebellion searching for liberty's rights, / They will find neither Brutus nor Riego."[39] Throughout his memoir, Bestuzhev depicts Ryleev as the hero of a romantic tale, blurring the boundaries between literature and biography to provide a captivating portrait of Ryleev as a heroic opponent of tyranny along the lines of classical models.[40]

Nikolai Bestuzhev and Ryleev were not the only ones who invoked Brutus. Nikolai's more famous sibling, the writer, critic, and staff captain of the Light Guard Dragoons Alexander Bestuzhev-Marlinsky (1797–1837), began studying English in 1824 and shortly thereafter began reading Byron and Shakespeare in the original. Notably, Bestuzhev-Marlinsky quickly learned Brutus's speech from *Julius Caesar* by heart,[41] and his critical articles, published in the *Polar Star* (*Poliarnaia zvezda*), are full of praise for Shakespeare. His careful reading of Shakespeare during the months immediately before the Decembrist revolt (March through August 1825) raises the question of Bestuzhev-Marlinsky's commitment to the conspiracy. On December 14, 1825, he was the first Decembrist officer to bring troops to the square, and had he not appeared, the revolt would have been a nonstarter. Yet immediately after the rebelling troops were routed, he donned his dress uniform and surrendered himself to the tsar at the Winter Palace. During his incarceration in the Peter-Paul Fortress, he penned one of the most revealing documents regarding the goals and methods of the Decembrists, as well as several letters professing his loyalty to Tsar Nicholas I. As Bestuzhev-Marlinsky's behavior after the revolt suggests, he may well have been as uncertain as Shakespeare's Brutus. Attesting to the lasting impression the play made on him, he continued to read and refer to Shakespeare throughout his exile, and specifically quoted Mark Antony's speech on Brutus's death ("Nature might stand up / And say to all the world 'This was a man!'") in his tale "The Frigate *Hope*" (written in 1832, published in 1833).[42]

But Ryleev and other Decembrists were not the only Russian writers who explored the complex of ideas associated with *tiranoborchestvo,* a common thematic at the time. Alexander Pushkin's "The Dagger" ("*Kinzhal,*" 1821), which invoked the names of Brutus and Karl Sand, among other freedom fighters, and "Liberty" ("*Vol'nost',*" 1817) are considered the best examples of the theme in Russian poetry and undoubtedly influenced the Decembrists' writings, not to mention their deeds. Numerous Decembrists mentioned that Pushkin's aforementioned poems inspired them to freethinking when questioned by the Investigating Commission after the revolt. Commenting on the appropriation of the codes of classicism for uses other than the glorification of patriotism in Russia after the wars against Napoleon, Monika Greenleaf notes that "by the 1820s the mythology of the Roman Republic had been thoroughly assimilated into French revolutionary-republican, then Byronic-libertarian rhetoric," and that Pushkin and the Decembrists were "following the well-established subversive track of Byron, Shelley and other political radicals."[43]

Yet the Decembrists' cult of antiquity continued to play an important role even after their arrest and exile. Their lasting interest can be seen in their numerous translations of Greek and Latin historical sources. Briggen translated in their entirety Julius Caesar's memoirs of the wars with the Gauls, as well as the works of Sallust. Kornilovich and M. M. Spiridov (1796–1854) also translated Sallust, Livy, Tacitus, and Cicero. But their greatest achievement may well have been their collective translation of Gibbon's *The Rise and Fall of the Roman Empire.*[44] The Decembrists' study of antiquity broadened in its orientation over the years. Kornilovich suggests a change in a note from July 11, 1830, in which he discusses the influence of Plutarch and Tacitus on their youth. He observes that they were very impressionable and that their teachers encouraged an unquestioning veneration of the heroes of old, so that "our years then were years of day-dreams and enthusiasm."[45] Though perhaps some Decembrists were initially motivated to delve into classical writings in search of historical models for emulation because of their interest in political assassinations, their study over time modulated into more mature and self-conscious scholarship focused on the examination of the root causes of successful political organization.

The French Revolution: Mass Terror and Regicide

Needless to say, the makers of the French Revolution also invoked the figures of antiquity for legitimacy in deposing and executing Louis XVI and Marie Antoinette. In postrevolutionary France, contemporaries remarked on the mania for all things related to the Roman Republic, ranging from the arts to fashion to names.[46] It was not only the ancient references that resonated with the Decembrists; so too did the so-called innovations of the French Revolution. For the Decembrists, however, the legacy of the French Revolution was mixed, providing both negative examples to avoid and positive examples for emulation. Many Decembrists changed their thinking over time as they learned more about the revolution, either as a result of discussions with émigrés (of all affiliations) who fled to Russia during the revolution or because of their reading of contemporary works such as Madame de Staël's *Considérations sur les principaux événements de la Révolution Francaise*.[47] First and foremost, numerous Decembrists wanted to avoid the excesses—the mass uprising and copious bloodshed—of the French Revolution. During their questioning, Pestel, Bestuzhev-Riumin, Bestuzhev-Marlinsky, and Prince S. P. Trubetskoi (1790–1860) all discussed their desire to effect change without unnecessary loss of life. As Pestel attested, "The terrible events occurring in France during the Revolution forced me to find means to avoid similar events, and thus later led me to the idea of the necessity of provisional rule and to my discussions then of how to prevent all kinds of civil strife."[48] Their distaste for extremes found reflection in Pestel's programmatic *Russian Law*, which sought institutional solutions within Russia's future government to prevent similar excesses after a successful military revolution.[49]

For their study of political processes the Decembrists turned to the philosophers who shaped the thinking of the men who made the French Revolution. Pestel commented, "Political books were in everyone's hands, political science is taught everywhere, political news spreads everywhere. This taught everyone to judge the actions and deeds of the government—to praise some and to censure others."[50] Pestel and his colleagues made a thorough reading of Montesquieu, Voltaire, Rousseau, Beccarria, and Destutt de Tracy while stationed in the south for military duty. Of all the political philosophers mentioned in their testimony, Montesquieu came up most frequently, with no fewer than twenty members expressing their familiarity with the writer, though most did not name a specific tract that was especially influential.[51] For the purpose of our discussion, Montesquieu stands out among other thinkers, since he has been called the source of the "first systematic theory of terror." In Montesquieu's schematic of the constitutive principles of different forms of governments, he proposes that only for despotic governments is "terror consistent with the political structure."[52] We may speculate that the Decembrists thus saw terror more as a weapon of despotism than of any other form of government, and that Montesquieu's theory convinced them of the necessity of promoting either a constitutional monarchy or a republic to guarantee against capricious rule.

As A. V. Semenova has suggested, Montesquieu greatly influenced Nikita Muraviev and Pestel, both of whom worked on constitutional projects and plans for the future government of Russia with Montesquieu's principal forms of political structure in mind.[53]

Though a study of Pestel's republicanism is beyond the scope of this essay, one or two common points between the French example and his future plan should be mentioned here. Assessing the French Revolution according to its tangible political results, Pestel found that several institutional changes after the revolution were beneficial to the people. However, Pestel did not turn a blind eye to the horrors of the Terror. As a solution to the excesses, he called for the creation of a "Provisional Supreme Government," a "dictatorship" of five to ten years' tenure to stabilize the postrevolutionary internal and external political situations. He looked to the Jacobin model of a centralized bureaucracy with deputy commissars in the provinces for the future political structure of the Russian state. Yet in Pestel's plan to avoid terror, he used the name of the same governmental body that carried out the Terror in France, an irony on which Odessky and Feldman have already commented. They also note the similarities between the chosen names not just for various departments in Pestel's Russian postrevolutionary government and their Jacobin precursors but also for the secret societies, which eventually became simply known in "politically neutral terms" as the Northern and Southern Societies, remarking that the Decembrists were working with the same "terrorist thesaurus" as the Jacobins.[54]

The French Revolution also influenced the Decembrists' everyday experience. The Decembrists' and their contemporaries' inclination to model themselves as historical personalities can be seen in relationship to French revolutionaries, akin to their aesthetic role-playing as Brutus. Sometime during the 1810s, Briggen closed a letter to one of his acquaintances with the words "Farewell my dear Jacobin," a comment more openly incendiary than a related remark made by Karamzin to his friend I. I. Dmitriev, "*Salut et fraternité.*"[55] Though some of these gestures were part of the spirit of the time—as was the singing of revolutionary songs among progressive members of the elite—the Decembrists again took their deeds to another level. Members of the Society of United Slavs wrote the months according to the revolutionary calendar rather than the Orthodox one,[56] and some Decembrists continued to sing the "Marseillaise," the anthem of the French Revolution, years into their exile in Siberia. Among the Decembrists and their contemporaries, Pestel was frequently compared to Robespierre (a "living Robespierre") and accused of behaving like Napoleon.[57] For his contemporaries, both comparisons were obviously negative and an indication of their distrust and dislike of his ambition and coldness.[58] General Chernyshev, one of the key members of the Investigating Commission, called Pestel "a demagogue combining all the characteristics of the Robespierres and Marats of this world."[59]

Other Decembrists sought to avoid comparison to the Jacobins. A. N. Muraviev, "valuing his good name," did not want to be taken for a "so-called Jacobin." Trubetskoi, aware of the parallels between them, explained that he did not take part in the revolt in Senate Square because he did not want to become "the very devil incarnate, some kind of Robespierre or Marat."[60] The act of taking up arms against the state and tsar for Trubetskoi takes on an almost magical, transformative quality and would immediately change him into an anathema. The equation of Jacobins with the devil speaks volumes about Trubetskoi's relationship to these figures of the Terror. By purposefully avoiding their mention during testimony, the majority hoped to downplay the magnitude of their conspiracy and to obscure their regicidal plans, which they knew would surely condemn them in the eyes of the government.[61]

This leads to the most important elements appropriated by the Decembrists from the French Revolution and revolutionary terror: the efficacy of regicide and the notion of the *cohorte perdue,* or suicide squad. A surprising number of Decembrists contemplated regicide or volunteered to assassinate Alexander I at different times in the secret society's history. The earliest plot—"an intriguingly modern terrorist tactic," in the words of one historian—featured a number of masked men who would be dispatched to kill the tsar as he was on the road from Tsarskoe Selo and was suggested by Lunin sometime in 1816 or 1817. According to several Decembrists' testimony, the assassins would be recruited from outside the secret society's membership to keep the conspirators free from the stain of the crime so they could wield their subsequent authority without shame in the public eye.[62] Early in his involvement with the secret society, Yakushkin offered to be the sacrificial assassin of Alexander I. His colleagues convinced him that the time was not right for such a deed and that premature action would be most harmful to Russia.[63] Lunin's plan and Yakushkin's offer were never implemented, but other plots built on the idea of assassins in disguise.[64]

One plan, proposed by Sergei Muraviev-Apostol and Mikhail Bestuzhev-Riumin, proposed that Alexander I be arrested and assassinated at his review of the Ninth Infantry Division in Bobriusk, Belorussia. According to Bestuzhev-Riumin, "Several officers deemed ready to commit such a crime (some of them retired) in soldiers' uniforms at the changing of the guard would break into the pavilion in the Alexandria park, penetrate the emperor's apartment and kill him."[65] Since the above leaders did not obtain the agreement of the secret society's members, they never undertook the plan. However, they returned to the idea when they believed that Tsar Alexander was due to review the Third Infantry Corps at Belaia Tserkov in the summer of 1824. This plan was also foiled when the tsar canceled his visit, though Muraviev-Apostol and Bestuzhev-Riumin discussed it as a possibility if the tsar came to review the unit in the summer of 1825.

In the Northern Society, the idea of *cohorte perdue* also prevailed. Ryleev told his colleagues he was preparing Petr Kakhovsky to be the tsar's sole assassin should the chance provide itself. Ryleev's testimony affirmed that Kakhovsky offered to kill the tsar either before or during the uprising on December 14, 1825. But on the eve of the uprising, Kakhovsky apparently decided he did not want to act alone, and reneged. Nechkina discusses Kakhovsky's decision, proposing that he changed his mind because he wanted to act not as a solitary outsider but as a participant in a larger revolutionary action.[66] Alexander Yakubovich, another voluntary assassin, was not a member of the secret society, though he participated in the uprising, frequented the apartment of Ryleev, and took part in many of the Decembrists' discussions. He had a personal grievance against Alexander I and spoke of his intention to avenge his honor for demotion to the ranks in 1817 after having served as a second in a duel. On the day of the uprising, Yakubovich also took back his word and said he would not be involved in a plot to kill Nicholas, since he did not consider him a personal enemy.[67] Be that as it may, the society counted among its associates at least two men in Petersburg who initially wanted the distinction of killing the tsar. Kakhovsky came closest to their original intention in assassinating Count Miloradovich and General Sturler, the tsar's emissaries to the rebels, during the uprising in Senate Square. This futile and unpremeditated action sealed his fate and affirmed his death sentence despite his confession, later disavowal of revolution, and professions of loyalty to Nicholas. Of the other four Decembrists who were hanged, Pestel, already under arrest by the December 14 uprising, was given a death sentence for his espousal of regicide and convicted for his intention alone rather than for participation in the northern or southern uprisings.

Though the Decembrists did not think of themselves as terrorists, members of the Investigating Commission did, as is evident in their description of Bestuzhev-Marlinsky and Kakhovsky as "fiery terrorists, prepared for the most horrifying evil actions."[68] However, among contemporaries, at least a few individuals recognized the harshness of the sentence decreed by the government. In 1826, Prince Petr Viazemsky commented,

> Those thinking about a change in our political system were in a fateful wave brought to the calamitous necessity of regicide and with the same force repelled from it: and the proof of this is that the regicide

> was not carried out. Everything remained in words and on paper, because in the conspiracy there was not a single regicide. I did not see them on Senate Square, just as I did not see a single hero in any war on the battlefield. . . . You don't give a St. George's cross for intention alone and in hope of future heroic deeds, why should you execute prematurely? You will place on the same level with already accomplished murder murderous chatter (*bavardage atroce,* as I called it, having read everything said about them in the commission's report).[69]

Viazemsky here recognizes the important distinction between words and deeds: no one actually attempted regicide, though all five leaders were condemned to death for their belief in its necessity. But the Investigating Commission considered the act's contemplation equal to its attempt and judged the conspirators harshly—too harshly, in some contemporaries' eyes. Though Miloradovich and Sturler were killed by Kakhovsky in Senate Square, his act appears almost accidental, carried out in the heat of the moment. In contrast to Kakhovsky, Decembrist and poet Wilhelm Kiukhelbeker shot at the Grand Duke Michael, but his pistol misfired. Yet Kiukhelbeker was not considered a regicide, nor was he condemned to death. The standards of judgment were not evenly or consistently applied to the various Decembrists within the confines of the questionable legal process of the so-called trial.

European Models of the 1820s

Though older historical models played an immense role in the Decembrists' conceptualization of the uses of political violence, there were more immediate events at hand to influence them as well. As Pestel remarked in his testimony, "Every century has its distinguishing feature. The current century is marked by revolutionary thoughts. . . . From one end of Europe to the other the same thing is visible everywhere from Portugal to Russia, not excepting a single government, not even England or Turkey, the two opposites. All of America presents the same spectacle. The spirit of reform everywhere compels minds to seethe."[70] The Decembrist movement was very much a part of the era of revolutions in Europe, and the Decembrists paid particular attention to the cataclysmic events that rocked absolutist governments across Europe, ascertaining the successes and failures of other revolutionary movements. Two primary contemporary events of political terrorism were the assassination plot carried out by Karl Sand against a Russian government agent in Germany in 1819 and the military uprising led by the officer Rafael Riego against the king of Spain in 1820.[71]

Karl Ludwig Sand (1795–1820), a German theological student at Jena, assassinated the German writer August von Kotzebue in March 1819 for his service to the Russian government, considered by German radical student associations of which Sand was a member to be tantamount to espionage. Kotzebue was employed by Alexander I at the rank of privy counselor and was charged with writing monthly reports on cultural and political issues in Germany. Kotzebue carried out his duties from his residence in Baden, where he also worked as a playwright and publicist. The sensational case garnered a great deal of publicity, perhaps in part because of Sand's garrulousness after his capture and arrest and his citation of historical models of tyrannicide. Sand had a second dagger on hand for his suicide if he was in danger of being caught; though he attempted suicide before his arrest by the authorities, it is not clear that he intended to sacrifice or "martyr" himself rather than flee.[72] Franklin L. Ford assesses the act within the context of the harsh political reaction to the assassination: "Considering this official backlash, unaccompanied by any surge of revolutionary élan in Biedermeier Germany, the assassination of Kotzebue might appear to have been just one more example of counterproductive histrionics. Nevertheless, Sand's undertaking remains an uncommonly emphatic demonstration of political romanticism. . . . In so doing he found as well some vocal admirers, not only in his own country but also abroad."[73] The Decembrists should be numbered among Sand's admirers particularly for the so-called political romanticism of his gesture. Ryleev's poetry specifically mentions both Sand and Riego as positive heroic examples, naming both the assassin and the military revolutionary leader in the final stanza of his aforementioned poem, "Will I be at the fateful time?" Again employing a dualistic model of behavioral codes, contemporaries, including Ryleev, saw Kakhovsky as a "Russian Sand" or "second Sand," equating Kakhovsky's social alienation and proclaimed willingness to assassinate Alexander I with Sand's political plot.[74]

In contrast to Sand's act of individual terror, the Spanish Revolution of 1820 provided a powerful example of a military uprising that accomplished its goals without excess violence. Led by Major Rafael Riego y Núñez (1785–1823), who was joined by Lieutenant Antonio Quiroga and his troops, Spanish troops in Cadiz revolted against the government and compelled King Ferdinand VII to reestablish the 1812 constitution. Among liberal-thinking circles the Spanish Revolution was greeted with enthusiasm. Nikolai Turgenev (1789–1871) wrote in his diary, "Glory to you, the excellent Spanish army! Glory to the Spanish people! For the second time Spain has shown what national spirit means, what love for the fatherland means!"[75] Decembrist A. P. Beliaev (1803–87) recalled, "Fervid enthusiasts like us were made ecstatic by the revolution in Spain with Riego at its head, wresting the former constitution from Ferdinand."[76] In a letter to Nicholas, Kakhovsky characterized Riego as "a holy martyr, a hero, renouncing the throne offered to him, a friend of the people."[77] Indeed, the name of Riego "was on everyone's lips," and he was spoken of in admiration by numerous educated Russians throughout the empire.[78] Though Petr Chaadaev (1794–1856) hoped that the revolution might provide a productive model for Russia ("All the masses rose up, the revolution [was] completed in 8 months and during this time not a single drop of blood spilled, no carnage, no destruction, the complete absence of violence, in a word nothing that could sully such a beautiful cause"), Viazemsky and Karamzin expressed their doubts regarding the outcome and reserved final judgment. Of course, the Russian government and the conservative members of the elite watched the events with trepidation, fearing that Europe's revolutionary outbursts might portend further instability closer to home.[79] In the long term, the reaction of Viazemsky and Karamzin proved to be most astute, as positive change lasted only three years, until the monarch could reestablish his stronghold and take revenge on the revolutionaries.

Several aspects of Riego's revolution recur in the military uprising led by Muraviev-Apostol and his colleague Bestuzhev-Riumin in January 1826. Muraviev-Apostol knowingly exploited the analogy by telling his troops about the Spanish Revolution and its leader and saw it as a productive example of a swift military uprising that took the minimum number of victims.[80] Muraviev-Apostol even copied one of the primary documents of that revolution, penning a "revolutionary catechism" to read to his soldiers and villagers in the occupied towns to persuade them of the rightness of their cause. Though tailored to the unique conditions of Russia, it also echoed the "Civil Catechism or the Short Review of the Duties of a Spaniard," published in the French novel *Don Alonzo, ou L'Espagne, histoire contemporaine* (1824) and known to the Decembrists in its French original and Russian translation. This conscious modeling in decisive moments of revolution testifies to the power of intergeneric dialogue connecting life, history, and literature, both in the political symbolism and in the actuality of Riego and his undertaking.[81]

Yet despite the Decembrists' study of Russian history, contemporary revolutions, and political theory, they failed to comprehend fully the importance of military action without observing the rules of the game, or to use Whittaker's words, an "etiquette of accession," which included election by the political elite, endorsement by acclamation of the guards and other nobility closest to the throne, the proclamation of an accession manifesto and oath swearing, and elaborate coronation rituals and celebrations.[82] Naturally, the last two points would be moot, since they did not envision another absolute monarch, but the fact that there was no certainty about the form of government or leader after a successful outcome indicates a surprising lack of political foresight. Though they designated the reluctant Trubetskoi as dictator, it was not clear whether he would lead the uprising and subsequent government or would cede leadership upon formation of the new ruling order. Moreover, the Decembrists did not have the full support of the two guards' regiments closest to the throne, they did not have highly placed government officials to assist them in their acclamation, and they did not have a developed program of how to rule the country once they overthrew the autocracy. Certainly their goals were more radical than in any past uprising since they sought the complete change of the political and social structures as they knew them. Yet they still felt they needed to frame their own revolt within past schematics as a question of legitimacy, as they believed it would be safer to mobilize the troops by playing on their preference for Constantine over Nicholas. It is uncertain how much military support they would have garnered had they told the troops the truth about their mission. They justified their deception as necessary to avoid involving the masses in the uprising and to prevent the loss of lives and property they believed would occur if they revealed their true goals. But to most uninformed observers, their actions must have looked like power grabbing, plain and simple. Under these circumstances, they were doomed to failure.

Despite their general disavowal of terror, the Decembrists provided direct links to later generations of Russian terrorists. These connections were both literal and symbolic. Though the Decembrists' children remained loyal to their parents' cause and validated their struggle, many were politically conservative, and several even became a part of the tsarist bureaucracy during the 1860s and participated in the reforms undertaken by Alexander II's government. However, a few second- or third-generation descendants of the Decembrists followed a more radical political path and became terrorists. Olga Bulanova-Trubnikova (1858–1942), who joined the Black Repartition but later belonged to the Left Socialist Revolutionaries (SRs), was the daughter of Maria Trubnikova, the daughter of Decembrist Vasily Ivashev and a feminist and social activist in her own right. Irina Kakhovskaia (1888–1960), great-granddaughter of a Decembrist, was a maximalist who later joined the SRs and assassinated General Eickhorn during the civil war, and Petr Filippovich Yakubovich (1860–1911), organizer of the Young People's Will party, which espoused agrarian and factory terror, was the grand-nephew of Alexander Yakubovich.[83] Raised in a milieu of open discussion of democratic ideas and the valorization of self-sacrifice for the betterment of their people, these revolutionary terrorists felt the direct influence of the Decembrists' heroic example and used it to inform their own self-sacrifice for political causes. Bulanova-Trubnikova recalled her childhood: "In our family there was a cult of the Decembrists. They were always spoken of with reverence, a fact which was aided by the presence of our elderly nanny, a living witness to their life in penal servitude and exile. . . . She always spoke of the Decembrists with tears in her eyes and cursed their tormentor, Tsar Nicholas, whom we children were accustomed to hate practically since infancy."[84] Bulanova-Trubnikova's apartment became a meeting place for revolutionaries: "V. N. Figner, her sister Evgenia, Morozov, O. Liubatovich, S. L. Perovskaia, Bogdanovich, Kolotkevich, M. N. Olovennikova, Gesia Gelfman, and later Stefanovich and Deich would come to our place. They all, especially Perovskaia, treated my mother with great respect and always tried to steal a moment to speak with her. Mother warmly sympathized with their goals but decisively rejected terror and this was an eternal source of arguments."[85] It is notable that political engagement emerged as a "hereditary" trait among some Decembrists' descendants despite tsarist repression, and that in some cases that very repression caused the opposite effect of what was desired, further radicalizing later generations.

The self-sacrificial image also resonated beyond the Decembrists' intimate domestic circle to a larger group of political activists through the Decembrists' writings, word of mouth, and the writings of Alexander Herzen, Nikolai Ogarev, and Nikolai Nekrasov, among others, who propagated a mythic depiction of the Decembrists and their deeds.[86] Because of their willingness to die for their political cause, the Decembrists became inspirational figures. Vera Zasulich, the assassin of General Trepov, governor of St. Petersburg, in 1877, valorized the self-sacrifice of the Decembrists, specifically Ryleev's, in her memoirs: "Somehow I had gotten hold of Ryleev's poem *Nalivaiko* and it became one of my holy relics. 'I know that ruin awaits the one who . . .' and so forth. And I did indeed know Ryleev's fate. Everywhere heroism, struggle, and revolt were always connected with suffering and death."[87] Another terrorist, Elizaveta Kovalskaia, also speaks of the Decembrists' influence on her early thinking: "Images of the Decembrists passed through my childhood like dim phantoms. Among my father's relatives, there was a very young officer, a Prince Volkonsky. I don't know whether he was related to the Decembrists in any way, but he . . . told me how there had once been good people who were imprisoned by the tsar for wanting to change things so that no one could sell people anymore."[88] Vera Figner also lauded the Decembrists and their wives in her writings during the Soviet era, memorializing them as the progenitors of revolutionary activism despite the gap between their generation and hers.[89]

The Decembrists' example became influential for another element of their insurrectional strategy as rebels who planned to assassinate the tsar. Though by far the anomaly and not the norm, the figures of Kakhovsky and Yakubovich as isolated individuals willing to commit regicide captured the imagination of later generations.[90] In addition to the imperial government's insistence that the Decembrists were terrorists at the time of the uprising, in 1906 a commemorative postcard was issued which underlined the connection by including portraits of Ryleev and Pestel along with S. V. Balmashev (1881–1902), the assassin of Minister of the Interior D. S. Sipiagin in 1902, and Lieutenant P. P. Schmidt (1867–1906), one of the leaders of the Sevastopol uprising of 1905.[91] However, a remarkable shift in emphasis had taken place in the interim, and the Decembrists went from being anathematized as terrorists by the establishment to being lauded for their potentially regicidal actions. This paradigm change illustrates how far educated Russian society had traveled in its political convictions over the course of eighty-one years, from a point where no one would or could speak against the tsar's treatment of the Decembrists to a time when they could openly be feted, along with "terrorist" heroes of the revolutionary cause. Or to put it another way, the genealogies of Bulanova-Trubnikova, Kakhovskaia, and Yakubovich illustrate quite literally the radical polarization of tsarist opposition over three generations from noble revolutionaries to terrorist assassins.

Notes

The epigraph to this essay is from Hannah Arendt, *On Revolution* (New York: Penguin, 1965), 112.

1. All dates are given according to the Gregorian calendar as they were observed in Russia before the revolution.

2. My brief account of the Decembrist uprising is primarily based on W. Bruce Lincoln's *Nicholas I: Emperor and Autocrat of All the Russias* (DeKalb: Northern Illinois University Press, 1989), 17–47, and Anatole Mazour's *The First Russian Revolution, 1825: The Decembrist Movement* (Stanford: Stanford University Press, 1963). A readable recent account can be found in Peter Julicher's *Renegades, Rebels and Rogues Under the Tsars* (Jefferson, N.C.: McFarland, 2003).

3. Franklin L. Ford, *Political Murder: From Tyrannicide to Terrorism* (Cambridge, Mass.: Harvard University Press, 1985), 45.

4. A. M. Murav'ev, *Mon Journal,* excerpted from Theodor Schiemann, *Zur Geschichte der Regierung Paul I und Nikolaus I,* 2nd ed. (Berlin, 1906), 111–76, in Marc Raeff, *The Decembrist Movement* (Englewood Cliffs, N.J.: Prentice Hall, 1966), 168.

5. Cynthia Hyla Whittaker, *Russian Monarchy: Eighteenth-Century Rulers and Writers in Political Dialogue* (Dekalb: Northern Illinois University Press, 2003), 59–63.

6. Raeff, *The Decembrist Movement,* 167.

7. For a discussion of the various claims of Russian political parties before and after the 1917 revolution on the Decembrists as forefathers, see Ludmilla A. Trigos, *The*

Decembrist Myth in Russian Culture (New York: Palgrave/Macmillan, 2009), chaps. 3 and 4.

8. Nechkina authored and edited a variety of publications on the Decembrists. Among other works, see her two-volume study, *Dvizheniia dekabristov* (Moscow: Akademiia Nauk, 1955), and *A. S. Griboedov i dekabristy* (Moscow: Akademiia Nauk, 1951). For a discussion of the ideological orientation of Nechkina's work and her polemics against other interpretations of the Decembrists' legacy, see John Gooding, "The Decembrists in the Soviet Union," *Soviet Studies* 40, no. 2 (April 1988): 196–209.

9. See Walter Laqueur, *Terrorism* (Boston: Little, Brown, 1977), 4–10.

10. See Iu. M. Lotman, "The Decembrist in Everyday Life: Everyday Behavior as a Historical-Psychological Category" and "Theater and Theatricality as Components of Early Nineteenth-Century Culture," in *The Semiotics of Russian Culture,* ed. Iu. M. Lotman and B. A. Uspensky, Michigan Slavic Contributions (Ann Arbor: University of Michigan, Department of Slavic Languages and Literatures, 1984), respectively 71–123 and 141–64; M. P. Odesskii and D. M. Fel'dman, "Dekabristy i terroristicheskii tezaurus," *Literaturnoe obozrenie* 1, no. 254 (1996): 65–80, and *Poetika terrora i novaia administrativnaia mental'nost': Ocherki istorii formirovaniia* (Moscow: Rossiiskii gosudarstvennyi gumanitarnyi universitet, 1997).

11. Odesskii and Fel'dman, "Dekabristy," 42.

12. E. V. Walter, "Theories of Terrorism and the Classical Tradition," in *Political Theory and Social Change,* ed. David Spitz (New York: Acherton, 1967), 133–34. Odessky and Feldman also examine this topic in *Poetika terrora.*

13. In my discussion, I distinguish between a tyrant and a despot by relying on the original Greek definition of the word *tyrannos* as an illegitimate ruler who employs a bodyguard and incites fear to maintain his rule. For more on the distinction between tyranny and kingship, see Walter, "Theories of Terrorism," 135, 145, and Deborah Tarn Steiner, *The Tyrant's Writ: Myths and Images of Writing in Ancient Greece* (Princeton: Princeton University Press, 1994), 163.

14. Harold T. Parker, *The Cult of Antiquity and the French Revolutionaries* (Chicago: University of Chicago Press, 1937), as paraphrased in Walter, "Theories of Terrorism," 143.

15. Lotman, "Theater and Theatricality," 160.

16. Ibid., 150.

17. Walter Laqueur, "Interpretations of Terrorism: Fact, Fiction and Political Sci ence," *Journal of Contemporary History* 12, no. 1 (January 1977): 1–42, esp. 15–42.

18. Andrew Baruch Wachtel, *An Obsession with History: Russian Writers Confront the Past* (Stanford: Stanford University Press, 1994), esp. 1–65.

19. These documents include Pestel's *Russkaia pravda* (*The Russian Law*) and his testimony to the Investigating Commission, in which he discussed his thoughts on regicide, the French Revolution, and political organization in general. For a thorough study of Pestel's thinking, see Patrick O'Meara, *The Decembrist Pavel Pestel: Russia's First Republican* (Hampshire, Eng.: Palgrave/Macmillan, 2005). For a discussion of the contradictions inherent in his views, see Arthur E. Adams, "The Character of Pestel's Thought," *American Slavic and East European Review* 12, no. 2 (April 1953): 153–61.

20. O'Meara, *The Decembrist Pavel Pestel,* esp. 17–48, 72–89.

21. S. S. Volk, *Istoricheskie vzgliady dekabristov* (Moscow and Leningrad, 1958), 44–45, 59–60, 291.

22. TsGIAM, f. III otd., 1 eks. 1826, g. 61, ch. 79, l. 202 ob., cited in Volk, *Istoricheskie vzgliady dekabristov,* 45.

23. M. S. Lunin, *Sochineniia i pisma* (St. Petersburg, 1923), 82, cited in Volk, *Istoricheskie vzgliady dekabristov,* 46.

24. See Militsa Nechkina's introductory article and critiques written by Nikita Muraviev and Mikhail Orlov in *Dekabristy-literatory, Literaturnoe nasledstvo* 59 (Moscow: Akademiia Nauk, 1954), 557–67 and 569–86, and Volk, *Istoricheskie vzgliady dekabristov,* 288–99. The Ryleev quotation comes from A. G. Cross, *N. M. Karamzin: A Study of His Literary Career, 1783–1803* (Carbondale: Southern Illinois University Press, 1971), 225.

25. See P. G. Kakhovsky's letter to General Levashev, February 24, 1826, in *Izbrannye sotsial'no-politicheskie i filosofskie proizvedeniia* (Moscow: Gosudarstvennoe izdatel'stvo politicheskoi literatury, 1951), 502. The *veche* was the popular assembly in towns in medieval Russia, and the *velikie sobory* were the great councils that met a few times during the reign of Tsar Alexei Mikhailovich (1645–76). See Nicholas V. Riazanovsky, *A History of Russia* (New York: Oxford University Press, 1984), 50–51, 79–83, 177–82.

26. K. F. Ryleev, *Polnoe sobranie sochinenii* (Leningrad: Sovetskii pisatel', 1971), 14, quoted in Wachtel, *Obsession,* 241n36. Wachtel also discusses the intergeneric dialogue between Ryleev's *Dumy* and Karamzin's history, focusing specifically on Ryleev's *Vadim,* 84–87.

27. Whittaker calls this genre "advice literature" in her work on the Russian monarchy and political discourse. See also A. K. Borozdin, *Iz pisem i pokazanii dekabristov* (St. Petersburg, 1906), esp. the letters of Kakhovsky and A. Bestuzhev, 1–32, 33–44.

28. M. K. Azadovskii, *Stranitsy istorii dekabrizma* (Irkutsk: Vostochnoe knizhnoe izdatel'stvo, 1991), 1:266–67.

29. See Andrew Kahn, "Readings of Imperial Rome from Lomonosov to Pushkin," *Slavic Review* 53, no. 4 (Winter 1993): 745–68, and V. E. Vatsuro, ed., *Pisateli-dekabristy v vospominaniiakh sovremennikov* (hereafter cited as *PD*) (Moscow: Khudozhestvennaia literatura, 1980), 1:16. For a discussion of Nikita Muraviev's knowledge of Latin, see Andrew Kahn's introduction to M. N. Murav'ev, *Institutiones rhetoricae* (Oxford: Willem A. Meeuws, 1995).

30. Lynn Ellen Patyk, "'The Double-Edged Sword of Word and Deed': Revolutionary Terrorism and Russian Literary Culture" (Ph.D. diss., Stanford University, 2005), 74–75.

31. See Iu. D. Levin, *Shekspir i russkaia literatura* (Leningrad: Nauka, 1988), for details on the various translations of *Julius Caesar* available in the early nineteenth century.

32. Ryleev, *Polnoe sobranie stikhotvorenii,* 57. All subsequent quotations from Ryleev's poetry are from this volume and the page and line numbers are indicated in the text.

33. Voinarovsky was the nephew of the Ukrainian Hetman Mazepa, a close adviser to Peter the Great, who in 1708 allied himself and Ukrainian Cossack forces with King Charles XII of Sweden when he invaded Russia. The ultimate goal was an independent Ukrainian state. Though Mazepa died before he could be properly pun-

ished, the nephew survived and was exiled for his involvement in the treachery. For more detail on the poem's composition, see Iu. G. Oksman, "K istorii poemy Ryleeva 'Voinarovskii,'" in his *Ot Kapitanskaia dochka A. S. Pushkina k Zapiski okhotnika A. S. Turgeneva* (Saratov: Saratovskoe knizhnoe izdatel'stvo, 1959), 134–59.

34. See M. L. Clarke, *The Noblest Roman: Marcus Brutus and His Reputation* (London: Thames and Hudson, 1981).

35. T. Snytko, "Ryleev na sledstvii," *Literaturnoe nasledstvo* 59, 1:177, 236.

36. Ryleev's phraseology "Moia otchizna stradaet" recalls P. A. Katenin's earlier poem, dating from sometime between 1816 and 1820, which begins, "Otechestvo nashe stradaet / Pod igom tvoim, o zlodei! / Kol' nas despotism ugnetaet, / To svergnem my tron i tsarei" (Our fatherland suffers beneath your yoke, O villain! If despotism oppresses us, then we will overthrow throne and tsars). This poem became a "revolutionary hymn" for the Decembrists and their generation (*PD*, 1:21).

37. S. G. Nechaev (1847–82), espousing violent means of taking over the state, wrote about the characteristics necessary for the most effective real-life revolutionary. They included a complete dedication to the cause beyond any personal or social attachments and a consuming passion for the political and conspiratorial activities of revolution, combined with a lack of egotism or vendetta against political enemies. My thanks to Anthony Anemone, who reminded me of the parallel between Rakhmetev and Nechaev. For more on Nechaev, see Philip Pomper, *Sergei Nechaev* (New Brunswick, N.J.: Rutgers University Press, 1979), and Val Vinokur's contribution to the present volume.

38. N. A. Bestuzhev, "Vospominaniia o Ryleeve," in *PD*, 2:65. According to Nikolai Bestuzhev's brother, Mikhail, Nikolai wrote reminiscences about Ryleev at the beginning of their incarceration in Petrovsky zavod prison. Scholars believe that they were written no later than 1832, though they were published only in 1861 (*PD*, 2:343–44).

39. *PD*, 2:81. Major Rafael Riego y Núñez (1785–1823) led a successful military insurrection against the Spanish government in 1820 and forced King Ferdinand VII to reestablish the 1812 constitution. Riego is discussed at greater length later in this essay. For more information, see the informative introduction and biographical note in Rafael del Riego, *La revolución de 1820, día a día: Cartas, escritos y discursos,* prólogo, biografía sucinta, notas y recopilación de documentos por Alberto Gil Novales (Madrid: Editorial Tecnos, 1976). Here we should also note that other Decembrists saw these lines as a "practical call to action": the Decembrist Lieutenant Bulatov allegedly rephrased them while loading his pistol and speaking to his brother in Senate Square on December 14, "and here come Brutus and Riego and perhaps they will surpass those revolutionaries." See Snytko, "Ryleev na sledstvii," 1:173–74.

40. For a discussion of the romantic traits exploited by N. Bestuzhev, see Azadovskii, "Memuary Bestuzhevykh kak istoricheskii i literaturnyi pamiatnik," in *Stranitsy istorii dekabrizma,* 1:267.

41. Levin, *Shekspir,* 20.

42. Lauren G. Leighton, *The Esoteric Tradition in Russian Romantic Literature: Decembrism and Freemasonry* (University Park: Pennsylvania State University Press, 1994), 107. Elsewhere Leighton calls Ryleev "the Brutus of the Decembrist conspiracy" (72).

43. Monika Greenleaf, *Pushkin and Romantic Fashion: Fragment, Elegy, Orient, Irony* (Stanford: Stanford University Press, 1994), 61.

44. Azadovskii, *Stranitsy istorii dekabrizma,* 1:179.

45. TsGIAM, f. III otd., 1 eks., 1826, g. 61, ch. 79, l. 199 ob., cited in Volk, *Istoricheskie vzgliady dekabristov,* 165.

46. Odesskii and Fel'dman, "Dekabristy," 60–61.

47. I am necessarily focusing my discussion on the Decembrists' relationship to terror in the French Revolution. For a thorough discussion of the Decembrists' wider perspective on the French Revolution, see Volk, *Istoricheskie vzgliady dekabristov,* 251–68. F. F. Vigel states that Decembrists Nikita and Alexander Muraviev acquired their Jacobin views from their French tutor, Magier. See F. F. Vigel', *Zapiski* (Moscow, 1929), 1:81–83, cited in Leonid Ignatieff, "French Emigrés in Russia After the French Revolution: French Tutors," *Canadian Slavonic Papers* 8 (1966): 129.

48. *Vosstanie dekabristov,* 4:90–91 (hereafter abbreviated *VD*), as cited in Odesskii and Fel'dman, *Poetika terrora,* 90.

49. Odesskii and Fel'dman, "Dekabristy," 68.

50. *VD,* 4:105, cited in Nechkina, *Dvizhenie,* 1:348.

51. Volk, *Istoricheskie vzgliady dekabristov,* 34. Elsewhere Volk specifically cites two works, *The Spirit of the Laws* and *The Reasons for the Rise and Fall of Rome,* as being especially influential among the Decembrists (157).

52. Walter, "Theories of Terrorism," 153–54.

53. See A. V. Semenova, "D. Didro i dekabristy," in *Velikaia frantsuzskaia revolutsiia i Rossiia* (Moscow, 1989), 366–73.

54. This revolutionary vocabulary consisted of the terms salvation (*spasenie*), welfare (*blagodenstvie*), happiness (*schast'e*), son of the fatherland (*syn otechestva*), and directory (*directoriia*). For a more detailed discussion of the exact referents in both the French and American revolutionary experience (where applicable), see Odesskii and Fel'dman, "Dekabristy," 68–72.

55. Volk, *Istoricheskie vzgliady dekabristov,* 254.

56. M. V. Nechkina, "Tri pis'ma dekabrista P. I. Borisova," *Katorga i ssylka* 6 (1926): 56, cited in Volk, *Istoricheskie vzgliady dekabristov,* 162.

57. "Pestel, the head of the southern society, is a living Robespierre, intelligent, clever, enlightened, cruel, persistent and enterprising." This observation was made by A. Borovkov, scribe to the Investigating Commission. TsGVIA, F. VUA, ch. 1, d. 40681, cited in Iu. M. Lotman, "Ob otnoshenii Pushkina v gody iuzhnoi ssylki k Robesp'eru," in Iu. M. Lotman, *Izbrannye stat'i v 3 tomakh* (Tallinn, 1992–93), 3:406. Lotman affirms that Pushkin held a very negative assessment of Marat but that his attitude to the "incorruptible Robespierre," as he called him, was more complex.

58. Trubetskoi's memoirs attest that some Decembrists feared Pestel's radicalism, especially his positive references to the achievements of the French Revolution such as the benefits of the Jacobin's Committee of Public Safety: "The protest against this was universal; it left behind an unfavourable impression which could never be eradicated and gave rise to a lasting distrust of Pestel'" (O'Meara, *The Decembrist Pavel Pestel,* 55).

59. Ibid., 165.

60. *VD,* 1:39, cited in Odesskii and Fel'dman, *Poetika terrora,* 101.

61. See V. M. Bokova, "Bol'noi skoree zhiv, chem mertv: Zametki ob otechestvennom dekabristovedenii 1990-kh godov," *14 dekabria 1825,* vyp. 4 (St. Petersburg, 2002), 512–14, for a refutation of Odessky and Feldman's theory that there was a taboo against using terminology borrowed from the French Revolution.

62. O'Meara, *The Decembrist Pavel Pestel,* 145–46.

63. Odessky and Feldman provide an interesting analysis of Yakushkin's plot within the context of the duel (*Poetika terrora,* 109–12).

64. Interestingly, neither Lunin nor Yakushkin participated in the northern or southern uprisings, but because of their espousal of regicide they belonged to the first category of criminals and were sentenced to penal servitude for fifteen years.

65. *VD,* 4:104, cited in O'Meara, *The Decembrist Pavel Pestel,* 148.

66. Nechkina, *Dvizhenie,* 2:258–60.

67. When he heard that Alexander I had died, Yakubovich purportedly said to the Decembrists, "It is you who snatched him away from me" (*VD,* 1:182, cited in Nechkina, *Dvizhenie,* 2:259).

68. *VD,* 17:51, cited in Odesskii and Fel'dman, "Dekabristy," 73.

69. Iu. M. Lotman, "P. A. Viazemskii i dvizhenie dekabristov," in *Trudy po russkoi i slavianskoi filosofii, t. III, Uchennye zapiski Tartuskogo gosudarstvennogo universiteta,* vyp. 98 (Tartu, 1960), 94, cited in Iu. M. Lotman, "Ideinaia struktura poemy Pushkina 'Andzhelo,'" in *Uchenye zapiski: Pushkinskii sbornik* (Pskov: Pskovskii universitet, 1973), 11–12.

70. *VD,* 4:105, cited in Nechkina, *Dvizhenie,* 1:305.

71. Though the Decembrists also mentioned the Greek Revolution, the stories of Sand and Riego recur with greater frequency and clearly made a stronger impression on them.

72. Using a dagger to kill a political figure was a transparent reference to the classical practice of tyrannicide, especially the assassination of Julius Caesar.

73. Ford, *Political Murder,* 215–16. I am relying primarily on Ford's discussion for my treatment of Sand's case.

74. E. P. Obolenskii, "Vospominaniia o Ryleeve," in *PD,* 2:103. See also Azadovskii, "Stern v vospriiatiiakh dekabristov," in *Stranitsy istorii dekabrizma,* 2:143.

75. N. I. Turgenev, diary entry of March 24, 1820, cited in M. P. Alekseev, *Ocherki istorii ispano-russkikh literaturnykh otnoshenii XVI-XIX vv.* (Leningrad: Izdatel'stvo Leningradskogo universiteta, 1964), 120.

76. A. P. Beliaev, *Vospominaniia dekabrista o perezhitom i perechusvstvovannom* (St. Petersburg, 1882), 155, cited in Alekseev, *Ocherki,* 317.

77. *Iz pisem i pokazanii dekabristov,* 13, cited in V. Bazanov, *Uchenaia respublika* (Moscow and Leningrad: Nauka, 1964), 244.

78. Alekseev, *Ocherki,* 123.

79. P. Ia. Chaadaev, *Sochinenii i pis'ma* (Moscow, 1924), 2:53, cited in Alekseev, *Ocherki,* 121. A more detailed treatment of the governmental reaction to the Spanish and Neapolitan revolutions and the concurrent wave of peasant unrest in Russia is beyond the scope of this discussion. For information on this topic and its influence on the Semenov troop uprising in 1820, see Nechkina, *Dvizhenie,* 1:305–13.

80. Alekseev, *Ocherki,* 123, and *VD,* 4:130, cited in O. I. Kianskaia, "Glavar' shaiki zloumyshlennikov . . . : Iz razmyshlennii nad biografiei S. I. Murav'eva-Apostola," *Literaturnoe obozrenie* 1, no. 254 (1996): 82.

81. According to one Decembrist, Ryleev's lines invoking Brutus and Riego were heard in Senate Square on December 14 as well as in the south in January 1826 (M. P. Alekseev, *Russkaia kul'tura i romanskii mir* [Leningrad: Nauka, 1985], 134–35).

82. Whittaker, *Russian Monarchy,* 63.

83. See Amy Knight, "Female Terrorists in the Russian Socialist Revolutionary

Party," *Russian Review* 38, no. 2 (1979): 157, on I. Kakhovskaia, and B. N. Dvinianov, *Mech i lira: Ocherk zhizni i tvorchestva P. F. Iakubovicha* (Moscow: Nauka, 1967), 9–10, on P. F. Yakubovich. Dvinianov points out that, as a nod to his ancestor, Yakubovich took the name Alexander in his underground revolutionary work.

84. See Olga Bulanova-Trubnikova's autobiographical note in *Deiateli SSSR i revoliutsionnogo dvizheniia Rossii: Entsiklopedicheskii slovar' granat* (Moscow: Sovetskaia entsiklopediia, rpt, 1989), 29. For more information on her experiences, see her memoir, *Tri pokoleniia* (Moscow and Leningrad: Gosudarstvennoe izdatel'stvo, 1928).

85. Bulanova-Trubnikova, autobiographical note in *Deiateli SSSR i revoliutsionnogo dvizheniia Rossii,* 30. Perovskaia also became acquainted with the family of Decembrist Alexander Poggio in Switzerland when she was an adolescent. See Cathy Porter, *Fathers and Daughters: Russian Women in Revolution* (London: Virago Press, 1976), 180.

86. See L. Frizman, *Dekabristy i russkaia literatura* (Moscow, 1988), and Trigos, *Decembrist Myth.*

87. Vera Zasulich, *Vospominaniia* (Moscow, 1931), in *Five Sisters: Women Against the Tsar,* ed. and trans. Barbara Alpern Engel and Clifford N. Rosenthal (New York: Routledge, 1975), 69.

88. Engel and Rosenthal, *Five Sisters,* 208.

89. See her article "Zheny dekabristov" in *Katorga i ssylka* 21 (1925): 227–37 and her speech to the All-Union Society of Political Prisoners and Exiles on the centennial of the Decembrist uprising and the twentieth anniversary of 1905.

90. O. Budnitskii, *Terrorizm v rossiiskom osvoboditel'nom dvizhenii* (Moscow: Rossiiskaia politicheskaia entsiklopediia, 2000), 6. See also Nikolai Starikov, *Ot dekabistrov do modzhakhedov: Kto kormil nashikh revoliutsionerov?* (St. Petersburg: Piter, 2008).

91. N. L. Brodskii, "Dekabristy v russkoi khudozhestvennoi literature," *Katorga i ssylka* 21 (1925): 217.

All of a Sudden: Dostoevsky's Demonologies of Terror

Val Vinokur

According to a Sufi tradition, Iblis, Islam's version of Lucifer, is the embodiment of the perfect lover, an angel who fell because he had clung to absolute monotheism even after Allah had asked that his angels bow before Adam. Perhaps no other story better captures the intersection of desire, rebellion, intolerance, and ideological purity that gives rise to evil in its grandiose mode. Relying as it does on a principled individual stubbornness (and on an ambivalent portrayal of Allah, punishing his most devoted angel), this is a supremely sentimental image of cosmic evil, the opposite of Hannah Arendt's banal one—and it is closely associated with the romance of terrorism. After all, the ideal terrorist must possess an impossible self-righteousness, godly beyond God, as well as the faith that a brave new world can be formed from rubble and wounds. The ideal terrorist is an expert draftsman of theodicies, even as he rejects those seemingly paltry ones that justify the status quo.

The recent emergence of catastrophic terrorism has confounded a culture that has been questioning theodicies since the Lisbon earthquake of 1755. Indeed, if a globalist West has, to a significant extent, become a "telephone book" culture,[1] all pluralistic middle and no extremes, no wonder al Qaeda's largely cosmopolitan and urbane victims cannot coherently address its dualism. This impasse has prompted some commentators to reach for the comfort of historical parallel.[2] A favorite has been Dostoevsky's portrayal of nineteenth-century Russian radicals. While one should not suggest that we have finished understanding Verkhovensky or Raskolnikov, at least we can *read* these imaginary characters in ways that we cannot seem to read Zawahiri's communiqués or the video testaments of suicide bombers. Slavists declare, "We have read Dostoevsky, and we have seen all this before!" and feel strangely useful again, two decades after the end of the cold war. As Nina Pelikan Straus puts it, "Individuals who would plan or commit a terrorist act are of a complexity that requires not social science but Russian fiction to comprehend them."[3] In this reading, Islamic terrorists generally resemble the reckless, conflicted, overeducated, homosocial, sexually frustrated, and misogynistic "superfluous men" of Russian letters. But whatever the truth of the comparison, in the effort to show social science a thing or two, literary criticism risks becoming an eccentric branch of social psychology.[4] If anything truly useful is to emerge from literary connections, we must first treat the different historical and cultural terms as distinctly as possible.

Terror mocked seems, at least for a moment, a little less terrifying. So perhaps the other unspoken reason for the popularity of Dostoevsky-as-bin-Laden-expert is that most of Dostoevsky's terrorists are satirically portrayed: they are exposed, literarily. Raskolnikov, for one, is a most pathetic terrorist, if he is one at all. As Ilja Kostovski writes, "By the murder of one old woman, Raskolnikov wanted to save dying horses, perishing prostitutes, starving children, and drunken fathers. He wanted too much for such small a portion of blood. What poor mathematics. What blood! The blood of an old woman. What bad esthetics."[5]

Our focus here will be on *Demons* (1871), the novel begun as a pamphlet about the 1869 Nechaev-Ivanov affair and its revelations about Russia's violent young radicals, and generally considered to be Dostoevsky's chief commentary on the culture of revolutionary terror.[6] Sergei Nechaev, Bakunin's upstart protégé and purported lover, was the reputed author of the *Catechism of a Revolutionary,* which justified any means in the service of revolution. He founded a small secret revolutionary group, the People's Retribution (*Narodnaia rasprava*), also called the Society of the Axe, based on the principles of the *Catechism* and requiring its members to submit unquestioningly to his leadership. When I. I. Ivanov (whom Dostoevsky had heard about as a school companion of his brother-in-law) challenged his methods and his authority, Nechaev and his conspirators beat, strangled, and shot him, dumping the body in a frozen pond through a hole in the ice. When the crime was discovered, Nechaev escaped to Switzerland, but sixty-seven members of his organization were brought to trial. At the request of the Russian government, Nechaev was arrested in 1872 and extradited to stand trial in Russia, where he was convicted and sentenced to twenty years imprisonment in the Peter-Paul Fortress.

Yet even in *Demons,* it is difficult to find a terrorist worth taking seriously. Dostoevsky splits his historical model, the scheming and charismatic Nechaev, into the charismatic shell of Stavrogin and the scheming snake Verkhovensky; Nechaev's "barracks Communism" (as Marx and Engels would later call it) is doled out to a third and minor character, the bloodless theoretician Shigalev, whose "research" forces him to conclude that 90 percent of humanity must be reduced to slavery (or, as Liamshin suggests, eliminated) so that the "useful" remainder could rule and achieve social progress. In the radical prototype the manipulative scheming and half-baked theories are masked by seductiveness; the split in the novel is therefore already a demystification of Nechaev. In his working notes for the novel, Dostoevsky explains that "Nechaev is not a socialist but a rebel. His ideal is insurrection and destruction and then, whatever might come." Verkhovensky, on the other hand, is an utterly cynical ringleader, "not a socialist but a crook,"[7] as he confesses to Stavrogin; Stavrogin has no clear desire for anything or anyone; and Shigalev seems almost hesitant to share his "findings." Moreover, the novel excludes perhaps the most important feature of Nechaev's appeal, the proletarian earnestness of this provincial sign painter's son, which overwhelmed the better judgments of Bakunin, Herzen, Vera Zasulich, and even his guards at the Peter-Paul Fortress.[8] As a "bored squire" lacking conviction or biographical pathos, Stavrogin's charisma is much easier for a reader to dismiss: he is a blank slate upon which others project their ideas and desires. Unlike his historical prototype, Stavrogin's charm is purely aesthetic, without any real moral, political, or ideological claims, however insane these may be in Nechaev's case.

Although Nechaev's traits were doled out among several characters partly to allow for the possibility of narrative tension and redemption, the effect is nevertheless to make them transparent and demystified. Whether such demystification is valid or not, one might observe, as Lynn Ellen Patyk does in her recent work, that *Demons* is hardly a novel about terrorism at all.[9] With the exception of Shatov's murder (which is arguably a blood pact between revolutionaries and not a public act of terror) and the burning of Zareche, nearly everything that can be defined as terrorism occurs offstage as hearsay. Many argue that Dostoevsky died before writing his true opus on Russian terrorism: the "second book" of *The Brothers Karamazov,* in which, according to the evidence marshaled by James Rice, Alyosha Karamazov and Kolya Krasotkin would have become revolutionaries and tsar killers.[10] And aside from the projected second novel, it may be true that *The Brothers Karamazov* presents the author's mature thought about the psychology of the Russian terrorist of the 1870s. In this respect one looks to Ivan and his Grand Inquisitor, Krasotkin, Rakitin, and perhaps most of all to the description of Smerdyakov as Kramskoi's *Contemplator,* who "perhaps suddenly, having stored up his impressions over many years, . . . will drop everything and wander off to Jerusalem to save his soul, or perhaps he will suddenly burn down his native village, or perhaps he will do both."[11] The psychological types found in *The Brothers Karamazov* reflect the most compelling aspect of Russian terrorism of the People's Will (Narodnaia volia) variety: it was the product of a satanically proud form of compassion, an apocalyptic and heroic spiritual calling, and not simply the inauthentic and anarchic criminality portrayed in *Demons,* a novel that predated the People's Will. Patyk writes,

> The purpose of *Demons* was to (dis)abuse Dostoevsky's political opponents, to malign and vent his spite upon them; the purpose of *The Brothers Karamazov* was to "teach." In *Demons,* Dostoevsky uses caricature and satire to great effect: he demonstrates the bankruptcy of abstract ideas by exposing their disastrous, rather than regenerative effects on the individuals who embrace them, as well as on the larger community. Yet Dostoevsky purposefully—and to the detriment of the persuasive force of his argument—distorts his opponents' political ideas, makes their spokesmen singularly unattractive embodiments, and allows no true scope for the revolutionaries' most compelling argument: justice.[12]

It is tempting on this basis alone to dismiss the ability of *Demons* to teach us anything profound about radical terrorism.

Dostoevsky's attempt at rapprochement with the young radicals in an 1873 article hardly addressed the dismissive tone in the novel:

> In my novel *Demons* I attempted to depict those diverse and multifarious motives by which even the purest of hearts and the most innocent of people can be drawn into committing such a monstrous offense. And therein lies the real horror: that in Russia one can commit the foulest and most villainous acts without in the least being a villain. And this happens not only in Russia but all over the world, and it has happened since time began, in times of transition. . . . But let me say one thing about myself alone: a Nechaev I probably could have never become, but a Nechaevist—well, of that I can't be sure; perhaps I could have become one . . . in the days of my youth.[13]

Here Dostoevsky alludes to the possibility of his seduction by his own Nechaev—"my own Mephistopheles," Nikolai Speshnev, leader of the Petrashevsky splinter group to which Dostoevsky belonged before his arrest and mock execution. To be sure, Dostoevsky lent certain autobiographical traits to two of the more sympathetic radicals in *Demons,* the Slavophile Shatov (murdered like the real-life Ivanov) and the proto-epileptic Kirillov. But even these two sincere and decent characters are easy to dismiss ideologically, though their deaths in the novel are ones that a reader might actually mourn. The spastic ex-nihilist Shatov "believes in Russia . . . in her Orthodoxy" but can only promise that he "*will* believe in God" (253).[14] And Kirillov, with his Martian syntax and apparent ability to subsist entirely on tea, has convinced himself that he will become God through the free act of suicide—a deed that, like Raskolnikov's murder, is ultimately beyond Kirillov's intentionality and ends up being absurd, gruesome, and pathetic, anything but heroic and sublime. If *Demons* teaches anything at all interesting about terror, the lessons may lie beyond history and psychology.

Then again, one could argue that terrorism is larger than its history or its psychology, and that this is why *Demons* is relevant. Like the problem of evil, terrorism is cosmic: even though its physical destructiveness is always surpassed by that of conventional warfare, crime, accidents, and natural disasters, terror, as a rule-breaking "spectacle of the deed," seeks to disrupt the unconscious assumptions about a functional universe that make our daily lives possible. Like torture in Elaine Scarry's analysis, terror is "world-unmaking."[15] This is its true "multiplier effect," for without these world-forming assumptions we ourselves become vulnerable to apocalyptic moods and politics. One might say that in our violent attempts to shake off the sense of terror awakened in us by the seeming boundlessness of another suicide car bomb, we become open to demonic possession. And in *Demons,* Dostoevsky constructs a *demonology* of terror, that is, an account of how cosmic evil possesses us. Or rather he constructs two dueling demonologies, framed by the novel's dueling epigraphs.

The first is from Pushkin's 1830 poem, which is, like the novel, titled "*Besy,*" the native Russian word for demons (as opposed to the Western variant *demony*).[16] The speaker of the poem finds himself and his coachman caught in the archetypal whiteout of a Russian blizzard; the coachman is the speaker in the first stanza used by Dostoevsky, while the other is in the voice of the passenger-poet:

> Upon my life, the tracks have vanished,
> We've lost our way, what shall we do? [*sic:* "!" in Pushkin]
> It must be a demon's [*bes*] leading us
> This way and that around the fields.
>
> . . . .
>
> How many are there? Where are they rushing?
> Why do they sing so plaintively?

> Are they burying some household spirit [*domovogo li khoronyat'*]?
> Is it some witch's wedding day?

In light of Pushkin's earlier "*Demon*" (1823), which features a classically Western and romantic interlocutor-demon (a Mephistopheles, "an evil genius/spirit—*zlobnyi genii*"), this later poem is a decidedly post-Byronic, folkloric invocation of Slavic "unclean forces," and begs to be read as an allegory for Russia's destiny. Pushkin's demons, *besy,* suggest a "deep Russia" that is not simply pagan but godforsaken. They represent the plenitude of being in all its terrifying white noise—a plenitude best captured in Emmanuel Levinas's discussion of the inescapable "*il y a,*" the rustling "there-is" of an existence "without existents," in which even nothing is something.[17] To be sure, Pushkin goes out of his way to name these existents, but his fancy strikes me as an imaginative conceit, the Westernized passenger-poet's exaggerated attempt to cast a folkloristic sheen over the coachman's fear (while betraying his own anxiety, perhaps). Though Dostoevsky cites only the two stanzas above, Pushkin's poem concludes essentially where it begins, although with the speaker's heart strained ("*Nadryvaia serdtse mne . . .*") by the plaintive howling of the blizzard spirits.[18] This epigraph frames a hopeless, godless Russian demonology. A telling throwaway detail here is the paradoxical funeral of the *domovoi,* a touchy but generally benevolent spirit who must be appeased in order to ensure—and often assist—in the smooth functioning of the household.[19] A *domovoi* is not supposed to die; in fact, he is like a member of the family, like a grandfather, who must be coaxed and brought along if his mortal kin move to a new house, and to lose a *domovoi* is a disaster for the family. What hope is there if the most helpful *bes* of the Slavic spirit realm is being buried in Pushkin's allegory for Russia's destiny? Interestingly, however, Dostoevsky softens this hopelessness somewhat in the second line of the epigraph when he substitutes Pushkin's (or the coachman's) exclamation point (". . . what shall we do!") with a question mark.[20]

The second epigraph, often referred to as the tale of the Gadarene swine, is from the Gospel of Luke. The demonology here could not be more different from that of Pushkin's "*Besy*":

> Now a large herd of swine was feeding there on the hillside; and they begged him to let them enter these. So he gave them leave. Then the demons came out of the man and entered the swine, and the herd rushed down the steep bank into the lake and were drowned. When the herdsmen saw what had happened, they fled, and told it in the city and in the country. Then people went out to see what had happened,

> and they came to Jesus, and found the man from whom the demons had gone, sitting at the feet of Jesus, clothed and in his right mind; and they were afraid. And those who had seen it told them how he who had been possessed with demons was healed. (Luke 8:32–36, Revised Standard Version)

Here the demonic plenitude of being is literally corralled and submerged by a heroic Christ who restores narrative order. In Luke 8, Christ not only casts out demons, he calms a storm at sea, heals a woman, and raises the dead—his goal throughout to engender fear or awe, to the extent that the Gadarenes (Luke 8:37) beg him to leave (if only, perhaps, to spare the rest of their livestock!). Where Pushkin's "*Besy*" concludes with free-ranging demons and a poet's lacerated heart, the epigraph from Luke ends with a healed mind and a frighteningly immanent kingdom of God. Between these two epigraphic demonologies lies the relevance of *Demons* to an understanding of terrorism.

The two epigraphs also correspond to the splitting of the historical Nechaev prototype into Verkhovensky and Stavrogin (setting aside Shigalev for the moment). The Pushkin poem gestures toward the chaos wrought by Verkhovensky, while the story of the Gadarene swine tempts the reader into hoping that Stavrogin will be cured (and perhaps even cure others) by the end of the novel—which ends not with a demoniac cured and "in his right mind" but with Stavrogin's autopsy, which mysteriously and "emphatically ruled out insanity." Even the importance of Stavrogin's halfhearted attempt at confession is undermined by the ambiguous status of the appended chapter "At Tikhon's," which Dostoevsky wrote out of sequence and neglected to insert into the chronology of the novel after it was no longer suppressed by the publisher.[21] The appended chapter, in which Stavrogin recounts how he seduced the adolescent Matryosha,[22] who then hanged herself, might have suggested an echo of atonement in Stavrogin's eventual suicide by hanging. But the way the chapter physically dangles, sideshadowing the rest of the novel, makes Stavrogin's death seem little more than an extension of his death-in-life.[23] After all, the narrator likens him to "an inanimate wax figure" (229), and Stavrogin himself compares Darya Shatov's affection for him to the way "certain pious old women who hang about at funerals prefer certain nice little corpses that are comelier than the others" (*Demons,* 292–93).

Such characters as Maria Lebiadkina and Peter Verkhovensky associate Stavrogin with the pretender-czar Grigory Otrepev,[24] and his very name (the Greek *stavros* means cross, the Russian *rogi* means horns) evokes the Antichrist. Although half the characters in the novel claim that Stavrogin had at one point or another before the action of the novel inspired and in a sense "possessed" them, his inanimate qualities suggest that he is less a false messiah or a demon than he is—like the demoniac in Luke, or like the unclean dead of Russian folk belief (generally suicides like Stavrogin)—a body prone to possession.

Furthermore, Stavrogin seems like an uncanny illustration of Kierkegaard's expansive definition of the demonic in *The Concept of Anxiety* (1844) as an "unfreedom [that] wills something, when in fact it has lost its will"[25] and that is characterized by "brooding inclosing reserve," "silence," by boredom and a lack of content, and by "the sudden [which] knows no law [and is] an expression of unfreedom. . . . Freedom is tranquil in continuity. Its opposite is the sudden, but also the quietness that comes to mind when one sees a man who looks as if he were dead and buried."[26] In his recent past, Stavrogin's rebellious charm was characterized by his shameless and anarchic suddenness. Pulling a nose here, biting an ear there, he would give in to the fleeting demonic urges that most of us overcome for moral or practical reasons. By the beginning of the novel, he has become bored with his old self, recognizing that such spontaneity is fundamentally unfree and that it would be far more challenging to decide to be normal.

Of course, Stavrogin is bad at normal. He can embrace neither good nor evil, his "desires . . . far too weak" (*Demons,* 675), like the "lukewarm" church of Laodicea in Revelation 3:14, to which the novel refers. And he is so fettered by his own reputation and by the expectations of others that he cannot spare Gaganov's life in a duel without unintentionally giving offense. The Stavrogin we see in the novel is little more than a brooding zombie, exuding an "oppressive lethargic motionlessness," occasionally shifting "a little, somehow suddenly, with some strange movement in his face" (*Demons,* 229, 228).

Kierkegaard adds that one of the results of this demonic suddenness, when "all the ethical dimensions of evil are excluded, and only metaphysical determinants of emptiness are used, . . . is the trivial, which can easily have a comic aspect"[27]—which suggests that although Dostoevsky expressly set out to deride the Russian Left in *Demons* through satire, the "comic aspect" is also a natural side effect of the demonic. And while Dostoevsky's understanding of humor was a complex hybrid of Russian and Western views, the fused demonic-comic, as Sergei Averintsev reminds us, is the *only* approach to laughter in the Russian Orthodox tradition: *Gde smekh, tam i grekh*—"Where there is laughter, there is sin," goes the proverb.[28] Given the way laughter can physically seize and *possess* us, this is an unsettlingly intuitive approach—one that is also suggested by the somewhat silly descriptions of the *besy* in Pushkin's nevertheless "heartrending" poem. Indeed, most of the novel lacks the Western option of divine comedy. The guffawing that follows Yulia Mikhailovna's absurd and diversionary literary fete gives way to the horror of Zareche aflame, with her husband Governor von Lembke staring into the "black skeleton of a nearly burnt-down . . . wooden house, with holes instead of windows . . . and flames still snaking here and there" (*Demons,* 514)—an almost literal image of hell. Nor is there much comedy in the dramatic deaths of Shatov and Kirillov,[29] or in the matter-of-fact deaths of Liza Tushin, Captain Lebiadkin and his sister Maria, and Marie Shatov and her child.

Dostoevsky's theological approach to the problem of political terror recasts the romantic rebel, the "freedom-fighting" Nechaev figure, into a paragon of unfreedom, possessed of demonic suddenness.[30] It is important to recall that Dostoevsky took seriously a key variant of this figure—the Byronic rebel—and understood him sympathetically as the product of disillusionment with both autocracy and the tragic outcome of the French Revolution.[31] As Patyk notes in this volume, Dostoevsky's radical heroes suggest that for him the "Byronic 'moment' was a protracted one indeed, as the revolutionary movement was bound to produce a succession of disillusioned heroes marooned between bankrupt new idols and the old world." Some of Dostoevsky's readers (like Voloshin and Rice) believe that the projected second volume of *The Brothers Karamazov* would have decided the "questions that remain unanswered in *Demons*" (as though the prospect of Alyosha-as-revolutionary might square the circle of divine and political justice).[32] The fact that this book was never written—and, as Robert Belknap has argued, was perhaps never intended[33]—would mean that *Demons,* in all its "unanswered questions," remains the supreme expression of Russia's spiritual and political "protraction."[34] And if the Pushkin epigraph—with its invocation of a teeming, interesting, and seemingly unresolvable native Russian demonism—frames this expression, we must conclude by returning to the more hopeful epigraph from Luke to see if anything in the novel emerges from its counterdemonology. Is this demonic protraction, of which political terror is the secular manifestation, transcended? Is anyone really healed?

The only possible candidate would seem to be Verkhovensky's father, Stepan Trofimovich, the washed-up liberal of the 1840s, who wanders off at the end of the novel, like a Russian holy tramp or an ersatz Hebrew patriarch. On his deathbed, Stepan muses about the Gadarene swine:

> This wonderful and . . . extraordinary passage has been a stumbling block for me all my life. . . . These demons who come out of sick man and enter into swine—it's all the sores, all the miasmas, all the uncleanness, all the big and little demons accumulated in our dear and

> sick man, in our Russia, for centuries, for centuries! *Oui, cette Russie que j'aimais toujours.* But a great will and a great thought will descend to her from on high, as upon that insane demoniac, and out will come all the demons, all the uncleanness, all the abomination that is festering on the surface . . . and they will beg of themselves to enter into swine. And perhaps they already have! It is us, us and them, and Petrusha . . . *et les autres avec lui,* and I, perhaps, first, at the head, and we will rush, insane and raging, from the cliff down into the sea, and all be drowned, and good riddance to us, because that's the most we're fit for. But the sick man will be healed and "sit at the feet of Jesus." (*Demons,* 655)

Stepan does not claim to be the cured demoniac—in fact, he suggests he is one of the demons possessing "the sick man" that is Russia. But one may connect him to the healed man from the epigraph precisely because he also identifies himself at the head of the raging Gadarene swine (those sacrificial vessels of the exorcism), an acknowledgment of his irresponsible paternity—biological and spiritual—of "Petrusha . . . *et les autres.*" After all, to accept responsibility is, in a sense, to be healed. A sick man cannot be fully responsible for himself, much less for others.

Stepan's acceptance of responsibility may also explain some of the mysterious aspects of Luke 8:32–36: How do the demons know Jesus is God? Why do they beg to enter the swine? And why are witnesses afraid? Again, Kierkegaard provides the relevant gloss when he describes the demonic as an "anxiety about the good," which "manifests itself clearly only when it is in contact with the good. . . . For this reason, it is noteworthy that the demonic in the New Testament first appears when it is approached by Christ." If the demonic becomes evident only in proximity to "the restoration of freedom, redemption, salvation, or whatever one would call it,"[35] then it is understandable that the demons recognize Christ and bargain with him. Likewise, the Gadarenes' pleading with Jesus to leave their shores after the exorcism may be attributed to their fear of the demonism suddenly manifest among them or, just as plausibly, to their fear of the disruptive immanence of salvation. As Jesus and his followers will discover, not everyone wants to be "saved" right away. "If the demonic is a fate, it may happen to anyone," writes Kierkegaard, a fact that we Gadarenes are inclined to deny or forget with the help of "diversions and the Turkish music of loud enterprises."[36] The demons and the swine, in this sense, may be more commendable than the squeamish Gadarenes, just as Stepan emerges as a better man than his friend, the narrator-chronicler, who had set out to mock and blame him for the town's demonism and who comments skeptically on Stepan's last words, as though the narrator himself were not yet another demonic presence in the novel.[37]

Moreover, Stepan's declaration echoes Shatov's about his former comrades, shortly after his wife gives birth and before he is murdered, that "convictions and the man [. . . are] two different things in many ways. Maybe in many ways I'm guilty before them!" (*Demons,* 584). These are awkward precursors to the ethical maxim introduced on Markel's deathbed in *The Brothers Karamazov:* "Each of us is guilty for everyone in everything, and I more than the others."[38] This maxim precludes terror as an option for achieving justice, for if I am indeed responsible more than the others, then I have no right to impose my radical solution upon them, to make them equally or more responsible than I am. Faisal Devji suggests that al Qaeda—arrogating to individuals a religious authority that was heretofore collective and hierarchical—is a perversely "democratizing" and modernizing force in the context of traditional Islam.[39] So, too, was Russian terror in the late nineteenth century, although the Bolshevik regime it eventually produced was in most ways less democratic than that of the Romanovs. Democratization does not necessarily lead to democracy.[40]

Luke's heroic, miracle-working Christ, who—in keeping with the apocalyptic dualism that characterized late biblical Judaism—directly wages war against Satan in this world,[41] is here transmuted through Stepan's "*profession de foi*" into something less dramatic. Indeed, if, as Adam Weiner suggests, *Demons* "is about the evil that postlapsarian man does out of the best motives, in his impatience to be reunited with God,"[42] then Stepan's dying words almost seem like an ebbing away of such impatience and of its demonic politics. We must recall that both the politically demonic and the Godly seek to overrule matters personal and biological. In 1 Kings 19, Elisha abandons his prosperous family to follow Elijah. In Mark 3 and Luke 8 (the chapter that includes the tale of the Gadarene swine), Jesus rejects his own skeptical relatives and enjoins his followers to reject theirs as well,[43] just as elsewhere in the Gospels one finds allegories about offending eyes and hands to be plucked or severed if they put the soul in mortal peril (Mark 9:42–47 and Matthew 18:9). Similarly, Nechaev's *Catechism* reminds us that

> A revolutionary is a dedicated man. He has no interests of his own, no affairs, no feelings, no attachments, no belongings, not even a name. Everything in him is absorbed by a single exclusive interest, a single thought, a single passion—the revolution. . . . All the tender and effeminate emotions of kinship, friendship, love, gratitude and even honour must be stifled in him by a cold and single-minded passion for the revolutionary cause. There exists for him only one delight, one consolation, one reward and one gratification—the success of the

> revolution. Night and day he must have but one thought, one aim—merciless destruction. In cold-blooded and tireless pursuit of this aim, he must be prepared both to die himself and to destroy with his own hands everything that stands in the way of its achievement. The nature of the true revolutionary has no place for any romanticism, any sentimentality, rapture or enthusiasm. It has no place either for personal hatred or vengeance. The revolutionary passion, which in him becomes a habitual state of mind, must at every moment be combined with cold calculation. Always and everywhere he must be not what the promptings of his personal inclinations would have him be, but what the general interest of the revolution prescribes. . . . The revolutionary considers his friend and holds dear only a person who has shown himself in practice to be as much a revolutionary as himself. The extent of his friendship, devotion and other obligations towards his comrade is determined only by their degree of usefulness in the practical work of total revolutionary destruction.[44]

Intimacy is the chief obstacle of an apocalyptic or revolutionary politics, which reduces everyone to a bit part in a vast impersonal drama.

At the farcical meeting of revolutionaries in *Demons,* we are treated to the comedy of the "girl student" and her uncle, the major, who can't reconcile the rude young radical with the girl he used to carry in his "arms, danced the mazurka with her when she was ten years old. . . . She came in today, naturally I flew to embrace her, and she announces to me from the second word that there is no God. If it had been from the third word, not from the second—but no, she's in a hurry!" (*Demons,* 397). *Pospeshysh', liudei nasmeshysh',* goes the Russian proverb: If you hurry, people will laugh. Everyone in the novel is in a hurry, rushing into the Galilee like the Gadarene swine. Stepan recognizes this, sees his ideological and biological connection to it, and understands that this impatience is a lie, a form of vanity that has little to do with the patience required for true political compassion.[45] Moreover, by invoking and embodying the episode from Luke, Stepan softens the Gospels' own political impatience. The unspecified "great will and great thought" will come after Stepan. When it comes doesn't really matter; what matters is the faith that it will and must require—a faith that permits us to live in this world without succumbing to demonic impatience.

And while there is as much bathos as pathos in Stepan's confession, the comedy is, for perhaps the first time in the novel, gentle and not derisive. Dostoevsky, after all, also believed in the redemptive possibility of humor and considered Don Quixote to be an exemplary Christian character;[46] and in *The Brothers Karamazov* Zosima recalls how after his conversion his former comrades "laughed at [him] and yet they loved" him (300). As Varvara Petrovna explains to the priest, Stepan "is the sort of man [who will] have to be reconfessed again in an hour." His deathbed revelation, suffering as it does from his characteristic Gallicisms and "artistic receptivity" (*Demons,* 663), suggests that a modern exorcism will not so much be a complete transformation as it might reveal a cultural "middle." And it is this middle that can defend itself against the sort of world-unmaking reflected by political terror—of the demonic suddenness that destroys the boring and vital continuity of imperfectly free human beings.

The project of a viable middle is one that has perplexed Russia—so notoriously bipolar—for hundreds of years. For instance, the same Nikolai Berdiaev who could invoke the Russian maximalist creed that "culture . . . and institutions belittle life itself," also realized that "in its struggle against mediocrity and moderation, every culture will tend downward, toward the nether abyss, rather than the chasm above. These modern Scythians sing hymns not to a super-cultural, but to a pre-cultural condition."[47] Mikhail Epstein identifies this Russian preoccupation with mediocrity and *poshlost,* this suspicion of the sorts of "neutral" cultural and civic institutions that came to define the West, as demonic precisely in Kierkegaard's sense of the sudden.[48] And, uncharacteristically for Dostoevsky's world, Stepan's "conversion" is anything but sudden. It is dragged out and ungainly, fed by human and sensory encounters on the road—peasants "studying [him as if he] were guilty before them," blini and vodka at the tavern, Sofia Matveevna the bible-seller who takes care of him, etc. (*Demons,* 634–44)[49]—and will forever beg interpretation. This is its key difference from the legend Kierkegaard cites as an exemplar for the demonic, in which "the devil for 3,000 years sat and speculated on how to destroy man—finally, he did discover it."[50] Nor is Stepan like the atheist philosopher in the allegory recounted by Ivan's devil in *The Brothers Karamazov* who sings hosanna two seconds upon reaching the gates of heaven after refusing for a thousand years to approach them out of principle.[51] Stepan's confession contains no such demonic drama; and yet it cannot be dismissed despite—and perhaps precisely because of—its apparent mediocrity and muddle. The laughter it induces is potentially redemptive, in a very un-Russian way.

The novel that began with a sneering biography of Stepan as an effete and grossly irresponsible romantic ends with a loving if ridiculous portrait of his final days as a penitent. The novel that began as a polemic framed by two juxtaposed demonologies ends in a modest synthesis that sets aside both. And it is appropriate that this synthesis, this middle, takes the shape of comedy—in counterpoint to the basic humorlessness of terror, a parallel and opposite response to human corporeality. Comedy is life-as-theater, figuratively loosening us from our bodies. Terror is theater-as-life, literally removing us from our bodies. If, as Kierkegaard suggests, demonic suddenness is "*almost* comic in [its] involuntary anxiety,"[52] then the ability to laugh at it, to extend it into narrative continuity, is already not demonic.

If *Demons* is ultimately not about terror per se, the novel certainly revolves around its culture. And the most basic lesson in this sense is that the goals of political terror are of secondary importance. The more sincere and compassionate the terrorist, the more maximalist his goals. As the experience of post-truce IRA and ETA splinter groups suggests, it is difficult to cease terror even after "victory." After all, what earthly goal can be worth such world-unmaking means? The logic goes, "We have spilled too much blood to accept anything short of total victory, whatever that is." *Demons* is not simply a full-frontal satirical attack on the Russian Westernizers and nihilists, as Dostoevsky initially intended. The right-wing fans who still invoke the novel as an exposé of every liberal tendency seldom mention the fact that there are no attractive *political* alternatives in the novel: the conservative Governor von Lembke—who does "not allow youth" (*Demons,* 447)—with his Germanisms and his paper sculptures, is an idiot whose sanity is overcome by the events in the town. Indeed, the novel should perhaps be read as a warning about *any* form of political earnestness. Dostoevsky's point (confirmed in his 1873 *Diary* article about Nechaevism)[53] is that, inasmuch as we are vulnerable to the brooding suddenness of ideological demons, each of us is an unwitting terrorist-in-waiting, a passive nihilist in Nietzsche's sense,[54] rehearsing that specific scene that would prompt one to disrupt life's muddy and relentless stream.

What, then, is literature's role in understanding terror? My reading of *Demons* leads me to suggest not that fiction merely lends additional complexity to the explanations offered by the social sciences but that it challenges the very basis of their authority. After all, social science is conditioned by the premise that the human can be reduced to knowledge, to typologies—a demonically impatient premise, as Dostoevsky might argue. Instead, literature defers knowledge and offers us the immersive, imaginative, and forever ambiguous experience of characters, narrative, and linguistic subtlety. In this experience, the souls of Stepan "and Petrusha . . . *et les autres avec lui*" do not become known to us but, rather, mingle with our own.[55] By this I do not mean that Dostoevsky's fiction simply urges a kind of political quietism—after all, even in his skepticism, Dostoevsky preferred ideas that were passionately *felt* and not just sensible. Indeed, the right kind of moral and political impatience has freed slaves and given women the vote. But liberal *outrage* is very different from the self-righteous *rage* of the terrorist, who strikes at a civilian target to emphasize—as philosophy and social science, in their more deterministic moods, are often wont to do—that every part and person represents the corrupt whole of "the system."[56] The best writers, on the other hand, show us how even the sorriest parts can exceed the whole, how no one—not even the manipulative Peter Verkhovensky, when he is called "Petrusha" by his father—can fully represent any system. Unfortunately, if, as one critic puts it, "writers philosophize not with a hammer but with a feather,"[57] terrorists do so with a bomb.

Notes

I thank Anthony Anemone, Keith Gessen, and Lynn Ellen Patyk for their generous and indispensable criticism, suggestions, and encouragement in the revision of this essay.

1. See Avital Ronell, *The Telephone Book: Technology, Schizophrenia, Electric Speech* (Lincoln: University of Nebraska Press, 1991).

2. Among the better scholarly treatments is Nina Pelikan Straus, "From Dostoevsky to Al-Qaeda: What Fiction Says to Social Science," *Common Knowledge* 12, no. 2 (Spring 2006): 197–213; others are cited below. An even more telling barometer may be the recourse to Dostoevsky's *Demons* on a variety of blogs (and recent course syllabi) about terrorism: see Justin Raimondo's comparison of George W. Bush to Governor von Lembke, "W and Dostoevsky: George W. Bush Is a Man Possessed," *Antiwar.com,* comment posted January 21, 2005, http://antiwar.com/justin/?articleid=4515 (accessed May 8, 2009); and Chris Floyd's comparison of neoconservative foreign policy to Shigalevism, "Fatal Vision: The Strategy of Chaos and Ethnic Cleansing," *Empire Burlesque,* comment posted September 12, 2006, www.chris-floyd.com/index.php?option=com_content&task=view&id=842&Itemid=135 (accessed May 8, 2009). Perhaps most striking is the statement on the Web site of the 2007 Summer Program of the European College of Liberal Arts in Berlin, "The Mantle of the Prophet: Demons, Saints, and Terrorists," http://www.h-net.org/announce/show.cgi?ID=154119, which takes *Demons* as the "keystone text in exploring the historical and intellectual roots of terrorism, its embodiments from state terror to individual violence, and its expression of nihilist and existential questions."

3. Straus, "From Dostoevsky to Al-Qaeda," 198. The tendency to treat Russian fiction as a source or confirmation for social psychology is at least as old as Nietzsche and Freud, the latter of whom understood the "death instinct" as a Russian cultural contribution. See James Rice, *Freud's Russia: National Identity in the Evolution of Psychoanalysis* (New Brunswick, N.J.: Transaction Publishers, 1993), 17–19.

4. This is perhaps the chief problem with a work like André Glucksmann's otherwise provocative *Dostoïevski à Manhattan* (Paris: Laffont, 2002). See also Andrew McKenna, "Scandal, Resentment, Idolatry: The Underground Psychology of Terrorism," *Anthropoetics* 8, no. 1 (Spring–Summer 2002), www.anthropoetics.ucla.edu/ap0801/resent.htm (accessed May 8, 2009). See also André Glucksmann, "Bin Laden, Dostoevsky and the Reality Principle: An Interview with André Glucksmann," *OpenDemocracy.net,* posted March 31, 2003, www.opendemocracy.net/faith-iraqwarphiloshophy/article_1111.jsp (accessed May 8, 2009). Glucksmann's rather unprescient comments on Iraq underscore the risks involved in making policy by way of literary generalization.

5. Ilja Kostovski, *Dostoevsky and Goethe: Two Devils—Two Geniuses* (New York: Revisionist Press, 1974), 104.

6. See Paul Avrich, *Bakunin and Nechaev* (London: Freedom Press, 1974); Konstantin Mochulsky, *Dostoevsky: His Life and Work,* trans. Michael Minihan (Princeton: Princeton University Press, 1967), 404–32; Joseph Frank, *Dostoevsky: The Miraculous Years, 1865–1871* (Princeton: Princeton University Press, 1996), 397–500, and *Dostoevsky: The Mantle of the Prophet, 1871–1881* (Princeton: Princeton University Press, 2002), 1–102.

7. Fyodor Dostoevsky, *Demons,* trans. Richard Pevear and Larissa Volokhonsky (New York: Vintage, 1995), 421. All further quotations from the novel in this chapter are from this edition.

8. The strength of Nechaev's convictions so impressed his guards that, by the late 1870s, he was using them to pass correspondence to revolutionaries on the outside. By this means, by 1880 Nechaev and the leadership of Narodnaia volia were able to begin plotting his escape, an effort that was ultimately abandoned because he did not want to distract the organization from the effort to assassinate Alexander II.

9. Lynn Ellen Patyk, "By the Double-Edged Sword of Word and Deed: Revolutionary Terrorism and Russian Literary Culture, 1871–1917" (Ph.D. diss., Stanford University, 2006), 26.

10. Of course, even if Dostoevsky had not died in February 1881, the successful assassination of Alexander II a month later would have rendered any fictional depiction of tsar killing unlikely due to censorship.

11. Dostoevsky, *The Brothers Karamazov,* trans. Richard Pevear and Larissa Volokhonsky (New York: Farrar, Straus and Giroux, 2002), 126. Dostoevsky's narrator is comparing Smerdyakov to the 1876 painting by Ivan Kramskoi (1837–87) of a ragged peasant with a vacant expression, walking on a forest trail; the narrator sees a stereotypically Russian bipolarity in the peasant's act of "contemplation." All further translations in this chapter are from this edition.

12. Patyk, "By the Double-Edged Sword," 30–31.

13. Dostoevsky, *The Diary of a Writer,* trans. Boris Brasol (New York: Charles Scribner, 1949), 286. Dostoevsky, *Polnoe sobranie sochinenii,* 30 vols. (Leningrad: Nauka, 1972), 21:131, 21:129 (henceforth *PSS*).

14. Nikolai Berdiaev viewed this belief "in a 'Russian Christ,' who is a national god, a peasant god with their own characteristics" as a "pagan tendency in the very bosom of Orthodoxy"—a tendency that "can be seen in Dostoevsky himself." See Berdiaev, *Dostoevsky,* trans. Donald Attwater (Cleveland: Meridian Books, 1968), 184–85.

15. Elaine Scarry, *The Body in Pain* (New York: Oxford University Press, 1985).

16. *Bes* and *beshenstvo* might be related to *Bessesenheit,* the German word for possession. See also Georg Krotkoff, "Zum ägyptischen Ursprung des slawischen Bes Dämon," in *Zwischen den beiden Ewigkeiten: Festschrift Thausing* (Vienna: Eigenverlag des Institutes für Ägyptologie der Universität Wien, 1994), 143–45, which discusses the iconography of *Bes* on objects of Iranian nomadic tribes in Altai and suggests the possibility that the name of the Egyptian demon god Bes may lie at the origin of the Ukrainian *bis* and Russian *bes.* In an interesting parallel, the word "demon" comes from the Greek *daimone* or spirit, a neutral or positive polytheistic term that was likewise transformed into something negative by the church fathers.

17. See Emmanuel Levinas, *Time and the Other,* trans. Richard Cohen (Pittsburgh: Duquesne University Press, 1987), 50.

18. In his excellent chapter, "Narrative Possession in *The Devils*," Adam Weiner notes that the Pushkin poem contains the voices of a coachman, who is the first to identify the *besy* and fears them, and his master (the poet), who comes to pity them. See Weiner, *By Authors Possessed: The Demonic Novel in Russia* (Evanston, Ill.: Northwestern University Press, 1998), 93–137. Weiner also points out that the narrator of *Demons* expresses awareness only of the epigraph from Luke and not the other, which suggests that the Pushkin stanzas were chosen by an "implied author" who, like the poet, comes to sympathize with the demonic (130–31). See also Michael Brewer's detailed and cogent "'Besy' na sluzhbe u *Besov:* Analiz stikhotvorenia Pushkina i ego roli v epigrafe k romanu Dostoevskogo," *Graduate Essays on Slavic Languages and Literatures* (University of Pittsburgh Center for Russian and East European Studies), 11–12 (1999): 18–27, which suggests that the Pushkin epigraph provides the crucial local historical context for the eschatological "History" of the passage from Luke. I would qualify this argument by questioning the assumption behind it—that Dostoevsky was truly convinced by his own rhetoric about the centrality of the "God-bearing Russian people." Even Vladimir Soloviev doubted Dostoevsky's faith in this respect; see Marina Kostalevsky, *Dostoevsky and Soloviev* (New Haven: Yale University Press, 1997), 144. René Girard writes that Dostoevsky "fully understood the negative usefulness of religion as a social prop against anarchy and chaos but was personally unable to believe." Girard, *Resurrection from the Underground: Feodor Dostoevsky,* trans. James G. Williams (New York: Crossroad, 1997), 162–63. James Rice argues persuasively, however, that Dostoevsky never gave up the radical politics of his youth, and that his reactionary outbursts were a smoke screen for a profoundly pessimistic view of the very possibility of "the Russian idea." See Rice, "Dostoevsky's Endgame: The Projected Sequel to *The Brothers Karamazov,*" *Russian History/Histoire Russe* 33, no. 1 (Spring 2006): 45–62.

19. See Linda Ivanits, *Russian Folk Belief* (Armonk, N.Y.: M. E. Sharpe, 1992), 169–77.

20. Dostoevsky's question mark also links Pushkin's language—*chto delat' nam*—to the political discourse of the 1860s and beyond: *Chto delat'?* or *What Is to Be Done?* (an ideological successor to Alexander Herzen's *Who Is to Blame?*) was the title of Nikolai Chernyshevsky's 1863 socialist novel (and, later, Lenin's tract). Dostoevsky began *Demons* partly as an ironic response to Chernyshevsky's question.

21. For a persuasive explanation of the circumstances of Dostoevsky's decision, see Frank, *Dostoevsky: The Miraculous Years,* 434.

22. Oddly, Matryosha is described both as a fourteen- and a ten-year-old. The first variant casts Stavrogin as a statutory rapist, the second as a pedophile.

23. See Mochulsky, who argues that the deletion of the Tikhon chapter reflected Dostoevsky's hope that Stavrogin might yet be healed like the demoniac in the second epigraph, who "was destroyed and only the dark panel of the diptych remained: the picture of hell, of universal ruin, of the raging of the demonic snowstorm . . . [of] Pushkin's verses" (*Dostoevsky,* 466).

24. The identification of the monk Otrepev (1580–1606) with the first "False Dmitry" is uncertain and owes as much to the propaganda of Dmitry's enemies as it does to Pushkin's immortalization of Otrepev as the pretender-czar in *Boris Godunov.* Weiner and Brewer note that the Time of Troubles, or *Smuta,* that devastated Russia during the early seventeenth century is a connective subtext shared by *Demons, Boris Godunov,* and Pushkin's "*Besy,*" in which *mutno* (a cognate of *smutno*) appears in a

thrice-repeated refrain: "Clouds race, clouds swirl; / The hidden moon / Lights up the flying snow; / The sky is hazy [*mutno*], hazy [*mutna*] is the night." Pushkin, *Polnoe sobranie sochinenii,* 10 vols. (Moscow, 1956), 3:176.

25. Søren Kierkegaard, *The Concept of Anxiety,* ed. and trans. Reidar Thomte with Albert Anderson (Princeton: Princeton University Press, 1980), 135.

26. Ibid., 130–33.

27. Ibid., 133.

28. Sergei Averintsev, "Bakhtin and the Russian Attitude Toward Laughter," trans. Tom Cunningham, in *Critical Essays on Mikhail Bakhtin,* ed. Caryl Emerson (New York: G. K. Hall, 1999), 278.

29. Kirillov's grotesque and undignified suicide, preceded by his biting Peter's finger, might arguably seem comical only if the reader had no sympathy for Kirillov to begin with.

30. The quotation marks here reflect the fact that Nechaev's revolutionary *Catechism,* written together with Bakunin in 1869, actually has little to do with freedom. Here is a typical passage, translated by Hilary Sternberg and Lydia Bott, from *Daughter of a Revolutionary: Natalie Herzen and the Bakunin-Nechaev Circle,* ed. Michael Confino (London: Alcove Press, 1974), 226: "Each comrade should have under him several revolutionists of the second or third categories, that is, comrades who are not completely initiated. He should regard them as portions of a common fund of revolutionary capital, placed at his disposal. He should expend his portion of the capital economically, always attempting to derive utmost benefit from it. Himself he should regard as capital consecrated to the triumph of the revolutionary cause; but as capital which he may not dispose of independently without the consent of the entire company of the fully initiated comrades." The revolutionary is utterly unfree here, ironically reduced to "capital" at the disposition of the movement. Translations of Nechaev's *Catechism* may be found on several "alternative" and "radical" Web sites; the Russian is available at www.hrono.ru/dokum/katehizrev.html (accessed May 10, 2009).

31. See Frank, *Dostoevsky: The Mantle of the Prophet,* 333.

32. Maksimilian Voloshin, *Istoriia moei dushi* (Moscow: Agraf, 1991), 57; the passage is translated in Patyk, "By the Double-Edged Sword."

33. Robert Belknap, *The Structure of "The Brothers Karamazov"* (Evanston, Ill.: Northwestern University Press, 1989), 98–104. Belknap's case for the projected sequel's status as a literary device rests on the fact that Dostoevsky did no work on it after submitting the last installment of *The Brothers Karamazov,* that the fictional "author" makes almost the same remark about incompleteness at the end of *Crime and Punishment* as he makes at the beginning of *The Brothers Karamazov,* and that Dostoevsky may have been inspired by the romantics' use of incompleteness as a "roughening device [. . . that] disturbs the impact of the existing novel and suggests a grand scheme."

34. It has been suggested that *Demons* is a novel written on "the second day," between the Crucifixion and the Resurrection. A most protracted second day, indeed! For more on "the second day," see Caryl Emerson, "Word and Image in Dostoevsky's Worlds: Robert Louis Jackson on Readings That Bakhtin Could Not Do," in *Freedom and Responsibility in Russian Literature: Essays in Honor of Robert Louis Jackson,* ed. Elizabeth Cheresh Allen and Gary Saul Morson (Evanston, Ill.: Northwestern University Press, 1995), 246–306.

35. Kierkegaard, *Anxiety,* 119.

36. Ibid., 120.

37. Weiner makes a compelling argument for the narrator's demonism in *By Authors Possessed,* 93–137.

38. Levinas adopts this credo to express his own philosophical project. For more on this connection, see Val Vinokur, "Levinas's Dostoevsky," *Common Knowledge* 9, no. 2 (2003): 318–40, and *The Trace of Judaism: Dostoevsky, Babel, Mandelstam, Levinas* (Evanston, Ill.: Northwestern University Press, 2008).

39. Faisal Devji, *Landscapes of the Jihad* (Ithaca, N.Y.: Cornell University Press, 2005).

40. Jonathan Raban links this paradox to a more general, parricidal "theology of rebellion, rooted in hostility and contempt"—a theology that, as Raban's own experience as a British antinuclear "fundamentalist" underscores, may also be militantly atheist. Raban, "My Holy War," *New Yorker,* February 4, 2002, 33, 35. Examples of democratization eating its own tail are almost too many to list; they include Weimar Germany, the post-Soviet states, Algeria in the 1990s, and post-Saddam Iraq.

41. See Jeffrey Burton Russell, *The Prince of Darkness* (Ithaca, N.Y.: Cornell University Press, 1992), 44–47: "The struggle between God and the Evil One is at the heart of the New Testament. In the New Testament worldview, either you follow God or you are subject to Satan. Because of sin, the world lies under the Devil's power; Christ comes to break that power and to heal the alienation between humanity and God. . . . By exorcising the demons and by curing diseases sent by them, Jesus makes war upon Satan's kingdom and thereby makes known to the people that the new age is coming. 'If I drive out demons by the power of God it is because the kingdom of God is come among you' (Matthew 12:28). The exorcism of demons represents no quirk here, no irrelevant accretion of superstition, but rather is central to the war against Satan and therefore to the meaning of the gospels. Each act of exorcism represented one installment of the destruction of the old age, one step closer to the time when Satan will no longer control the world."

42. Weiner, *By Authors Possessed,* 133.

43. "My mother and my brethren are these which hear the word of God, and do it" (Luke 8:21).

44. Quoted in Confino, *Daughter of a Revolutionary,* 224–26.

45. For more on such impatience, see Claudia Verhoeven, "The Wait, and Then Any Moment: On the Temporality of Revolutionary Terrorism," paper presented at the conference panel "New Directions in the Study of Russian Revolutionary Terrorism," AAASS, Washington, D.C., November 16, 2006.

46. See R. L. Busch, *Humor in the Major Novels of F. M. Dostoevsky* (Columbus, Ohio: Slavica, 1987).

47. Nikolai Berdiaev, "Filosofia neravenstva" (1923), in *Sobranie sochenenii,* 4 vols. (Paris: YMCA Press, 1990), 4:573, 571.

48. Mikhail Epstein, "Russian Spirituality and the Theology of Negation," paper presented at the international conference, "Russian Culture at the Crossroads: Art and Society," University of Nevada, Las Vegas, November 24, 1997. Available at www.unlv.edu/centers/cdclv/archives/nc2/epstein_demonic.html (accessed May 14, 2009). See also Yuri Lotman, "'Agreement' and 'Self-Giving' as Archetypal Models of Culture," trans. N. F. C. Owen, in *The Semiotics of Russian Culture* (Michigan Slavic Contributions 11), ed. Jurij M. Lotman and B. A. Uspenskij (Ann Arbor: Department of Slavic Languages and Literatures, University of Michigan, 1984); or Iurii Lotman, *Izbrannye stat'i,* 3 vols. (Tallinn: Alexandra, 1993).

49. Of all this Stepan observes, as only he could, "This 'real life' has something rather characteristic about it" (*Demons,* 634).

50. Kierkegaard, *Anxiety,* 131.

51. Ivan's devil notes that the philosopher "oversweetened it so much that some persons there, of a nobler cast of mind, did not even want to shake hands with him at first: he jumped over to the conservatives a bit too precipitously. The Russian character" (*Brothers Karamazov,* 644). This is Dostoevsky's dig both at himself and at the liberal critics who said that he "oversweetened it" with his own sudden embrace of Orthodoxy.

52. Kierkegaard, *Anxiety,* 129 (my emphasis).

53. Dostoevsky, *Diary,* 286. Dostoevsky, *PSS,* 21:129.

54. A "normal condition," according to Nietzsche, in *The Will to Power,* trans. Walter Kaufmann and R. J. Hollingdale (New York: Random House, 1967), 18. See Straus, "From Dostoevsky to Al-Qaeda," 204. For a chilling example of "normal" nihilism, see Peter Landesman, "A Modest Proposal from the Brigadier," *Atlantic Monthly,* March 2002, 37–38, in which a retired Pakistani general expresses his hopes for a nuclear exchange with India: "We should fire at them and take out a few of their cities. . . . They should fire back and take Karachi and Lahore. . . . It would teach all of us a lesson. There is no future here and we need to start over. So many people think this. . . . There is nothing but dire poverty and pain. . . . My children have no future. . . . Millions should die away. . . . Before I die I hope I should see it."

55. Keith Gessen notes this essential conflict between knowledge and narrative in his analysis of the *9/11 Report:* "We were going to *know* the enemy. And then? Well, and then—we were going to kill him. The trouble for the producers of this knowledge is that narrative demands sympathy and identification." Gessen, "Torture and the Known Unknowns," *n+1* 5 (Winter 2007): 125. Gessen argues convincingly that the most compelling literature to come out of 9/11 so far has been journalism and transcripts, not fiction. The current "war on terror" has not found its Dostoevsky. See also Michael Walzer's discussion of the Orwell episode in *Just and Unjust Wars* (New York: Basic Books, 1992), 140–41.

56. Any useful definition of terrorism should exclude asymmetrical warfare and suicide attacks against military or command targets. Insurgents and regular soldiers become terrorists only by deliberately targeting civilians. *Jus in bello* is not a bourgeois nicety; it represents the acknowledgment that even in wartime human identity remains complex. During the Spanish Civil War, George Orwell trained his rifle on an enemy soldier taking a bathroom break: "I had come here to shoot at 'Fascists'; but a man who is holding up his trousers isn't a 'Fascist,' he is visibly a fellow-creature, similar to yourself, and you don't feel like shooting him." Orwell's insight, while less than categorically normative, is also more than empirically psychological: it is profoundly literary in the way it makes the primary experience of empathy instantly recognizable to the reader without any claim to reproducible truth. See Orwell, "Looking Back on the Spanish War," in *My Country Right or Left 1940–1943: The Collected Essays Journalism and Letters of George Orwell,* ed. Sonia Orwell and Ian Angus (Jaffrey, N.H.: Nonpareil Books, 2000), 254.

57. Gary Saul Morson, *Narrative and Freedom* (New Haven: Yale University Press, 1994), 4.

Fool or Saint? Writers Reading the Zasulich Case

Donna Oliver

In 1873, in *The Diary of a Writer*, Dostoevsky offered the following explanation for the behavior of his misled revolutionaries in *The Devils:*

> I made the attempt to depict the manifold and heterogeneous motives which may prompt even the purest of heart and the most naive people to take part in the perpetration of so monstrous a villainy. The horror lies precisely in the fact that in our midst the filthiest and most villainous act may be committed by one who is not a villain at all! . . . This is the most pathological and saddest trait of our present time—the possibility of considering oneself not as a villain, and sometimes almost not being one, while perpetrating a patent and incontestable villainy—therein is our present-day calamity![1]

Dostoevsky wrote *The Devils* in response to the notorious Nechaev affair, yet his postscript here makes clear the persistence of his concern for the idealistic youth of his time, whose well-intentioned attempts to effect meaningful change by joining the revolutionary cause could lead them to make moral compromises that would undermine the very ideals that motivated them in their quest. As such, his comments are prophetic in that they aptly capture the contradictory ethical basis of the Russian revolutionary period and correctly predict the violent consequences that were to come once political terror was adopted as a means to a greater good. Yet the act that launched the terrorist stage in the Russian revolutionary movement was not regarded by the majority of educated Russian society—or by Dostoevsky himself—as such a "monstrous villainy"; in fact, its "villainous" aspects were for many eclipsed by that very moral idealism that lay at its base.

On January 24, 1878, twenty-eight-year-old Vera Zasulich, posing as a petitioner, shot at point-blank range the governor-general of St. Petersburg, F. F. Trepov, in his reception hall. At her trial two months later, Zasulich testified that her motive for shooting Trepov was revenge for his role in ordering the beating of a political prisoner, Arkhip Bogoliubov, who had refused to remove his cap when addressing the governor-general. Zasulich reported that although she did not know the prisoner Bogoliubov, the news of his beating had made a tremendous impression on her. She confessed at her trial that the attempt on Trepov had been completely premeditated, but that the consequence of her attempt for the general—that is, whether she killed him or merely wounded him—was immaterial to her, since her goal was simply to make sure that an act of such arbitrary tyranny did not pass without punishment. Zasulich's attorney produced as witnesses other political prisoners who testified with tears in their eyes about Bogoliubov's brutal beating with birch rods, a punishment that was both rare and cruel. The defense attorney successfully turned the case into a trial of the victim and concluded by elevating Zasulich to the role of martyr-avenger, a woman whose conscience was so alert to acts of injustice that she was simply unable to sit back idly and let them go unpunished.

Zasulich testified at her trial that she experienced deep dismay when she realized that Trepov's actions would pass without reprimand:

> I waited for some response, but everyone remained silent. . . . There was nothing to stop Trepov, or someone just as powerful as he, from repeating the same violence over and over. I resolved at that point, even if it cost my life, to prove that no one who abused a human being that way could be sure of getting away with it. I couldn't find another way of drawing attention to what had happened. I saw no other way. . . . It's terrible to have to lift a hand against another person, but I felt that it had to be done.[2]

According to Zasulich, it was not the harshness or the cruelty of the punishment that outraged her; rather, she was upset by "the despotic tyranny over the human dignity of powerless, defenseless people." Zasulich herself had spent two years in prison and two more in exile for accidental complicity in the Nechaev affair. Thus, Zasulich's attorney argued, she well understood the sufferings and spiritual torment of people deprived of freedom, and as a result, she "came to love with her whole soul all those who suffer for their convictions."[3] The jury deliberated less than an hour and returned a verdict of not guilty.

By the time it was tried, the Zasulich case had already acquired tremendous notoriety and had taken on a truly sensational aspect. When the verdict was announced, the spectators in the courtroom—administrative powers, representatives of the press, and members of high society—broke into thunderous applause; the enormous crowd waiting on the street reacted with a joy that soon led to near-riot conditions. Zasulich was almost mobbed when she was escorted from the court building, and the crowd accompanied her carriage through the streets of St. Petersburg. The furor surrounding Zasulich increased even more when the tsar, outraged at the verdict, ordered her arrested again. Aided by liberal sympathizers who vied with each other in offers to help her leave Russia, Zasulich went into hiding, where she remained until she was smuggled out of the country a few months later.[4]

Though the verdict delivered by the jury may have defied the letter of the law,[5] it was the public response to the verdict that was in many ways the more notable event. How did educated members of Russian society come to sympathize with Vera Zasulich and, in some cases, excuse her actions on the basis of a moral imperative? The answer to this question is far from easy. Certainly, part of it lies in the sensational nature of the crime itself, as well as in the age and gender of its perpetrator. But the more compelling reason seems implicit in Zasulich's motive, in her determination to avenge an injustice and her willingness to accept whatever consequences she herself might face as a result. This higher purpose driving Zasulich's rebellion, along with the thirst for self-sacrifice and martyrdom that drew her to it, clearly resonated with the Russian national consciousness, inspiring many of her contemporaries to view her action as an example of supreme virtue and moral integrity.

This compulsion for self-sacrifice, with its origins in the kenoticism so revered by Russian Orthodoxy, was in fact what drew many young Russians to the radical cause and resulted ironically in a conflation of the ideals of Christianity with the ideals of revolution.[6] Vera Zasulich was no exception. In her memoirs, she wrote how she felt little connection in her childhood and youth to God but tremendous devotion to Christ and the idea Christ represented: "What bothered me most was that everyone, absolutely everyone had fled and abandoned Him, even the children who had greeted Him with palm branches and hosannas." Zasulich's love for Christ was a love borne out of a desire to emulate him, to sacrifice herself in the same way he had sacrificed himself, to be *his* savior: "I didn't want His intercession, I wanted to serve Him, to save Him." By age fifteen, Zasulich no longer believed in God, but she continued to cherish the idea of Christ: "Of my earlier religious beliefs, only Christ remained with me, engraved in my heart. In fact, it was as if I were more closely tied to Him than ever."[7]

What is ironic about this desire for self-sacrifice is that it became for many revolutionary women a goal in itself: the consequence of helping others was in some ways secondary to the true goal of satisfying the thirst for martyrdom. Zasulich made it quite clear in her memoirs that her motivation for joining the revolutionary struggle was not to help the suffering masses but to help those who were struggling to help the masses. She quotes her hero, the Decembrist poet Ryleev: "'There are times, there are entire ages, when there is nothing more beautiful and desirable than a crown of thorns.'" Zasulich recognized that her own actions were motivated by that desire:

> That crown of thorns attracted me to those who perished, inspiring my passionate love for them, too. And undoubtedly, that love resembled the love I had felt for Christ when I read the Gospel for the first time. I had not betrayed Him: both He and they were great enough to merit a crown of thorns. . . . I would seek them out and try to make myself useful to their struggle. Sympathy for the sufferings of the people did not move me to join those who perished.[8]

Though Zasulich could not, of course, carry out her dream of being Christ's savior, she could nonetheless function in that role for someone else—such as Arkhip Bogoliubov and other struggling, suffering revolutionaries.

But perhaps an equal culprit in nurturing this thirst for self-sacrifice among revolutionary youth was Russian literature, with its prescriptive models of behavior and firm ethical base. The habit of looking to literature for cues about how to behave in real life was a well-established practice by the mid-nineteenth century and had even become the subject of literary works themselves, most notably Pushkin's *Eugene Onegin* and *Tales of Belkin.* Boris Gasparov in his introduction to *The Semiotics of Russian Cultural History* contextualizes this habit in a broader practice of using literature "as an all embracing 'guide to life'": "Literature was regarded, and even regarded itself, as containing the solution to moral problems and the answer to cardinal philosophical questions. It was a political program for the transformation of society, a codex of individual behavior, a way of understanding the national past, and a source of prophesy about the future." The civic criticism of Belinsky and others further contributed to the "sanctification of literature"[9] among Russia's educated classes. The literary text and the characters it portrayed became not only sources for knowledge of the world but also arbiters of ethical behavior and stimulants of social consciousness.

For Vera Zasulich, it was the literature introduced to her by her governess that kindled her moral awareness—the poetry of Lermontov, Nekrasov, and especially Ryleev, whose works revealed to her a "world of heroism, struggle, and moral virtue" far different from the reality of her existence growing up unwanted and unloved in the home of relatives. Ryleev's own fate, brought about, in Zasulich's view, by his struggles "to reduce the material and spiritual impoverishment of the masses,"[10] convinced Zasulich that meaningful civic engagement rested on the Christian ideals of suffering and self-sacrifice. According to Yuri Lotman, Ryleev's poetry was in fact responsible for helping to define the cultural norms of heroic behavior for his contemporaries. For women, such norms included the practice of following one's husband into exile, an act that became "a manifestation of civic virtue on a par with all others." Thus, the Decembrist wives who accompanied their husbands to Siberia were following a "program of behavior" based not only on "religious norms" but also on the literary model promoted by Ryleev and other writers of "a feminine counterpart to the heroic citizen."[11]

These same factors were clearly in operation for women of later generations, including Zasulich. But they faced a different social reality, and the sphere in which they could actually demonstrate their "civic virtue" and readiness for self-sacrifice had extended well beyond the act of following one's husband into exile. The revolution provided them with an opportunity not simply to be the "feminine counterpart" but actually to be "the heroic citizen." To follow the socially prescribed path for young women like Vera Zasulich meant following a gendered path—in most cases, becoming a governess. But Zasulich was determined not to succumb to her seemingly inevitable fate. She understood that her gender limited her possibilities to act on her desire for sacrifice, for meaningful activity, but she also recognized that revolutionary activity was both a liberating force and an equalizing force, a force that had the power to transform her: "It would have been far easier, of course, if I had been a boy: then I could have done anything.... And then, the distant specter of revolution appeared making me equal to a boy; I, too, could dream of 'action,' of 'exploits,' and the 'great struggle.' I too could join 'those who perished for the great cause of love.'"[12] Revolutionary activity freed Russian women like Vera Zasulich from the confines of their prescribed roles and offered them an outlet for their altruistic urges. But the ideals Zasulich cites here—"action," "exploits," "struggle"—are the ones Ryleev wrote about, and the quotation with which she concludes the passage comes from Nekrasov's "Knight for an Hour." Together, they serve as further proof of the extent to which literature provided Zasulich and others like her not only with the models of behavior but also the language with which to talk about that behavior.

Yet there remains an essential incongruity between Zasulich's apparent self-abnegating motives and the self-asserting consequences they produced, especially given the fact that her case launched the first wave of terrorist violence in the Russian revolutionary movement, a wave that culminated three years later in the assassination of Tsar Alexander II.[13] Zasulich's background as an active member of revolutionary circles meant that she had had occasion prior to her attempt on Trepov to ponder the role of violence in that "great struggle" in which she was now taking part. Though in her later writings she made clear her rejection of terror as an effective means of revolutionary activity, her thoughts at the time of her attempt on Trepov do not seem to have been as clearly defined. In retrospect, she came to characterize her action and similar actions by others in those years not as deliberate acts of terror or revolutionary struggle but rather as "a psychological burst, expressing feelings of despair and pain, a weapon of last resort."[14] Yet as a member of the "Southern Rebels,"[15] Zasulich knew of and apparently condoned Lev Deich's attack in 1876 on suspected police informant N. E. Gorinovich. Deich, who was Zasulich's lover at the time, beat Gorinovich with a ball and chain and poured acid on his face, leaving him blind and physically maimed.[16] Though the revolutionary movement in general had moved onto a nonviolent path after the Nechaev affair, by the mid-1870s such incidents of violence within the movement—primarily of the sort involving revenge against a police informer—were on the increase. Their scope, however, was fairly limited: self-defense, freeing imprisoned comrades, and exacting vengeance against traitors.[17] Jay Bergman in his biography of Zasulich suggests she had initially accepted this generally held view that violence against informants and spies was justified, but then changed her mind: "It may be that it was only as the full import of Gorinovich's blinding and disfigurement became clear to her that she began to realize that terrorism could only be justified as a gesture of moral conscience and as a means to avenge unpunished acts of official brutality."[18] Thus, Zasulich's attack on Trepov represented a clear departure from the previous code of conduct in that it switched the focus of violence from threats within the movement to public figures, whose punishment then assumed a moral character.

It is also important to note that the attempt on Trepov was not an individual act of vengeance but part of a larger plot that was to include the simultaneous assassination of Zhelikovsky, the prosecutor in the Trial of the 193.[19] Zasulich, who was working as a typesetter in St. Petersburg at the time, and her roommate, Masha Kolenkina, were joined by coconspirators from the south, members of the Southern Rebels group, who had come to St. Petersburg for that purpose and were to return south upon completion of the assassinations to help free several of their comrades from prison. Deborah Hardy argues that Zasulich and Kolenkina eventually grew impatient with the slow approach of their male counterparts and decided to act on their own. If true, Zasulich's eagerness to act becomes even more complicated by the fact that, according to Hardy, Lev Deich was one of those awaiting rescue.[20] Zasulich and Kolenkina chose to carry out the assassinations on the day after the completion of the Trial of the 193 so as not to jeopardize its outcome; some speculate that they even drew straws to see who would shoot whom.[21] Kolenkina's attempt on Zhelikovsky failed when she was unable to gain entrance to his quarters, and thus Zasulich accidentally emerged alone as the one who was able to carry out the plot. Such facts certainly complicate the portrait of Zasulich as a lone avenger, compelled to act by an outraged moral sensibility, but it was nonetheless that picture, despite evidence of her act's more textured background, that Russian society chose to embrace.[22]

At the same time, many did recognize an essential contradiction in the characterization of a violent act against an individual as morally justified. A closer look at the response to her trial by three major Russian writers of that time—Dostoevsky, Turgenev, and Tolstoy—reveals that each writer in his own way recognized that the path taken by Zasulich, however noble in its origin, led to a slippery slope that quickly and decisively lost sight of the moral ideal that served as its source.

Dostoevsky was the only one of the three to be present at the Zasulich trial itself, having gained entrance through one of the special tickets that had been issued to members of the press. When the jury recessed for their deliberations, Dostoevsky was asked by his acquaintance, the liberal journalist G. K. Gradovsky, what he thought the verdict should be. Dostoevsky had already told acquaintances before the trial that Zasulich should not be convicted, and he repeated this belief to Gradovsky. He said that to convict her of this crime would be impossible, that punishment would be inappropriate and unnecessary, and that they should just say to her instead, "Go, but don't do that again" ("*Idi, no ne postupai tak v drugoi raz*").[23] This response, though it sounds like a rebuke one might give a child, in actuality echoes Christ's words to the woman taken in adultery in the Gospel of John. After the crowd that has come to stone her disperses because none can say that he is without sin, Christ similarly refuses to judge: "Neither do I condemn you. Go your way, and from now on do not sin again" (John 8:11). Dostoevsky would have had the court respond as Christ did, with a benevolent refusal to judge and a gentle redirection onto the path of righteousness. In other words, he wished both for a flexible judicial system that would recognize the extenuating circumstances motivating the crime and for a penitent criminal who would accept forgiveness and be redeemed by it. The culmination of Dostoevsky's religious thinking, soon to be expressed in the figure of Father Zosima in *The Brothers Karamazov,* as well as his aversion to rational formulas and categorical absolutes put him at odds with the operating principles of the relatively new institution of trial by jury, principles based on rationality and objectivity. But Dostoevsky understood that such a stance was inimical to the notion of any kind of judicial system, and he acknowledged that incompatibility in his subsequent comments to Gradovsky: "No, it seems we don't have such a juridical formula, and, what's more, she will now be elevated to a heroine."[24] Despite his skepticism, Dostoevsky's desired outcome for the criminal ironically worked out: though she remained active in the revolutionary movement, Vera Zasulich renounced terror after the Trepov incident; she did not, in fact, "do that again."[25]

But Dostoevsky's other prediction, that Zasulich's actions would come to be perceived as heroic, was realized, evident both in the immediate response to the verdict and in her subsequent canonization in the liberal and radical press. In his ecstatic account of the trial in the liberal newspaper *Golos* (*The Voice*), Gradovsky took the defense attorney's attempts to put the victim on trial even further, arguing that it was in fact not Zasulich who was being tried but rather all of society.[26] His description of the jubilant courtroom on the announcement of the verdict and his speculation about the greater significance of the Zasulich case now read like tremendous irony: "Can there really again begin discord between word and deed? Can there really again be misunderstandings, mistrust, fears? . . . No, one wants to believe that the Vera Zasulich affair will leave a mark upon our inner life, that this is that crisis, that turning point that is an ordinary part of any serious illness; this is that desired, albeit difficult moment with which recovery begins."[27] The affair was indeed a "turning point," but not toward the "recovery" Gradovsky no doubt had in mind.

The revolutionary writer Sergei Stepniak-Kravchinsky, who was living in exile in Switzerland at the time, wrote about Zasulich in similarly ecstatic terms that only served to heighten the perception of her as the ideal of self-abnegation. He called the shooting of Trepov "an event of the most unself-centered selflessness, of the highest heroism," and depicted her as a model worthy of emulation: "The wondrous form of the young avenger, flowing with radiance, has stamped itself upon the imagination of everyone. And the world bows before her."[28] That Zasulich did indeed become a model to emulate is evident in the escalation of terrorist activity after her trial. Stepniak-Kravchinsky's own terrorist act, the assassination of the chief of the Third Section, Mezentsev, in August of that same year, was by his admission inspired by Zasulich's act.[29] But she also became a role model for other young women seeking opportunities to demonstrate their civic idealism by sacrificing themselves for a higher good. This response by a young woman enrolled in the women's medical courses in St. Petersburg expressed not only admiration of Zasulich but also envy: "We were sorry that this self-sacrificing girl . . . was not one of us. . . . What endeared her to us and made her such a heroine was her willingness to sacrifice her young life. . . . We thought her the luckiest person in the world, and each of us would have liked to exchange places with her. We felt that the anxiety of the headmistress about the integrity of the courses was very petty in comparison to the great deed that this unknown but precious girl had undertaken."[30]

Though Dostoevsky expressed apprehension regarding this inevitable recasting of Zasulich in the role of martyr for a virtuous cause, he retained his sympathy for her long after the trial had ended. In part, he appreciated the ideal of self-sacrifice she embodied—a virtue he regularly bestowed on his positive female characters—even if he felt less comfortable with the way in which she pursued that goal. But perhaps more important, he was struck by the moral awareness Zasulich exhibited in her confession that she did not find it easy to shoot Trepov. In one of his notebook entries two years after the trial, he quotes from Zasulich's testimony: "Zasulich: 'It is hard to raise a hand to shed blood'—this vacillation is more moral than the shedding of blood itself."[31] Just as he values more his scoundrels who are aware that they are scoundrels, Dostoevsky values this wavering in a morally complex situation over the self-righteous assertion of moral certitude. Zasulich's vacillation, for Dostoevsky, confirmed her moral consciousness, and it is in that consciousness rather than in the act of avenging an injustice that true moral values lie.

Turgenev, who was living in Paris at the time, shared Dostoevsky's concern for the potential consequences of Zasulich's act. His initial response to the shooting was expressed succinctly in a postscript in a letter to his editor Stasiulevich: "The story with Trepov is a new illustration of the old saying: 'the echo responds to the call.'"[32] Similarly, he characterized Zasulich's acquittal two months later in a letter to Lavrov as a "sign of the times" (Turgenev, *PSS,* 12:304). Turgenev understood that Zasulich's action—the echo that responded to Trepov's brutality—represented an overdue, inevitable protest from a class no longer content to accept its subordination. And her acquittal, consequently, appeared just as inevitable and symbolic of the changing dynamic in Russian society. That change, however, would come at great cost, as he wrote to Annenkov: "You and I were born too early, dear Pavel Vasilevich; we will see only monstrosities from the new time that is coming into being—and that it is coming, I have no doubt" (Turgenev,

PSS, 12:308). The extent to which the events surrounding the Zasulich trial preoccupied the ex-patriot Turgenev can be seen in his comment in a letter to Stasiulevich a week later, reporting sleepless nights during which Zasulich and other names in the news performed a "fantastic waltz" in his head (Turgenev, *PSS,* 12:312).[33]

The European response to the trial was not dissimilar to the Russian one, with expressions of both ecstatic excess and indignant disbelief. In that same letter to Stasiulevich, Turgenev wrote that the French newspaper *Bien Public* had printed an article entitled "Let Us Celebrate Our Heroes" ("*Fêtons nos héros*"), with the "heroes" in question being Voltaire and Zasulich (Turgenev, *PSS,* 12:312). The German and Austrian papers, on the other hand, seemed less enthusiastic, with one publishing an article entitled "Russia—The Typhus of Europe" (Turgenev, *PSS,* 12:477). The Western press's interest in the Zasulich case put Turgenev in the awkward position of resident expert, a position he assumed with some reluctance. German journals had taken to calling him *der Prophet,* noting a similarity between Zasulich and Marianna, Turgenev's heroine in his novel *Virgin Soil.* Paul Lindau, the editor of the German weekly *Gegenwart,* even asked him to write an article about the trial, but Turgenev politely refused the offer (Turgenev, *PSS,* 12:477). In explaining his reasoning to Lindau's brother, Rudolf, Turgenev admitted with evident frustration that he agreed with the sentiments expressed in the coverage of the Zasulich affair by German newspapers, which described it "as proof of something 'foul' in [Russian] customs." He knew, however, that if he were to voice his opinion, those papers would point to his "prophetic vision" ("*Seherblick*"), seize upon his words, and quote them as confirmation of their views. As a result, he wrote, Russian society would view him as "an enemy, a compatriot of those who attack it and want to bring it to its senses" (Turgenev, *PSS,* 12:477).

Turgenev reveals in these letters a certain uneasiness and even ambivalence toward his own role as a writer who depicted revolutionary youth in his works. Unlike Dostoevsky, Turgenev's depictions of such youth, though not idealized, are largely sympathetic. *Fathers and Sons, On the Eve,* and *Virgin Soil* in particular had made his reputation as the chronicler of the revolutionary movement, but his attempts to tread a middle ground and offer an objective depiction of these types often resulted in criticism from both sides of the political debate. The expectation that he function in this role of resident authority clearly raised concerns for Turgenev about his reputation and the perception of him back in Russia, but perhaps what we also see here is a reluctance to align himself with the implication that he had rightly predicted the violent turn the revolutionary movement would take. Perhaps Turgenev's discomfort was in fact apprehension that his positive portrayals of pure-hearted, noble-minded young women caught up in the idealism of the revolutionary cause might in some way make him complicit in the events unfolding in Russia.

Yet this apparent reluctance to antagonize the right was followed a month later by a creative act that was soon to be embraced by the radical left. In May 1878, in all likelihood in response to the Zasulich case, Turgenev wrote "The Threshold" ("*Porog*"), a prose poem that depicts the final moments before a young Russian woman decides to cross the line and follow the revolutionary path. In response to a faceless voice coming from the gloomy darkness beyond the threshold the girl replies that she is ready to suffer, to endure hardship, contempt, even death. She will accept thankless self-sacrifice and, in the poem's most controversial lines, she asserts that she is ready to accept crime. The voice's final warning—that she might one day come to regret her decision and cease to believe what she now believes—is met by the girl's firm determination to go forward. As she steps across the threshold, the voices of onlookers reflect the bifurcated view of her contemporaries: "Fool!" "Saint!"[34]

Turgenev withheld "The Threshold" from publication, however, until October 1882, when he submitted the poem in a group of other "poems in prose" to Stasiulevich for publication in the journal *Vestnik Evropy* (*Herald of Europe*). When Stasiulevich expressed concern about the censor and suggested eliminating the passage about crime and altering the final lines, Turgenev changed his mind and asked Stasiulevich to exclude it from the collection, noting that if it were allowed, it was a "threshold" over which he "could stumble" (Turgenev, *PSS,* 13:67). This first letter, dated October 13, 1882, was followed by another letter on the following day urgently requesting Stasiulevich to omit the work: "I repeat my request: exclude 'The Threshold.' Or else I won't be calm" (Turgenev, *PSS,* 13:68). Though Turgenev's artistic integrity rightly resisted Stasiulevich's suggestion that he change the poem's ending, his willingness not to publish it indicates his complex and unresolved response to the revolutionaries, especially in the period following the 1881 assassination of Alexander II.

Though no decisive connection exists between Turgenev's poem and the Zasulich case, the timing of its composition surely suggests the influence of her recent trial. At the same time, its similarity to the scene in Turgenev's *On the Eve,* in which Insarov asks Elena if she is ready to accept the consequences of joining the revolutionary cause, has also been noted by Turgenev scholars.[35] Others have pointed to the closing scene in *Virgin Soil,* in which Paklin presses Mashurina to tell him what lies ahead for her.[36] But the fact that Turgenev had explored such a scenario in previous works does not exclude the possibility of the Zasulich case serving as an inspiration for this particular version. If Turgenev was indeed plagiarizing himself in the composition of "The Threshold," he was nonetheless doing so from a perspective enhanced by the Zasulich trial. Moreover, the European public's casting of Zasulich in the roles of Elena and Marianna presents a compelling case for a complex creative layering: art imitating life imitating art. Zasulich's action, which Turgenev prophesied in his earlier novels, impelled Turgenev to recycle his previous work into a new work based on her act.

In some respects, however, the poem's origin is not as important as its potential consequences. Though the female protagonists in Turgenev's novels never actually crossed the line that led to terror, his portrayal of a girl ready to do so in "The Threshold" was clearly read by some as tacit approval on the part of the author. Moreover, the references to his works by the foreign press in the context of the Zasulich case, including the labeling of him as "prophet," remind us that his works and the models of behavior he set forth in them did play a role in shaping how young Russians viewed the revolutionary cause. Turgenev's apparent nervousness about the publication of "The Threshold" and his urgent and repeated requests that Stasiulevich not include it for publication with the other prose poems indicate that the writer had at least an inkling that the ambiguous ending of the work might lead some readers to conclude that he approved of terrorism.[37] The work was in fact excluded from the collection and did not appear in print officially until 1905.[38] Nonetheless, it was circulated widely in manuscript form both in Russia and abroad and was well known among revolutionary circles as early as 1882–83.[39] Perhaps its broadest circulation in those years occurred on the occasion of Turgenev's funeral on September 27, 1883, when members of the People's Will (Narodnaia volia), despite the presence at the funeral of more than 130 police agents, managed to circulate the poem as part of a revolutionary pamphlet commemorating Turgenev's work.[40] Printed on high-quality paper on an illegal press and written by the radical poet P. F. Yakubovich, the piece ridicules conservatives and liberals alike for their attempts to use the occasion of Turgenev's funeral to promote their own versions of the writer's significance. The "Russian revolutionaries," on the other hand, had at their disposal "the palpable, real facts" that allowed them to proclaim "loudly" who Turgenev was and what he meant for their cause: "A nobleman by birth, an aristocrat by upbringing and character, a 'gradualist' by convictions, Turgenev, perhaps unconsciously even for himself, with his sensitive and loving heart sympathized with and even served the Russian revolution."[41] He was for them "an honest herald" of the idealism, inner torments, and spiritual struggle of Russian youth over several generations.

Yakubovich goes on to draw a connection between Turgenev's literary heroes and the young people who read about them: "The images of Rudin,

Insarov, Elena, Bazarov, Nezhdanov and Markelov are not only living and true-to-life images, but, no matter how strange this appears at first glance—these are the types that youth imitated and that themselves created life [*sozdavali zhizn'*]."[42] Such types, Yakubovich emphasizes, have "historical significance"—that is, Turgenev's literary characters played a role in the events that transpired in real life.

Yuri Lotman, in "The Decembrists in Daily Life," makes a distinction between the ways in which life and the text interact in romanticism and in realism, and uses Turgenev to illustrate his point: "With realism, it is characteristic for a type of behavior to arise first in real life and then appear on the pages of the literary text (Turgenev, for example, was known for his ability to spot new modes of thought and behavior in real life.) In the romantic work, the new type of human behavior is conceived in the pages of the text and then transferred to life."[43] In "Concerning Khlestakov," he elaborates further on this concept: unlike romantic texts, which offer readers "a straightforward program for behavior," realist texts are "less directive." Instead, "they *give a name* to patterns of behavior that are present as spontaneous and unconscious elements of a particular social fabric, and in so doing they bring these elements to the level of social and conscious." Once named, the pattern of behavior "now appears on an altogether new level, in the category of culturally recognized forms of behavior."[44] Thus, one can argue that Turgenev's labeling of Bazarov and his like-minded followers as "nihilist" functioned as the naming of a "pattern of behavior" already present in Russian society of the time, though not yet defined as a social phenomenon. Yet, as Yakubovich's pamphlet makes clear, Turgenev's heroes functioned not only as representations of types observed in real life, but also—and no less than their romantic predecessors—as behavioral models for young Russians of that time.[45]

Though Yakubovich acknowledges and accepts Turgenev's irony in his depiction of the naïveté of the early populists in *Virgin Soil,* he asserts in conclusion—somewhat contradictorily—that it does not matter what Turgenev himself thought about the revolution; his works nonetheless served it:

> The Stasiuleviches, Polonskys, and company, supposed friends of the deceased, have published both written and verbal views of I. S. Turgenev about the Russian revolution, which he ostensibly did not believe in and did not serve. But we are not maintaining that he did believe. No, he doubted its closeness and its feasibility through heroic skirmishes with the government; perhaps he even didn't want it and was a sincere gradualist—this doesn't matter to us. For us it is important that he served the Russian revolution through the heartfelt meaning

of his works, that he loved revolutionary youth, calling them "saintly" and selfless.[46]

Yakubovich concluded by noting that the government's advance attempts to suppress reporting about Turgenev's funeral offered the final proof that the writer did in fact have revolutionary significance, since it clearly expected some kind of response to his death from Russia's youth.[47]

The word Yakubovich puts in quotation marks at the end of the passage cited above, "*sviatye*," can function in this context either as an adjective ("saintly") or noun ("saints"). Either way, the fact that it appears in quotation marks strongly suggests Turgenev's use of the word in "The Threshold," a copy of which followed shortly after these comments in the leaflet. Lavrov similarly uses the word in his tribute to Turgenev published in 1884 in *Vestnik narodnoi voli* (*Herald of the People's Will*): "He declared the women martyrs of the Russian revolution 'saints.'" (Neither, of course, allowed for the possibility that he was also calling them "fools.") Though Lavrov had quoted Turgenev's 1880 assertion that he was "a liberal of the old style, . . . awaiting reform only from above—a principled opponent of revolution," he concluded his piece with an assertion similar to Yakubovich's: though Turgenev may have played his role unconsciously or unintentionally, he nonetheless did "prepare and participate in the development of the Russian revolutionary movement." Lavrov also uses Turgenev's own words from one of his prose poems, "What will I think when I have to die—if only I am able to think?" to introduce an unsubstantiated rumor he had heard about that very subject: "A person whom I have reason to believe told me that apparently, in a delirious state before his death, Ivan Sergeevich declared that 'terrorists are great people.'" Lavrov went on to say that he could not, however, place as much trust in those who had told his acquaintance this story.[48] True or false, in reporting the story, Lavrov enters it into the complex historical record of Turgenev's relations with the revolutionary movement. It is ironic, of course, that Turgenev's "fence-sitting" in respect to that movement, for which he was criticized by both sides, resulted in his appropriation after death by the revolutionaries as a supporter of their cause in all of its forms—including terror.[49]

Tolstoy was more removed from the Zasulich affair than the other two writers, but he too grasped its larger significance; in particular, he recognized that the public response to Zasulich's action was as important as the action itself. He declared in a letter to Strakhov that "the Zasulich affair is no joke," and stressed that the people's support of Zasulich was a portent of more serious things to come: "The Slavic folly was a harbinger of war;

this is like a herald of revolution."[50] Tolstoy was the one to articulate most clearly the real consequences of the Zasulich case: the act itself and its acquittal and forgiveness by large segments of Russian society did indeed set the course for the terrorist activity that emerged in its wake, culminating in the revolution itself.

Having finished *Anna Karenina* the year before, Tolstoy was immersed at the time of the trial in his own spiritual crisis, wrestling with the "cursed questions" that his hero Levin had seemingly solved for himself. His comments nonetheless reflect the moral lucidity one might expect from him. He clearly felt no sympathy for Trepov, quipping in a letter to Alexandra Tolstoy after the trial that politics are "as red as the blood of the repulsive Trepov" (Tolstoi, *PSS,* 62:409), but he also recognized that Zasulich's action had its own repellent aspects. For Tolstoy, the actors represented two sides of an equally ugly battle. Both sides were brutal, and their differences appeared to be irreconcilable:

> It is clear to me from afar, as to one who stands outside the battle, that the animosity for each other of the two extreme parties has reached the point of brutality. For Maidel [commandant at the Peter-Paul Fortress] and others, all these Bogoliubovs and Zasulichs are such trash, that he does not see them as human beings and cannot pity them; for Zasulich, Trepov and the others are evil animals whom one can and should kill like dogs. And this is no longer merely indignation, but a battle. (Tolstoi, *PSS,* 62:409)

Tolstoy recognized that the verdict and the public response to it contained a dangerous contradiction of the requirements of a civil society, and he again noted with dread his sense that the consequences of the case would be far-reaching:

> All of those who justify murder and sympathized with the acquittal know very well that for their own safety it is impossible and they cannot justify murder, but for them the question was not who is right, but who will win, who will be victorious. All of this, it seems to me, foretells much misfortune and much sin. There are good people in both camps. Can there really not be such conditions in which they would stop being animals and begin again to be people? God grant that I may be mistaken, but it seems to me, that all the eastern questions and all the Slavs and Constantinople are trifles in comparison with this. And since I read about this trial and about this commotion, it has not left my head. (Tolstoi, *PSS,* 62:409)

Tolstoy had ridiculed educated Russian society's preoccupation with the Pan-Slavic cause in part eight of *Anna Karenina.*[51] But his comments here shed a different light on "the Slavic folly": Russian society, in immersing itself with the problems of its Slavic brethren, was failing to perceive the very real threat of violence and upheaval facing them at home.

Though perhaps merely a coincidence, Tolstoy wrote a letter that same day (April 6, 1878) to Turgenev proposing that they put aside their long-standing animosity and reconcile: "In our time there is only one good thing—loving relationships with people. And I would be very glad, if they were restored between us" (Tolstoi, *PSS,* 62:407). Annenkov reported that Turgenev wept when he read it. Perhaps what Tolstoy saw in the bestial behavior of both the tsarist officials and those involved in the revolutionary movement convinced him that in a time fraught with hatred and hostility, there is no sense for good men to live in enmity over trifles.

Three years later, when Tolstoy wrote his famous letter to Alexander III following the assassination of his father, he had fully embraced the ethos of nonresistance to evil and had rejected the very concept of civil authority and, by association, civil society. The critical distance that led him to articulate in that letter to Alexandra Tolstoy his recognition that Zasulich's acquittal contradicted society's own interests by seemingly condoning violence and murder is replaced in this letter by a serious—albeit idealistic and futile—attempt to engage instead the rhetorical question he had posed then: "Can there really not be such conditions in which they would stop being animals and begin again to be people?" Not surprisingly, Tolstoy proposes that the answer to this question—the requisite conditions that would restore the two sides' essential humanity—can be found through the imitation of Christ. He urges the new tsar not only to show mercy to the terrorist assassins but also to follow the teachings of Christ: to forgive his father's murderers and thereby repay evil with good.

Reading Tolstoy's impassioned rhetoric, certainly sincere and just as certainly self-deceptive, one is struck by the willful intellectual naïveté that he stubbornly adopts in arguing this tack. The perceptive, rational apprehension of reality that characterized the remarkable works of his most prolific creative period has been replaced by earnest idealism and hyperbolic prophecy. Descending more than once into self-abnegating obeisance, Tolstoy concludes his plea for clemency with a prediction that even without the benefit of hindsight was surely unrealistic in the context of the times:

> If you were to do this, summon these people, give them money and send them off somewhere to America and write a manifesto above them with the words: "Verily I say unto you, love your enemies"—I

> don't know about others, but I, a poor faithful citizen would be your dog, your slave. I would cry from tenderness, as I now cry every time I hear your name. But what am I saying that I don't know about others? I do know that a flood of goodness and love would spread over Russia at these words. The truths of Christ are alive in the hearts of people, and they alone are alive, and we love people only in the name of these truths. (Tolstoi, *PSS,* 63:50)

In repaying evil with good, Tolstoy writes, the tsar will have the power to change the tenor of the debate by encompassing the terrorists' goals and ideals within the larger, greater ideal of forgiveness and love. Revolutionaries, Tolstoy writes, "hate the existing order of things" and propose destroying that order in the name of a higher good—"common prosperity, equality, freedom." Such ideas, he writes, must be dealt with "spiritually" by placing in opposition to them "an ideal that would be higher than theirs, that would include their ideal within itself," that is, "the ideal of love, forgiveness and the repayment of good for evil. Only one word of forgiveness and Christian love uttered and enacted from the height of the throne, and the path of Christian reign onto which you will step can destroy the evil that is oppressing Russia" (Tolstoi, *PSS,* 62:52).

Though such an approach reveals the moral idealism of Tolstoy's new-found religion, it also reveals the ineffectuality of such a stance—extreme in its own way—in the context of political terror. Dostoevsky had advocated a similar response to the Zasulich affair three years earlier, but he also well understood the incompatibility of his Christian ideal with the requirements of civil order. One could argue that Tolstoy, in adopting Christian idealism, has abrogated his role as critical social commentator in favor of the ultimately ineffectual role of good shepherd and utopian prophet. To oppose the death penalty is one thing; to propose that Christlike forgiveness from the tsar would produce "a flood of goodness" in Russia and deflect the revolutionary movement from a path of violence onto a path of productive cooperation seems at best uncharacteristically naive of the wise Tolstoy and at worst stubbornly self-deceptive. Just as the jury's moral act of forgiveness of Vera Zasulich three years earlier had not changed the hearts of the revolutionaries, a similar act on the part of the tsar would not likely have stemmed the tide of revolution.

Clearly, the attempt by Vera Zasulich on the life of Governor-General Trepov set the tone for much of what followed in the Russian revolutionary period, and it contributed to the acceptance of violence as a means of achieving social and political progress. The portrait of passionate commitment and willing self-sacrifice that Zasulich presented not only became a model for emulation by her contemporaries but also the source of some confusion among some of those who have subsequently written about her and other women revolutionaries. In their introduction to *Five Sisters: Women Against the Tsar,* for example, Barbara Alpern Engel and Clifford N. Rosenthal write that the women featured in the book—revolutionaries, including Zasulich, who accepted terrorism and participated in terrorist acts—"possessed a passionate and lucid moral vision which neither exile, imprisonment, nor imminent death could destroy"; the book is, in fact, dedicated "to the women fighting for freedom throughout the world."[52] In her introduction to *Mothers and Daughters: Women of the Intelligentsia in Nineteenth-Century Russia,* Engel writes in a similar vein, describing the radical women she writes about as "awe-inspiring," and expressing deep admiration for their strength of character: "I have never met the like of the women who appear in this book. I feel privileged to have lived with them for ten years and to have been able to learn so much from them."[53] The role played by women in the Russian revolutionary movement was indeed central, and those women's experiences certainly merit further study and analysis. But in the context of the contemporary world order, it goes without saying that passionate commitment, living according to convictions, and willingness to sacrifice oneself for a political cause do not in themselves amount to virtue. In the case of Vera Zasulich, what merits particular attention is not simply that she chose to fight evil by violent means in response to a supposed moral imperative but rather that she *renounced* violence and terror almost immediately after her own act. Therein lies the real irony of the Zasulich affair—its heroine bears responsibility for launching the first significant wave of terror in Russia, yet she failed to convey the lessons of her own act to others. The moral vacillation on Zasulich's part that Dostoevsky admired gave way in many revolutionaries who followed her lead to an absolutism based in a more cynical argument that the ends justify the means. In this regard, Zasulich's action did indeed become the "herald of revolution" that Tolstoy predicted, a revolution accomplished not through the grassroots methods envisioned by the populists but by the implementation of systematic terror embraced by the People's Will.

Notes

My thanks to Lynn Patyk, who offered comments on an earlier version of this paper.

1. Feodor Dostoievsky, *The Diary of a Writer,* trans. Boris Brasol (Salt Lake City, Utah: Gibbs M. Smith, 1985), 149. Val Vinokur in his essay in this volume refers to this passage as "Dostoevsky's attempt at rapprochement with the young radicals."

2. Quoted in Barbara Alpern Engel and Clifford N. Rosenthal, eds., *Five Sisters: Women Against the Tsar* (Boston: Allen and Unwin, 1987), 78.

3. This summary, as well as the quoted passages, come from the account of the trial published in the conservative paper *Moskovskie vedomosti:* "Zasedanie 1-go otdeleniia peterburgskogo okruzhnogo suda po delu Very Zasulich," April 3, 1878, 2. Unless otherwise noted, all translations are mine.

4. For firsthand accounts of the days surrounding the Zasulich trial, see S. F. Librovich, *Na knizhnom postu* (Petrograd and Moscow, 1916), 40–43, and I. I. Popov, *Minuvshee i perezhitoe* (Moscow and Leningrad: Akademiia, 1955), 51–52.

5. Gary Rosenshield points out that the instructions given to the jury by the presiding judge A. F. Koni, which directed the jury to arrive at a verdict consistent with "'the voice of conscience,'" left open the possibility of "jury nullification, that is, sanctioning the right of the jurors to take into consideration the nature and situation of the defendant in their verdict and rule against the strict interpretation of the law." See Gary Rosenshield, *Western Law, Russian Justice: Dostoevsky, the Jury Trial, and the Law* (Madison: University of Wisconsin Press, 2005), 103, 139. For a similar observation, see Jay Bergman, *Vera Zasulich* (Stanford: Stanford University Press, 1983), 50.

6. Kenoticism, from the Greek *kenosis,* refers to the willing acceptance of suffering and death in imitation of Christ. As Peter Scotto and Lynn Ellen Patyk in this volume have pointed out, many revolutionaries retained religious ideals even when they were no longer religious, and ironically, those ideals served as the basis for many of their actions. A striking example is found in Andrei Zheliabov's testimony at his trial for the assassination of Alexander II, in which he cites the tenets of Christianity as the basis of his terrorist actions: "I was baptized in the Orthodox Church but I reject Orthodoxy, although I acknowledge the essential teaching of Jesus Christ. This essential teaching occupies an honored place among my moral incentives. I believe in the truth and the righteousness of that teaching and I solemnly declare that faith without works is dead and that every true Christian ought to fight for the truth and for the rights of the oppressed and the weak, and even if need be, to suffer for them. Such is my creed." Cited in Nikolai Berdyaev, *The Russian Idea* (Hudson, N.Y.: Lindisfarne Press, 1992), 144.

7. Engel and Rosenthal, *Five Sisters,* 67–68.

8. Ibid., 69. For a fuller discussion of the influence of the Decembrists on subsequent generations of Russian revolutionaries, and in particular Ryleev's "valorization of self-sacrifice," see Ludmilla Trigos's essay in this volume.

9. Boris Gasparov, introduction to *The Semiotics of Russian Cultural History* (Ithaca, N.Y.: Cornell University Press, 1985), 13.

10. Bergman, *Vera Zasulich,* 3, 6.

11. Iurii M. Lotman, "The Decembrists in Daily Life," in *The Semiotics of Russian Cultural History,* 121, 122, 123.

12. Engel and Rosenthal, *Five Sisters,* 69.

13. For a discussion of the extent to which Zasulich's action inspired subsequent terrorist acts, as well as her own dismayed response to those acts, see Bergman, *Vera Zasulich,* 57–59.

14. E. B. Shubina, *Filosofsko-sotsiologicheskie vzgliady V. I. Zasulich, 1867–1903 gg.* (Leningrad: Nauka, 1984), 7. For further discussion of Zasulich's views on terrorism after the Trepov shooting, see Bergman, *Vera Zasulich,* 59–62.

15. The Southern Rebels (*Iuzhnye buntari*) were a revolutionary group based in Kiev. Heavily influenced by the ideas of Bakunin, they advocated violent, spontaneous uprisings as a means of advancing the revolutionary cause. See J. Frank Goodwin, "Violence and the Legacy of 'Bakuninism' in the Russian Revolution," in *Times of Trouble: Violence in Russian Literature and Culture,* ed. Marcus C. Levitt and Tatyana Novikov (Madison: University of Wisconsin Press, 2007), 105.

16. Bergman rightly points out that Zasulich's support of the Gorinovich attack does not entirely jibe with her rejection of Nechaev's attack on Ivanov. Bergman, *Vera Zasulich,* 28.

17. Deborah Hardy, *Land and Freedom: The Origins of Russian Terrorism, 1876–1879* (Westport, Conn.: Greenwood Press, 1987), 55.

18. Bergman, *Vera Zasulich,* 28.

19. The Trial of the 193 was one of the mass trials of revolutionaries who had "gone to the people" as part of the populist movement. The trial, which began in October 1877, ended the day before the Trepov shooting. Franco Venturi, *Roots of Revolution: A History of the Populist and Socialist Movements in Nineteenth-Century Russia* (New York: Knopf, 1960), 587–96.

20. Hardy, *Land and Freedom,* 60.

21. Bergman, *Vera Zasulich,* 37n; Hardy, *Land and Freedom,* 60. The plot against Zhelikovsky, who, as prosecutor, was just doing his job, also raises questions about changes in the revolutionaries' attitude toward violence. Kolenkina's choice of him as her victim—unlike Zasulich's selection of Trepov—was a symbolic one. Nevertheless, the belief of both women that they acted as surrogates of those incapable of acting for themselves was strikingly at odds with the common justification of terrorism in the 1870s as a "defensive measure" directed at informers and police infiltrators (Bergman, *Vera Zasulich,* 37n).

22. Sally A. Boniece's account of the less than virginal "SR Madonna" (*Esserskaia Bogoroditsa*), Maria Spiridonova, in her essay in this volume similarly offers a substantially more complex portrait than the one embraced by public opinion.

23. G. K. Gradovskii, "Iz vospominanii 'Rokovoe piatiletie. 1878–1882,'" in *F. M Dostoevskii v vospominaniiakh sovremennikov v dvukh tomakh* (Moscow: Khudozhestvennaia literatura, 1990), 233. The writer S. F. Librovich reports a similar pronouncement from Dostoevsky before the trial at one of the regular gatherings of literati at the store of Petersburg bookseller M. O. Volf: "To convict this girl is impossible. . . . Punishment here is inappropriate and pointless. . . . On the contrary, the jury should say to the accused: 'You have a sin on your soul, you wanted to kill a man, but you have already atoned for it—go and don't do that again.'" Librovich reported that Dostoevsky became excited when uttering these thoughts and repeated them several times in front of different people (Librovich, *Na knizhnom postu,* 42).

24. Gradovskii, "Iz vospominanii," 233. Rosenshield presents a different interpretation of this incident. He characterizes Dostoevsky's response to the trial and Zasulich's acquittal as an "outrage," and places little emphasis on this exchange. Rosenshield neither makes the connection between Dostoevsky's repetition of this phrase and the biblical verse, nor does he mention that Dostoevsky uttered this pronouncement before the trial and in more than one venue. Rosenshield, *Western Law,* 125, 135.

25. The Zasulich trial provided Dostoevsky with much of his material for the jury trial depicted in *The Brothers Karamazov.* Zasulich's attorney, Alexandrov, for example, served as the model for Fetiukovich (Rosenshield, *Western Law,* 29–30, 179).

26. G. K. Gradovskii, *Itogi: Ocherki, stat'i, vospominaniia, fel'etony* (Kiev, 1908), 430.
27. Ibid., 436.
28. Quoted in Hardy, *Land and Freedom,* 69.
29. For a fuller discussion of the ways in which Stepniak used the trope of martyrdom and self-sacrifice in his revolutionary writings, see Peter Scotto's essay in this volume.
30. Barbara Alpern Engel, *Mothers and Daughters: Women of the Intelligentsia in Nineteenth-Century Russia* (Cambridge: Cambridge University Press, 1983), 165.
31. Joseph Frank, *Dostoevsky: The Mantle of the Prophet, 1871–1881* (Princeton: Princeton University Press, 2002), 374.
32. I. S. Turgenev, *Polnoe sobranie sochinenii i pisem v dvadtsati vos'mi tomakh* (Moscow and Leningrad: Nauka, 1960–68), *Pis'ma,* 12:275. Hereafter cited as *PSS,* with page references given parenthetically in the text.
33. M. P. Dragomanov, a Ukrainian historian and one of Turgenev's acquaintances, nonetheless noted that when he met Turgenev in Paris, the writer said to him "with visible joy: 'and do you know, Vera Zasulich is already abroad.'" See M. P. Dragomanov, "Znakomstvo s I. S. Turgenevym," in *I. S. Turgenev v vospominaniiakh revoliutsionerov-semidesiatnikov* (Moscow and Leningrad: Academia, 1930), 174.
34. Turgenev, *PSS,* 13:168–69. Here is the full text in my translation.

> I see a huge building.
>
> A narrow door stands wide open in the front wall; behind the door—a gloomy darkness. In front of the high threshold stands a girl. . . . A Russian girl.
>
> That impenetrable gloom breathes frost; and from the depths of the building along with a stream of icy air comes a slow, hollow voice.
>
> "O you, why do you wish to cross this threshold, do you know what awaits you?"
>
> "I know," answers the girl.
>
> "Cold, hunger, hatred, mockery, contempt, insult, prison, sickness and death itself?"
>
> "I know."
>
> "Complete estrangement, solitude?"
>
> "I know. I am ready. I will endure all sufferings, all blows."
>
> "Not only from enemies, but also from loved ones, from friends?"
>
> "Yes, even from them."
>
> "Good. Are you ready for sacrifice?"
>
> "Yes."
>
> "For anonymous sacrifice? You will perish—and no one, no one will even know, whose memory to honor!"
>
> "I need neither gratitude nor pity. I don't need a name."
>
> "Are you ready for crime?"
>
> The girl lowered her head . . .
>
> "I am ready for crime."
>
> The voice did not immediately renew its questions.
>
> "Do you know," it began finally, "that you may lose faith in what you now believe, you may come to understand, that you have been deceived and have ruined your young life in vain?"
>
> "I know this as well. And I still want to enter."

"Enter!"

The girl stepped across the threshold—and a heavy curtain fell behind her.

"Fool!" someone snarled from behind.

"Saint!" came from somewhere in response. (May 1878)

35. See Turgenev, *PSS,* 8:94, for the passage from *On the Eve.* See *PSS,* 13:655, for the commentary.

36. See Turgenev, *PSS,* 12:300, for the passage from *Virgin Soil.* See also *Russkaia literatura ot Gertsena do Brodskogo: Khrestomatiia dlia srednikh i starshikh klassov* (Nizhni Novgorod: Russkii kupets i Brat'ia slaviane, 1995), 130.

37. Ironically, most commentators have ignored the ambiguity of the poem's final lines. The revolutionary underground in Russia clearly seized on the piece as an unequivocal praise of the young woman's action, and some of Turgenev's early Western biographers also asserted that the piece offers unambiguous praise of the girl's actions. Avrahm Yarmolinsky, for example, claimed that the poem "canonized the revolutionists," while Harry Hershkowitz wrote that it expressed Turgenev's "admiration for those women who gave their lives for the revolutionary movement and went on the scaffold, without being even understood at the time by those for whom they died." See Harry Hershkowitz, *Democratic Ideas in Turgenev's Works* (New York: Columbia University Press, 1932), 113; Avrahm Yarmolinsky, *Turgenev, the Man, His Art, His Age* (New York: Century, 1926), 373. Even some later works perpetuate the picture of Turgenev's intention as being firmly on the side of sainthood: Leonard Shapiro writes that the poem reflects Turgenev's "revolutionary ardor" of those years, and notes that its ending "was typical of Turgenev's romantic mood at that date." (Shapiro goes on to challenge Turgenev's view by questioning whether the assassins of Alexander II, whose first bomb missed and killed an innocent child, were the "saints" Turgenev had in mind.) See Leonard Shapiro, *Turgenev: His Life and Times* (New York: Random House, 1978), 287, 302. Later Soviet sources perpetuated the interpretation of the poem as an unambiguous hymn in honor of women terrorists: "He praised the 'saintly' Russian women-revolutionaries in their courageous struggle." See Galina Vinnikova, *Turgenev i Rossiia* (Moscow: Sovetskaia Rossiia, 1977), 399. At least one more recent study has reestablished the ambiguity: according to Frank Seeley, the piece demonstrates Turgenev's belief that "the value of action—and of the agent—is to be measured not by results but by the intensity of the love-and-faith that fuels the action. Folly or sainthood: the distinction may be in the eye of the beholder." See Frank Friedeberg Seeley, *Turgenev: A Reading of His Fiction* (Cambridge: Cambridge University Press, 1991), 333.

38. It was V. V. Stasov who sent "The Threshold" to S. S. Vengerov for publication in the journal *Russkoe bogatstvo* in April 1905, citing it, along with *Fathers and Sons,* as the work by Turgenev that he valued most. See V. V. Stasov, *Pis'ma k deiateliam russkoi kul'tury* (Moscow: Akademiia Nauk, 1962), 1:227–28. "The Threshold" was published by Vengerov in *Russkoe bogatstvo* that fall (1905, nos. 11–12).

39. Since the date of the poem's composition (May 1878) became known only after 1905, several misperceptions persisted about its inspiration. Lavrov, for example, thought it was inspired by Sof'ia Perovskaia, as did some of Turgenev's earlier biographers. See P. L. Lavrov, "Iz stat'i 'I. S. Turgenev i razvitie russkogo obshchestva,'" in *I. S. Turgenev v vospominaniiakh sovremennikov v dvukh tomakh* (Moscow: Khudozhestvennaia literatura, 1969), 2:418; see also Yarmolinsky, *Turgenev,* 373; Hershko-

witz, *Democratic Ideas,* 113. A later edition of Yarmolinsky's biography (1959) corrects the mistake.

40. B. N. Dvinianinov, *Mech i lira: Ocherk zhizni i tvorchestva P. F. Iakubovicha* (Moscow: Nauka, 1969), 48.

41. P. F. Iakubovich, "I. S. Turgenev," in *Literatura partii Narodnoi voli* (St. Petersburg: Energiia, 1905), 952.

42. Ibid.

43. Lotman, "Decembrists," 112.

44. Iurii M. Lotman, "Concerning Khlestakov," in *The Semiotics of Russian Cultural History,* 186.

45. Iakubovich's dissertation, in which he compares Lermontov's Tamara to the women of the revolutionary underground like Sof'ia Perovskaia and Vera Figner, further illustrates the habit of Russian youth to search for models of behavior in literary characters (Dvinianinov, *Mech i lira,* 44).

46. Iakubovich, "Turgenev," 952–53.

47. For a detailed account of the furor surrounding Turgenev's funeral, see Iu. Nikol'skii, "Delo o pokhoronakh I. S. Turgeneva," *Byloe* 4 (1917): 146–56.

48. Lavrov, "Iz stat'i," 424, 391, 424, 423.

49. M. O. Ashkenazi is an exception. In his memoir, "Turgenev and Terrorists," he tells how the writer helped him get his novel, *Les victimes du tsar,* published, even though he did not approve of the way the novel condoned political murder. Turgenev declared to Ashkenazi in 1881: "I can never condone any kind of murder. . . . I mourn the tsar just as I mourn his murder." See M. O. Ashkenazi, "Turgenev i terroristy," in *I. S. Turgenev v vospominaniiakh revoliutsionerov-semidesiatnikov* (Moscow and Leningrad: Academia, 1930), 200.

50. Lev N. Tolstoi, *Polnoe sobranie sochinenii* (Moscow and Leningrad, 1928–58), 62:411.

51. As a result, Katkov had refused to publish the final part in *Russkii vestnik.*

52. Engel and Rosenthal, *Five Sisters,* xxxii.

53. Engel, *Mothers and Daughters,* viii.

The Terrorist as Novelist: Sergei Stepniak-Kravchinsky

Peter Scotto

> Murder is a terrible thing. Only in a moment of the most intense passion, reaching even to a loss of self-consciousness, can a man who is not a monster and a degenerate deprive another like himself of life.
>
> —*DEATH FOR DEATH!*

At around 9:00 A.M. on August 4, 1878,[1] Adjutant General Nikolai Mezentsev, chief of Russia's gendarmes and head of its secret police, was assassinated in Mikhailovsky Square in St. Petersburg. Coming a little more than six months after Vera Zasulich's sensational attempt on the life of Petersburg governor-general Fedor Trepov, Mezentsev's murder was a signal event in the wave of revolutionary terror that convulsed Russia at the end of the 1870s, reaching its zenith in the assassination of Tsar Alexander II by members of Narodnaia volia (the People's Will) on March 1, 1881.[2]

After driving a dagger into his victim, Mezentsev's assassin managed a daring escape, galloping away from the scene of the crime in what one source later described as an "elegant carriage."[3] Within days of the event, a pamphlet with the bloodcurdling title *Death for Death!* rolled off a secret printing press in St. Petersburg.[4] The title offers a key to its reasoning: Mezentsev was executed by "revolutionary-socialists" in retaliation for the arbitrary imprisonment, abuse, torture, and death of comrades at the hands of the secret police. If the government wanted an end to the terror, it had to give up its own deadly campaign against the revolutionaries. As it was, the revolutionaries had been pushed beyond human endurance. They had no choice but to act. From here on in, death would be answered by death.

***

Sometime on the afternoon of December 29, 1893, Olivia Garnett of Bloomsbury made an agitated entry in her diary: "I must say that the article 'Anarchists' II was a blow to me. . . . Selfishly I feared that I might lose 'my Stepniak'—the artist—in the nihilist, terrorist and ______________."[5] (The long dash belongs to the diarist.) Twenty-two years old when she made this entry, "Olive" was the daughter of Richard Garnett—poet, writer, scholar, and Keeper of Printed Books at the British Museum. She was also the sister-in-law of Constance Garnett. Constance Garnett (née Black) had married Olive's brother Edward in 1889 and, at the end of 1893, had only just begun her life's work as a translator of Russian literature. Through Constance, Olive had become acquainted with the community of Russian political exiles in London. Like Constance, she had developed a deep emotional attachment to one of its most charismatic figures, Sergei Stepniak.[6]

Stepniak was well known in the city's literary and political circles. His *Underground Russia,* first published in Britain in 1883, had met with instant success, and was in its fourth edition by 1892.[7] His accounts of life under the tsar had become familiar to readers of the *Times,* the *Contemporary,* and the *Fortnightly,* and, drawing on this journalistic work, he had put together and published in rapid succession three substantial volumes on the origins, practices, and consequences of tsarist despotism: *Russia Under the Tzars* (1885), *The Russian Storm-Cloud* (1886), and *The Russian Peasantry* (1888).[8] He had been instrumental in founding the Society of Friends of Russian Freedom in 1890, editing its newspaper, *Free Russia,* from 1890 to 1893,[9] and, together with fellow émigrés, had organized the Russian Free Press Fund to publish Russian-language books, pamphlets, and tracts for the revolutionary movement inside Russia and abroad.[10] Buoyed by the success of lectures throughout Britain, he undertook a five-month tour of the United States in 1890–91, speaking and raising money for the revolutionary cause in New York, Boston, and Chicago.[11]

In Britain, he could number among his friends and acquaintances William Morris, George Bernard Shaw, Annie Besant, and Herbert Burrows. On the other side of the Atlantic, he could count George Kennan a close friend, William Dean Howells an admirer, and Samuel Clemens an acquaintance. All but forgotten today, Stepniak was, throughout the 1880s and up until his death in 1895, one of the two most important interpreters of the Russia revolutionary movement for the English-speaking world. His only rival was George Kennan, whose famous series of articles on the Russian exile and prison system began to appear in *The Century Magazine* in 1887.[12] However, unlike his American friend, Stepniak was the living embodiment of the revolution.

What so upset Olive on that day in late December 1893 began with a report from Constance the previous day: "a clever attack has been made on Stepniak, Volkhovsky & others . . . & calculated to do much harm to the Cause. . . . I had heard of the attack . . . but had not read it and treated it lightly."[13] By the next afternoon, she had obtained and read the piece ("Anarchists" II) that had been published in the January issue of the *New Review.* The article charged that Mezentsev's murderer was living in London "under an assumed name." Although it did not mention Stepniak by name, the article included more than enough biographical detail so that, to those who knew him, the accusation was clear and unmistakable. Even more upsetting, it contained a substantially accurate—if sensationalized—account of the circumstances, planning, and execution of Mezentsev's murder:

> This man, then came back to Russia, where he became the warmest partisan of terrorism, giving himself up entirely to the plot for the murder of General Mezentzeff, whilst the latter would be taking, as usual, his morning walk through the streets of St. Petersburg.
>
> In order to perpetrate this crime, he had provided himself with a kitchen knife, and, to secure his flight, he and his confederates had secured the victoria of Dr. Weimar, their friend and associate, who had often lent him his carriage, especially on the occasion of the ovation of Prince Krapotkine.
>
> General Mezentzeff went out on the fourth of August, 1878, at nine o'clock in the morning, and accompanied by one of his friends—a Russian colonel—and whilst walking, they were talking together without the least anxiety. All at once the murderer, sneaking up on tip-toe, assaulted the General, plunging the kitchen knife into his abdomen; then after having turned and re-turned the knife in the open wound, he rushed with his confederate to the victoria, into which they jumped. The carriage started at such a tremendous pace that it was soon out of sight throughout the streets of the Russian capital. All these facts have been proved by unimpeachable evidence, and also on the testimony of Mikhailoff and one Goldenberg.[14]

The article's revelations clearly came as a shock to Olive, who confided her confusion to her diary: "the article is a clever mixture of truth unfavourably represented & falsehood in the guise of truth. . . . When I had finished reading—& from my own knowledge I was unable to separate truth from falsehood."[15] The word replaced by that long dash, then, the dash Olive had recorded earlier—the word too horrible for her to contemplate—was clearly either "assassin" or "murderer." Whatever Olive believed or could not bring herself to believe, there was far more truth in "Ivanoff's" article than falsehood. The charismatic Russian whom Olive knew as Sergei Stepniak—and with whom she was more than a little in love—was Sergei Mikhailovich Kravchinsky, the murderer of General Mezentsev and the author of *Death for Death!*

Sergei Kravchinsky was born on July 1, 1851, in the village of Novyi Starodub in Kherson province.[16] (In those parts of the Russian Empire, the Eurasian steppe stretched northward from the shores of the Black Sea; hence the pseudonym "Stepniak," which can be translated as "born of the steppe.") His father, Mikhail Fadeevich, was the son of an "Orthodox churchman of minor orders" who had made a career for himself as an army doctor. For his service, Mikhail Fadeevich was granted hereditary nobility, which conferred noble status on him and his descendants. Sergei's mother, Liubov Yakovlevna, was from south Russian gentry, and "had a good command of French, wrote gracefully and was quite well-read."[17] In his social origins, Kravchinsky was, in fact, remarkably similar to Evgeny Bazarov, the nihilist hero of Turgenev's *Fathers and Sons.*

Kravchinsky appeared destined to follow his father into the military. After completing the six-year course of study at the Orlov-Bakhtin Military Academy, he went to Moscow, where he spent two years at the Third Aleksandrovsky Military Institute. By the summer of 1869, the eighteen-year-old Kravchinsky had transferred to the Mikhailovsky Artillery Institute in St. Petersburg to complete his education. To this point, there is nothing remarkable about Kravchinsky's career: for an educated son of minor nobility, service as an artillery officer was a wholly suitable and honorable path in life.

This was, however, the 1860s—the decade that had begun with the Great Reforms, an end to serfdom, newfound freedom for the press—and the birth of Russian radicalism. Even during the period of growing government reaction after 1866, the walls of the Artillery Institute could not keep the ferment out. Taking advantage of the permissive post-reform atmosphere, the cadets managed to organize a radical study group. Kravchinsky joined. Leonid Shishko, who founded the group, later recalled that Kravchinsky soon came to dominate, pushing it further to the left. Writing considerably later, Shishko has left us this portrait of his friend:

> He was a young man of an extraordinarily serious and even gloomy appearance—somewhat round-shouldered, with a large head, a massive forehead and sharply-defined features. He was forever sitting at his desk behind his books, and would rarely speak to anyone. . . . All of his energy was directed toward developing himself intellectually. . . .

> At that time he could already read several foreign languages, and, given a great memory, he would stun us with his knowledge of the social sciences.[18]

Crucial to his future career, Kravchinsky had apparently inherited his mother's facility for languages, while the intensity that Shishko recalls here would forever remain a striking aspect of his personality.

On July 21, 1870, just a few weeks after his nineteenth birthday, Kravchinsky completed the course of study at the institute, received the rank of second lieutenant, and began a brief career as an instructor at the Kharkov Military District Bombardiers' School.[19] After only a year's service, he resigned his commission and returned to St. Petersburg, this time to matriculate at the St. Petersburg Agricultural Institute. What is much more important, sometime in the fall of 1871 or the spring of 1872, he was accepted into the Chaikovsky Circle, whose members were collectively know as the Chaikovtsy. At that time, it was directing its energies toward establishing workers' study groups in the Russian capital, and Kravchinsky quickly distinguished himself as one of the group's most able propagandists. By all accounts, he had a special talent for getting his point across to his working-class audiences in accessible and vigorous language.

Equally important, as one of the Chaikovtsy, Kravchinsky got to know many of the comrades who would remain important for him for the rest of his life. In addition to his old friend Leonid Shishko, the organization had among its members Peter Kropotkin, the "Anarchist Prince"; Sofia Perovskaia, one of the organizers of the dynamite plot that killed Alexander II; and lesser-known figures, such as Dimitry Klements and Yakov Stefanovich.[20]

By the fall of 1873—well in advance of the great "going to the people" movement (*khozhdenie v narod*) of the summer of 1874, when several thousand enthusiastic young propagandists made their way to the villages—Kravchinsky was already in the countryside, having decided it was time to carry socialist propaganda to the peasantry. He and a friend from the Artillery Institute, Dmitry Rogachev, disguised themselves as woodcutters, filled their knapsacks with revolutionary leaflets, and went to work preaching revolution to the sometimes less-than-receptive *muzhiks* of Tver province.[21] Taken into police custody, he made a miraculous escape and spent the winter of 1873–74 in hiding along the Volga in Nizhny Novgorod and Kazan.

Stung by the failure of the "going to the people" movement, and mindful of the waves of arrests that had come in its wake, Kravchinsky left Russia sometime in the spring of 1875. That summer, together with anarchists, revolutionaries, and rabble-rousers from all over Europe, he set off for the

Balkans to fight against the Turks in the Herzegovinian uprising. His aims were twofold: to aid the cause of Balkan liberation and to gain experience in guerrilla warfare for possible application back home. His military training went to good use here: he was put in command of the one cannon the rebels had in their armory.[22]

By 1877 he was in southern Italy. The crushing poverty of the *Mezzogiorno* was among the very worst in Europe—Kravchinsky would later write that its rival could be found only in Russia[23]—and Italy's south was fertile ground for anarchist agitation. Together with Italian Bakuninists Errico Malatesta and Carlo Cafiero, he helped lead an armed insurgency in the Matese hills around Benevento. He was captured by carabinieri a few days before the three-day revolt got under way and spent the next ten months in prison awaiting trial, reading Marx, and using the time to perfect his knowledge of Italian. Once again luck seemed to be with him: at the end of January he was out of jail, released as part of a general amnesty that followed the accession of Umberto I to the Italian throne.[24]

Kravchinsky was in Geneva writing for the émigré press when word came of Vera Zasulich's attempt on the life of General Trepov in February 1878, and of her stunning acquittal by a sympathetic jury in April. By May he had slipped back into Petersburg to begin work as an editor on the first issue of *Zemlia i volia* (*Land and Freedom*), the underground newspaper of the Russian Revolution. Inspired by Zasulich's example and enraged by the mistreatment of comrades languishing in prison, he proposed, planned, and carried out the murder of General Mezentsev. He stabbed the general with a stiletto he had brought back from Italy (not a "kitchen knife"). He was not yet twenty-seven years old.[25]

When Olive Garnett first met Stepniak, in October 1892, he was forty-one and had been living in England with his wife, Fanny, since 1884. In her diary entry for November 9, 1892, Olive recorded this reaction: "[Constance and I] began to talk about *him.* We agreed that he overwhelmed us not only morally and mentally but physically. In argument he comes up and literally towers over one. . . . Stepniak did not talk much at first, he observed one, then another & pondered, afterwards he thundered."[26] In his memoirs, James Mavor offers this characterization of Stepniak: "The cast of Stepniak's temperament was that of an artist rather than that of a political philosopher or a revolutionist. Yet I never met an artist who was so amiable and so gentle in his judgments."[27] Mavor, a Scottish-born economist and later professor of political economy at the University of Toronto, knew Stepniak quite well during the 1880s. Although set down in the 1920s, his memory of Stepniak as "an artist," that is, as a writer rather than a revolutionary, is entirely congruent with Olive's fear of losing Stepniak "the artist" to Stepniak "the nihilist" and "the terrorist."

Like his facility for languages, Kravchinsky's love of literature showed itself during his student years. Evidence of this comes from, of all places, the protocol of an interrogation conducted by the Third Department—the secret police—in 1874. Unlike the fictional Bazarov, he seems to have combined an interest in natural science (proper to a young radical) with a passion for poetry: "He would occupy himself mainly with reading in all branches of knowledge, and not be satisfied with any one branch; he loved the poets, would declaim poetry, excelled in languages, and kept himself busy with translations."[28]

Another clue to Kravchinsky's literary formation comes from Peter Kropotkin, who reports, "Serghei, who knew the New Testament almost by heart, spoke to the peasants as a religious preacher, proving to them by quotations from the Bible that they ought to start a revolution. Sometimes he formed his quotations from the economists."[29] Taratuta notes that, as a child, "he was very religious."[30] Although as an adult he would become a thoroughgoing atheist, as a writer he would never abandon the religious rhetoric he had absorbed as a child as a means to move an audience in favor of his cause.

The "going to the people" movement of 1873–74 also provides the first evidence of the intersection of the literary with the revolutionary that would define Kravchinsky's career. During these years he began work on a series of *propagandistskie skazki* (propagandistic fairy tales) that combined folk imagery, demotic language, and sometimes elaborate allegory to introduce his readers to the fundamentals of Marxist economic and historical thought.[31] Whatever we may think of this project, Kravchinsky took his work as a writer seriously. In a letter to Peter Lavrov, the émigré activist and publisher who was editing the *skazki* for publication, he observed, "I'm always changing, redoing, revising endlessly. I read my works to any and all and I always listen carefully to all opinions. . . . Criticism, polishing—that's something essential. Without it you won't write anything that gets you anywhere. . . . We, sinners that we are—if we have at least some talent, however modest, we have to hammer our works out like Bessemer steel."[32] Kravchinsky was not the only one who took his writing seriously. Ivan Turgenev read one of the *skazki* and offered these comments in a letter to Lavrov:

> The author is a man of talent, he commands the language, and his entire work is warmed through by the fire of youth and conviction. However, the tone is not sustained. The author hasn't managed to figure

> out for whom he's writing—for exactly which segment of the reading public? The consequence of this is an inconsistency and unevenness of exposition. First it's written for the people, then for—if not exactly a more educated—a more "literary" segment. But I repeat, your acquaintance does have talent and may he continue to labor in this field.[33]

Turgenev puts his finger on a problem that would grow ever more acute for Kravchinsky as he emerged fully as a writer: the problem of an audience. His two most important works—*Underground Russia* and *The Career of a Nihilist*—were originally written in foreign languages for foreign (i.e., non-Russian) audiences. Although both were eventually translated into Russian, this fact hindered Stepniak's reception as a writer in his native land. Unlike Nabokov or Brodsky, who began to write in English only *after* producing a substantial body of work in Russian, Stepniak (*skazki* and journalism aside) only began to produce a substantial body of original work in Russian during the last six years of his life, beginning in 1889.

Kravchinsky left Russia reluctantly following the assassination of General Mezentsev in 1878. He spent several years in Switzerland, having been persuaded by his comrades that he could be of more use to the revolution testing explosives in the Swiss mountains than sitting in a Russian prison.[34] In addition to purely journalistic work, he supported himself by literary translation. Pressing his Italian into service, he translated *In risaia* (*In the Ricefields*), a verismo novel by the proto-feminist Maria Torriani Torelli-Viollier, who wrote under the pseudonym Marchesa Colombi, and *Spartaco* (*Spartacus*), a historical novel about the Roman slave revolt by Garabaldisti writer Raffaello Giovagnoli. But in the months following the assassination of Alexander II in May 1881, Kravchinsky's position in Switzerland became increasingly untenable. Fearing imminent arrest and extradition, he made his way over the Alps—in secret and on foot—and, eventually, to Milan, where by October 1881 he had already set about writing the work that would bring him an international reputation.

Composed in Italian, *Underground Russia* was first published in the newspaper *Il Pungolo* as a series of "letters from a Russian patriot." While the first letter was printed anonymously, the second was signed "Stepniak," marking the first appearance of the pseudonym under which Kravchinsky would become famous. Revised and expanded, *Underground Russia* first appeared in a separate edition in May 1882 as *La Russia sotterranea: Profili e bozzetti rivoluzionarj dal vero di Stepniak gia diretorre di "Zemlia i Volia" (Terra e Liberta).*

Alexander's assassination had raised interest in Russia—and more particularly in Russian revolutionaries. Reliable information, however, was scarce. Stepniak knew what he was talking about, and his "revolutionary sketches"—the accuracy of which was guaranteed in an introduction by the better-known Lavrov—could not have appeared at a more opportune moment. Even before *La Russia sotterranea* was brought out separately in Italian, Stepniak was negotiating with publishers in London and Paris regarding publication of his work in English and French. Things moved more quickly in England than in France: a publisher and translator were found, and *La Russia sotterranea* was rushed into print as *Underground Russia: Revolutionary Profiles and Sketches from Life* (March 1883). An American edition followed immediately, and within the next three years the book had been published in full or in part in Swedish (1883), German (1884), French (1885), Dutch (1886), and Hungarian (1886). The first Russian edition finally saw the light of day in 1893, two years before Stepniak's death.[35] Published in London by the Russian Free Press Fund, it was illegal in Russia.

Stepniak outlined the plan for *Underground Russia* in a letter to his wife written from Milan toward the end of 1881:

> I told [my Italian publishers] that I would come up with 13 letters in all (I picked a devil's dozen on purpose). And here's how I'm thinking of arranging them: The first two—historical. After that 8 biographies: 4 men and 4 women. . . . After that the last three letters will depict three facts—one escape (probably Kropotkin's—it's worth saying something about him since he's quite well-known), the Hartmann mine—only to the extent that it was revealed at the trial—with a few belletristic additions based on Morozov's stories. Then a separate letter—the secret press. This will be the final and the darkest—and maybe the best. I can write about this too because it's been written about in the papers. All together it will make really good material for a future historian or novelist.[36]

Two things are worth noting here. The first is the constraints under which Kravchinsky was operating. He could not allow anything he wrote to compromise his comrades in the ongoing struggle with the Russian government. In that same vein, the subjects of the eight biographies had to be either in exile abroad without hope of return, or in prison without hope of escape, or already dead. The second thing to note is Stepniak's sense that the material he had brought together for *Underground Russia* was on its way to becoming a novel.

In a draft of a wide-ranging letter intended for the Executive Committee of the People's Will written in March 1882, Stepniak informed his comrades of the imminent publication of his book and outlined his own role in addressing them:

> The fact is that Russian socialists are at present trying to win what Europeans already won several generations ago—also at the cost of bloody exertions. Therefore they can sympathize with our struggle only if its true meaning and character at the current moment are made clear to them. But up until now this hasn't been done. Up until now "nihilism" has remained a monster for Europe, a "monster huge, unruly and hundred-mawed."[37] [. . .] Europe has its own affairs, its own troubles, and up to now it has been interested in "nihilists" more as a rare and wondrous beast, more as an amusement, as a kind of curious gladiatorial combat. It does not recognize in them any particle of itself, and we have to hammer and keep hammering away at one point, so that we can hammer it into their skull that our contemporary terrorists are the men of '93 and '89 in France to whom all Europe gives pride of place. What comes next, each of the sides decides that for itself. But since Russian socialists at this time are not going beyond the attainment of universal human rights, they are flesh of the flesh and bone of the bone of progressive Europe.
>
> It's not fitting, not possible and it's shameful to conceal our socialism from radical Europe in order to win its sympathy. And it's not even needed. But it's not in the name of this socialism that we can expect sympathy. Therefore you've got to acquaint Europe not with your program, but with the revolutionary struggle at the current moment. It has to be illuminated in a way that makes it clear that the aspirations of Russian socialists are identical—temporarily to be sure—with those of the radicals of European revolutions. We've finally got to reconcile Europe to the bloody measures taken by Russian revolutionaries, demonstrating, on the one hand, their inevitability under Russian conditions and, on the other, showing the terrorists themselves to be what they are in reality, that is, not cannibals, but humane, highly moral people who harbor a deep aversion for any kind of violence, but that only the government's measures compel them.
>
> That's how I look at the business of propaganda among a foreign audience [*publiki*] in foreign languages and that's what I will try to do to the extent that I can, and if up to now we've done very little in this area, then the blame for that is not any lack of good will, believe me.
>
> Propaganda in Russian for Russian youth should, of course, have a completely different character.[38]

In essence, Stepniak argues that in order to win over "progressive Europe," Russia's revolutionaries needed to provide a context for the terror, put a human face on the terrorists, and persuade Europe to see them as its own.

In the complete English-language edition of 1883, *Underground Russia* comprises three chapters of historical introduction, eight profiles, five "sketches from life" detailing the activities and adventures of the revolutionary movement (the "facts" mentioned in the letter to his wife), and a conclusion. As a final "note," Stepniak included a translation of the letter from the Executive Committee of the People's Will to Alexander III justifying the assassination of his father.

For his eight profiles Stepniak chose Yakov Stefanovich (in prison), Dmitry Klements (in Siberia), Valerian Ossinsky (dead by execution), Dmitry Lizogub (dead by execution), Peter Kropotkin (in exile abroad), Vera Zasulich (in exile abroad), Sofia Perovskaia (dead by execution), and Gesia Gelfman (died awaiting execution). With the exception of Gelfman, Stepniak knew every one of them personally and considered all of them his friends.

For his five sketches Stepniak eventually settled on the attempt to dynamite the emperor's train as it approached Moscow ("The Moscow Attempt"), the escapes of Kropotkin and the Ukrainian revolutionary Ivan Bokhanovsky from prison ("Two Escapes"), a chapter on methods used to avoid detection by the police ("The Ukrivateli"), an account of the underground press ("The Secret Press"), and a longish section recounting a clandestine journey across the border to St. Petersburg ("A Trip to St. Petersburg").

Stepniak's three historical chapters are meant to prepare the reader for the profiles and sketches that follow. They trace an arc from the emergence of the radicals of the 1860s ("Introduction"), through the appearance of the populists during the first half of the 1870s ("The Propaganda"), to the advent of the terrorists by the end of that decade ("The Terrorism"). In addition to providing an accurate (if abbreviated) historical account, Stepniak establishes a European pedigree for Russian socialism by way of Proudhon, Fourier, and Owen (significantly, Marx is not mentioned).[39] He takes pains to convince his readers that, in the absence of meaningful political reform, change by violence was, in fact, the only real hope of self-respecting people of conscience, intellect, and feeling:

> It may be fairly assumed that the public mind would have turned to legal and pacific means if, after having liberated the peasants from the bondage of their lords, the Emperor Alexander II had liberated Russia from his bondage, bestowing some kind of Constitution which would

> have made her the arbiter of her own destinies, or at least have afforded her the hope of becoming so. But this is precisely what he would not do on any account. Autocracy having retained all its power, nothing could be hoped for except from the good-will of the Emperor, and this hope went on diminishing as the years went by. Alexander II as a reformer stood the test for only a few years.
>
> The insurrection in Poland, stifled with a ferocity known to all, was a signal for a reaction, which grew more furious day by day. There was nothing to hope for in legal and pacific means. Everything must be uncomplainingly endured, or other ways of saving the country must be sought for. All those who had a heart in their breast naturally clung to the latter course. . . . Nay, after 1866, the reaction redoubled its fury. In a few months everything that maintained a semblance of the Liberalism of the early years was swept away. . . . After 1866 a man must have been either blind or a hypocrite to believe in the possibility of any improvement except by violent means. (*UR*, 15–17)

Into this historical and political account Stepniak weaves a narrative strand that goes to the heart of the belletristic or novelistic dimensions of *Underground Russia,* a strand that might best be characterized as religious-psychological.

Stepniak begins its development with his characterization of the nihilism of the 1860s. Rather than a genuine political movement, he presents it as a far-ranging, ground-clearing operation undertaken to liberate the individual ego from the constraints of tradition: "The fundamental principle of Nihilism, properly so-called, was absolute individualism. It was the negation, in the name of individual liberty, of all the obligations imposed on the individual by society, family life, and by religion. Nihilism was a passionate and powerful reaction, not against political despotism, but against the moral despotism that weighs upon the private and inner life of the individual" (*UR,* 4). In his account of this great campaign for the liberation of the "inner life," Stepniak maintains that the battle against religion, though crucial to the revolutionary movement, was won quickly and early on:

> The first battle was fought in the domain of religion. But this was neither long nor obstinate. It was gained, so to speak, in a single assault; for there is no country in the world where, among the educated classes, religion has such little root as in Russia. The past generation was partly Christian by custom, and partly atheist by culture. But once this band of young writers, armed with the natural sciences and positive philosophy, full of talent, of fire, and of the ardour of proselytism, was

> impelled to the assault, Christianity fell like an old, decaying hovel, which remains standing because no one touches it (*UR*, 4). . . .[40] The victory was of the highest importance. Absolute atheism is the sole inheritance [of the 1860s] that has been preserved intact by the new generation, and I need scarcely point out how much advantage the modern revolutionary movement has derived from it. (*UR*, 7)

While proclaiming the importance of "absolute" atheism to the revolutionary movement, however, Stepniak has rhetorically smuggled back into it something like "religious feeling" ("of talent, of fire, and the ardour of proselytism") even as he rejects the content of received religion (Christianity).

In the second chapter, the theme tentatively sounded here is realized in full in Stepniak's account of "the vast movement of 1873–74 which inaugurated the new Russian revolutionary era":

> Nothing similar had been seen before, nor since. It was a revelation, rather than apropaganda. [. . .] It was a powerful cry which arose no one knew where, and summoned the ardent to the great work of the redemption of the country and humanity. And the ardent, hearing this cry, arose, overflowing with sorrow and indignation for their past life, and abandoning home, wealth, honours, family, threw themselves into the movement with a joy, an enthusiasm, a faith, such as are experienced only once in a life, and when lost are never found again. . . .
>
> Yet it was not a political movement. It rather resembled a religious movement, and had all the contagious and absorbing character of one. People not only sought to attain a distant practical object, but also to satisfy an inward sentiment of duty, an aspiration to their own moral perfection. (*UR*, 22–23)[41]

While this can be seen as a version of the same tactics that Stepniak employed agitating among the peasants of Tver in 1873 (filling religious form with revolutionary content), there is nothing cynical, insincere, or inauthentic in any of it. Quite the contrary. For Stepniak, involvement in the revolutionary movement was a deeply transformative experience that inextricably linked redemption of society with self-redemption, change without with change within. And for this reason, it can be argued, he was ineluctably impelled toward the novel, particularly toward the realistic novel as it developed in Russia in the nineteenth century. For what is the Russian novel if not a record of self-change in a rapidly changing society?

The final stage in this process of revolutionary transformation is the birth of terrorism out of disillusionment with the faith that had animated the "propagandists" (i.e., populist agitators) of the early 1870s. To describe the emergence of the terrorist, Stepniak explicitly rejects Christian analogies, only to replace them with others of no less metaphysical import:

> The type of the propagandist . . . was religious rather than revolutionary. His faith was Socialism. His god the people. . . . Inexorable reality struck a blow at his enthusiasm and faith, disclosing to him his god as it really is, and not as he had pictured it. He was as ready for sacrifice as ever. But he had neither the impetuosity nor the ardour for the struggle. After the first disenchantment he no longer saw any hope in victory, and longed for the crown of thorns rather than the laurel. He went forth to martyrdom with the serenity of the Christian of the early ages. . . . He was full of love and had no hatred for anyone, not even his executioners.
>
> Such was the propagandist of 1872–75. This type was too ideal to withstand the fierce and imminent conflict. It must change or disappear.
>
> Already another was rising in its place. Upon the horizon there appeared a gloomy form, illuminated by the light of hell, who, with lofty bearing, and a look breathing forth hatred and defiance, made his way through the terrified crowd to enter with firm step upon the scene of history.
>
> It was the Terrorist. (*UR*, 28–29)

If the propagandists were Christlike in their acceptance of suffering and their ability to love even their enemies, Stepniak's terrorist breathes hatred, but combines within himself the martyr's readiness for self-sacrifice with the hero's drive to victorious action. To borrow Stepniak's own trope, he longs for both the crown of thorns *and* the laurel:

> He is noble, terrible and irresistibly fascinating, for he combines in himself the two sublimities of human grandeur: the martyr and the hero.
>
> He is a martyr. From the day when he swears in the depths of his heart to free the people and the country, he is consecrated to Death. He faces it at every step of his stormy life. He goes forth to meet it fearlessly, when necessary, and can die without flinching, not like the Christian of old, but like a warrior accustomed to look death in the face.
>
> He has no longer any religious feeling in his disposition. He is a

> wrestler, all bone and muscle, and has nothing in common with the dreamy idealist of the previous lustre. He is a mature man, and the unreal dreams of youth have disappeared with the years. He is a Socialist fatally convinced. [. . .] He has no other object than to overthrow this abhorred despotism, and to give his country, what all civilised nations possess, political liberty, to enable it to advance with firm step towards its own redemption. The force of mind, the indomitable energy, and the spirit of sacrifice which his predecessor possessed in the beauty of his dreams, he attains in the grandeur of his mission, in the strong passions which this marvelous, intoxicating, vertiginous struggle arouses in his heart. . . .
>
> Proud as Satan rebelling against God, he opposed his own will to that of the man who alone, amid a nation of slaves, claimed the right of having a will. (*UR*, 39–41)

In the final paragraphs of his historical introduction, Stepniak makes it clear that the struggle of the revolutionary terrorist is as personal as it is political. His commitment to his own dignity and his own freedom is as important as his commitment to the people in whose name he has taken up the fight, and, if it comes to it, even more so:

> He fights not only for the people, to render them arbiters of their own destinies, not only for the whole nation stifling in this pestiferous atmosphere, but also for himself; for the dear ones whom he loves, whom he adores with all the enthusiasm which animates his soul; for his friends who languish in the horrid cells of the central prisons. . . . He fights for himself. He has sworn to be free and will be free in defiance of everything. . . . And if the people, ill-counseled, say to him, "Be a slave," he will exclaim "No," and he will march onward, defying their imprecations and their fury, certain that justice will be rendered to him in his tomb.
>
> Such is the Terrorist. (*UR*, 42)

Love, which seemed to have been abandoned together with the shattered "dreams" of the propagandists, returns here in full force. But it is neither a Christlike love for one's enemy nor an "idealistic" love for "the people"—at best an abstraction. In place of these, the terrorist is left with only a deep emotional commitment—to friends and comrades in the struggle, to real people with real faces, each of whom has a story of his or her own. It is the impulse born of this commitment that lies behind Stepniak's decision to present "the peculiar life of this Revolutionary Russia" as a collection of "personal recollections," as "profiles" or "portraits" (*UR*, 46) meant to preserve the faces of those whom he loved.

The eight profiles that follow cannot really be called biographical. Rather, they are meant to evoke the salient features of each of Stepniak's subjects as revolutionary activists, and so focus on incidents and episodes rather than whole lives. The profile of Yakov Stefanovich ("Jacob Stefanovic"), for example, contains a brief account of his failed attempt to raise the peasants of Chigirino in 1877 and the circumstances of his arrest, an account of a clandestine meeting with Stepniak in St. Petersburg after Stefanovich's escape from prison, and, finally, an encomium to the hero meant to encapsulate his chief virtues (or failings, in some cases):

> He is a man of action exclusively; but yet not of immediate action like those whose hands itch to be at work. He knows how to wait. He is a man of far-reaching plans; he is the finest type of organizer whom I have ever known. His clear and eminently practical mind, his firm and cautious character, his knowledge of men . . . render him particularly adapted for this highly difficult office. . . . Notwithstanding the vicissitudes of his life, he had never broken off intercourse with his father, an old village priest; a somewhat dangerous thing in the case of a man who has thrown whole cities into commotion, when it was suspected that he would be found in them. He greatly loves and venerates his father and often speaks of him, relating with especial pleasure anecdotes of him, and quoting passages from his letters, which show his rude intelligence and his honest and upright heart. (*UR*, 58)

With variations suitable to his subject, at greater or lesser length, Stepniak repeats this pattern in each of his profiles. The net effect is rather like that of a collection of saints' legends—and no doubt intentionally so. Those familiar with Old Russian literature may be reminded of a *Paterikon,* a record of incidents from the lives of the saints connected with a particular monastic community and any miracles performed. But here again, Stepniak has filled religious form with revolutionary content: his monastery is underground Russia, and his saints are the revolutionaries who inhabit it. To complete the analogy, the miracles come in the third section of *Underground Russia,* the "revolutionary sketches." In the sketches, Stepniak offers his readers tales of daring escapes, ingenious ruses, and seemingly impossible feats undertaken in the name of the cause.

While working within this essentially hagiographic structure, Stepniak nevertheless incorporates unmistakably novelistic elements into his narratives, ransacking the catalog of nineteenth-century Russian fiction for his effects. Verbal portraiture figures prominently in almost all of the profiles, and in places is reminiscent of Turgenev:

> She is a strong, robust woman, and, although of middle height, she at first seems to be tall. She is not beautiful. Her eyes are very fine, large, well-shaped, with long lashes, and of grey colour, which become dark when she is excited. Ordinarily thoughtful and somewhat sad, these eyes shine forth brilliantly when she is enthusiastic, which not unfrequently happens, or sparkle when she jests, which happens very often. The slightest change of mind is reflected in the expressive eyes. The rest of her face is very commonplace. ("Vera Zassulic," *UR,* 107)

Descriptive passages—this one evoking the environs of the cottage rented by Perovskaia and Hartmann as headquarters for the plot to blow up the imperial train—have the flavor of Aksakov or Goncharov:

> Upon the outskirts of the old capital of Russia, just where that half Asiatic city, immense and antique as Babylon or Nineveh, is at last lost in the distance, and its houses, becoming fewer, are scattered among the market gardens and fields, and the immense uncultivated plains surround it on all sides, as the sea surrounds an islet; on these outskirts is a little cottage, one story high, old, grimy with age, and half in ruins. . . .
>
> There is no movement. From time to time a passerby is seen, and if he does not belong to the district the boys stare at him until he is out of sight. If by chance a carriage, or a hired vehicle, arrives in these parts, all the shutters, green, red, and blue, are hurriedly opened, and girls and women peep forth, curious to see such an extraordinary sight. ("The Moscow Attempt," *UR,* 137–138)

A clandestine nighttime journey through the streets of St. Petersburg launches a lyrical passage that sounds as if it might have been taken from the early Dostoevsky:

> It was one of those wondrous bright nights which are among the greatest beauties of St. Petersburg, when the dawn and the sunset seem to embrace each other in the pallid, starless sky, from which streams forth a rosy, soft, subtle and fantastic glow, and the light golden clouds float in an atmosphere of enchanting transparency. How I used to

> love those nights in times gone by, alone in a little *duscehubka* and with a single oar, I glided in the middle of the immense Neva, suspended between the arch of heaven and that other arch reflected in the black waters, which seemed of fathomless depth; and how I began to hate them afterwards, those accursed and dangerous nights! ("Jacob Stefanovic," *UR,* 54)

And, as unlikely as it may seem, there are even places where Stepniak's narrative takes on the antic quality of one of Gogol's *Dikanka* tales:

> When Krapotkine had finished his narrative [of his escape from prison], the turn came of John Bokanovski, surnamed the Cossack, because, being a native of the Ukraine, he resembled the ancient Cossacks of that country, by his courage, his imperturbable coolness, and his taciturnity.
>
> Everyone turned towards him. He took his little wooden pipe from his mouth and said: "Why, there's nothing to relate. He came, took us, and we went out; that's all."
>
> "No, no!" exclaimed those present. "Relate it all, from beginning to end."
>
> "Well then, when the day fixed arrived, he came with the keys of our cells—"
>
> "No, no," they broke in again. "Let us have it all. Relate everything from the commencement."
>
> The Cossack, seeing that every way of escape was closed against him, slowly filled his pipe with the air of a man preparing for a long journey, lit it, tried it to see if it drew properly, and began his narrative, which combined more words than the Cossack would ordinarily pronounce in three months at least. ("Two Escapes," *UR,* 158)

Whatever else *Underground Russia* may be, it is also a laboratory where Stepniak tried out techniques he would later put to use as a novelist.

By 1886, Stepniak was ready to write his novel. In August of that year he mentioned it in a letter to Edward R. Pease, a friend, fellow socialist, and later secretary of the Fabian Society: "You ask how my novel is going? It's coming along quite well. But my English gives me great cause for concern, and until I've made it through the most difficult, middle chapters, I can't say whether the book will be good or mediocre."[42] Again, Stepniak was writing in a language other than Russian, and again he had to keep a non-Russian audience in mind.

The Career of a Nihilist is set in the latter half of the 1870s, sometime after the "going to the people" movement of 1874 and not long before the final split of the Russian revolutionary movement into terrorist and gradualist wings in 1879.[43] That would place it sometime in 1877–78, precisely the period leading up to the assassination of Mezentsev after Stepniak's return to Russia from his first sojourn abroad. That period marks the final stage in a journey he described in the opening chapters of *Underground Russia,* the journey from propagandist to terrorist. The crucial difference is that what Stepniak presents in *Underground Russia* as a change of "generations" was in fact the psychological distance he himself had traveled between 1873 and 1878, between his own "going to the people" and the murder in Mikhailovsky Square. What the novel could offer that the ten-page profiles of *Underground Russia* could not was the capaciousness to encompass this distance. Above all, Stepniak's novel is a record of this journey, the travel notes of someone who finally arrives at a place where he is prepared to "deprive another like himself of life."

The prototype for Stepniak's hero, Andrey Kojukhov,[44] is, it will come as no surprise, Stepniak himself. Like his creator, Andrey is "strong and well-shaped" (*CN,* 4), "restless" and eager for action (*CN,* 13), "not insensible" to art and poetry (*CN,* 13), and adept at picking up languages (*CN,* 14). Unlike Stepniak, however, he has been "denied . . . any literary talent" (*CN,* 13). Although he is deeply committed to the cause, he was never intended to be an ascetic superman. Stepniak made this point forcefully in a letter to Pease from March 1889, when his novel was nearing completion:

> There is no superior man among them, no leader of men. Andrey himself is the commonest of all. You say "he is not merely a fanatic." He is not a bit of a fanatic. He is a most matter of fact, placid and unexacting man, born to be a father of a prosperous family and nothing else, I think he is not even particularly clever and there is certainly in his character a good deal of what may be called "wooden" element.[45]

Andrey is tough, disciplined, resourceful, and committed, but he is not without doubts, weaknesses, and flaws. At issue for Andrey is a deeply felt tension between the demands of radical commitment and the imperatives of personal life, the same tension that animates so many of Turgenev's novels. Unlike the liberal Turgenev's protagonists, who more often than not are crippled by their dilemma, Andrey always decides the issue in favor of the cause: he is, after all, a *revolutionary* hero. Nevertheless, his decision does not come without cost.

The human center of this conflict is Tania Repina, the beautiful nineteen-year-old daughter of a successful Petersburg lawyer, Grigory Repin. The embodiment of Russian liberalism, Repin sympathizes with the aims of Andrey and his comrades while harboring serious reservations about their methods. New to the movement, Tania has been drawn into the world of the underground by Andrey's close friend George. Andrey first meets Tania at her father's luxurious apartment, where the revolutionaries have gathered to discuss plans to free Boris, a comrade who has fallen into the hands of the police. Boris is being held prisoner in Dubravnik (a provincial Ukrainian town), and Andrey has only just returned to Russia, summoned back from exile abroad, in order to effect his escape.

Andrey falls in love with Tania that night, although he is not fully aware of it himself (an example, surely, of the "wooden element" in his character). As a revolutionary, he has to choose between acting on principle and acting on emotion. As the novel unfolds, Andrey wrestles with his feelings for Tania, at times giving in to intense and very uncomradely jealousy:

> It was at this very moment that a pang of jealousy tore away the scales covering his eyes. He saw, as by a lightning flash, what had been at the bottom of his attachment to Tania since the first day of their acquaintance. He loved this charming girl, loved her face, her blouse, the very bit of floor she was standing upon. And at the same moment a maddening conviction pierced his heart like a knife: that if she should ever love anybody, it would be this glib-tongued flatterer [George], who at the moment was positively hateful to him. A fit of furious irrepressible jealousy made his head swim. It required a desperate effort to maintain his self-control. He was afraid to betray himself if this lasted much longer. (*CN*, 96)

Later, when the party needs to bolster its propaganda effort in the working-class Narva district of St. Petersburg, the assembled comrades decide that Andrey and Tania are the two people best suited for the job. Andrey is deeply troubled by this unexpected turn of events but resolves to master his feelings and do whatever needs to be done:

> Andrey looked timidly at Tania, who was next to him. The girl seemed troubled and perplexed at the unlooked-for proposal. This hurt Andrey profoundly. . . . From her he certainly did not expect this.
>
> Love or no love, he was not a milksop; and he would prove to them that in all matters connected with the cause, he would never be influenced by considerations touching his personal feelings.

> His mind was made up at once, and he gave his full and unreserved consent to the new arrangement. (*CN,* 189)

Tania, of course, loves Andrey every bit as much as he loves her. Their work together soon leads to a mutual confession of feelings, followed by a proper revolutionary marriage:

> They were married soon after. No priest or policeman was requested to interfere in the matter. The union was completed by giving publicity to their intentions, as is the rule in the world in which they lived.
>
> The marriage changed in no way the external part of their life. They resumed the same work as before, though they had to settle at the opposite end of the capital, as the old district became too hot for them. In one of the bye-streets near the Cronversky they found small lodgings, consisting of two rooms, with a kitchen in which Tania cooked their meals.
>
> The rooms were small, and shabbily furnished. The floor was bare, the ceiling not very lofty. . . . On a sunny day they could enjoy the view of a block of ugly monotonous houses on the opposite side of the street. . . . Yet this was their paradise. . . .
>
> They were as fully and completely happy as they ever dreamed of being. (*CN,* 207)

This is the closest Andrey will ever get to being the "father of a prosperous family" that, in more normal circumstances, he might otherwise have been. But circumstances are not normal (this is Russia), and he will be brought to the point where he will choose to sacrifice what is most dear to him. When he decides that he must make an attempt on the life of the emperor, he knows that he is giving up everything—his life, and, what is perhaps even more difficult, Tania along with it. How he reaches this point is the very core of Stepniak's novel.

Andrey is not by nature a martyr. Certainly, he has learned to live with the knowledge that, as a revolutionary, his life and freedom hang by the slenderest of threads, but he is "too full of vigorous health" to "court the ghastly goddess of self immolation" (*CN,* 208). Nevertheless, as energetic as Andrey is, as happy as he is working for the cause shoulder to shoulder with Tania, any success he has had is far outweighed by painful failure and irrecoverable loss.

Sent to Dubravnik to rescue the imprisoned Boris, he fails in his mission: while he does manage to free two other comrades being held together with

Boris, he makes a crucial mistake in a battle with the gendarmes, leaving Boris a prisoner (*CN,* 159). As bad or worse: Boris's wife, Zina, one of Andrey's closest friends, cannot reconcile herself to the loss of her husband. Despite Andrey's stern admonitions reminding Zina that the needs of the cause must be put above "personal feelings," Zina decides to stay in Dubravnik in the hope of freeing Boris, even though all real hope has been lost:

> "You understand now, I suppose," she added, in a calmer tone raising her head again, "that considerations of a personal nature must also be taken into account sometimes."
>
> He sat down on the stool opposite her, and taking her hand raised it gently to his lips.
>
> Zina's reluctant confession only confirmed what he said to himself long ago. She was consumed by a slow fire. The constant suspense, the constant brooding over the affair on which depended Boris's life, was more than flesh or blood could bear. A sudden bereavement was easier to support than this. And now her pain had reached the point when reason ceased to control her feelings. If she remained in Dubravnik she would do something desperate and ruin herself on purpose. (*CN,* 176)

Andrey will reach his crisis later. Back in Petersburg, just at the moment of his greatest happiness with Tania, news of a "disaster" arrives from Dubravnik: Zina, together with another comrade who had helped Andrey organize the escape attempt, has been arrested in a shoot-out with the police. Three other comrades involved in the escape attempt have been rounded up. All are going to be tried together with Boris—and the sentence will inevitably be death. Andrey, already familiar with the situation on the ground, is put in charge of organizing the rescue. He returns to Dubravnik and sets about it with characteristic energy. His plan is as risky as it is daring: as the prisoners are being taken from prison to the place of execution, brigades of handpicked comrades led by trusted lieutenants will attack the convoy with revolvers and dynamite bombs and free the prisoners. Andrey's planning is meticulous, but at the last moment, bad news: Andrey's bomb maker has been severely wounded in an explosion, and the bombs that were to have been used in the operation have fallen into the hands of the police. Over the objections of hotheaded younger comrades, Andrey reluctantly calls off the attempt:

> Nobody spoke again. The meeting dispersed mournfully, . . . and Andrey hastened to fulfill his last duty to his friends, to let them know

> everything, that they might have no vain hope. They must go to meet their fate, with eyes open as became people such as they.
>
> He took the letter to the prison warder who carried his correspondence for him. He learned afterwards that his letter reached its destination that very evening. It was even answered by Zina, in the name of her companions. Her letter was not a sad one; if anything, it was rather cheerful. But the reading of it tore Andrey's heart, and made him, the man of iron nerve, cry like a child, because, delayed in transmission, it reached him two days after it was all over, and the hand that wrote those touching lines was cold and stiff, and the heart that inspired them had ceased to beat. (*CN*, 244)

On the day of the execution, Andrey reaches a tipping point. Helpless to free his friends, the last service he can perform for them is to "take his stand in some conspicuous place on the way to the scaffold, so that they might see each other" (*CN*, 253). Moved by the sight of his friends being carted to their death, he is most affected by Zina:

> She expected that Andrey would come, and was seeking him in the crowd. She discovered him at once. There he stood, directly under her feet, with head raised towards her. Their eyes met.
>
> Neither then nor afterwards could Andrey understand how it came to pass, but in that moment everything was changed in him, as if in that kind pitying look there was some spell. Anxieties and fears, nay, even indignation, regrets, revenge—all were forgotten, submerged by something thrilling, vehement, undescribable. It was more than enthusiasm, more than a readiness to bear everything. It was a positive thirst for martyrdom—a feeling he always deprecated in others, and never expected himself to possess—which burst forth within him now. To be there, among them, upon the black car of infamy, his shoulders fastened to the wood like those of that woman, bending her radiant brow above the crowd, this was not punishment, this was not horror, it was the fulfillment of an ardent desire, of a dream of supreme happiness! Forgetting the place, the crowd, the dangers, everything,—conscious of an irresistible impulse,—he made a step forward, stretching both his hands towards her. He did not cry aloud words that would have ruined him irrevocably, only because his voice forsook him; or perhaps the words were lost in the noise of the drums, as his movement was in the rush of the crowd which closed on him from both sides, swelling the enormous following of the advancing procession. (*CN*, 253)

Andrey's reaction is profoundly personal: it is a desire for an ecstatic communion in death with "the dear ones whom he loves, whom he adores with all the enthusiasm which animates his soul." But this "irresistible impulse" as yet has no political content. That comes only later, when Andrey realizes that half measures are useless, and that he must strike at the very heart of the evil—the emperor Alexander himself:

> What a mass of victims! Zina dead, Boris, Vasily, Botcharov dead also. The two Dudorovs and so many, many others buried alive, as good as dead. He himself would be arrested one of these days, for he could not always expect to slip through the enemy's fingers, as he had until now. He too would be put to death, and who would be the better for all these hecatombs?
>
> The vision of the crowd returning from the place of execution passed before him and sent a chill through his brain. But he shook it off.
>
> No, that was not the upshot of his experiences and meditations! These people had not died in vain. They were the skirmishers who had perished in starting from its lair the great beast. For the survivors to grapple with it now!
>
> The idea, which . . . had been hovering over him at a distance, like a hawk making its circles above its prey, now swooped upon him, demanding immediate and final solution.
>
> Half dressed and barefooted, he took to pacing up and down the room noiselessly, so as not to awaken George.
>
> His idea was clearly formulated in his own mind. The struggle with the menial tools of autocracy had had its day. An attempt must be made against the Tzar himself and he was the man to make it. (*CN*, 272–273)

In this final act, the personal and the political will be seamlessly merged, and in this moment the hero and the martyr become one. The making of the terrorist is complete.

The attempt will fail. There is still too much of Andrey that is bound too closely to life by his love for Tania. Distracted by agonizing efforts to detach himself from her, he neglects to test a newly acquired revolver, an inexcusable oversight that will prove to be a fatal mistake. Even as he makes his way to the appointed place—a trip he has practiced and timed again and again—he unconsciously slows his pace at the sight of a young girl who reminds him of Tania (*CN*, 315–16), and he is almost too late.

Andrey's last moments are seen only at a distance. George, who has posted himself in the window of a house overlooking Palace Square, watches as Andrey approaches the emperor:

> In breathless suspense George watched as the distance between the two diminished step by step until they seemed to have come within a few paces of each other and nothing yet had happened and they were advancing. . . . Why does he wait? What could it mean? . . . But it was a delusion; the distance which appeared in perspective so short was about fifteen yards.
>
> Here according to regulations Andrey had to take off his hat and stand bareheaded until his master should pass. But instead of doing that act of obeisance, he plunged his hand into his pocket, drew a revolver, pointed and fired at the Tzar instantaneously.
>
> The ball struck in the wall of a house at the Tzar's back some forty yards off, almost under the cornice. The shot had missed; the revolver kicked strongly, and had to be pointed at the feet for a fatal shot. This Andrey discovered too late. For a moment he stood petrified with consternation, both hands hanging down. The Tzar, pale likewise, the flaps of his long overcoat gathered up in his hands, ran from him as quickly as he could. But he did not lose his presence of mind; instead of running straight, he ran in zigzags, thus offering a very difficult target to the man running behind him. That saved him. . . .
>
> In less than a minute, Andrey's six shots were spent. The flock of spies [bodyguards], who at first had made themselves scarce, now appeared from all sides, their numbers growing every moment. George saw Andrey encompassed at all points by the crowd of them, wild at having eluded their vigilance. For a moment they stood at a distance, cautious, none daring to be the first to approach him. Then, seeing him disarmed, they rushed on him all at once. George heard only fierce shouts and cries, for he had covered his face with both his hands and saw nothing more.
>
> Andrey was thrown into prison half dead. He recovered, and was in due time tried and executed.
>
> He had perished. But the work for which he dies did not perish. It goes on from defeat to defeat toward the final victory, which in this sad world cannot be obtained save by the sufferings and sacrifice of the chosen few. (*CN*, 319–320)

There is a serious moral evasion in Stepniak's work that cannot go unmentioned. He does not, either in *The Career of a Nihilist* or in *Under-*

ground Russia, depict a successful assassination: his terrorists remain victims, and the terrible moment when one human being actually takes the life of another "like himself" is passed over in silence. Indeed, in the account of Mezentsev's death offered in *Underground Russia,* Stepniak himself is strangely absent: "On August 16, 1878, that is five months after the acquittal of Zasulic, the Terrorism, by putting to death General Mesentzeff, the head of the police and the entire *camarilla,* boldly threw down its glove in the face of the autocracy" (*UR,* 39). The real terrorist dissolves in an abstraction called "the Terrorism."

There is a record of other such evasions. The *New York Times* published this account of an exchange with Stepniak which took place during a meeting with the press on the day of his arrival in New York for his American tour:

> "Stepniak is not your name; what is your name? They call you by five or six names in this country; which is the right one?"
>
> The Russian laughed at this question and then he answered: "My name is Stepniak. That is the name I will be known by. I was born 'Stepniak' when I wrote my book 'Underground Russia' down in Italy. I choose to conceal my real name. Let the Russian government know me as 'Stepniak.' I have never done aught that I am ashamed of or regret, but I do not wish to give my name and it is my right to withhold it."
>
> "Have you ever killed anybody?" mildly inquired one of the journalists.
>
> Stepniak opened his eyes at this question, as well he might, but he answered it promptly in the negative.
>
> "I didn't suppose that you had," said the inquirer.[46]

Stepniak may well be forgiven for not wishing to admit he was a murderer at his first press conference on his first visit to a new country. However, not long after the article about Mezentsev's assassination appeared in the *New Review,* Olive came over to help him draft a rebuttal. As Thomas Moser cannily notes, Olive was more than ready to "delud[e] herself into believing that, though he accepted responsibility for the violence of others in the cause, he himself, like Kropotkin, did not commit violent acts." And Stepniak did not have the courage to disabuse her. Her diary records this exchange:

> I said "There is nothing in Ivanoff's article which is not in 'Underground Russia,' nothing." And he said "Absolutely nothing." "Moreover," I continued "from their point of view it would have been

> enough to have said—'Read this book, this is the man who wrote it, this man'—and these things of which they accuse you, are they not included? If you were a terrorist you are morally responsible for every act of the party, even if you sat all the time in your own armchair." Stepniak nodded, & blushed.[47]

After publishing *The Career of a Nihilist,* Stepniak abandoned English for his literary pursuits, and wrote instead in Russian.[48] He was killed on December 23, 1895, when he was struck by a train as he was making his way across the tracks at a dangerous crossing.

Olive never married. She visited Russia, eventually producing a volume of short stories[49] and a novel[50] based on her experiences. The journal she kept of her travels is, at this writing, being prepared for publication.

Constance Garnett went on to become the single most important translator of Russian literature into English who ever lived. She had begun studying Russian during her pregnancy at the urging of Felix Volkhovsky, putting Goncharov's *Obyknovennaia istoriia* (*A Common Story*) into English to distract herself. But she owed her career as a translator to Stepniak. Thirty-five years after first meeting him, she would write in her autobiography,

> This was one of the most important events of my life. Stepniak read my Goncharov translation, undertook to go over it with me, urged me to finish it. [He said I] ought to get it published. I sent it to Heinemann . . . to my intense joy I received £40 for it & a commission to translate Tolstoy's *The Kingdom of God Is Within You*. . . . From that time up to now I have never been without a Russian translation to do—& have by now some 70 volumes finished.[51]

This, finally, may have been Stepniak's most important contribution to Russian literature.

Notes

Unless otherwise indicated, all translations are mine.

1. For events in Russia, dates are given old style.

2. Narodnaia volia was the terrorist wing of the main revolutionary movement after its bifurcation in early 1879.

3. George Brandes, "Sergei Stepniak," in Sergey Stepnyak, *Andrey Kozhuhkov* (Geneva: Tipografiia Soiuza Russkikh Sotsial-demokratov, 1898), vii.

4. Reprinted in O. V. Budnitskii, *Istoriia terrorizma v dokumentakh, biografiiakh, issledovaniiakh,* 2nd ed. (Rostov-na-Donu: Feniks, 1996), 77–88.

5. Barry C. Johnson, ed., *Olive and Stepniak: The Bloomsbury Diary of Olive Garnett, 1893–1895* (Birmingham, Eng.: Bartletts, 1993), 19.

6. Thomas C. Moser, "An English Context for Conrad's Russian Characters: Sergei Stepniak and the Diary of Olive Garnett," *Journal of Modern Literature* 11, no. 1 (March 1984): 3–44. I am greatly indebted to Moser's splendid article for my account of Stepniak's relations with the Garnett family. See also Anat Vernitski, "Russian Revolutionaries and English Sympathizers in 1890s London: The Case of Olive Garnett and Sergei Stepniak," *Journal of European Studies* 35, no. 3 (2005): 299–314.

7. Throughout the 1880s and into the 1890s, Stepniak's work was published simultaneously in London and New York.

8. *Russia Under the Tsars* (London: Ward and Downey, 1885); *The Russian Storm-Cloud, or Russia in Her Relations to Neighboring Countries* (London: Swan Sonneschein, 1886); *The Russian Peasantry: Their Agrarian Condition, Social Life and Religion* (London: Swan Sonneschein, 1888). For the first two, Stepniak's New York publisher was Charles Scribner's Sons, and for the third, Harper and Brothers.

9. For the society and its activities, see Barry Hollingsworth, "The Society of Friends of Russian Freedom: English Liberals and Russian Socialists, 1890–1917," *Oxford Slavonic Papers,* n.s., 3 (1970): 45–64.

10. James W. Hulse, *Revolutionists in London: A Study of Five Unorthodox Socialists* (Oxford: Clarendon Press, 1970), 44.

11. For a brief account of Stepniak's American tour, see Charles A. Moser, "A Nihilist's Career: S. M. Stepniak-Kravchinskij," *American Slavic and East European Review* 20, no. 1 (1961): 55–77.

12. Published as a book in 1891 as *Siberia and the Exile System.*

13. Olive Garnett, diary entry of December 28, 1893, quoted in Moser, "English Context," 15; also Johnson, *Olive and Stepniak,* 1. "Volkhovsky" is Feliks Vadimovich Volkhovsky (1846–1914), a comrade, friend, and collaborator of Stepniak. On Volkhovsky, see Donald Senese, *S. M. Stepniak-Kravchinskii: The London Years* (Newtonville, Mass.: Oriental Research Partners, 1987), 49–51.

14. "Anarchists: Their Methods and Organization (Part 2)," *New Review* 56 (January 1894), quoted in Johnson, *Olive and Stepniak,* 5.

15. Ibid., 19.

16. Present-day Ukraine.

17. Quoted in Evgeniia Taratuta, *S. M. Stepniak-Kravchinskii: Revoliutsioner i pisatel'* (Moscow: Khudozhestvennaia literatura, 1973), 14. For this and for many of the details of Stepniak's life presented in this article, I am deeply indebted to Taratuta's meticulously researched biography. Taratuta is the author of several books and articles on Kravchinsky, including the entry on Kravchinsky in *Kratkaia literaturnaia entsiklopediia,* ed. Aleksei Aleksandrovich Surkov (Moscow: Surkov, 1962–78), 3:794.

18. Quoted in Taratuta, *Stepniak-Kravchinskii,* 20.

19. Ibid., 24.

20. For a history of the Chaikovsky Circle, see Franco Venturi, *Roots of Revolution: A History of Populist and Socialist Movements in Nineteenth Century Russia,* rev. ed. (London: Phoenix Press, 2001), 469–506.

21. Peter Kropotkin, *Memoirs of a Revolutionist,* 2 vols. (London: Smith, Elder, and Co., 1899).

22. Taratuta, *Stepniak-Kravchinskii,* 124.

23. Sergei Kravchinskii, "Beneventskaia popytka," *Obschina* 2 (February 1878): 29–32.

24. E. A. Taratuta, "S. M. Stepniak-Kravchinskii v Italii," *Rossiia i Italiia: Iz istorii russko-ital'ianskikh kul'turnykh i obshchestvennykh otnoshenii* (Moscow: Nauka, 1968).

25. Although Zasulich's attempt on Trepov has always received far more attention, it has been argued that Kravchinsky's action was historically the more important. Senese writes that "because of the meticulously prepared escape, Mezentsev's murder can be justly regarded as the first planned terrorist act of *Zemlia i volia* [Land and Freedom]" (*Stepniak,* 5) and moreover that "the brilliant attack on Mezentsev was the model for a series of terrorist attacks that led to the fatal infatuation with terror which within the year was to split *Zemlia i volia*" (*Stepniak,* 7).

26. Quoted in Moser, "English Context," 7.

27. James Mavor, *My Windows on the Street and the World,* 2 vols. (London: J. M. Dent and Sons, 1923), 1:253.

28. Quoted in Taratuta, *Stepniak-Kravchinskii,* 28.

29. Kropotkin, *Memoirs,* 2:113–14.

30. Quoted in Taratuta, *Stepniak-Kravchinskii,* 15.

31. On the *skazki,* see T. P. Maevskaia, *Slovo i podvig: Zhizn' i tvorchestvo S. M. Stepniaka-Kravchinskogo* (Kiev: Naukova dumka, 1968), 22–49.

32. Quoted in ibid., 24.

33. I. S. Turgenev, letter of September 9, 1875, in *Sobranie sochinenii v dvenadtsati tomakh* (Moscow: Gosizdat, 1953–58), 12:479.

34. E. [A]. Taratuta, *Podpol'naia Rossiia: Sud'ba knigi S. M. Stepniaka-Kravchinskogo* (Moscow: Kniga, 1967), 17.

35. *Podpol'naia Rossiia* (London: Izdanie fonda Russkoi Vol'noi Pressy, 1893).

36. Taratuta, *Podpol'naia Rossiia,* 49.

37. This quotation is a somewhat altered version of the epigraph to Radishchev's *Journey from St. Petersburg to Moscow* (1790), where it appears as "A monster gross, unruly, huge hundred-mawed, and howling," and is clearly meant to apply to the Russian state. Radishchev gives his source as book 18 of the *Telemakhida,* Trediakovskii's translation (1766) of Fénelon's epic, *Télémaque* (1699).

38. "Otvet S. M. Kravchinskogo na pis'mo Ispol'nitel'nogo komiteta Narodnoi voli," *Revoliutsionnoe narodnichestvo 70-kh godov XIX veka,* t. 2, 1876–82 (Moscow and Leningrad: Nauka, 1965), 342.

39. Stepniak, *Underground Russia,* 13. Hereafter cited as *UR.* Page numbers in the text citations refer to the second American edition, *Underground Russia: Revolutionary Profiles and Sketches from Life* (New York: Charles Scribner's Sons, 1883).

40. Stepniak's description of the latent unbelief of Russia's educated classes is consistent with the account of his own experience Tolstoy offers at the beginning of *A Confession* (1879) (Leo Tolstoy, *A Confession and Other Religious Writings,* trans. Jane Kentish [New York: Penguin, 1987], 20). Born in 1828, Tolstoy belonged to the "older generation" of educated Russians that Stepniak has in mind.

41. The "essentially religious" character of the Russian revolutionary movement is by now a well-established historiographic commonplace. The question for scholarship is, what influence did Stepniak have on the genesis of this idea?

42. Quoted in Taratuta, *Stepniak-Kravchinskii,* 343. Although the original of this letter is in English, I have had to translate back from Russian. Stepniak's papers were given by his wife to TsGALI in the 1930s.

43. See [S. M.] Stepniak, *The Career of a Nihilist* (New York: Harper and Brothers, 1889), 112. Hereafter cited as *CN,* with page references noted in parentheses.

44. In my discussion of *The Career of a Nihilist,* Russian names and places are spelled as they are in the English text.

45. Quoted in Moser, "Nihilist's Career," 61.

46. "Nihilist Stepniak Here," *New York Times,* December 31, 1890, 8.

47. January 13, 1894. Quoted in Moser, "English Context," 18–19; also Johnson, *Olive and Stepniak,* 27.

48. For a discussion of Stepniak's later Russian fiction, see Maevskaia, *Slovo i podvig,* 179–216.

49. Olive Garnett, *Petersburg Tales* (Boston: Houghton Mifflin, 1900).

50. Olive Garnett, *Russia's Night* (London: W. Collins, 1918).

51. As quoted in Moser, "English Context," 6.

The Spiridonova Case, 1906: Terror, Myth, and Martyrdom

Sally A. Boniece

Reflecting in the early 1950s on the "legitimization of murder" that had "culminate[d] in . . . the Hitlerian apocalypse," Albert Camus upheld the Russian Socialist Revolutionary (SR) terrorists of the early twentieth century as "fastidious assassins" whose "voluntary assumption of guilt and death" and "respect for human life in general and contempt for their own lives" he contrasted to the "nihilism" practiced by "the totalitarian theocrats of . . . state terrorism."[1] In the 1970s, Michael Walzer echoed this theme in discussing "the revolutionary 'code of honor'" by which the SRs and other earlier terrorists had operated prior to "the systematic terrorizing of whole populations" that developed in the course of World War II.[2] Well before World War II, however, the Left SR leader Isaak Zakharovich Steinberg, commissar of justice in the short-lived Bolshevik–Left SR government of 1917–18, emphasized the difference between the principled "individual" or oppositional terrorism of the SRs and the unprincipled state terrorism of the subsequent all-Bolshevik regime.[3]

One century ago, terrorism as conceptualized by the Russian SRs was limited in scope and moral in purpose. To the SRs and their supporters, "terrorist" was a heroic label, because "terrorism" meant a righteous violence in the cause of political change, employed against a corrupt autocracy on behalf of an oppressed and helpless people. Occurring in what Luigi Bonanate has characterized as a "blocked society,"[4] with no national forum for political participation let alone toleration of political opposition, the SR Party's assassinations of tyrannical government officials met with acclaim rather than fear from the greater part of the Russian population. Although SR terrorism did not lead to a radical overturn of the tsarist system as intended, its power to attract popular sympathy was especially noteworthy in the case of Maria Spiridonova.

The public legend or myth that developed around the Spiridonova case is illustrative of the interactive aspects of political terrorism in the modern era. Mark Juergensmeyer, building on earlier definitions by Martha Crenshaw, has described terrorism as "performance violence" insofar as it communicates with multiple audiences, both sympathetic and antagonistic, through actions, images, and symbols.[5] The technological achievements of the modernizing state—railroads, telegraph, photography, mass-circulation newspapers—brought the theatrical events of terrorism, as Russian revolutionaries of 1905–6 were well aware, to national and even international attention. In the argument of Claudia Verhoeven, Russian terrorists staged acts of violence to speed up progression toward modernity's ultimate goal of "universal redemption and autonomy"; for terrorism, she writes, "is violence perpetrated by those who think they can deliver the future from the past by intervening in the present."[6]

Furthermore, the multiple audiences that reacted to the Spiridonova case within the Russian Empire—ranging from the peasants to the propertied, from the revolutionary underground to the tsarist bureaucracy—can be viewed in correspondence to the subcultures, or semiotic systems, that constitute the cultural space or semiosphere of Russian society, in Yuri M. Lotman's model.[7] Spiridonova herself, as a participant in Russian revolutionary subculture, was conforming to an existing behavioral text or myth of that subculture in committing her terrorist act.[8] This particular behavioral text, which might be titled the myth of the revolutionary martyr-heroine,[9] had resonance beyond the revolutionary subculture in the chaotic period of 1905–7. Hence Spiridonova became perhaps the supreme incarnation of the Russian myth of female revolutionary martyrdom.

On the morning of January 16, 1906, at the Borisoglebsk railroad station in Tambov province, twenty-one-year-old Maria Aleksandrovna Spiridonova, daughter of a nonhereditary noble and member of the SR Party, shot and fatally wounded provincial councilor Gavril Nikolaevich Luzhenovsky, notorious for his suppression of peasant unrest in the Tambov countryside. One of close to two hundred acts of SR "individual terror" occurring throughout the Russian Empire of Nicholas II during the revolution of 1905–7, the Luzhenovsky assassination received little more than local attention until the following month. On February 12 a liberal newspaper in St. Petersburg published a letter from the imprisoned Spiridonova that not only detailed her beating and torture by Cossacks and police during her arrest and initial detention but also hinted at sexual abuse.

Spiridonova, beloved by Tambov peasants as their deliverer from Luzhenovsky, now gained national recognition for her heroism, from educated society as well as from the lower classes. Liberals exalted her for her sufferings at the hands of a despotic state, equating her violation by Cossacks with the violation of Russia itself by the bureaucracy and autocracy; peasants and workers revered her for sacrificing her own life to liberate others from injustice. A liberal investigative journalist's series of articles contrasting the courage and gentility of Spiridonova with the callous cruelty of Russian officialdom provided the public with additional ingredients of what would become the Spiridonova myth. Leading members of the SR Party, while regretting the sensationalism and distortions of the journalist's account, were likewise bent on popularizing her martyrdom—as was indeed Spiridonova herself.

The tsarist government subdued the furor over the Spiridonova case by removing Spiridonova, together with five other convicted female SR terrorists, to a remote Siberian penal complex. Nevertheless, Spiridonova's eleven years of imprisonment only enhanced the myth of her revolutionary martyrdom. When the February Revolution of 1917 brought down the autocracy and freed its political prisoners throughout the empire, Spiridonova returned to European Russia in glory as a heroine of the 1905 revolution. In Petrograd and Moscow, she became a charismatic leader of the breakaway Left SR Party and, for a time, a supporter of the Bolshevik Revolution.

Spiridonova's influential role in the political events of 1917–18 testifies to the enduring power of her myth among intellectual and less educated classes alike. To Spiridonova and her SR comrades, the primary purpose of her myth was to advance the revolutionary cause. As the myth was evolving in 1906, she and the Tambov SR committee sought to shape it into a propaganda tool; after the Bolshevik Revolution of 1917, the Left SR leadership relied on Spiridonova and her myth to promote the party's program among peasants and workers.

In exploring how the Spiridonova myth was created, I have uncovered four different layers to the story of Spiridonova's controversial arrest and detention in 1906: the version advanced by Spiridonova and the SRs, the version portrayed in the liberal press, the version published by the tsarist government, and a more private dimension to the case that Spiridonova wished to conceal and the Tambov authorities did conceal. These variants of the Spiridonova story reflected the subcultures that produced them and the audiences for which they were intended. Thus the variants exhibited differing degrees of "mutual translatability," in Lotman's phrase,[10] while sharing an overall intelligibility, just as their creators and audiences shared the semiosphere of Russian culture.

Spiridonova's public legend originated with her letter from Tambov prison describing the assassination and her brutal arrest at the scene to her SR comrades. To propagandize Spiridonova's self-sacrifice on behalf of the revolution, the Tambov SR committee sought publication for her letter in the national press. The letter's publication in the liberal newspaper *Rus* provoked an official investigation of the Spiridonova case that was expeditiously completed but not made public for many weeks. In the meantime, *Rus* sent a journalist to Tambov to conduct his own research. His findings, which he presented in a series of dramatic articles for *Rus,* only exacerbated popular indignation about the case and the government's handling of it.

In essence, the conclusions reached by the government investigators contradicted those of the liberal journalist and also disputed certain claims made in Spiridonova's published letter. An additional complication is that Spiridonova herself took issue with the journalist's version of her story: at her urging, the leader of the Tambov SRs repudiated it in an accusatory pamphlet. Both the Tambov SRs and, ironically, their erstwhile enemies in the Tambov provincial administration further contributed to the evolution of the Spiridonova myth by withholding some potentially damaging personal information about her. Spiridonova had asked her SR comrades to conceal this information, probably because it would have lessened her appeal had it been made public; Tambov administrators neither passed the information on to their superiors in St. Petersburg nor revealed it in their local press organ. My comparison of the various versions of the Spiridonova story thus reveals crucial differences between the idealized and the actual Spiridonova while illuminating class and gender values during a period in which political violence had become a norm.

The disturbances that erupted across the empire in 1905, set off by the government's massacre of peacefully petitioning St. Petersburg workers in January, expressed an accumulation of political and economic grievances that had been exacerbated by Russia's recent humiliating defeat in a war with Japan. Despite the deep societal fissure between upper and lower classes, many propertied citizens of the empire found themselves at one with peasants and workers in opposing the autocratic rule of the tsar. Peasants, the majority of the population, were desperate for sufficient allotments of land to support their families; the tiny but growing working class, concentrated in the largest cities, was suffering the rawest phase of industrialization; and the landed and professional classes, unlike their European counterparts, had no voice in the national government. If socialist intellectuals encouraged urban and agrarian protest, liberal intellectuals showed active sympathy and support for it, in the hope that rampant social disorder would force major political changes on the rigid tsarist system.

Widespread urban and rural disturbances culminated in a general strike in October 1905 that crippled the entire country and forced the tsar to issue a manifesto promising basic civil liberties and an elected legislative assembly. Nevertheless, a new wave of rural violence then broke out across European Russia to rage most seriously in Tambov and other provinces of the Central Black Earth and Volga regions. Their anxieties intensified by a poor harvest, peasants interpreted the tsar's October Manifesto as granting them the "freedom" to seize land and attack the gentry. In Tambov as in the neighboring provinces, peasants confiscated their landlords' grain and timber, set fire to estate buildings, and refused to pay taxes.[11]

At the peak of agrarian unrest in November, the tsarist government imposed a state of "reinforced security" on the disorderly provinces and dispatched a number of adjutant-generals to assist local military and police authorities in "pacifying" the countryside. In early December, martial law was declared in the cities of Tambov and Kozlov, while the remaining cities of Tambov province were placed under conditions of "extraordinary security."[12] Tambov's governor Vladimir Fedorovich von der Launits appointed Luzhenovsky, a landowner and attorney who had been serving as senior provincial councilor since April, to the additional post of security chief in one of the most unruly districts of the province, Borisoglebsk, on November 2. Luzhenovsky became as well a leader of the Tambov branch of the Union of the Russian People, an organization recently formed under the patronage of the tsar and the Orthodox Church that united extreme right-wing, nationalist, and anti-Semitic elements known as Black Hundreds; its mission was to restore the autocratic order by attacking liberals, socialists, and Jews.[13]

Peasant land seizures in the Black Earth and Volga provinces had the support of the SR Party so long as they were carried out in the spirit of egalitarian redistribution—that is, socialization—of the land rather than merely appropriation. Encouraging "constructive" actions such as strikes and boycotts, the SRs repudiated raids, arson, and other "destructive" actions of agrarian terror.[14] At the same time, however, the party itself employed the tactic of political terror, which the leadership justified as fulfilling three purposes: to arouse the revolutionary consciousness of peasants and workers, to threaten the government with retaliation for further repression, and to force concessions from the state by disrupting the social order.[15]

As numerous studies of political violence have indicated, historical and societal contexts, rational choices made by terrorist organizations, and psychological motivations and interactions of the terrorists themselves all play a role in the phenomenon of terrorism.[16] Strategically, terrorists select targets of violence, victims who symbolize the wrongs they oppose, with the aim of influencing targets of demands, such as governments, and/or targets of attention, such as public opinion.[17] The SR Combat Organization's assassination of two unpopular high-ranking Russian officials in 1904 and 1905, Minister of the Interior Viacheslav Konstantinovich von Plehve and Moscow's governor-general, the Grand Duke Sergei, gratified rather than horrified many members of the propertied and professional classes in a society becoming ever more hostile toward the autocratic system.[18] Local SR groups in the provinces conducted their own terrorist activities against lower-ranking political, military, and police officials independently of the party's Central Committee and Combat Organization. According to party statistics, SRs committed a total of two hundred acts of terrorism during the years of the first Russian Revolution: fifty-four in 1905, seventy-eight in 1906, and sixty-eight in 1907.[19]

The SR Party adopted the tactic of individual terror, or oppositional terrorism targeting representatives of the tsarist regime,[20] in the tradition of its populist-terrorist predecessor, the People's Will (Narodnaia volia). The ultimate "heroic deed" (*podvig*) in the eyes of the People's Will was to strike down the tsar himself in 1881. Hanged for their success, the conspirators of the party's Executive Committee ennobled the act of political assassination and established what Philip Pomper terms "the mystique of the virtuous terrorist" in the radical subculture of Russian society. Although the government annihilated the party leadership, the myth of the heroic assassin attracted new members to the People's Will, who continued its terrorist mission well into the 1890s. A number of the founders of the SR Party in fact began their revolutionary careers as members of the People's Will.[21]

These revolutionaries and terrorists populated a shadowy illicit world known as underground Russia (*podpol'naia Rossiia*), where they lived according to a strict code of behavior embodied in certain texts and myths. Marina Mogilner considers the formative behavioral text for this "radical microcosm" to have been Sergei Mikhailovich Stepniak-Kravchinsky's hagiographic "profiles" of his populist-terrorist comrades, written and first published in Italian in 1882 under the title *Underground Russia.*[22] But Stepniak-Kravchinsky's profiles, and the subjects of the profiles themselves, reflected an earlier, more foundational behavioral text: Nikolai Gavrilovich Chernyshevsky's novel *Chto delat'?* (*What Is to Be Done?*), which influenced every generation of Russian radicals from its publication in 1863 onward, whether nihilist, populist, or Marxist. In his minor character Rakhmetov, Chernyshevsky provided the archetype of the professional revolutionary. Rakhmetov, who gave away his inherited wealth, allowed himself only peasant fare to eat, and slept on a bed of nails to test his own endurance, was an ascetic, single-minded hero with no life beyond the cause.[23]

All of Stepniak-Kravchinsky's subjects, the populist-terrorist heroes of the 1870s and 1880s, adhered to this behavioral code in his portrayal of them; consequently, his profiles presented their revolutionary lifestyles and accomplishments as model behavior for aspiring radicals. Of one male comrade, for example, Stepniak-Kravchinsky wrote, "His convictions were his religion, and he devoted to them not only all his life, but what is much more difficult, all his thoughts. He had no other thought than that of serving his cause." Stepniak-Kravchinsky portrayed Vera Ivanovna Zasulich, who had attempted to kill the governor-general of St. Petersburg for flogging a political prisoner, as "the angel of vengeance, and not of terror . . . a victim who voluntarily threw herself into the jaws of the monster in order to cleanse the honor of the party from a mortal outrage," while Sofia Lvovna Perovskaia of the People's Will, executed for her role in the conspiracy to kill the tsar, was an "inspired priestess" imbued with "moral elevation and boundless devotion."[24]

Latter-day SR terrorists, modeling themselves after these mythologized first-generation populist heroes as well as the fictional Rakhmetov, sought to abandon all inner struggles and private desires in their absolute dedication to the revolution. Yet as Aileen Kelly has observed, the terrorists' rigidly suppressed egoism often evolved into an obsession with self-sacrifice and death, in which their own guilt for killing played an active role.[25] Many SR terrorists experienced severe moral qualms about committing murder, however just the cause, and expected to compensate for taking others' lives by losing their own on the gallows. "From a moral-philosophical viewpoint," Vladimir Mikhailovich Zenzinov, a member of the SR Combat Organization, explained, "the act of killing must at the same time be an act of self-sacrifice."[26] Women radicals seem to have been particularly vulnerable to the sacrificial component of terrorism.

Historians such as Barbara Alpern Engel, Maureen Perrie, Amy Knight, Beate Fieseler, and Barbara Evans Clements have established that women's contribution to the Russian revolutionary movement was significant. A valued minority of the People's Will, women controlled one-third of the party's original Executive Committee in 1879.[27] In 1905, women composed around 15 percent of the total membership of both the SR and Social Democratic (SD) parties.[28] Fifteen percent of the SR terrorists listed by name in party statistics were women as well.[29] Female SRs and SDs tended to be of higher social origin and better educated than their male counterparts, perhaps because lower-class women, in comparison to lower-class men, were much more restricted in mobility and much less literate in the strongly patriarchal society of tsarist Russia. One factor motivating upper-class women like Spiridonova to join the revolutionary underground was their frustrating lack of education and career opportunities.[30]

Perhaps even more important to female radicals was their perception that in underground Russia, they enjoyed more rights, opportunities, and recognition than the larger society was willing to grant them. The men of the SR and SD parties, like those of the earlier People's Will, at least paid lip service to the socialist principle of gender equality, though they did not always treat women as their equals. Historians have noted that women revolutionaries were rarely admitted into the top ranks of leaders and theorists; instead, they tended to devote their working hours to organizational, secretarial, and housekeeping duties.[31] As terrorists, however, women SRs were able to achieve a status commensurate with that of the men of their party.[32]

Within the revolutionary movement, as in Western society as a whole, women were valued for their virtue rather than for their intellect. In Russia, the Western feminization of virtue was reinforced by the state Orthodox Church, which sanctified the practice of humility and self-sacrifice. Women's social inferiority to men therefore gained for them a certain moral authority, a belief that was shared by various subcultures within the Russian semiosphere. As studies by Engel and Knight have demonstrated, the radicals of underground Russia considered women, who were spiritually exalted by their humbler position in life, to be natural candidates for revolutionary martyrdom.[33] "Women," wrote Stepniak-Kravchinsky in his reflection on Perovskaia, "are much more richly endowed with [a] divine flame than men. This is why the almost religious fervor of the Russian revolutionary movement must in great part be attributed to them."[34]

In general, the women of underground Russia appear to have had a more intense and absolute commitment to the cause than their male comrades, perhaps because women were less likely to practice a profession but more likely to have suffered a serious break with their families for joining the radical movement.[35] Moreover, the association of members of the so-called gentler, fairer sex with political violence and state retaliation for it created a cognitive dissonance in Russian society that rendered terrorism all the more effective as a weapon against tsardom. The public outcry against the state's execution of Sofia Perovskaia of the People's Will in 1881 gave the SR women terrorists an example to emulate;[36] it also caused the government to refrain from hanging another woman for a political crime for twenty-five years.[37]

Thus, political and socioeconomic constraints, the glamour of the radical fringe, and individual psychology all factored into the making of a woman terrorist during the first Russian Revolution. Like historians of Russian radicalism, scholars who study later twentieth-century terrorism have postulated that the "maternal-sacrificial affective code" imposed by Western society convinces participants in radical subcultures, male and female alike, of women's special suitability for martyrdom.[38] Studies of more recent terrorism also indicate that societal myths of womanly virtue and womanly weakness intensify the shock of female political violence for its targeted audiences.[39] Nevertheless, I would argue with Oleg Budnitsky for the uniqueness of the Russian context, in which "an assassination was proclaimed a heroic deed and an assassin, whatever his or her motives, a national hero"—not only by fellow revolutionaries but also by broad segments of Russian society.[40]

The case of Maria Spiridonova epitomizes the uniqueness of Russian revolutionary terrorism while bringing to light certain values of Russian social culture in the era of the first revolution, when terrorist activity reached what Anna Geifman calls "its most explosive stage."[41] Indeed, Spiridonova's terrorist action in January 1906 was immediately preceded by those of the five other women SR terrorists with whom she would subsequently be sent to Siberia. Jewish dressmaker Revekka Moiseevna Fialka, aged eighteen, was arrested in Odessa in June 1905 for constructing bombs. Lidia Pavlovna Ezerskaia, a thirty-nine-year-old dentist born into the Belorussian nobility and married to a Polish landowner, attempted to kill the governor of Mogilev province in October 1905. Thirty-year-old Anastasia Alekseevna Bitsenko, born into a Russian peasant family, educated as a teacher, and married to a Ukrainian radical, assassinated General V. V. Sakharov, "the butcher of Saratov," in November 1905. Maria Markovna Shkolnik, a Jewish factory worker aged twenty-three, attempted to kill the governor of Chernigov province on January 1, 1906. In the last of these five terrorist actions preceding Spiridonova's, Alexandra Adolfovna Izmailovich, the twenty-seven-year-old daughter of a Belorussian general, attempted to kill the police chief of Minsk on January 14, just two days before Spiridonova fatally wounded Luzhenovsky.[42]

What set Spiridonova apart from her future prison companions Fialka, Ezerskaia, Bitsenko, Shkolnik, and Izmailovich was her myth. None of the other women received the public attention that Spiridonova did, nor did they solicit such attention in the manner of Spiridonova and the Tambov SRs. Perhaps most important, Spiridonova alone of this terrorist *shesterka* (six), as they became known to their party comrades, possessed all of the attributes that seemed to hold the greatest public appeal: youth, beauty, maidenhood, good breeding, and a Russian surname. Izmailovich was a Belorussian name, Bitsenko Ukrainian, Ezerskaia Polish or Jewish. Fialka and Shkolnik were also Jewish names, exemplifying the high percentage of Jews within the Russian revolutionary movement as a whole and particularly among female SR terrorists.[43] Only Spiridonova, therefore, could represent the ideal of Russian womanhood or even, as some of her admirers contended, Russia itself.

The Spiridonova case entered Russian revolutionary mythology when the liberal newspaper *Rus* published Spiridonova's letter from Tambov prison on February 12, two days after Luzhenovsky died of the wounds Spiridonova had inflicted on him at the Borisoglebsk railroad station in January. The editors of *Rus,* one of the numerous new periodicals flourishing since the government's relaxation of press controls in the fall of 1905,[44] claimed to have been provided with "a completely authentic copy" of Spiridonova's original letter by some unnamed individual. Addressing her "dear comrades" of the Tambov SR committee who had sentenced the hated district security chief to death, Spiridonova began her letter with a rather oblique statement of her success in felling him: "Luzhenovsky was riding on that railroad for the last time."[45]

Tersely, the letter related how Spiridonova had stalked Luzhenovsky for several days as he traveled around the Borisoglebsk district by train. "I spent 24 hours at one station, the same at another and 48 hours at a third. The next morning, I determined from the presence of Cossacks meeting a train that Luzhenovsky was riding on it. I bought a second-class ticket for the coach next to his. Dressed as a gymnasium (secondary school) student, rosy-cheeked, cheerful and calm, I attracted no suspicion whatsoever. But he did not get off at that station."

Watching from her coach window as the train pulled into the next station, the district center at Borisoglebsk, Spiridonova saw Cossacks and police driving people off the platform to clear it, as she correctly deduced, for Luzhenovsky's arrival. With increasing dispassion, her letter explained how she entered the neighboring coach and fired at Luzhenovsky as he was stepping down from the train, surrounded by his Cossack bodyguard. "Because I was very calm, I was not afraid of missing him, although I had to aim across a Cossack's shoulder. I fired shots for as long as I could. After the first shot, Luzhenovsky squatted, grabbed at his stomach and started to rush away from me along the platform. At that time I ran down from the coach to the platform and fired three more bullets quickly, one after another, continually changing my aim." Spiridonova stated that according to a surgeon, Luzhenovsky had received a total of five wounds: "two in the stomach, two in the chest and one in the arm."[46]

The tone of Spiridonova's letter then grew dramatic as she described how Luzhenovsky's Cossack bodyguard, "stupefied" by her first shot at their employer, "recovered their senses" after several more shots and swarmed all over the station platform, shouting, "Beat her! Seize her! Shoot her!" and drawing their swords. "When I saw those glittering swords," she wrote, "I decided my end had come, and not to let myself be taken alive. I started to raise the revolver to my temple, but halfway there my hand fell and I was lying on the platform, stunned by blows [from the butts of the Cossacks' guns]." In intense pain, she begged the Cossacks to execute her, but the beating continued. "I would cover my face with my hands; they would remove my hands with the butts of their guns. Then the Cossack officer wound my braid around his hand and lifted me up; with one powerful thrust, he threw me back down on the platform. . . . Then they dragged me by the foot down a staircase, my head striking against the steps; I was lifted by my braid into a cab."

"At the [Borisoglebsk] police station," Spiridonova wrote, "I was stripped, searched and taken away to an unheated cell with a stone floor that was damp and filthy." Around noon Cossack officer P. F. Avramov and assistant police superintendent T. S. Zhdanov entered her cell to begin a torturous interrogation that lasted until 11:00 that night. "Swearing terribly, they would beat my naked body with their whips and say, 'Come now, my fine young lady, give us a stirring speech!' . . . They would pull hairs from my head, one hair at a time, and ask where the other revolutionaries were. They put out a burning cigarette on my naked body and said, 'So scream, you piece of trash!' To make me scream, they crushed the soles of my 'elegant' feet—or so they called them—with their heavy boots, like in a vise, and roared at me, 'Scream!'—with more cursing." The two officials threatened to "hand [Spiridonova] over to the Cossacks for the night," but only after first having their way with her themselves, and one of them forced on her "a crude embrace" while ordering her to scream. "Not once," Spiridonova added, "neither during my beating in the railroad station nor later in the police station, did I scream. I was completely delirious."

Later that night, after a court investigator took her deposition, Spiridonova was put on a special train to the provincial capital, the city of Tambov, with Avramov and his Cossacks as escorts. In her letter, Spiridonova skillfully employed a cryptic literary present to portray Avramov as an inebriated and menacing lout. "The train is traveling soundlessly. It's cold and dark. The crude swearing of Avramov lingers in the air. He is cursing me terribly. I can feel the breath of death. Even the Cossacks are terrified. . . . I'm delirious; I must have water—there is no water." Spiridonova's descriptive style then became fuller, detailing certain facets of the officer's behavior toward her that strongly implied an end result of rape. "He is drunk and affectionate; his hands are on me, unbuttoning my clothing; his drunken lips whisper repulsively, 'What satin breasts, what a graceful body.' . . . I don't have the strength to struggle, I don't have the strength to push away. . . . I did not sleep the entire night, fearing violence ultimately."[47] Daylight brought Spiridonova no respite from Avramov's sexual harassment: "In the afternoon, he offers me vodka and chocolate; when [the other passengers] go away, he caresses me. Right before [we reached] Tambov, I slept for an hour. I awoke because the officer's hand was on me."

On their arrival at Tambov prison, Spiridonova wrote, Avramov embraced her in farewell, leaving her still "delirious and very ill." Her letter next recorded for her SR comrades the deposition she had given to court authorities: "Yes, I wanted to kill Luzhenovsky . . . according to a resolution by the Tambov SR committee, for his criminal flogging to death and excessive torturing of peasants during the agrarian and political disorders and, after that, in the districts where Luzhenovsky was present; for Luzhenovsky's murderous adventures in Borisoglebsk as security chief; for his organization of the Black Hundreds in Tambov; and as a response to the introduction of martial law and the increase of police authority in Tambov and other districts. The Tambov SR committee passed the [death] sentence on Luzhenovsky; in full agreement with this sentence and in full consciousness of my action, I took it on myself to carry out this sentence."

In terrorist subcultures, the terrorists are the rational beings, acting legitimately and righteously against the symbols of an irrational evil. Spiridonova in her deposition both proclaimed herself a voluntary executor of SR justice and exonerated herself for attempting to take a life. By demonizing Luzhenovsky as the willing tool of an inhumane system, she made her victim responsible for his own assassination; indeed, she intimated that the far greater misdeed would have been *not* to shoot him.[48] In the conclusion of her letter, Spiridonova further justified her terrorist act by underlining how she was suffering for it. "Up to now I have been very ill; I am often delirious. If they kill me, I will die at peace with myself," she wrote, expressing both a lack of regret about the attempted murder and a willingness to sacrifice her own life in restitution, just as Ivan Platonovich Kaliaev, the SR assassin of the Grand Duke Sergei, had declared before his execution that he would die proud of having fulfilled his duty to Russia.[49] The letter was signed simply "Spiridonova."

Through elliptical descriptions of Avramov's unwelcome familiarities and reiterations of her own escape into delirium, Spiridonova gave the impression that she had been violated but could not bear to admit to it directly. In addition to the probability of rape, the letter established certain attributes of Spiridonova herself that were essential elements of the myth of female revolutionary martyrdom: her youth, signaled by the school uniform she wore; her physical beauty and desirability, voiced, in an adroit use of dialogue ("elegant feet," "satin breasts"), by the men who assaulted her; her chastity, conveyed by her shocked response to their crude language and sexual advances; her upper-class origin, implicit in her moral refinement as well as her literary style; and her courage, evinced by her silence under torture. Spiridonova and the SRs projected this compelling image of her sufferings to promote the SR message behind her act, which she emphasized in her deposition: she shot Luzhenovsky for his oppression of peasants and revolutionaries. The liberal press, having different interests, would dwell instead on the personal attributes of Maria Spiridonova while bypassing her political affiliation.

The medium through which *Rus* received the Spiridonova letter appears to have been Maria's older sister Yulia, a close associate if not a member of the Tambov SR committee. In a search of Yulia's apartment on February 19, the Tambov police recovered a copy of a letter Yulia had written to the editors of *Rus* verifying the authenticity of her sister's prison letter.[50] The Tambov SRs sought publication of Maria's letter in the national press to propagandize her self-sacrifice on behalf of the revolution, a break with the usual SR policy of concealing the identity of terrorists,[51] as Tambov leader Stepan Nikolaevich Sletov later acknowledged. "Our personal feelings [about publicizing the case] had to be overcome, and however difficult it was to bring a comrade's sufferings and sores to light, we did this . . . and did this, as it turned out, not in vain," Sletov wrote. "The case of M. A. Spiridonova did not pass over in silence—it resounded as a loud slap in the face of despotism. The name of our comrade became a symbol of suffering Russia, a symbol of struggle to the end."[52]

Yet SR aims in publicizing the Spiridonova case differed from the aims of the liberal press that brought her story to the attention of the nation. *Rus*, in common with other liberal mass-circulation newspapers then profiting from the temporary suspension of censorship restrictions, had a mission to mobilize public opinion as a force for reform; the editors firmly espoused the rule of law and insisted that government officials respect it when arresting political terrorists.[53] A *Rus* editorial accompanying the Spiridonova letter expressed outrage about Spiridonova's "torture" by police and military officials, who had the duty of "defending the lawful order" in Russia. Although the editors viewed terrorism as "a political crime," they argued that such crimes failed to provide "even the slightest justification for treating a human being as Spiridonova was treated" and urged the minister of justice to prosecute Avramov and Zhdanov for misuse of authority against "this helpless, weak, underage girl."[54]

On the same day that Spiridonova's letter was published in *Rus,* its major episodes of beating, torture, and sexual threat were excerpted in another leading liberal newspaper, *Nasha zhizn* (*Our Life*). Similarly taking issue with the unwarranted violence of Spiridonova's arrest, the editors of *Nasha zhizn* commented that her story would seem "monstrous and improbable" in any other era but the present one.[55] Readers' responses to the Spiridonova letter that were printed in *Rus* over the course of the next month echoed the basic concern of these liberal editors: that the rule of law prevail in Russia, thus safeguarding the rights of the individual and eliminating the arbitrary use of corporal punishment.[56]

Male and female readers of *Rus* alike characterized Spiridonova as a virgin just emerging from childhood and decried the abuse of her youth and gender by agents of the government. A number of readers protested against Avramov's and Zhdanov's actions as an insult to human dignity in general, while others encouraged all of civil society, which had an obligation "to protect its members from any sort of violence," to speak out on behalf of Spiridonova. Several female readers exhorted "all Russian women," especially those who were mothers, to "demand justice" for "our desecrated sister" and enlist their husbands in Spiridonova's defense. The bulk of letters printed were, in fact, from women; nevertheless, the respondents represented a cross section of Russian society, including workers and peasants of both sexes, male university students and noblewomen, military men of various ranks and officers' daughters, from Warsaw to Yaroslavl.[57]

In contrast to the indignant credulity of liberal editors and their readership, the leading conservative newspaper, *Novoe vremia* (*New Times*),[58] voiced doubts about the veracity of the Spiridonova letter because its numerous references to the author's delirium seemed inconsistent with its polished literary style. Listing all these references (e.g., "I was completely delirious," "I was often delirious," "I was delirious the entire time"), *Novoe vremia* remarked that Spiridonova's constant delirium had not prevented her from relating her experiences in graphic detail, interspersed with "gleaming literary phrases such as 'I can feel the breath of death' and so forth." In the editors' opinion, this document was not a "letter" but a "story," probably based on Spiridonova's own account of what had happened but "written and given to the newspaper by someone else." Indeed, the editors found "impossible to believe" the letter's description of drunken officials beating a delirious female terrorist while complimenting her on her "elegant feet" and "graceful body."

Regardless of whoever had authored the published version of the Spiridonova letter, *Novoe vremia* judged Spiridonova to be "a sick soul, perhaps stunned by her own crime and the preparations for it."[59] Epitomizing "the one-sided understanding of revolutionaries," she was "morally blinded" to the "double terror" portrayed in her letter, for she seemed not to recognize that "her own savagery" as a political assassin was "completely equivalent to the savagery of her torturers." The editors deplored the increasing devaluation of human life in the current era of unrest, when "servants of the revolution" armed with guns and bombs were being hailed as "heroic vigilantes" and "freedom fighters"[60]—a theme to which they would return as the Spiridonova controversy continued.

Whereas the nation's preeminent conservative newspaper suggested that the published Spiridonova letter had been fictionalized from Spiridonova's actual, possibly incoherent, testimony, the reactionary press organ of the Tambov provincial administration—and, unofficially, of the Tambov Union of the Russian People—denounced it as a complete invention, "a loathsome document whose mendacity and improbability could be doubted only by those capable of applauding such human monsters as Spiridonova and her like" and "a work of pornography that under no circumstances should fall into the hands of children." The *Tambovskie gubernskie vedomosti* (*Tambov Provincial Gazette*) professed to understand neither how Spiridonova's womanly morals could have sunk so low as to allow her to write a letter of this nature nor how any letter from "so consequential a criminal" could have passed outside the prison walls unknown to the prison administration. Despite such insinuations as to where the blame lay if the letter proved to be authentic, the local editorial concluded with the statement "We are sooner inclined to think that this letter is apocryphal."[61]

Within days of the Spiridonova letter's appearance in *Rus*, the Ministry of Justice ordered the Tambov public prosecutor to investigate the Spiridonova case, during the course of which investigation local officials were able to uncover how Maria's prison correspondence had reached her sister Yulia and the Tambov SRs. The results of the local investigation, including various eyewitness accounts of Spiridonova's arrest, detention, and conveyance to Tambov, were reported to St. Petersburg in late February but withheld from the public pending a military inquiry into the conduct of Zhdanov and Avramov.[62] The delay, interpreted by the liberal press as reluctance on the part of the government to prosecute its own officials, only increased the controversy over the Spiridonova case. *Rus*, meanwhile, had sent an investigative reporter, V. E. Vladimirov, to Tambov to ferret out additional information, which he presented in seven dramatic articles published between March 7 and 18. Coinciding with the peak of popular participation in the national parliamentary election that had been promised in the October Manifesto, Vladimirov's provocative revelations further exacerbated liberal suspicions and public furor over the government's handling of the Spiridonova case.[63]

Not only did Vladmirov's articles contradict many findings of the official investigation, they also much dismayed Spiridonova and the Tambov SRs. Ignoring Spiridonova's political intentions, the liberal journalist portrayed her as a genteel, high-principled victim of the tyrannical Russian system. Moreover, his articles tended to leap to conclusions and to indulge in histrionics, in contrast to the dry but carefully detailed official documents on the Spiridonova case. Although Vladimirov, like other early twentieth-century reporters, would have argued it was his duty to supply facts that the public had a right to know, he evidently did not scruple to enhance those facts or even to invent racier ones in the interest of correcting the injustices of tsarism.[64]

The extent to which Vladimirov sensationalized the case can be seen by comparing some of his more flamboyant assertions with related material gathered by Tambov investigators. Two issues worthy of question concern the testimony of Dr. Fink, the physician who examined Spiridonova on her arrival in Tambov prison: first, the extent of her injuries from the beatings she had received; and second, the possibility that Avramov had infected her with syphilis. Claiming to have gained access to Dr. Fink's testimony, Vladimirov reported that the doctor found Spiridonova to be "constantly delirious," her face and body covered with welts "from the Cossacks' whips," her left eye swollen shut and the retina hemorrhaged, her lungs damaged and hemorrhaged so that she was "continually coughing blood."[65] Fink's actual testimony, in contrast, stated that Spiridonova was in too much pain to sit or stand but did not seem delirious; that she had welts on one shoulder and bruises on one thigh; that her right eye was swollen shut—and made no comment on the condition of her lungs.[66]

Vladimirov also disclosed evidence, purportedly from Fink, that Spiridonova suspected she had contracted syphilis from her rape by Avramov. This impelled her to ask Fink, on one of his subsequent prison visits, about the signs of the disease. In Vladimirov's story, Fink told Spiridonova he could have established the rape if she had allowed him to examine her when she first arrived in Tambov, but now it was too late. Vladimirov added that Spiridonova, "a pure, chaste young girl," had refused the gynecological examination out of a desire to keep secret "the foul violence done to her."[67] What Fink actually testified, however, was that Spiridonova questioned him about syphilis because a rash had recently appeared on her shoulder, which he found to be a simple irritation of the skin; he did not mention her accusing Avramov of rape. Afterward, Fink noted, Spiridonova never complained to him of any other signs of the disease.[68]

The public responded with horror to these new disclosures about the Spiridonova case, *Nasha zhizn* bemoaning the fall of "a pure, virginal being, a flower of spiritual beauty that only the highest culture of Russia could produce . . . into the shaggy paws of brutally repulsive, brutally malicious, brutally salacious orangutans."[69] The myth of the revolutionary martyr-heroine was, as Mogilner has emphasized, the myth of a pure and delicate young girl, a kind of secular Blessed Virgin (*bogoroditsa*);[70] a more repugnant proof of a virgin's desecration than syphilis could hardly be imagined. Spiridonova herself, however, evinced even greater horror over Vladimirov's latest revelation than did her sympathizers.

From her prison cell, Spiridonova managed to smuggle out an urgent request to Tambov SR leader Sletov that the SRs publicly refute the Vladimirov articles. Spiridonova explained to Sletov that the syphilis story, excepting her initial query about the signs of syphilis, was a fabrication; thus she unknowingly verified Fink's testimony to the Tambov investigators. In compliance with Spiridonova's request to repudiate the story, the SR leader produced an accusatory pamphlet entitled *Spekuliatsiia na chuzhikh ranakh* (*Profiteering from Others' Wounds*). Here Sletov discussed Spiridonova's strong objections to the Vladimirov articles, which he labeled "pulp literature" because they omitted the political convictions that had inspired Spiridonova's terrorist act.[71]

Just as Spiridonova and Sletov charged, Vladimirov did not depict Spiridonova as a dedicated SR but rather as a heroic individual, highlighting her cultured background as well as her present sufferings. He wrote that a close girlfriend of hers from secondary school described her as "pretty, tiny but well-proportioned, with light chestnut hair . . . a small, delicate face, very clear skin and bluish, wide-open eyes."[72] One of five children of a banking administrator in Tambov, Maria loved to play Beethoven sonatas on the piano, excelled in the classroom, led a citywide circle of student radicals during her gymnasium days, and steadfastly challenged the injustices of what Vladimirov characterized as a "coldly formalist" secondary school system. When Vladimirov inquired about possible "influences" compelling Spiridonova to activism, her former schoolmate replied that a certain "unknown gentleman" in Tambov, who had been exiled to his native province under police surveillance, lent Spiridonova illegal publications and "supplemented her education" in radicalism.[73]

According to Vladimirov, Spiridonova's open support of a student rebellion at the Tambov seminary during her eighth and final year at the women's gymnasium resulted in her expulsion with a negative attestation designed to prevent her from continuing her education elsewhere.[74] The unexpected death of Spiridonova's father in the same period left the family without an income and forced Spiridonova to seek employment, which she obtained as a clerk for the Tambov gentry assembly. She lost this position in March 1905, when she was arrested and imprisoned six weeks for participating in a local demonstration.[75]

Tambov police records tell a somewhat different story of Spiridonova's background, however. Although a "politically unreliable" male teacher at the women's gymnasium inspired the girls in her class to set up a circulating library of illegal literature that they shared with students at other secondary institutions in the city,[76] there is no indication in police files that Spiridonova was at the hub of these activities, as Vladimirov maintained, or involved in them at all. Moreover, rather than being expelled from the women's gymnasium, Spiridonova withdrew by her own petition in 1902, explaining to the Tambov pedagogical council that "ruined health and domestic circumstances" forced her to give up her studies.[77] Her health may have been "ruined" by a bout with tuberculosis, the chronic disease that flared up in periods of stress, especially coupled with imprisonment, throughout Spiridonova's adult life;[78] the "domestic circumstances" probably concerned her father's death.

Vladimirov's claim that an attestation was issued against Spiridonova at the time of her withdrawal from the gymnasium also appears to have been false, for Maria enrolled in dentistry courses in Moscow, where her family had relatives, shortly after leaving school. It was not until she suddenly quit these courses and returned to Tambov that Spiridonova showed an interest in the revolutionary movement, local citizens told a correspondent for the liberal newspaper *Nasha zhizn*.[79] The reasons for her return, though unknown, may have been financial, for Spiridonova began work as a clerk for the Tambov gentry assembly in 1903.[80] She appears to have first attracted the attention of the Tambov police in November 1904, when her apartment was searched for suspected concealment of an illegal press operation.[81] Arrested during the student demonstrations of March 1905 and imprisoned for three weeks,[82] not six, as Vladimirov claimed, Spiridonova applied to the Tambov school for medical assistants (*fel'dshery*) in September 1905, only to be rejected on the basis of her "political unreliability."[83]

Career frustration, along with penury, most likely increased Spiridonova's radicalism, which in turn increased her career frustration. Vladimirov was at least accurate in his implications, if inaccurate in his facts. The journalist also put his finger, albeit unwittingly, on the hidden dimension to the Spiridonova case when he quoted her former schoolmate's perhaps sly reference to the "unknown gentleman" who had played revolutionary mentor to Spiridonova. As Tambov authorities would learn, this man, twenty-eight-year-old local SR leader Vladimir Kazimirovich Volsky, was not only Spiridonova's mentor but also her lover. Furthermore, though he declared Spiridonova to be his fiancée, Volsky was already married to someone else.

The relationship between Spiridonova and Volsky only came to the attention of Tambov authorities following Spiridonova's trial on March 11, at which a court-martial condemned her to death by hanging but simultaneously petitioned the commander of the Moscow military district to commute her sentence to penal servitude in Siberia due to "extenuating circumstances."[84] According to a statement made to the liberal press by Spiridonova's defense attorney Nikolai Vasilevich Teslenko, Dr. Fink testified at the trial that Spiridonova had developed "severe" tuberculosis "as a result of her tortures," in addition to poor vision, near deafness, and reduced memory.[85] Teslenko, like Tambov SR leader Sletov, eloquently compared the "oppressed, desecrated and sick Spiridonova" to "sick and desecrated Russia," and warned the court that should Spiridonova be sentenced to death, "the entire country will flinch from the anguish of state terror."[86] Although Spiridonova herself, coughing into a bloodstained handkerchief at her trial, asserted that she was "happy to stand in defense of the Russian people and to die for them,"[87] the Moscow military commander on March 20 approved the commutation of Spiridonova's death sentence to penal servitude for life, "in view of her incurable illness—tuberculosis of the lungs."[88]

Vladimirov reported that Spiridonova was not informed of the commutation of her death sentence until March 27.[89] According to documents preserved in the Tambov archive, on March 25, Maria petitioned the governor of the province, Bronislav Mstislavovich Yanushevich, "to allow me a meeting with my fiancé Vladimir Kazimirovich Volsky, [also] incarcerated in Tambov prison, as soon as possible because of the imminent confirmation and carrying out of my sentence." Governor Yanushevich, after investigating their "engagement" and discovering that Volsky had been married to another woman for the past six years, rejected Spiridonova's petition on April 17. Ten days later Volsky wrote to the governor to defend his relationship with Spiridonova, arguing that their engagement was legitimate insofar as his legal spouse had left him for a lover four years ago. "I love [Spiridonova] as my wife," Volsky declared, "and if, beyond all expectation, she does not die from those abominably foul tortures criminally visited on her by the government, but is released from prison, then she will be my wife."[90]

The provincial governor seems not to have forwarded copies of Spiridonova's and Volsky's letters to his superiors in St. Petersburg; nor did he forward copies of their confiscated correspondence with each other, despite the damage these letters would have done to Spiridonova's reputation.[91]

Public knowledge of her affair with a married man would have destroyed the popular myth of a noble virgin ravaged by a loutish government agent. Indeed, Spiridonova's relationship with Volsky puts a different complexion on her published letter, for the letter implied her maidenly offense at Avramov's advances when in reality she was romantically involved, perhaps even sexually involved, with another man—though she would undoubtedly have been shocked and insulted by Avramov's crudity regardless of her personal experience.

Yet Yanushevich elected to keep Spiridonova's love affair with Volsky quiet. The most likely reason for his reticence was a desire to protect two respected local families, but it had the effect of protecting the Spiridonova myth as well. That Spiridonova herself wished this aspect of her life to remain private is clear from her request, in a letter confiscated from her sister Yulia by the Tambov police, for silence about what she called her "romantic history." Tambov deputy prosecutor N. V. Kamenev quoted her request in his late February report to St. Petersburg.[92] At the time he was unaware of its significance, for Spiridonova did not make her "engagement" known to Tambov authorities until the end of March.

It was the murder of Avramov, Spiridonova's chief tormentor, on April 2[93] and the ensuing public uproar that finally compelled the Ministry of Justice to publish a summary of the Tambov investigation of the Spiridonova case on April 8. During the six days before the official statement was released, liberal and conservative newspapers alike condemned the government for allowing the revolutionaries to bring Avramov to justice. But whereas liberal *Nasha zhizn* and *Dvadtsatyi vek* (*Twentieth Century*) deplored the missed opportunity to prosecute Avramov in a courtroom, conservative *Novoe vremia* pointed to "the bloody chain of violence" that the government had done nothing to prevent in the Spiridonova case. "First the Tambov peasants slaughtered their landlords; then Luzhenovsky cruelly punished the peasants; then Spiridonova killed Luzhenovsky; then Avramov tortured Spiridonova; and now some unknown person has killed Avramov" before he could be brought to trial. Thus, "the government's complete silence" on the Spiridonova case had provoked "societal hysterics" over a deranged young girl and "a bloody scandal [that] dragged on for months."[94]

Nevertheless, the government's ending of that silence by publishing an official summary of the investigation failed to still the controversy. Liberal editors, their self-confidence undoubtedly bolstered by the Constitutional Democratic (Kadet) Party's ongoing triumph in the parliamentary election, were as incensed as they were incredulous in their reaction to the report, particularly concerning Spiridonova's quoted request to suppress her "romantic history."[95] *Strana* (*The Country*) attacked the official statement for making "indecent and filthy insinuations" about Spiridonova's morals;[96] *Dvadtsatyi vek* protested that quoting private correspondence out of context gave Spiridonova's "innocent maidenly request" an aura of "vile suspicion."[97] In *Rech* (*Speech*), the Kadet press organ, an article by Spiridonova's defense attorney Teslenko accused the Ministry of Justice of directing its report "not against Spiridonova's torturers, but against Spiridonova herself."[98]

Teslenko contended that both the Spiridonova letter and the Vladimirov series were "only feeble attempts to depict the inexpressible sufferings and torments that [Spiridonova] underwent." His client had confided "everything" to him when he visited her in prison before her trial, he wrote, "and I shuddered at the terrible moral sufferings this young girl has endured as a consequence of all that happened to her on the train to Tambov. Her sufferings from physical pain and torture pale in comparison to her moral torment." So great was Spiridonova's shame that she had made her attorney promise not to disclose the full story "as long as she is alive."[99]

Teslenko's indignant response to the official statement concerned the government's refutation of certain claims and insinuations made by Spiridonova in her published letter, in addition to various conflicts between the official summary and the findings of Vladimirov. According to the Ministry of Justice, the Tambov investigation established that Zhdanov and Avramov, assisted by several lower-ranking Cossacks, did in fact kick and beat Spiridonova with their whips and fists at the Borisoglebsk railway station. With regard to the alleged rape, however, the report quoted Spiridonova's statement to the Tambov court investigator that she had "avoided sexual assault only because she was awake the entire night of the journey to Tambov." The injuries Spiridonova received did not endanger her life, and she was neither raped nor infected with syphilis, as several newspapers had charged; nor was she beaten in the Borisoglebsk police station, although witnesses earlier had seen Avramov slap her across the face. A number of witnesses also testified that during the train ride to Tambov, Avramov abused Spiridonova verbally, "with inappropriate and indecent expressions, but allowed himself no other insults to her womanly honor."[100]

A review of Spiridonova's central police file, which contains copies of the investigators' documents received by the Ministry of Justice, indicates that the official summary of the investigation was accurate. On January 20, a few days after Spiridonova arrived in Tambov, the court investigator recorded her testimony that she had been sexually threatened but not actually raped by Avramov.[101] Spiridonova's published letter to the Tambov SRs, though it did not contradict this testimony outright, was far more equivocal, stating, "I did not sleep the entire night, fearing violence ultimately" and implying, by sentences such as "I don't have the strength to struggle . . . besides, it would be of no use," that rape did occur.[102] But several male passengers on the train, among them a railroad *fel'dsher* (medical attendant) and a civilian police employee, testified that while Avramov "treated [Spiridonova] rudely and swore at her with unprintable words," he committed no sexual assault or battery on her.[103]

If Spiridonova was sexually harassed rather than assaulted, and sexually experienced rather than chaste, then questions arise as to why she gave the impression in her published letter that she had been raped, why she asked Dr. Fink about the first signs of syphilis, and why she convinced her attorney in a private interview that she had been raped and infected with syphilis. Perhaps the differences in sexual behavior between the coarse, forty-year-old Cossack officer Avramov and the younger radical intellectual Volsky, combined with Spiridonova's badly injured and semiconscious condition, magnified Avramov's lewd innuendos into actions in her perception. She may herself have been unsure of exactly what transpired on the nighttime train ride to Tambov.

Another possibility is that Spiridonova's letter, though addressed to the Tambov SRs, was written to provoke a public reaction, for there exists some evidence that Spiridonova had an intentional hand in the shaping of her myth. In addition to asking that her "romantic history" be kept quiet, she confided in letters to her friends and sister Yulia other concerns about her public image. This illicit correspondence, smuggled out of prison by cooperative female criminal inmates and male guards, was seized by the Tambov police in their February 19 raid on Yulia's apartment and reported to central authorities by Tambov deputy prosecutor Kamenev. As Kamenev paraphrased the letters,

> Maria Spiridonova discusses how she is awaiting her verdict, either death or penal servitude. She decides it will probably be penal servitude and declares that in such a case, "I need to show that I am not dead but something a little more elegant." After this, she expresses her agreement with the request of her comrades "to create a scandal about the autocracy and then escape," but "only providing this could be completely successful, for it is better to die five times than to be caught." . . . Spiridonova further requests that her defense attorney, when appointed, be given some personal information about her, apparently attesting to her "painful modesty," such as: her refusal to partake of appetizing dishes when she was still living in her father's house; her attempt to drink carbolic acid, when she desired to work but not to be a slave, etc.[104]

More mystifying than enlightening, the excerpts Kamenev selected from Spiridonova's secret correspondence hinted of a troubled adolescence and her own attempted suicide. Career frustration was denoted by Spiridonova's wish "to work but not to be a slave," most likely in reference to the period after her father's death, when additional family income may have become a necessity. Her enigmatic "refusal to partake of appetizing dishes" may have been a teenaged effort to emulate Rakhmetov, the self-denying model revolutionary in Chernyshevsky's *Chto delat'?* which was banned by the Russian government until 1905 but circulated covertly among the student youth of Tambov.[105] Also curious is the indication that Spiridonova and her SR comrades were plotting her escape from prison not long after her arrest, which contradicted Spiridonova's professed desire to die for the revolutionary cause.[106]

More important about these tantalizing excerpts from Spiridonova's private correspondence, however, is their revelation that Spiridonova participated in the construction of her own myth, the Spiridonova variant of the myth of the female revolutionary martyr. Certain details about her life and personality were to be made public, while others were to be suppressed, according to Spiridonova's directives. Also important is the implied role of Spiridonova's sister and comrades in the creation of her myth: they gave her advice as well as followed her directives. Was the Tambov SRs' proposal that Maria "create a scandal about the autocracy" the impetus behind the letter that found its way into the liberal press on February 12? Is it possible that Yulia, who appears to have sent the letter to *Rus,* either coauthored the account or revised it on behalf of her younger sister lying ill and injured in Tambov prison? Taken in conjunction with *Novoe vremia*'s quite reasonable doubts that such a literary epistle could have been penned by the recent victim of a police beating, these scraps of correspondence suggest that some of the letter's more artful effects might be attributed to one or more of the Tambov SRs.

Whatever the degree to which the making of the Spiridonova myth was a collaborative effort, Spiridonova's purpose in presenting herself as a martyr-heroine to multiple audiences was not personal gratification but service to the revolution. Her gallant performance during an exhausting monthlong train journey across the empire to eastern Siberia attests to her commitment to the SR mission.[107] Together with five other women terrorists—Bitsenko, Ezerskaia, Fialka, Izmailovich, and Shkolnik—Spiridonova traveled from the Moscow transit prison to their final destination, the Nerchinsk penal complex, in the summer of 1906. Crowds of workers, peasants, and more prosperous citizens thronged their train at every stop, according to police records as well as the recollections of Alexandra Izmailovich, who became Spiridonova's intimate companion in Siberia.[108]

Day and night Spiridonova would stand at the windows of the women's coach to speak with the people who came to meet the train, many of them weeping with emotion, in Izmailovich's description. Although between stops Spiridonova lay motionless and feverish, coughing up blood, her face twitching with nerves, she always greeted her audience with smiles, patiently answered their numerous questions, and discussed with them in clear and simple language the SR Party program. "The crowds did not know the rest of us," wrote Izmailovich, "but who did not know her name? . . . It had become a banner uniting all who seethed with holy indignation—SRs, SDs, Kadets, ordinary people unaffiliated with parties. She belonged not only to the SR Party. She belonged to all who carried her in their hearts as a banner of their protest."[109]

The most famous terrorist act committed by a woman in the era of the first Russian Revolution, Spiridonova's assassination of Luzhenovsky had been preceded by the political crimes of the five other SR women with whom she was sent to Siberia. However, the Spiridonova case differed from all five of the others in ways significant to public mythmaking, namely, concerning Spiridonova's ethnicity, age, class origin, marital status, and behavior. Among this *shesterka* of terrorists, only Spiridonova had a Russian surname; only Spiridonova combined the four appealing attributes of youth, beauty, chastity, and upper-class origin; and only Spiridonova, therefore, could be elevated to a national symbol "of young, struggling, determined and self-sacrificing Russia," as three male SR terrorists hailed her from their prison cells.[110] Furthermore, only Spiridonova, and the Tambov SRs on her behalf, made deliberate efforts to publicize and even dramatize the story of her arrest and detention by tsarist authorities, for the sake of advancing the revolution.

A comparison of the Spiridonova myth with information available on Spiridonova's life indicates that her act of martyrdom may have stemmed from personal frustration and the influence of her lover-mentor as well as from opposition to a despotic regime and a genuine concern for the underclass of Russian society. Although some studies of terrorism focus on the psychopathology of terrorists, I would argue with the majority of analysts that an integrative model linking individual, group, and societal factors is more efficacious in determining causation.[111] To me, the political and social constraints of late tsarist Russia were paramount in turning Spiridonova toward revolutionary terrorism. At the end of her teenage years, Spiridonova suffered a series of personal crises: the loss of a parent, a reduction in family income, and a flare-up of a chronic disease. But had she not been living in a society wracked by the conflicting forces of modernization and autocracy, she may not have sought to subsume her private trauma in an underground struggle against the collectively inflicted injustices of the government.

Novoe vremia labeled Spiridonova "a sick soul"; I see her as more of a lost soul, who found an identity in the radical subculture and conformed to the radicals' behavioral code. Yet what gave underground Russia meaning and purpose but the autocratic regime? Furthermore, it was precisely the collective application of tsarist injustices and the lack of legal redress against them that made national heroes of SR terrorists. By 1905, Russia's government and society had reached what Budnitsky describes as "a moral impasse" at which political violence appeared to be the only effective method of opposing the arbitrary rule of the tsarist system.[112] Not only was terrorism a rational mode of political expression to the very small minority of revolutionaries who practiced it; more significantly, terrorist acts and terrorist ethics held powerful resonance throughout the semiosphere of Russian society. The mutual translatability of grievances and values across the various subcultures of the Russian semiosphere was most fully manifested in the widespread appeal of the Spiridonova myth.

For much of the Russian public, Spiridonova, the assassin of a government official, was not some filthy or foreign fanatic with evil in her heart; she was one of their own—indeed, one of their best, "a flower of spiritual beauty that only the highest culture of Russia could produce," as the liberal press enthused. Much of the public accepted wholeheartedly Spiridonova's claim to have carried out the death sentence on Luzhenovsky "in the name of human dignity, in the name of respect for the individual, in the name of truth and justice"[113]—that is, in the name of values deemed to be universal by Europe's modernizing societies and cultures. To many Russian citizens, as to the SR terrorists, the irrational and inhumane actions were Luzhenovsky's violence against the peasants and Avramov's violence against Spiridonova, not Spiridonova's violence against Luzhenovsky. Spiridonova became the SR Blessed Virgin, a title the Bolsheviks would twist into mockery after she repudiated the Soviet regime in 1918.[114] Over thirty years of imprisonment and exile under autocracy and communism that ended with her execution in 1941 were the price Spiridonova paid for her populist politics and her compelling image as a revolutionary heroine.

Notes

1. Albert Camus, *The Rebel,* trans. Anthony Bower (New York: Knopf, 1954), 14–15, 135–47.

2. Michael Walzer, *Just and Unjust Wars: A Moral Argument with Historical Illustrations* (New York: Basic Books, 1977), 197–201. Defining terrorism as "the random

murder of innocent people," Walzer maintained that SR political violence was not "terrorism" per se.

3. I. Z. Steinberg, *Nravstvennyi lik revoliutsii* (Berlin: Skify, 1923), 171–72. Here Steinberg rather sidestepped the fact that Left SRs served as members of the Cheka from December 1917 to July 1918.

4. A "blocked society," according to Bonanate, is "incapable of answering the citizens' requests for change but nevertheless capable of preserving and reproducing itself." The blockage, he adds, "is not a sign of good functioning but of little or no functioning." See Luigi Bonanate, "Some Unanticipated Consequences of Terrorism," *Journal of Peace Research* 16, no. 3 (1979): 197–211.

5. Mark Juergensmeyer, *Terror in the Mind of God: The Global Rise of Religious Violence,* 3rd ed. (Berkeley and Los Angeles: University of California Press, 2003), 124–28. On myth and the subjective contexts of terrorism, see Martha Crenshaw, "Thoughts on Relating Terrorism to Historical Contexts," in *Terrorism in Context,* ed. Martha Crenshaw (University Park: Pennsylvania State University Press, 1995), 4, 7–12.

6. Claudia Verhoeven, *The Odd Man Karakozov: Imperial Russia, Modernity and the Birth of Terrorism* (Ithaca, N.Y.: Cornell University Press, 2009), 4–7, 174.

7. Yuri M. Lotman, *Universe of the Mind: A Semiotic Theory of Culture,* trans. Ann Shukman (London: I. B. Tauris, 1990), 123–30.

8. The Soviet school of semiotics defined myth as "a system that models the surrounding world or portions of it in the minds of individuals belonging to the group" and emphasized "the modeling capacity of myth and its influence on behavior." In contrast to other theorists of myth, Soviet semioticians also distinguished between myths of primitive tribes and modern myths, which concern "a more complexly organized world" and are "linked to external events." See D. M. Segal, "Problems in the Semiotic Study of Mythology," in *Soviet Semiotics: An Anthology,* ed. and trans. Daniel P. Lucid (Baltimore: Johns Hopkins University Press, 1977), 59–64. On the other hand, Ivan Strenski has maintained that "myth is everything and nothing at the same time" and therefore essentially without definition; see Ivan Strenski, *Four Theories of Myth in Twentieth-Century History: Cassirer, Eliade, Lévi-Strauss and Malinowski* (Iowa City: University of Iowa Press, 1987), 1–2. Nevertheless, conceptualizations of myth implicit in the works of social scientists and humanists such as George L. Mosse, Ian Kershaw, Richard Wortman, and Katerina Clark seem to include strands of definitions by Claude Lévi-Strauss (myth as a highly structured story of some significance, which may include a number of variants) and Roland Barthes (myth as a complex system of beliefs and symbols constructed by a society for its own self-authentication). On myth as defined by Lévi-Strauss and Barthes, see Strenski, *Four Theories,* 130, and Terence Hawkes, *Structuralism and Semiotics* (Berkeley and Los Angeles: University of California Press, 1977), 44–45, 131. Finally, myth is explicitly defined by Peter Heehs in his article "Myth, History and Theory" as "a set of propositions, often stated in narrative form, that is accepted uncritically by a culture or speech-community and that serves to found or affirm its self-conception" (*History and Theory* 33, no. 1 [1994]: 1–19).

9. This title I derive from Barbara Alpern Engel, who perceived an evolving "mythology" among nineteenth-century Russian radicals that "defined the revolutionary woman as limitlessly devoted and endlessly self-sacrificing, a martyr-heroine" (*Mothers and Daughters: Women of the Intelligentsia in Nineteenth-Century Russia* [Cambridge: Cambridge University Press, 1983], 155).

10. Lotman, *Universe of the Mind,* 125.

11. Abraham Ascher, *The Revolution of 1905: Russia in Disarray* (Stanford: Stanford University Press, 1988), 267; Maureen Perrie, *The Agrarian Policy of the Russian Socialist-Revolutionary Party, from Its Origins Through the Revolution of 1905–1907* (Cambridge: Cambridge University Press, 1976), 118–20; P. N. Chermenskii, *1905: Khronika revoliutsionnykh sobytii Tambovskoi gub.,* ed. P. Kroshitskii (Tambov: Tipografiia Proletarskii svetoch, 1925), 15–21.

12. Ascher, *Russia in Disarray,* 268–69; Chermenskii, *Khronika,* 20, 23, 27; Howard D. Mehlinger and John M. Thompson, *Count Witte and the Tsarist Government in the 1905 Revolution* (Bloomington: Indiana University Press, 1972), 87–90; Jonathan W. Daly, *Autocracy Under Siege: Security Police and Opposition in Russia, 1866–1905* (DeKalb: Northern Illinois University Press, 1998), 175. The "temporary" security law of 1881 had established the progressively more stringent categories of reinforced security and extraordinary security. Under reinforced security, authorities could prohibit gatherings, detain and search individuals on suspicion alone, and transfer cases to military courts; under extraordinary security, authorities could seize the property of suspicious individuals, exact heavy fines, shut down publications, and close or otherwise impede the functioning of public institutions (Daly, *Autocracy,* 33–34).

13. Chermenskii, *Khronika,* 21–22; K. V. Ostrovitianov, *Dumy o proshlom: Iz istorii pervoi russkoi revoliutsii, bol'shevistskogo podpol'ia i oktiabr'skikh boev protiv kontrrevoliutsii v Moskve* (Moscow: Nauka, 1967), 11–12. On the Union of the Russian People, see Hans Rogger, *Jewish Policies and Right-Wing Politics in Imperial Russia* (Berkeley and Los Angeles: University of California Press, 1986), 198, 202–6.

14. Perrie, *Agrarian Policy,* 59, 102–4, 120–22.

15. V. M. Chernov, "Terroristicheskii element v nashei programme," in *"Krov' po sovesti": Terrorizm v Rossii; Dokumenty i biografii,* ed. O. V. Budnitskii (Rostov: Izdatel'stvo Rostovskogo gosudarstvennogo pedagogicheskogo universiteta, 1994), 127–41; Maureen Perrie, "Political and Economic Terror in the Tactics of the Russian Socialist-Revolutionary Party Before 1914," in *Social Protest, Violence and Terror in Nineteenth- and Twentieth-Century Europe,* ed. Wolfgang J. Mommsen and Gerhard Hirschfeld (New York: St. Martin's Press, 1982), 65; Manfred Hildermeier, "The Terrorist Strategies of the Socialist-Revolutionary Party in Russia, 1900–14," in Mommsen and Hirschfeld, *Social Protest, Violence and Terror,* 82–83; Anna Geifman, *Thou Shalt Kill: Revolutionary Terrorism in Russia, 1894–1917* (Princeton: Princeton University Press, 1993), 46–47. I note that Brian Jenkins's explication of what he called "the purposes of terrorism" in 1974 closely approximates the stated purposes of the SRs (*International Terrorism: A New Mode of Conflict,* Research Paper no. 48, California Seminar on Arms Control and Foreign Policy [Los Angeles: Crescent Publications, 1975], 4–7).

16. See, for example, Jerrold M. Post et al., "The Radical Group in Context: 1. An Integrated Framework for the Analysis of Group Risk for Terrorism," *Studies in Conflict and Terrorism* 25, no. 2 (March–April 2002): 73–100; Jeffrey Ian Ross, "The Psychological Causes of Oppositional Political Terrorism: Toward an Integration of Findings," *International Journal of Group Tensions* 24, no. 2 (1994): 157–85; Martha Crenshaw, "The Causes of Terrorism," *Comparative Politics* 13, no. 4 (July 1981): 379–99; Crenshaw, "Thoughts on Relating Terrorism to Historical Contexts," in Crenshaw, *Terrorism in Context,* 3–24; and Donatella della Porta, "Political Socialization in Left-Wing Underground Organizations: Biographies of Italian and German

Militants," in *Social Movements and Violence: Participation in Underground Organizations,* ed. Donatella della Porta (Greenwich, Conn.: JAI Press, 1992), 259–90.

17. Alex Schmid, "Goals and Objectives of International Terrorism," in *Current Perspectives on International Terrorism,* ed. Robert O. Slater and Michael Stohl (New York: St. Martin's Press, 1988), 48–50; see also Martha Crenshaw, "The Logic of Terrorism: Terrorist Behavior as a Product of Strategic Choice," in Walter Reich, ed., *Origins of Terrorism: Psychologies, Ideologies, Theologies, States of Mind* (Cambridge: Cambridge University Press, 1990), 7–24, esp. 16–20.

18. Ascher, *Russia in Disarray,* 54–55; L. G. Praisman, *Terroristy i revoliutsionery, okhranniki i provokatory* (Moscow: Rosspen, 2001), 84–88; M. I. Leonov, "Terror i russkoe obshchestvo (nachalo XX v.)," in *Individual'nyi politicheskii terror v Rossii, XIX–nachalo XX v.* (Moscow: Memorial, 1996), 37–38; Marina Mogil'ner, *Mifologiia "popol'nogo cheloveka": Radikal'nyi mikrokosm v Rossii nachala XX veka kak predmet semioticheskogo analiza* (Moscow: Novoe literaturnoe obozrenie, 1999), 57. One Russian psychiatrist even considered terrorism a "healthy" rebellion against the autocracy; see Laura Engelstein, *The Keys to Happiness: Sex and the Search for Modernity in Fin-de-Siècle Russia* (Ithaca, N.Y.: Cornell University Press, 1992), 259.

19. M. I. Leonov, *Esery v 1905–07 gg.* (Samara: Samarskii gosudarstvennyi universitet, 1992), 23. Perrie's figures for these years are slightly lower, totaling 191 terrorist acts; see Perrie, "Political and Economic Terror," 67. Leonov further breaks down the figures for 1907: thirty-eight terrorist acts were committed before June 3.

20. It was the Russian Social Democrats (SDs) who labeled the SRs' brand of terrorism "individual" during their ongoing debate with the SRs over revolutionary tactics. The point for the SDs was to distinguish their "objective" Marxist class ideology from the SRs' "subjective" individualist orientation. The SRs subsequently adopted this label in their own discourse, finding that it appropriately expressed their emphasis on the efficacy of individual action against the state (Ze'ev Iviansky, "Individual Terror: Concept and Typology," *Journal of Contemporary History* 12, no. 1 [1977]: 44). However, the actual situation was far more complex than such labeling would suggest: there was a strong Marxist component to SR theory (Perrie, *Agrarian Policy,* 1, 6, 10–11), and the SDs themselves, Bolsheviks and Mensheviks alike, sometimes supported and even committed individual acts of terrorism (Geifman, *Thou Shalt Kill,* 84–122). Leading Bolsheviks and Mensheviks proposed a united terrorist struggle with the SRs against the autocracy in 1905; SDs in the provinces practiced terrorism, sometimes in conjunction with local SRs (O. V. Budnitskii, *Terrorizm v rossiskom osvoboditel'nom dvizhenii: Ideologiia, etika, psikhologii [vtoraia polovina XIX–nachalo XX v.]* [Moscow: Rosspen, 2000], 311–35).

21. Philip Pomper, "Russian Revolutionary Terrorism," in Crenshaw, *Terrorism in Context,* 64, 79–87, 99.

22. Mogil'ner, *Mifologiia,* 8–12, 27–30; details of publication are also provided by Peter Scotto in the present volume. As Mogilner notes, Russian translations of Stepniak-Kravchinsky's book led an illegal existence in his homeland before the 1905 revolution but attained widespread popularity among Russian readers nonetheless. Mogilner credits Stepniak-Kravchinsky with being "the creator of the term 'Underground Russia,'" as well as "one of [the radical subculture's] principal mythmakers" (*Mifologiia,* 27–28). But did the subculture title itself after his book, or vice versa? Certainly the term retained its symbolic power among revolutionaries long past the 1880s: in 1922, an émigré press in Berlin published a collection of letters and ac-

counts from the Left SR underground under Bolshevism entitled *Kreml' za reshetkoi (Podpol'naia Rossiia)* (Berlin: Skify, 1922).

23. Irina Paperno, *Chernyshevsky and the Age of Realism: A Study in the Semiotics of Behavior* (Stanford: Stanford University Press, 1988), 28–31. Banned virtually from its publication until after the 1905 revolution, the novel was nonetheless widely read in émigré editions that had been smuggled into Russia. The influence of Russian Orthodox hagiography on Chernyshevsky's depiction of Rakhmetov is mentioned in Paperno (*Chernyshevsky,* 207–8) and discussed at length in Marcia A. Morris, *Saints and Revolutionaries: The Ascetic Hero in Russian Literature* (Albany: State University of New York Press, 1993), 138–47. Donna Oliver in the present volume also discusses the double influences of Russian Orthodoxy and Russian literature on the "compulsion for self-sacrifice" among Russian radicals.

24. Stepniak [Sergei Mikhailovich Kravchinskii], *Underground Russia: Revolutionary Profiles and Sketches from Life,* trans. from Italian (New York: Charles Scribner's Sons, 1883; rpt, Hyperion, 1973), 96, 36, 126–27. See Scotto's analytical discussion of this work and its "essentially hagiographic structure" in the present volume.

25. Aileen Kelly, "Self-Censorship and the Russian Intelligentsia, 1905–14," *Slavic Review* 46, no. 2 (Summer 1987): 194–98.

26. V. M. Zenzinov, *Perezhitoe* (New York: Chekhov Publishing House, 1953), 108. Camus made this the central message of his play *Les justes* (*The Just Assassins*), which is based on the memoir of Boris Savinkov, the leader of the Combat Organization (*Vospominaniia terrorista* [Kharkov: Proletarii, 1926]). For a detailed discussion of Savinkov, see the essay by Lynn Ellen Patyk in this volume.

27. Engel states that eight out of eighteen original members were women (*Mothers and Daughters,* 173). Knight states that ten out of twenty-nine original members were women; see Amy Knight, "Female Terrorists in the Russian Socialist Revolutionary Party," *Russian Review* 38, no. 2 (April 1979): 139.

28. Maureen Perrie, "The Social Composition and Structure of the Socialist-Revolutionary Party Before 1917," *Soviet Studies* 24, no. 3 (October 1972): 235, and Beate Fieseler, *Frauen auf dem Weg in die russische Sozialdemokratie, 1890–1917: Eine kollektive Biographie* (Stuttgart: Franz Steiner Verlag, 1995), 20.

29. Perrie, who identified women terrorists only by "surnames with feminine endings," found 20 women out of 179 named terrorists, or 11.2 percent. Knight, however, identified 27 women out of the 179 terrorists, or 15 percent. See Perrie, "Social Composition and Structure," 235, and Knight, "Female Terrorists," 144.

30. Knight, "Female Terrorists," 140–41, 144–45; Perrie, "Social Composition and Structure," 235–36; Fieseler, *Frauen auf dem Weg,* 40–59; Barbara Evans Clements, *Bolshevik Women* (Cambridge: Cambridge University Press, 1997), 30–31, 40–45. See also Christine Johanson, *Women's Struggle for Higher Education in Russia, 1855–1900* (Montreal: McGill-Queen's University Press, 1987), 100–101.

31. Knight, "Female Terrorists," 147–48; Clements, *Bolshevik Women,* 66; Robert H. McNeal, "Women in the Russian Radical Movement," *Journal of Social History* 5, no. 2 (Winter 1971–72): 153–54; Engel, *Mothers and Daughters,* 173, 181–82; Fieseler, *Frauen auf dem Weg,* 261–72. Why were radical women generally excluded from party theory and polemics? McNeal blames the male revolutionaries and their "deep, tacit reluctance to share with women that most exalted of all male roles—the possession of sacred knowledge." Fieseler notes that women SDs acquiesced in their exclusion from policy-making; indeed, two female Bolsheviks confessed in their memoirs

that they felt themselves incompetent to participate in more intellectually demanding work (*Frauen auf dem Weg,* 263–64). Engel considers women's lack of intellectual contribution to have been far more a consequence of their inferior education than of gender prejudice; she also points to the difficulties of disguising illegal activities in a society bound by strict gender roles (*Mothers and Daughters,* 181, 183).

32. McNeal, "Women," 154; Knight, "Female Terrorists," 147–48.

33. Engel, *Mothers and Daughters,* 4–5, 173; Knight, "Female Terrorists," 143; see also Barbara Heldt, *Terrible Perfection: Women and Russian Literature* (Bloomington: Indiana University Press, 1987), 12. Bolshevik women, however, chose a different path to virtue than did the women populists of the People's Will and the SR Party. In common with all Russian radicals, the Bolsheviks aspired to be dedicated, principled, and selfless, but they also particularly prized "rock-hard" characteristics such as rationality, ruthlessness, and a lack of emotion or sentiment. Refusing to accept society's distinction of these characteristics as typically masculine, Bolshevik women followed Bolshevik men in considering *tverdost',* or hardness, to be the quality most appropriate in a professional revolutionary. Indeed, the Bolsheviks prided themselves that objective rigor, a legacy of Marx's "scientific socialism," set them apart from their subjective and therefore, to Bolshevik minds, sentimental SR rivals (Clements, *Bolshevik Women,* 60–65).

34. Stepniak [Kravchinskii], *Underground Russia,* 127.

35. Engel, *Mothers and Daughters,* 173, 189; Knight, "Female Terrorists," 142–44.

36. For example, one of Spiridonova's prison comrades, Maria (Mania) Shkolnik, said that Perovskaia inspired her "with special courage" to fulfill her "sacred obligation" as a terrorist (stated in a 1914 interview published by the New York Jewish SD newspaper *Forverts;* see the Russian police translation in GARF, f. 102, op. 241, d. 270, t.1, l. 191). Another prison comrade, Aleksandra Izmailovich, was begged by her SR lover not to imagine herself "a second Perovskaia" but to expect a commutation of her death sentence (A. Izmailovich, "Iz proshlogo," in *Zhenshchiny-terroristki v Rossii,* ed. O. V. Budnitskii [Rostov: Feniks, 1996], 367).

37. The next woman so hanged was Zinaida Konopliannikova on August 29, 1906, following the introduction of Prime Minister P. A. Stolypin's law on field courts-martial, which in its turn followed the bombing of Stolypin's summer home by SR maximalists on August 12. Konopliannikova was condemned to death for killing a general, also on August 12. For basic facts on Konopliannikova, see "Ukazatel' terroristicheskikh aktov, sovershennykh zhenshchinami-uchastnitsami eserovskikh boevykh organizatsii," in Budnitskii, *Zhenshchiny-terroristki,* 624, and also Anna Hillyar and Jane McDermid, *Revolutionary Women in Russia, 1870–1917: A Study in Collective Biography* (Manchester, Eng.: Manchester University Press, 2000), 135, table 4.3. On Stolypin and field courts-martial, see Abraham Ascher, *The Revolution of 1905: Authority Restored* (Stanford: Stanford University Press, 1992), 243–47.

38. See Luisella de Cataldo Neuburger and Tiziana Valenti, *Women and Terrorism,* trans. Leo Michael Hughes (New York: St. Martin's Press, 1996), 78–85; their argument is emphasized and amplified in Rhiannon Talbot, "Myths in the Representation of Women Terrorists," *Eire-Ireland* 35, nos. 3–4 (Fall–Winter 2000–2001): 165–86.

39. See, for example, Talbot, "Myths in the Representation of Women Terrorists," who discusses recent examples of female terrorism from the West Bank to Northern Ireland and Spain. See Talbot as well for other similarities to the Russian phenomenon, such as the fact that later women terrorists have been significantly more attracted

to and prominent in left-wing groups than right-wing groups, no doubt because of socialism's commitment to gender equality. Also like their Russian counterparts, later women terrorists have tended to be middle class, educated, and older than their male comrades.

40. Budnitskii, *Terrorizm,* 176. Even Anna Geifman, who criticizes Budnitsky for idealizing terrorists, quotes with approval his comment that Russian terrorism "has few analogues in world history." See her review of Budnitsky in *Kritika: Explorations in Russian and Eurasian History* 3, no. 4 (Fall 2002): 739. Budnitsky for his part likens Geifman's relentlessly negative depiction of terrorists and terrorism to "looking at events from the Police Department's window" (25). On Geifman's expressed purpose to "demystify and deromanticize the Russian revolutionary movement"—or rather, her refusal to "differentiate between revolutionaries and criminals in this period"—see Geifman, *Thou Shalt Kill,* 7–8.

41. Geifman, *Thou Shalt Kill,* 3.

42. Their stories are presented more fully in chapter 3 of my dissertation, "Mariia Spiridonova, 1884–1918: Feminine Martyrdom and Revolutionary Mythmaking" (Ph.D. diss., Indiana University, 1995).

43. Ezersky (Jezierski) could apparently be either a Jewish or a Polish surname: whereas Anzia Yezierska, the Polish-born American author, was Jewish, Lidiia Ezerskaia's husband, Stepan Ezersky, seems to have been Christian. Jews, 4 percent of the total population of the Russian Empire, comprised 13.5 percent of SR Party members (Perrie, "Social Composition," 236–37) and 30 percent of women SR terrorists (Knight, "Female Terrorists," 145–46). Intensified persecution, high literacy levels, and strongly traditional families are considered by Perrie and Knight to account for the high percentage of Jewish participation in radical politics.

44. On censorship and the press during the 1905 revolution, see Louise McReynolds, *The News Under Russia's Old Regime: The Development of a Mass-Circulation Press* (Princeton: Princeton University Press, 1991), 218–22; Ascher, *Russia in Disarray,* 275–76; Ascher, *Authority Restored,* 28–29; Mehlinger and Thompson, *Count Witte,* 67, 171–74.

45. Editors' comments and letter excerpts are from *Rus',* February 12, 1906.

46. She cited "Bogoroditsky's deposition"; V. M. Lavrov has identified Bogoroditsky as a Tambov surgeon (*Mariia Spiridonova: Terroristka i zhertva terrora: Povestvovanie v dokumentakh* [Moscow: Arkheologicheskii tsentr, 1996], 14n2).

47. In the original Russian text, an odd note is struck here by Avramov's use of the formal "you" (*vy*) during his clumsy attempts at seduction, whereas he and Zhdanov had insulted Spiridonova with the familiar "you" (*ty*) throughout her interrogation.

48. At her later court-martial, Spiridonova enumerated Luzhenovsky's crimes in greater detail, adding that the Tambov SR committee had therefore decided "he was an oppressor of the people, and there was no means of restraint on him besides death to be found" (*Dvadtsatyi vek,* March 27, 1906). On terrorists' dehumanization of their victims, see Albert Bandura, "Mechanisms of Moral Disengagement," in Reich, ed., *Origins of Terrorism,* 161–91; Martha Crenshaw, "The Subjective Reality of the Terrorist: Ideological and Psychological Factors in Terrorism," in Slater and Stohl, *Current Perspectives on International Terrorism,* 12–46; and della Porta, "Political Socialization," 278–79.

49. Kaliaev's speech is quoted in Savinkov, *Vospominaniia,* 110.

50. GARF, f. 102, op. 203, d. 8, ch. 58, t. 2, ll. 14–15. Yulia's name was not included

in either of two police listings of members of the Tambov SR committee, though Maria's was (GARF, f. 102, op. 202, d. 1526, ll. 4–6; GARF, f. 102, op. 233, d. 80, l. 22).

51. This was a rule of the party's central Combat Organization; see Savinkov, *Vospominaniia,* 60. In contrast to Spiridonova, Anastasia Bitsenko and Mania Shkolnik, both of whom were associated with the Combat Organization, refused to reveal their identities to authorities for months following their arrests, even appearing nameless at their trials.

52. S. Nechetnyi (S. N. Sletov), *Spekuliatsiia na chuzhikh ranakh* (n.p., n.d.), 100. Sletov, a Tambov native, was the brother-in-law of chief party theorist V. M. Chernov and a member of the SR Central Committee.

53. On the liberal press during the 1905 revolution, see McReynolds, *The News,* 198–222; on liberals and legalism, see Andrzej Walicki, *Legal Philosophies of Russian Liberalism* (Oxford: Clarendon Press, 1987), 1–7.

54. *Rus',* February 12, 1906.

55. *Nasha zhizn',* February 12, 1906.

56. Corporal punishment, which classical liberalism found incompatible with human dignity, had been virtually banned in Russia in 1863; moreover, Russia's upper classes had been exempt from it since 1785. See Bruce F. Adams, *The Politics of Punishment: Prison Reform in Russia, 1863–1917* (DeKalb: Northern Illinois University Press, 1996), 12–36. Reformers in Europe's "age of penal justice" dating from the eighteenth century held that punishment for those convicted of a crime should affect the soul rather than the body and consist of a suspension of personal rights (i.e., prison) rather than torture. See Michel Foucault, *Discipline and Punish: The Birth of the Prison,* trans. Alan Sheridan (New York: Vintage Books, 1979), 7–23.

57. These letters, published in *Rus',* February 14–March 4, 1906, also reflected two recent developments in educated Russian society: a public consciousness (*obshchestvennost'*) based on Western liberal values, and the beginnings of feminism as exemplified by two feminist groups organized in 1905. On *obshchestvennost',* see Edith W. Clowes, Samuel D. Kassow, and James L. West, eds., *Between Tsar and People: Educated Society and the Quest for Public Identity in Late Imperial Russia* (Princeton: Princeton University Press, 1991); on the beginnings of Russian feminism, see Linda Harriet Edmondson, *Feminism in Russia, 1900–1917* (Stanford: Stanford University Press, 1984), 27–54. Jeffrey Brooks has noted that for the most part in the late tsarist era, publishers targeted their mass-circulation newspapers toward "a relatively prosperous middle and upper-class audience," although a few newspapers geared their content toward a lower-class audience (*When Russia Learned to Read: Literacy and Popular Literature, 1861–1917* [Princeton: Princeton University Press, 1985], 118).

58. Its publisher, A. S. Suvorin, thought little of Nicholas II and preferred a parliamentary government dominated by Russia's elite, among whom he counted himself; see McReynolds, *The News,* 74–78, 208–9.

59. *Novoe vremia,* February 13, 1906.

60. *Novoe vremia,* February 15, 1906.

61. *Tambovskie gubernskie vedomosti,* February 19, 1906. Its editor, a personal friend of Luzhenovsky, according to the liberal press (see *Nasha zhizn',* March 9, 1906, and *Rus',* March 14, 1906), had publicly mourned the shooting of the security chief in January. One of his editorials proclaimed that "the treacherous bullets of some kind of insane, unscrupulous female revolutionary brought down a valuable employee, an upright man, a devoted son of his motherland, a loyal and incorruptible servant of the tsar" (*Tambovskie gubernskie vedomosti,* January 18, 1906).

62. *Russkie vedomosti,* February 25–26, 1906.

63. "It is said that the investigation into the cases of Zhdanov and Avramov has already begun, but no one believes that the government seriously intends to punish these torturers, for some reason," noted the editors of *Nasha zhizn'* (March 15, 1906). See similar editorial comments in *Rus',* March 7 and 9, 1906, and in *Nasha zhizn',* March 8, 1906. The indirect election of the 524 deputies to the Russian State Duma began in late February and ended in mid-April for most areas of the country (Ascher, *Authority Restored,* 43–45). With the SRs and SDs (or at least the Bolshevik faction thereof) boycotting the election, the liberal Constitutional Democrats (Kadets) emerged as the party of plurality by late March (Mehlinger and Thompson, *Count Witte,* 263, 281; Ascher, *Authority Restored,* 47–50).

64. On newspaper reporters in the late tsarist era, see McReynolds, *The News,* 145–67, esp. 155 and 164–65.

65. *Rus',* March 7, 1906.

66. GARF, f. 102, op. 203, d. 8, ch. 58, t. 2, ll. 54–55.

67. *Rus',* March 7, 1906.

68. GARF, f. 102, op. 203, d. 8, ch. 58, t. 2, l. 44.

69. *Nasha zhizn',* March 8, 1906.

70. Mogil'ner, *Mifologiia,* 50–51.

71. Sletov, *Spekuliatsiia,* 101–3.

72. *Rus',* March 8, 1906. More matter-of-factly, prison records from 1906 noted that Spiridonova was about two inches shy of five feet in height and weak in build, with a pale face, gray eyes, and light brown hair (GARF, f. 29, op. 2, d. 3790).

73. *Rus',* March 8, 1906.

74. Ibid. The eighth year was not obligatory but essentially a teacher's training course; see Sophie Satina, *Education of Women in Pre-Revolutionary Russia,* trans. Alexandra F. Pouschine (New York: self-published, 1966), 48–49.

75. *Rus',* March 8, 1906.

76. GARF, f. 102, op. 230, d. 855, l. 1; GARF, f. 102, op. 226, d. 3, ch. 102, l. 1; GARF, f. 102, op. 226, d. 3, ch. 160, l. 12. A "politically unreliable" person had been either "arrested, investigated or kept under surveillance in connection with politically criminal activity" (Daly, *Autocracy,* 68–69).

77. GARF, f. 102, op. 203, d. 8, ch. 58, t. 2, l. 77; S. V. Bezberezh'ev, "Mariia Aleksandrovna Spiridonova," in *Rossiia na rubezhe vekov: Istoricheskie portrety* (Moscow: Izdatel'stvo politicheskoi literatury, 1991), 335–36.

78. Her symptoms of fever, delirium, pain, emaciation, and coughing up of blood, observed by her female SR comrades during their train journey to Siberia in the summer of 1906, are all signs of an advanced state of tuberculosis. Descriptions of Spiridonova's symptoms are found in Izmailovich, "Iz proshlogo," 399–421.

79. *Nasha zhizn',* March 23, 1906.

80. GARF, f. 102, op. 203, d. 8, ch. 58, t. 2, l. 53

81. GARF, f. 102, op. 201, d. 3366, ll. 5–6.

82. GARF, f. 102, op. 202, d. 1526, ll. 3–9, 13; GARF, f. 102, op. 233, d. 80, ch. 35, ll. 20–22.

83. GARF, F. 102, op. 202, d. 1526, l. 17. Employment opportunities for women with a secondary education in this period were found only in teaching, medicine, and office work (Hillyar and McDermid, *Revolutionary Women,* 100).

84. *Rus',* March 12, 1906; GARF, f. 102, op. 203, d. 8, ch. 58, t. 2, l. 29.

85. *Rech',* March 13, 1906. This was the official Kadet press organ; Teslenko later

served as a Kadet deputy in the Second Duma (Ascher, *Authority Restored,* 296, 346–47). As I stated above, it is far more likely that Spiridonova's tuberculosis was contracted earlier and reactivated during her imprisonment (see note 78). Fink had, after all, made no note of a tubercular condition when he examined Spiridonova on her arrival at Tambov prison.

86. Teslenko reported this speech to Vladimirov; see *Rus',* March 18, 1906. In 1878, Vera Zasulich's defense attorney similarly "turned [her] case into a trial of the victim, and concluded by elevating Zasulich to the role of martyr-avenger"; see the essay by Donna Oliver in the present volume. With regard to Teslenko's interesting use of the term "state terror": the French Revolution of the 1790s had demonstrated that terrorism could be employed both by society against the state and by the state against society, marking an all-important development in the history of terrorism (Martin A. Miller, "The Intellectual Origins of Modern Terrorism in Europe," in Crenshaw, *Terrorism in Context,* 31).

87. Thus Spiridonova ended her speech to the court-martial, after outlining in extensive detail the crimes Luzhenovsky had committed against the people of the Borisoglebsk district. His victims, she stated, included "murdered peasants, ruined landlords, raped [*iznasilovannykh*] women and beaten children." (I note that she never used the word "rape" [*iznasilovanie*] when describing the Avramov incident.) Spiridonova's speech was printed in *Dvadtsatyi vek,* March 27, 1906. This newspaper was a new incarnation of *Rus',* appearing immediately after *Rus'* was shut down by the government—a common occurrence in the spring of 1906, when more stringent press regulations were coming into force (Ascher, *Authority Restored,* 28–30; Mehlinger and Thompson, *Count Witte,* 172).

88. GARF, f. 102, op. 203, d. 8, ch. 58, 2. 2, l. 32. Spiridonova's gender was probably another factor, though it was not mentioned. A court-martial in Saratov on March 3 sentenced peasant-born Anastasia Bitsenko to death while petitioning for commutation on the basis of "her insufficient intellectual development . . . and her female sex"; see GARF, f. 102, op. 203, d. 8, ch. 52, t. 1, l. 37. Mania Shkolnik, similarly sentenced to hanging, stated that the commutation of her sentence was based on her gender: "As a woman, I was 'spared' the death penalty" (GARF, f. 102, op. 241, d. 270, t. 1, l. 197).

89. *Dvadtsatyi vek,* April 5, 1906.

90. "'Blazhennaia' Mariia," in *Neizvestnaia Rossiia: XX vek,* vol. 2 (Moscow: Istoricheskoe nasledie, 1992), 25–31. Originals of the documents published herein are located in the Tambov provincial archive (GATO, f. 4, op. 1, d. 272, 356, 6368, and 6390). Yanushevich had recently replaced von der Launitz as governor. His less heavy-handed treatment of peasant rebels and revolutionaries, in comparison with his predecessor, earned him the contempt of the Tambov Black Hundreds, who maligned him as "that Polish Yid" ("'Blazhennaia' Mariia," 54n25). An American reporter who visited Spiridonova in prison with the permission of Yanushevich described the governor as "most affable and hospitable . . . a much more competent and conscientious administrator than other [Russian] governors whom I had met"; see Kellogg Durland, *The Red Reign: The True Story of an Adventurous Year in Russia* (New York: Century, 1908), 161.

91. There is no mention of Volsky's name in Spiridonova's central police records, now located in GARF; nor does his name appear among those of the Tambov SR committee members listed in GARF, f. 102, op. 202, d. 1526, ll. 4–6, or GARF, f. 102, op. 233, d. 80, l. 22. However, police records did note that Vladimir's brother, Mikhail

Volsky, was in prison as of January 4, 1906, apparently for serving as "secret editor" (at least until the police found out) of a radical newspaper, *Tambovskii golos* (GARF, f. 102, op. 233, d. 80, ch. 35, l. 31).

92. GARF, f. 102, op. 203, d. 8, ch. 58, t. 2, ll. 14–15.

93. GARF, f. 102, op. 203, d. 8, ch. 58, t. 4, l. 56. In 1910 the police learned that the Borisoglebsk SRs were responsible for this killing (GARF, f. 102, op. 240, d. 9, ch. 38, litera A, l. 23). Nor did Spiridonova's other tormentor, Zhdanov, escape retribution; he was shot to death on a street in Tambov on May 7, 1906 (GARF, f. 102, op. 236, d. 808, t. 2, l. 140).

94. *Novoe vremia,* April 5, 1906. The newspaper also derisively equated the charge that Avramov had "robbed [Spiridonova] of her innocence and infected her with syphilis" with the plot of "a very bad novel."

95. The summary appeared "in our semi-official organs, *Russkoe gosudarstvo* and *Novoe vremia,*" simultaneously, according to *Dvadtsatyi vek* (April 9, 1906). It was published in *Novoe vremia,* April 8, 1906.

96. *Strana,* April 9, 1906.

97. *Dvadtsatyi vek,* April 9, 1906.

98. *Rech',* April 12, 1906.

99. Ibid., April 13, 1906. Teslenko had earlier told Vladimirov that Spiridonova had confided to him "a terrible secret" and begged him not to publicize it until after her death; Teslenko also speculated to Vladimirov that Spiridonova's beautiful face and figure had aroused the "bestial lusts" of Avramov. See *Rus',* March 17, 1906.

100. *Novoe vremia,* April 8, 1906.

101. GARF, f. 102, op. 203, d. 8, ch. 58, t. 2, l. 53.

102. *Rus',* Feb. 12, 1906.

103. GARF, f. 102, op. 203, d. 8, ch. 58, t. 2, ll. 58, 60. I would add that the investigation strikes me as fair-minded and conscientious; the investigators appear to have conducted exhaustive interviews with every witness they could find. It is clear from the testimony of these witnesses, particularly those who saw Avramov's "extremely agitated" slapping of Spiridonova, that Avramov and the rest of the Cossack bodyguard were frightened as well as furious when they failed in their assigned duty of protecting Luzhenovsky. This may account for the force with which they turned on Luzhenovsky's assassin—or, as *Novoe vremia* might have put it, violence begets violence, and a despotic system creates despotic public servants.

104. GARF, f. 102, op. 203, d. 8, ch. 58, t. 2, ll. 14–15.

105. GARF, f. 102, op. 226, d. 3, ch. 104, l. 6. Émigré editions were published in 1867, 1876, and 1902; see Paperno, *Chernyshevsky,* 28.

106. As already noted, Spiridonova expressed her wish for a martyr's death in her deposition and at her trial. Shortly after her trial, Spiridonova wrote in another letter to her SR comrades that she so longed for her own death, because of its "value to society" in advancing the revolution, that she would regard the commutation of her sentence "as vengeance, as a fresh insult" from the government. This letter, along with several others she addressed to the Tambov SRs, was included in a collection of the Vladimirov articles published as a book in April (V. Vladimirov, *Mariia Spiridonova* [Moscow: Tipografiia A. P. Poplavskogo, 1906], 117). Spiridonova's lover Volsky chided her gently for her despair over the commutation, assuring her, "We [SRs] still need you, Marusia—we need you, and that is why you must live, you must live and live" (see their private correspondence in "'Blazhennaia' Mariia," 27). Spiridonova seems to have

preferred death on the scaffold to "the unavoidable abuses of a life in penal servitude," as she phrased it to her comrades (Vladimirov, *Mariia Siridonova,* 120).

107. Her sense of duty may have been reinforced by a letter she received from the incarcerated male SR terrorists G. A. Gershuni, P. V. Karpovich, L. V. Sikorskii, and E. S. Sazonov, published in the SR Party organ *Mysl'* (*Thought*) on July 5. Although the men exalted Spiridonova, "our glorious comrade," as "a symbol . . . of young, struggling, determined and self-sacrificing Russia," they also emphasized her responsibility "as a conscientious Socialist Revolutionary": "you will not put your own sufferings above the sufferings of the people to whose sacred cause you gave yourself without reservation" (reprinted in *Dvadtsatyi vek,* July 6, 1906).

108. Police reports on the crowds and the measures constantly undertaken to ensure order are found in GARF, f. 102, op. 236, d. 760. Not only was Spiridonova worshipped by ordinary people in Siberia—a peasant family in Voronezh province hung her portrait, framed in an icon-case, in their hut and kept a flame burning before it; Tambov peasants offered prayers for her health (Mogil'ner, *Mifologiia,* 59–60; also Vladimirov in *Rus',* March 14, 1906); a teenage schoolboy in Kiev drowned himself after learning of her prison sentence (Geifman, *Thou Shalt Kill,* 174–75).

109. Izmailovich, "Iz proshlogo," 400–416. Despite government pressure, the Kadet Party continually refused to denounce terrorism, even at the cost of remaining an "illegal" or "unregistered" party. In fact, on June 19, 1906, two days before the *shesterka* of women terrorists departed for Siberia, a Kadet deputy who also happened to be a priest made a speech on the floor of the Duma in which he compared Spiridonova and Izmailovich along with Zasulich to the nameless heroine of Turgenev's poem "The Threshold." Justifying all contemporary terrorists, the priest stated they were acting out of the legitimate fear that "some Luzhenovsky or his like" would perpetrate "further horrors" on the Russian population (Geifman, *Thou Shalt Kill,* 214–22). For a discussion of "The Threshold," see Donna Oliver's contribution to this volume.

110. *Dvadtsatyi vek,* July 6, 1906. Here the letter from Gershuni, Sazonov, and others. echoed the earlier accolades of Tambov SR leader Sletov ("The name of our comrade became a symbol of suffering Russia") and Spiridonova's defense attorney Teslenko ("Before you stands not only the oppressed, desecrated and sick Spiridonova. Before you stands sick and desecrated Russia").

111. A useful survey of developments in the field is Martha Crenshaw, "Psychology of Terrorism: An Agenda for the 21st Century," *Political Psychology* 21, no. 2 (June 2000), especially 407–11. Two historians of Russian terrorism, Knight ("Female Terrorists," 149–51) and Geifman, particularly in *Thou Shalt Kill* (167–72), emphasize psychological abnormalities among terrorists. See Budnitskii's more balanced interpretation in *Terrorizm,* 162–66.

112. Budnitskii, *Terrorizm,* 176.

113. In her speech at her trial, reported in *Dvadtsatyi vek,* March 27, 1906.

114. E. M. Iaroslavsky, future founder of the League of the Militant Godless, published an anti-Spiridonova pamphlet, *Trekhsviatitel'skaia bogoroditsa Mariia* (*The Blessed Virgin Mary of Three Prelates' Lane,* a reference to the location of the Left SR Party headquarters in Moscow), in 1919.

The Byronic Terrorist: Boris Savinkov's Literary Self-Mythologization

Lynn Ellen Patyk

> So do the dark in soul expire,
> Or live like Scorpion girt by fire;
> So writhes the mind Remorse hath riven,
> Unfit for earth, undoom'd for heaven,
> Darkness above, despair beneath,
> Around it flame, within it death!
> —GEORGE GORDON, LORD BYRON, "THE GIAOUR"

In January 1909, the appearance of the serialized novella *The Pale Steed* (*Kon' blednyi*) in the well-respected liberal journal *Russian Thought* (*Russkaia mysl'*) caused a brief furor among the reading public and won favorable notice in modernist literary circles for the unknown and pseudonymous author, V. Ropshin. In the temporal quagmire of the *bezvrem'e,* the period after the revolution of 1905 that saw the cultural intelligentsia's retreat from political activism to melancholy introspection, *The Pale Steed* presented itself as the fictionalized diary of a terrorist mastermind in the heyday of the 1905 revolution. Indeed, beneath the thin veneer of fiction, readers easily discerned that the novella referred to true events of just a few years before: the assassination of the Grand Duke Sergei, uncle of Tsar Nicholas II and the reactionary governor-general of Moscow. On February 4, 1905, as the Grand Duke proceeded along his customary route from his palatial residence to the chancellery, a lone attacker named Ivan Kaliaev, a member of the notorious Combat Organization of the Socialist Revolutionary (SR) Party, hurled a bomb at his ducal carriage from a distance of four paces.

Kaliaev was apprehended on the spot, tried before a special session of the Senate, and sentenced to hang, without betraying his coconspirators, who remained at large.[1]

Ropshin's novella appeared to be the work of an insider who possessed detailed knowledge of the planning and personalities involved in the assassination; it was also a sign of the times, the articulation of a nationally inflected Zeitgeist. The prominent symbolist writer and literary critic Dmitry Merezhkovsky heralded the novel's importance, attesting, "If they asked me now in Europe which book is the most Russian and allows one to foresee the future of Russia, after the great works of Tolstoy and Dostoevsky, I would point to *The Pale Steed.* . . . Here is the Russian style of the twentieth century, combining the smell of dynamite with apocalyptical incense."[2] Merezhkovsky was, as we will see, instrumental in forging the "Russian style" that joined the antitheses of socialist revolution to religious (Christian) revival.

Left-wing publicists, however, did not share Merezhkovsky's enthusiasm. They denounced Ropshin's portrayal of "national liberation fighters" as "slander of the revolution." The literary critic and foe of autocracy Alexander Amfiteatrov seethed that the novel might be a parody of the revolutionary movement had it not appeared in a respected journal. Amfiteatrov concluded his scathing review by contrasting the "delirium" of *The Pale Steed* to the truth and authenticity of countless notes and memoirs that had recently appeared in oppositional publications authored by real revolutionary "fighters steeped in sweat and blood." He advised his readers, "Take the notes of Gershuni. Read the latest article by Boris Savinkov. You will see that their worldview and the worldview of *The Pale Steed* are as distant from one another as Sirius from the Pinsky Swamp. And, even if we are prepared to pardon Mr. Ropshin: as experts in matters of revolutionary psychology, the world will believe, of course, Gershuni and Boris Savinkov, and not *The Pale Steed.*"[3]

Grigory Gershuni and his successor, Boris Savinkov, were well known to the radical reading public as the celebrated leaders of the SR Combat Organization. Under their direction, the terror of the People's Will (Narodnaia volia) had been resurrected and had achieved its most stunning blows against the regime: the assassination of Minister of the Interior Sipiagin in 1902, Minister of the Interior Viacheslav von Plehve in 1904, and the Grand Duke Sergei in 1905.[4] Gershuni's memoirs, *From the Recent Past,* had appeared in 1908, and Savinkov's memoirs of the von Plehve and Sergei assassinations, in which he depicted the knightly brotherhood of the Combat Organization, premiered in numbers one and two of the journal *Socialist Revolutionary* beginning in 1909, as well as in the revolutionary-historical journal *Byloe* (*The Past*). Savinkov's personal archive in the State Archive of the Russian Federation reveals that he assiduously clipped and saved his reviews, both of his literary works and of his terrorist activities.[5] We can only imagine the intense satisfaction that Savinkov, master of disguise and evasion, derived from Amfiteatrov's misapprehension, for the reprehensible Ropshin and the heroic Savinkov were in fact one and the same.

Boris Viktorovich Savinkov (1879–1925) riveted his contemporaries for two decades through the spectacle of his oscillation between the violent extremities of the revolutionary epoch. In 1903 he commenced his professional literary and revolutionary careers virtually in tandem: after his first story was published in the newspaper *Kurer* (*The Courier*) under the pseudonym Kanin, he applied in Geneva to the veteran revolutionary Mikhail Gots for admission to the exclusive SR Combat Organization, declaring his desire to participate in terror and only terror (as opposed to other revolutionary tasks). He won his revolutionary laurels first, for his orchestration of the von Plehve and Sergei assassinations; only in 1909 did he make his literary mark with the pseudonymous *Pale Steed*. Scholars have made sense of *The Pale Steed* by situating it within the history of the Russian intelligentsia and viewing it alongside the *Vekhi* (*Landmarks*) collection (published in April 1909) as a critique of revolutionary terrorism, and of the leftist intelligentsia more generally.[6] If Savinkov's novella is indeed a critique—moral or otherwise—of terrorism, then we have to come to terms with two puzzling facts: first, that he wrote it virtually simultaneously with his heroic memoir of the Combat Organization, and second, that the critique had no discernible effect on the behavior of its author, who continued to dabble in terrorist plots during the course of its writing.[7] No sooner did *The Pale Steed* appear in print, in fact, than Savinkov assumed the leadership of a reconstituted Combat Organization in order to "rehabilitate" terror, and went on to plot the assassination of Nicholas II and retribution against the agent provocateur Evno Azef, both of which efforts were unsuccessful.[8]

A close reading of *The Pale Steed* reveals that it lacks a coherent moral, ideological, or any other sort of idea and therefore should not be understood as a polemical utterance. Instead, the novel is best viewed as the first literary installment of Ropshin-Savinkov's self-mythologization. With "his magical ability," according to Savinkov's literary mentor, the poet Zinaida Gippius, "to perceive and grasp that which turned out to be necessary to him at a given moment,"[9] Savinkov chiseled his own myth from Russian modernism's neo-romantic cultural mythologies. As a member of the gentry, a cosmopolitan aesthete, and a dandy, Savinkov embraced a model of self-authorship bequeathed to Russian literature by the British romantic-era poet George Gordon, Lord Byron and nativized by Alexander Pushkin and Mikhail Lermontov, all of whom remained among Savinkov's favorites.[10] As Byron's previous Russian imitators had done, Savinkov funneled his ongoing biography—his revolutionary and amorous exploits, metaphysical questing, and malaise—into a series of literary works beginning with *The Pale Steed* and ending with "The Blue Cross" ("*Sinii Krest*"), written shortly before Savinkov's mysterious death in the Lubyanka in 1925.[11]

Of the three volumes comprising his revolutionary trilogy, the narrative persona, known only by his pseudonym, "George," unites the first (*The Pale Steed,* 1909) and third (*The Raven Steed,* 1922) volumes, and George's voice of disillusionment and damnation also resounds in Savinkov's posthumously published lyric poetry composed between 1911 and 1917.[12] While contemporaries and subsequent scholars have been quick to label George as a (pseudo-)Nietzschean type, "beyond good and evil," by excavating Savinkov's Byronic taproot we gain a more profound insight into George as a literary type, as well as into Savinkov's mode of self-authorship.[13] In understanding Savinkov as a latter-day Byronist, it is essential to note Dostoevsky's role in explicating and, in essence, adapting Byronism to its Russian habitat. Byronism was Dostoevsky's muse of "malediction and despair," and the most salient characteristics of the Dostoevskian hero, tormented consciousness and duality, were, according to Dostoevsky, the very essence of Byronism. This essay argues that Savinkov embraced Byronism as a model for transforming the terrorist's life into art, as well as a means for refuting the Merezhkovskys' attempt to sanctify the terrorist's tormented consciousness. Finally, Savinkov may be seen as the culmination of Byronism's hundred-year trajectory: the twentieth-century Byronist is a self-consciously literary terrorist.

"Not Right, but Justified": The Merezhkovskys' Christian Terrorist

> But some of them, albeit only a few, are very special people: they believe in God and are Christians, and at the same time Socialists. Those we fear most of all, they are terrifying people!
>
> —DOSTOEVSKY, *THE BROTHERS KARAMAZOV*[14]

On March 11 (March 24, old style), 1907, Dmitry Filosofov reported in the newspaper *Tovarishch* (*Comrade*) an event that had taken the émigré community in Paris by storm: Dmitry Merezhkovsky's lecture "On Violence" drew massive crowds of would-be listeners, so many that they overflowed the auditorium of the former Russian school and swamped the adjacent street. To avert a riot, the lecture was rescheduled. Subsequently, an audience of more than one thousand massed in the auditorium of the Masonic Lodge "The Great East": "The burning theme, involving the most pressing contemporary questions, electrified the audience."[15]

Public response to Merezhkovsky's controversial lecture (written in actuality by his wife, the poet Zinaida Gippius) demonstrates the intensity with which the Russian intelligentsia interrogated the ideological premises and tactics of the revolution and, needless to say, its own role, in the wake of the "failed revolution" of 1905.[16] For the Trio—Dmitry Merezhkovsky, Zinaida Gippius, and Dmitry Filosofov—transplanted in early 1906 from St. Petersburg to Paris, this interrogation culminated in a volume titled *Le tzar et la révolution,* conceived by Merezhkovsky as "militant miscellany-manifesto" addressed to the "entire Russian nation." *Le tzar et la révolution* was intended to elaborate the ideas adumbrated in Merezhkovsky's radical proclamation, "Appeal to the Church," which called on the Orthodox Church to condemn the autocracy for its violent repression of the revolution of 1905. Declaring that the autocracy had destroyed its connection to the people and had turned away from "the spirit of Christ, love, and freedom," the appeal presaged the Merezhkovskys' emerging conviction that the tsar was not God-anointed but the Antichrist, and that the revolution instead was the way of Christ.

Just as they had tried to build a bridge between the cultural intelligentsia and the Orthodox clergy prior to 1905, once in Paris the Merezhkovskys attempted to extend their religious civic consciousness to the firmly atheistic revolutionary intelligentsia in emigration, and in the process, to find justification for revolutionary violence within their neo-Christian framework.[17] To this end, the Trio organized not only stormy public lectures but also more intimate at-homes, where members of the cultural intelligentsia mingled with compatriots representing the most diverse political and philosophical tendencies. During this period, Gippius played dazzling hostess to those whom she fondly referred to as "killers" (*ubitsy*)—the members of the SR Combat Organization and their widows.[18]

In her article "Revolution and Violence" (on which Merezhkovsky's incendiary lecture was based), Gippius suggested that the Christian is in fact duty-bound to commit murder and that precisely the acknowledgment of the necessity of murder as well as the realization of its sinfulness is the true Christian's cross to bear. Gippius begins by standing Dostoevsky on his head, contending that "everything is permitted" applies not to the revolutionary but to the original nihilist—the autocrat—who views himself as "the *Übermensch,* God, standing outside of human laws. But whether he is Man or God, for him 'everything is permitted.'" According to Gippius, autocracy, in its various historical permutations (papism, Caesarism, or tsarism), is the apotheosis of egoism and survives only by a relentless war waged by the one against all, which brooks no compromise (neither reform, nor constitution, nor public opinion) and ends only with the crushing of all by the one or the destruction of the one by all. In this Manichean struggle, Gippius repeatedly compares the revolutionary martyrs to the Christian ascetics of the first centuries. Contending that the revolutionaries are atheists in name only and were forced to become atheists because the autocracy had co-opted Christianity, she insists, "but their nature, the deep and mute part of their soul, is not only in God, but in Christ, in his essence even if they don't know it and their reason opposes it."[19]

In support of her argument that revolutionary terrorists are at least subconsciously Christians,[20] Gippius relates a true anecdote about a veteran revolutionary ("one of the most active leaders of the terrorist party, who participated in the organization of four or five of the most famous assassinations which had such a fatal significance for the autocracy"), who was "drawn to expiation, the way a moth is drawn to the flame."[21] At the risk of being recognized and apprehended by the authorities, this notorious terrorist returns obsessively to the scene of the crime. He is plagued by guilt—not for the murder of his victims!—but because he alone remained alive while his comrades had perished on the scaffold. At his interlocutors' prompting, he confesses that he is "haunted" by the shade of his close comrade.

While admitting that in all probability, two-thirds of revolutionaries aren't troubled by such "nightmares," Gippius nonetheless adduces from this admitted anomaly a principle that not only justifies but mandates political murder.

> All who have upon their shoulders a murder that they have not redeemed with their own blood, in some way feel the burden of that cross. But regardless of how strongly they feel it, they carry that cross, to the extent that they believe in the rightness of their deeds (cause). Their cause is truly righteous, and to such an extent that if they did not fulfill it, if they did not assume the burden of the rock or death, if they stopped and reconciled themselves then in that case there would be no justification for them either on earth or in heaven.[22]

Gippius stops just short of asserting that because their cause is righteous, it would be a sin for the revolutionary terrorist to abandon it. This leads to her paradoxical conclusion that violence is not right, but justified (*ne pravo, no opravdano!*), and to her equally paradoxical parting salvo, "One must not spill blood, it's impossible. But in order for that impossibility to become real, it's imperative [to spill blood]!"[23]

The Byronic Moment

In fact, the Merezhkovskys' unconsciously Christian terrorist is recognizably cast in the mold of the Dostoevskian "great sinners," Raskolnikov, Stavrogin, and Ivan Karamazov, who in negating the existence of God and conventional morality commit crimes and are subsequently tormented by their guilt in the form of terrifying visions precisely because they remain devout in "the deep and mute part of their soul[s]." The monastery "confession scenes" in both *Demons* and *The Brothers Karamazov* stage an encounter between this antihero and Dostoevsky's embodiments of holiness, who expose the antihero's self-deception and compassionately call him to a new life. This new life, however, involves the overcoming of romantic individualism by self-humbling and expiation, which the antihero usually rejects and thereafter meets his doom. The confrontation between the apotheosis of individualism and spiritual authority is Dostoevsky's greatest debt to Byron, and "the refusal of confession" is the central scene of self-revelation/rebellion in Byron's 1813 orientalist poem, "The Giaour."[24]

Dostoevsky's attitude to Byron evolved throughout his career from a rather dismissive treatment to a tacit acknowledgment of Byronism as the cornerstone of his novelistic art. His early mentions of Byron(ism) emphasize personal egoism, aristocratic hauteur, and melancholy—in other words, the qualities of the Byronic hero that the romantic-era poets embraced (at first imitatively and then ironically) as they "overcame" romanticism and the Byronic apprenticeship that it implied.[25]

Dostoevsky thus begins with the inherited cliché and through fictional iterations restores to it an unprecedented psychological complexity and literary power.[26] While he erases from the text of *Demons* (1870) explicit reference to Nikolai Stavrogin's Byronic pedigree, Stavrogin is Dostoevsky's resuscitation of the cliché: his is the magnetic emptiness of "hopeless egoism" beneath an aristocratic exterior.[27] But only in December 1877, as he embarked on the writing of *The Brothers Karamazov,* did Dostoevsky definitively restore to Byron what had been taken away and exalt him as the reigning genius of the revolutionary age.

> And first of all, one shouldn't use the word "Byronist" as an invective. Byronism, though a momentary phenomenon, was a great, sacred and necessary one in the life of European mankind and, perhaps, in that of the entire human race. Byronism appeared at a moment of dreadful

> anguish, disillusionment and almost despair among men. Following the ecstatic transports of the new creed in the new ideals proclaimed at the end of the last century in France, then the most progressive nation of European mankind, the outcome was very different from what had been expected; this so deceived the faith of man that there has never perhaps been a sadder moment in the history of Western Europe. The new idols—raised for one moment only—fell not only as a result of external (political) causes, but because of their intrinsic bankruptcy—which was clearly perceived by the sagacious hearts and the progressive minds. The new outcome was not yet in sight; the new valve [*klapan*] was not yet revealed, and everybody was suffocating under the weight of a former world, which drew and narrowed itself down over mankind in a most dreadful manner. The old idols lay shattered.
>
> It was at that moment that a great and mighty genius, a passionate poet, appeared. In his melodies there sounded mankind's anguish of those days, its gloomy disillusionment in its mission and in the ideals which had deceived it. It was a novel, then unheard-of, muse of vengeance and Sorrow, malediction and despair. The spirit of Byronism, as it were, swept mankind as a whole, and everything responded to it.[28]

The Byronic moment is a tormenting in-between time when history stops, an agonizing caesura after the corrupt old and the false new worlds. In this "perhaps saddest moment" in the history of Western Europe, its genius channels a complex of virulent human emotions paired to action, which resonates and is imitated everywhere.

Perhaps because its pettiness impinges on the sublimity of his metanarrative, or because its paired action is most likely *inaction,* Dostoevsky doesn't mention boredom. Or perhaps boredom is implied in the deadly sin of despair (acedia) and is the necessary consequence of an in-between time without ideals to authorize action. Byronic boredom may manifest itself as social and trivial, or as existential and fatal (ennui). For Byronic knockoffs, boredom is something of a fashion accessory, the equivalent of white gloves worn to signal a privileged aloofness from life. But when it seeps into the skin, degrades, and recombines with other negative emotions, it unlooses mischief and tragedy that may ruffle those solipsistic selves embalmed in boredom.

It is important to underscore Dostoevsky's attitude toward Byronism as he defines it: he exalts it as "great, *sacred* [italics mine], and necessary," and goes so far as to criticize Mikhail Lermontov, perhaps the ultimate Russian Byronist, for reacting Byronically to his own Byronism:

> Of course, Lermontov was a Byronist, but because of his great and original poetic power he was a peculiar Byronist—some kind of sarcastic, capricious, surly Byronist, perpetually distrusting his own inspiration, his own Byronism. But if he had stopped fussing about the personality of the educated Russian tormented by his Europeanism, no doubt he would, just like Pushkin, have found the solution in the worship of the people's truth.[29]

Russian Byronism as a cultural (as well as temporal) in-betweenness is understandably uncomfortable, but once the fussing is done, one need simply imitate Dostoevsky's Pushkin and embrace a populist Christianity. Note that it is Dostoevsky who establishes these two poles of modern Russian culture, with the latter as the antidote to the former.

Dostoevsky makes the road sound easier—and shorter—than he knows it is; in fact, he goes on to identify Byronism as the wellspring of Russian poetry, especially of Nikolai Nekrasov's agonized civic poetry. If we situate Dostoevsky in his own metanarrative, his novels may be viewed as allegories that portray both the intrinsic bankruptcy of the "new idols" *and* the impossibility of the old world. His heroes are doomed to flounder in darkness and negation unless they embrace the "people's truth." Dostoevsky's Byronic creations suggest that the Byronic moment was a protracted one indeed, as the revolutionary era was bound to produce a succession of disillusioned heroes marooned between bankrupt new idols and the desacralized old world.[30]

While Dostoevsky had portrayed this malaise in his novels of the 1860s (in the wake of the disappointment following the Great Reforms) and 1870s, in the aftermath of 1905 Gippius perceived a similar crisis afflicting the actual revolutionary celebrities whose acquaintance she avidly cultivated in Paris. Thirty years after the fact, she still recalled the adolescent thrill of meeting the leader of the SR Combat Organization, Savinkov—a thrill that testifies to the charisma of terrorism more generally. "To know that there were and are somewhere terrorists—is one thing, but to see with one's own eyes, in one's own room the chief of the Combat Organization, who had prepared and carried out several murders almost yesterday—that's completely another thing."[31] With his keen understanding of Byronism, Dostoevsky anticipated Gippius's woozy fascination with Savinkov in his description of the "ladies'" reaction to Stavrogin: "Some were especially fascinated by the possibility of some fatal mystery in his soul; others positively liked his being a killer."[32]

Accompanied by the SR Ilya Fondaminsky, who had become acquainted with the Merezhkovskys in 1905, Savinkov indeed presented himself to the writing couple as possessing a "fatal mystery" in his soul, and he sought Dmitry Merezhkovsky's counsel and his definitive condemnation or benediction. Gippius's brief notation in her diary records Savinkov's confession to the writing couple: "The primary difficulty was that Savinkov felt that he himself was killed, in killing. He said that the blood of the murdered crushed him with its weight."[33] It is this intimate but clichéd scene of confession to Merezhkovsky, who had assumed the role of the Christian "elder" vis-à-vis socialist revolution, that Gippius describes in her article "Revolution and Violence." Clearly, Savinkov was the unnamed terrorist leader of Gippius's anecdote, and the shrouded specter was Savinkov's friend from childhood, Ivan Kaliaev, the assassin of the Grand Duke Sergei, who died on the scaffold without betraying his comrades. Disillusioned in his "idols," guilt-ridden for his crimes, yet unregenerate, Savinkov appeared to the writing couple as a Dostoevskian incarnation whose Byronic pedigree went temporarily undetected.

While Gippius later claimed that the couple's goal was to "drag Savinkov out of terror,"[34] her writings from this period suggest that, on the contrary, it was imperative that Savinkov remain a terrorist in order to incarnate the myth currently under construction—the more so as Savinkov appeared to be the aesthetically congenial embodiment of their religious-political ideas.[35] As a matter of fact, Savinkov brought with him not one myth, but two "polar" myths. The first was Savinkov's own—his inimitable aspect as the revolutionary aesthete, a dandyish decadent and Dostoevskian "great sinner." With Zosima's perspicacity but with her own snobbism, Gippius discerned Savinkov's duality, or, as she later put it, "the battle of spirits in that strong, powerful individual."[36] Gippius's later recollection preserves the titillating dark romanticism of Savinkov's initial impression: "He was a member of the Combat Organization, a man with a dark biography. He had the blood of many upon his soul."[37]

The second myth was that of the "ideal terrorist" as the Merezhkovskys conceived him or her: a terrorist who exemplified Christian virtues of humility and love and whose complete self-abnegation and self-sacrifice was unconsciously a Christian deed of heroic martyrdom (*podvig*).[38] Ivan Kaliaev was the unwilling embodiment of this second myth. In the two months between Kaliaev's arrest in February 1905 and his execution in April, the mass-circulation press had energetically promulgated an image of Kaliaev as a repentant (i.e., Christian) terrorist, an image that Kaliaev sought with equal energy to refute. Following the lead of Savinkov's contemporaries, scholars have frequently assumed that Ivan Kaliaev served as the prototype for Vanya, Savinkov's Christian terrorist in *The Pale Steed*.[39] By positing such a one-to-one correspondence, however, they have unwittingly subscribed to the press's Kaliaev myth while overlooking Vanya's purely literary origins. Vanya is better understood as the Merezhkovskys' mythical Christian terrorist, and in *The Pale Steed,* these polar myths of the revolutionary terrorist—the Christian and the Byronic—square off in reciprocal unmaskings.

Pro and Contra

The Pale Steed is in fact replete with Dostoevskian allusions and subtexts, and it is Savinkov's appropriation of Dostoevsky, particularly for his treatment of terrorism as a religious-philosophical problem, that partly redeems the novella's flimsy boulevard plot. *The Pale Steed* presents itself as the diary of "George," the leader of the terrorist conspiracy to assassinate "the Governor." When George is not overseeing his subordinates, Vanya, Genrikh, Fyodor, and Erna, in their preparations for the assassination, he is dallying with his emotionally fragile comrade, Erna, wooing a married woman, Elena, and nurturing a murderous hatred for her husband, an unnamed tsarist officer. Savinkov somewhat artlessly grafts his dialogues about terrorism and Christianity onto these parallel plots of illicit love and terrorist conspiracy.

Like *The Brothers Karamazov, The Pale Steed* approaches the question of violence as ultimately a question of faith, and follows Dostoevsky in exploring the nexus of faith, love, miracle, and violence through a (non)dialogue between the novella's polar heroes, George and Vanya. Merezhkovsky immediately noted the Karamazovian intertext and proclaimed George and Vanya "the incarnation of the same spirit, two sides of one face—as though the Ivan and Alyosha of the Russian Revolution."[40] In imposing this dichotomy on Savinkov's text, Merezhkovsky missed the point: in Vanya's voice we hear echoes of Alyosha *and* Ivan, the elder Zosima *and* the Grand Inquisitor. Vanya is an incarnation par excellence of Dostoevskian duality, and he conducts his dispute as much with himself as with his ostensible interlocutor, George.

Vanya explains the practice of revolutionary terrorism to George as the choice between two paths: the path of Christ, and Ivan Karamazov's moral philosophy distilled to the catchphrase "everything is permitted," which leads to Smerdyakov, Ivan's unsavory half brother, who puts his moral philosophy into murderous practice. Vanya implies that he has embraced the first while George has opted for the latter. For Vanya, however, the path to Christ does not preclude Smerdyakovian means (murder); instead, the great love of the Christian requires that he sacrifice his soul by committing the sin of murder: "But remember, there is no greater love than to lay down your soul for your brothers. Not your life, but your soul. Understand, you need to accept the suffering of the cross, and decide upon everything for love and out of love."[41] In other words, "everything is permitted" out of love for one's fellowmen. But Vanya readily admits that he is lacking in love ("there is little love in me"); therefore, Vanya's path to Christ leads in fact to Smerdyakov.

In Vanya, Savinkov fuses the religious-philosophical discourse of the Merezhkovskys to that of Dostoevsky's characters. Vanya's idea that "there is no greater love than to lay down one's soul for his fellow men" distinctly echoes Dostoevsky's Grand Inquisitor's contention that he and his fellow inquisitors have in essence laid down their souls for "thousands of millions" of their fellowmen's happiness. However, the Grand Inquisitor has no delusions about the implications of this act, and in his tête-à-tête with Christ he taunts him with his true affiliation: "We are not with you, but with him [i.e., Satan], that is our secret!"[42] While the Grand Inquisitor's declaration "we are not with you, but with him!" is an arrogant declaration of rebellion, Vanya's echo displays humility tainted with a touch of Smerdykovian presumption: "I am not worthy to be with him, for I am covered with dirt and blood. But Christ, in his infinite mercy, will be with me."[43]

Vanya's insistence that love distinguishes the path to Christ from the path to Smerdyakov and is sufficient to redeem sin recalls the elder Zosima's assurance to the penitent woman who had murdered her abusive husband that "with love, everything is bought, everything is saved."[44] Yet as the dialogue between Vanya and George progresses, Vanya confesses that it is his inability to love and his imperfect faith that lead him to resort to violence. Vanya sees revolutionary violence paradoxically as both his cross to bear and indicative of a lack of faith and weakness. His negative characterization of his fellow terrorists ("We are poor in faith and weak, like children, that is why we raise the sword. Not from our strength do we raise it, but from terror and weakness") echoes the Grand Inquisitor's cynical assessment of mankind, and his prescription of miracle, mystery, and authority.[45] As did Dostoevsky in the legend of the Grand Inquisitor and in *The Brothers Karamazov* more generally, Savinkov in *The Pale Steed* associates violence and miracle, and suggests that both are indicative of weakness, of a lack of faith. The Grand Inquisitor openly acknowledges miracle as a form of coercive trickery akin to violence and therefore antithetical to freedom: miracle in fact deprives man of freedom, which is the precondition of faith.

In *The Pale Steed,* before Vanya departs to assassinate the governor, he lingers on the miracles of Christ recounted in the Gospels, as if to spur himself and George to faith in Christ and as a final admission of his lack of faith. After he has performed his pseudo-miracle—the murder of the governor—and awaits his execution in prison, Vanya becomes more acutely aware of his own shortfall in love and faith. He realizes that he cannot live up to his (i.e., Zosima's) ideal of active love, but that the alternative of a sacrificial death still remains. "But I didn't find within myself the strength to *live* in the name of love, and understood, that I can and should *die* in its name."[46] Vanya, then, is not the "Alyosha of the Russian Revolution" but represents the clear defeat of Alyosha by Ivan, of faith in Christ by lack of faith in both Christ *and* the revolution, of love for individual men by "love for mankind."

Although Vanya has been most often identified as the fictionalized version of Ivan Kaliaev, the SR terrorist Egor Sazonov, the assassin of von Plehve, played a role in the character's genesis. In the winter of 1907–8 Savinkov conducted parallel dialogues with the Merezhkovskys and his imprisoned comrade.[47] If there remains any doubt whether Dostoevsky was read and relevant to active terrorists, it can be dispelled by Savinkov's and Sazonov's use of Ivan Karamazov's formulation of the question:

> Tell me straight out, I call on you—answer me: imagine that you yourself are building the edifice of human destiny with the object of making people happy in the finale, of giving them peace and rest at last, but that you must inevitably and unavoidably torture just one tiny creature, that same child who was beating her chest with her little fist, and raise your edifice on the foundation of her unrequited tears—would you agree to be the architect on such conditions?[48]

Sazonov agreed to this condition, maintaining that he had murdered von Plehve (a far cry from a "tiny creature") above all out of love. "I have love, love for the goal, there is the goal of acting in the name of love, even if it means sinning" (a far cry from love for a real person).[49] Savinkov, on the other hand, refused the proposition and concurred with Dostoevsky that love for those "far away" is often accompanied by hatred for those who are near.[50] Savinkov insisted to Sazonov that hatred, not love, was the basis of revolutionary terror, and he incarnated this idea in his Byronic literary persona, George.

A Terrorist of Our Time

It was not Vanya who raised the hackles of left-wing critics. Despite his peculiar "mysticism," Vanya's impassioned idealism and self-sacrifice were consonant with the mythology of heroic terrorism. The diarist George, on the other hand, was an abomination: not only did his ennui and cynicism cast an oppressive pall over the novella, but his position as "leader" of the terrorist brigade defiled the revolutionary movement. Savinkov's choices in this regard are interesting. He selected the intimate confessional and supremely subjective form of the diary with its first-person narration, and he cast the diarist George O'Brien (in the von Plehve assassination Savinkov had assumed the identity of a dapper British businessman, Arthur MacCullogh)[51] in *his* role, as the leader of the terrorist conspiracy. Although he ridiculed as "idiots" those readers and critics who confused the hero of the novel with its author, it is clear that Savinkov was, if not courting identification with his hero, then eschewing sensible measures to avoid it.[52]

In her extended epistolary criticism of the novel while it was still a work in progress, Gippius detected and sought to forestall with her advice the conflation of hero and author:

> Yes, an individual who understands everything, but only understands,—that's the true "hero of our time," the hero of a novel that is worth writing right now. But note: I'm not talking about the hero of life, but the hero of the novel. . . . The author should be higher than his hero and know even just a drop more than he. Be above him, master him. Remember that; you understand that perfectly. I emphasize it only because your task is made more difficult by the form you have chosen—first person narration—multiplies the danger of parity with the hero.[53]

Gippius homes in on the key relationships that defined (Russian) Byronism: the relationship of the hero to his time and the relationship of the author to his hero. The relationship between the author, Savinkov-Ropshin, and his hero George is not one of complete coincidence; rather, George O'Brien (a clear rhyme with George, Lord Byron) is to Savinkov as Childe Harold—and even more so, the Giaour—is to George Gordon, Lord Byron, and Pechorin is to his creator, Mikhail Lermontov. Savinkov endowed George with his own aspect (*oblik*), that of a revolutionary aesthete, renegade, and apostate from his revolutionary faith, and darkened the colors somewhat by depriving George of Savinkov's own irony and sense of humor.[54] À la Byron, Savinkov played hide-and-seek with his public (including his wife!) by filling a confessional genre with substance that seemed tantalizingly autobiographical, and then chaffed his audience for their naïveté, insisting that everything "was invented" but adding enigmatically that "it was invented as it could have been."[55]

Even more important for understanding the common underpinning of Savinkov's and George's Byronism is Gippius's designation of George as a "hero of our time." For Gippius, the "hero" of the period after the failed 1905 revolution (the *bezvremen'e*—literally "without time" and connoting a period of stagnation) was a hero of consciousness who was unable or unwilling to act upon this consciousness and who, moreover, acted deliberately against this consciousness. This dissonance between consciousness and action is the defining trait that Savinkov shared with his hero, George. The dissonance results because Savinkov's George is a hero of "the without time," another in-between time. His consciousness is shaped by disillusionment in old idols and new; his action—by Byronic boredom. What confused Savinkov's contemporary readers, as well as subsequent ones, is that George is actually an untimely hero, an anachronism, the jaded consciousness of 1907–8 superimposed on the fervor of 1905.

While critics and scholars have marveled at George as a "terrorist of a new type" (cold, efficient, professional), George's scandalous newness is replete with decadent behaviors. He is a Don Juan who beds and cruelly spurns his comrade Erna, loiters outside the building of his "Beautiful Lady," Elena, and haunts the urban spaces of Moscow and Petersburg—the café, the pub, the theater, and the public masquerade—like a Baudelairean flaneur, though on the knife's edge of police surveillance and arrest. Ostensibly a "man of action," George is striking for his lassitude and for his aestheticism. Although he is primus inter pares of the terrorist conspiracy, George is conspicuously inutile, especially compared to his comrades engaged in the arduous street work of surveillance and the perilous task of preparing the bombs. George is a laconic Nechaevist, but a notably bored and unconvinced one who bewails his incurable alienation and ennui by interweaving revolutionary cant with Revelation, decadent poetry, and cynicism.[56]

> I have become accustomed to illegal life. Accustomed to loneliness. I don't want to know the future. I try to forget about the past. I don't have a homeland, a name, or family. I say to myself:
>
> > Un grand sommeil noir
> > Tombe sur ma vie,
> > Dormez, tout espoir,
> > Dormez, toute envie.
>
> But after all, hope doesn't die. Hope in what? In "the morning star?"[57] I know: if we killed yesterday, we will kill today, and inevitably we will kill tomorrow. "And the third angel poured out his bowl upon the rivers and the fountains of waters; and they became blood."[58] Well,

> you don't wash out blood with water or burn it off with fire. With it [blood]—to the Grave.
>
> Je ne vois plus rien,
> Je perds la mémoire
> Du mal et du bien.
> Ô, la triste histoire!
>
> Happy is he who believes in the resurrection of Christ, in the resurrection of Lazarus. Happy is also he who believes in socialism, in the approaching heaven on earth. But these old fairy tales seem ridiculous to me, and fifteen *desiatins* of earth don't attract me. I said: I don't want to be a slave. Can my freedom really lie therein? What pitiful freedom. . . . And why do I need it? In the name of what do I kill? In the name of blood, for blood? . . .
>
> Je suis un berceau,
> Qu'une main balance
> Au creux d'un caveau
> Silence, silence . . .[59]

Here the novella fairly reeks "of dynamite with apocalyptical incense." We may also recognize the voice of "vengeance and Sorrow, malediction and despair" rendered in the Silver Age's most fashionable idioms. Even George's questioning seems less an expression of true existential angst and more a self-consciously struck pose, capped by the woeful silence of Paul Verlaine's "Un grand sommeil noir."[60]

Uniting the revolutionary (the prematurely dead man), the apocalyptical prophet, and the poète maudit is death and damnation. George knows that he is a damned spirit and a vampire (like Byron's Giaour) who kills not for ideas but "in the name of blood, for blood." It is Vanya, in fact, who unmasks George not as the avenging angel of the apocalypse but as a vampire, and prophesies George's fate in the words of St. John the Divine:

> "In those days people will seek death, but not find her, wish to die, but death will run from them."[61] Tell me what is more terrifying than if death runs from you when you seek it? And you will seek it. How do you spill blood? How do you break the law? . . . You are lawless, and blood for you is—water. But listen to me, listen to me: there will come a day, remember these words. You will seek the end, and not find it.[62]

Vanya's prophecy is indistinguishable from a curse and foreshadows George's inevitable doom. As for a vampire, amorous involvement and terror—the novella's sanguinary parallel plots—are the two activities that sustain George in his spiritual torpor. But even they would not be sufficiently compelling without obstacles to whet George's appetite. At first, George is both ideologically and personally indifferent toward the target of the terrorist conspiracy, the governor. When the conspirators' first attempt is thwarted by happenstance, George's nonchalance turns to hatred, which he projects onto his rival: "Our first failure gave birth in me to malice, and malice possesses me. I live inseparably from him, with the governor. At night I don't shut an eye: I whisper his name, in the morning,—my first thought is of him. There he is, the gray old man, with the pale smile on his bloodless lips. He despises us."[63] George's obsessive hatred is indistinguishable from obsessive love, and fuses him to his rival ("I live inseparably from him").

This pattern repeats itself with his mistress, Elena. At first George is indifferent to the fact that she is married, but gradually the husband, while offering no practical impediment to their liaison, becomes an intolerable rival. Although the terrorist brigade has by this time succeeded in assassinating the governor, in his obsessive hatred George conflates his political rival, the dead governor, with his romantic rival. Realizing that the sight of his lover's husband evokes the same reaction (hatred) in him as did the sight of the governor, George exclaims, "The Governor is still alive!" He is "haunted" not by guilt but by hatred provoked by his rival.[64]

Ultimately, George murders his beloved's husband in a cross between the ritualized violence of the duel and political assassination. George's shot results in an unexpected casualty: his love for Elena. Once his rival has been eliminated, so has his love. Without rivalrous hatred to stimulate desire, the boredom and indifference return. Savinkov has lifted this Byronic template of a fatal end to mimetic desire directly from Lermontov's *Hero of Our Time*, where Pechorin's love for Princess Mary evaporates as soon as he kills his rival for her affections in a duel.

After Vanya is executed and George has murdered his paramour's husband, he experiences an epiphany: "Christ said: 'Thou shalt not kill,' and His apostle Peter unsheathed his sword to kill. Christ said: 'Love one another', and Judas betrayed him. Christ said: 'I came not to judge, but to save,' and was condemned. And now Peter still is unsheathing his sword, Annas is judging with Caiaphas, and Simonov. And Christ is still being crucified."[65] George has ears to hear and eyes to see: he recognizes that despite two thousand years of the preaching of the kingdom of God, the world *still* remains in thrall to violence, and that this universal thrall obliterates the distinction between the two "camps"—the revolutionary Peters who unsheathe their swords and the reactionary judges (Annas and Caiaphas) who sentence to death. The repetition of the word "still" suggests a lack of historical progression, a stasis that is entirely in keeping with the "without time" of the *bezvremen'e.*

As does Smerdyakov vis-à-vis Ivan's "everything is permitted," George exposes the self-deception in Vanya's "everything is permitted in the name of love" and the fraudulent mythology spun from this premise. Violence, he avers, cannot end violence, or engender mythical "others," purified ones capable of the complete renunciation of violence, as Vanya believed. There is no difference between murder for one's own ends and murder for the good of humankind, between butchery committed by so-called savages and the equally savage butchery committed by the so-called civilized. The deed is the same, and only words endow it with or deny to it moral legitimacy. Savinkov, via George, therefore does not condemn revolutionary terrorism alone, but in the spirit of Tolstoyanism condemns all violence as evil and incompatible with Christianity.[66] The double irony is that the condemnation is issued by the atheist, George, and flouted by his creator, Savinkov.

The Fifth Act

Ultimately, George's apparent repudiation of terror at the end of the novella marks not a rejection of violence-death but a rejection of life, as he shuns solidarity with his fellow human beings. Virtuosic violence in which he takes the pride of a master craftsman is his means of distinction. "People are boring to me, their life. Between me and them—is a border. There are sacred borders. My border is the scarlet sword."[67] But terrorism and illicit love, both fueled by rivalrous hatred, prove a poor antidote to boredom. Forsaking both solidarity with people (earth) and faith in God (heaven), George sees his life of political and moral rebellion as puppet booth theater (*balagan*):[68]

> Here is the puppet booth theater. The curtain rises: we are on stage. Pale Pierrot has fallen in love with Pierretta. He swears eternal love. Pierretta has a fiancé. A toy pistol fires, blood flows—red cranberry juice. The barrel organ screeches behind the backdrop. Curtain. Number Two: the manhunt. He—wears a hat with a cock's feather, the admiral of the Swiss Fleet. We are in red cloaks and masks. With us is Rinaldo di Rinaldini. The carabinieri chase us, but can't catch us. Again the pistol fires, the barrel organ screeches. Curtain. . . . I am bored. Days again fly after days. The barrel organ screeches behind the

> scenes, and Pierrot saves himself by flight. Come on in—the puppet booth theater is open.[69]

The poet Alexander Blok's lyrical drama *Balaganchik* (1906), which scandalized its audience by presenting *balagan* as a metaphor for life, may have had particular relevance for Savinkov in 1908. His superior in the Combat Organization, Evno Azef, had just been conclusively unmasked as a double agent and appeared to his former comrades as a diabolical puppeteer. But no such unmasking figures in the plot of *The Pale Steed,* at least not explicitly. The metaphor of *balagan* floats like a corpse to the surface of the turgid waters of George's boredom.

The assertion that life is *balagan* is a form of metaphysical rebellion and despair that is more severe and debased than Ivan Karamazov's. Whereas Ivan, in expressing his intention to return his ticket to the inexplicable tragedy that is life, is oppressed precisely by his acute sense of sin, the suffering it engenders, and his need for a redeemer, George is troubled neither by sin nor by suffering, nor indeed by any of the sociopolitical questions related to revolutionary terrorism. George is concerned solely with himself and with the maximal assertion of his identity as a "free man" by means of violence. When he realizes that violence, far from being a means of distinction and liberation, is always the same, the identity he has founded on violence collapses. The metaphor of *balagan* as the ultimate expression of George's cynicism allows him at least to still maintain an aloof superiority over the life he despises because it is boring.

George's rebellion reveals itself as the tyranny of boredom in another guise, and his well-conditioned reflex is to rebel against his rebellion. "I will leave the boring *balagan.*" Inadvertently falling back on the equation freedom = violence, George seeks to demonstrate his own freedom not through murder but suicide. The irony is that George does not recognize the violence of suicide as the same futile, boring repetition. George accepts that life is theater but insists on playing the hero of a romantic-era tragedy, rather than being a mere puppet in a *balagan.* Of course, the diary form presents a technical difficulty in the staging of the supremely important fifth act. George cannot perform the finale (his suicide) for his audience, he can only rehearse it: "When the stars come out and the autumn night descends, I will say my final words: 'My revolver is with me.'"[70] George's parting shot is a restatement of his rebellion: Christ is not with him, but his gun is. The novella ends not with George's suicide but with his pseudo-suicide, not with a deed but with words and a pose. In contrast to the ignominious suicides that Dostoevsky allots his rebellious antiheroes, Stavrogin, Kirillov, and Smerdyakov, Savinkov notably permits George his heroic pose.

Like its hero, *The Pale Steed* defies. It resists the reader's attempts to derive any pat moral, philosophical, or narrative satisfaction. Meaning, like George's death, is deferred beyond the bounds of the novel. George sees everything in terms of polarities, but he doesn't know which term of the dichotomy is "true," and he denies the possibility of knowing. "So it is now. There are no features, no end and no beginning. Vaudeville or drama? Cranberry juice or blood? *Balagan* or life? I don't know. Who knows?"[71] George's bravado masks the terrifying nature of his condition—his radical epistemological, ontological, and moral disorientation. George can neither affirm nor deny, he rejects both his own and others' authority, and even his most profound insight regarding the illegitimacy of all violence is just another act of rebellion—another ripple in his boredom—rather than a moment of transformation.

As the Silver Age of revolutionary terrorism succeeded the Golden Age of the People's Will, Savinkov understood that the terrorist had come to exist as a literary construct in the Russian cultural imagination. While naive readers, as well as readers who should have known better, praised Savinkov's terrorist fictions as incarnating "real reality,"[72] Savinkov and his fictions were in fact saturated with literariness. His opportunistic appropriation and easy mastery of forms enabled Savinkov to create the terrorist's life as a work of art, to pour himself into inherited literary forms, and to incarnate his culture's most salient myths. Of these, Byronism was compatible with Savinkov's romantic individualism and, more important, congenial to his sensibility after the failure of the 1905 revolution and the eventual collapse of the SR Combat Organization.[73] Dostoevsky had explained why: the new idols of the revolution proved themselves fraudulent while the old world was impossible.

Notes

The epigraph to this essay is from George Gordon, Lord Byron, "The Giaour," in *Three Oriental Tales,* ed. Alan Richardson (Boston: Houghton Mifflin, 2002).

1. The Combat Organization of the Socialist Revolutionary (SR) Party was founded by Grigory Gershuni in 1902. The SRs were a conglomeration of populist groups that viewed themselves as heirs to the People's Will (Narodnaia volia) and formally embraced terrorist tactics as a revolutionary means. The conspiratorial Combat Organization operated largely independently from the SR Central Committee, and its membership was an exclusive group that never lacked for recruits to replace fallen comrades. For details on the membership of the Combat Organization and Kaliaev's assassination of the Grand Duke Sergei, see Boris Savinkov, *Memoirs of a Terrorist,* trans. Joseph Shaplen (New York: Albert and Charles Boni, 1931). See also Richard B. Spence, *Boris Savinkov: Renegade on the Left* (New York: Columbia University Press, 1991). For an account of the "epidemic of terrorism" that swept over Russia in the

early twentieth century, see Anna Geifman, *Thou Shalt Kill: Revolutionary Terrorism in Russia, 1894–1917* (Princeton: Princeton University Press, 1993). For a history of the SR Party in particular, see Manfred Hildemeier, *The Russian Socialist Revolutionary Party Before the First World War* (New York: St. Martin's Press, 2000).

2. Dmitrii Merezhkovskii, "Kon' blednyi," in *Bol'naia Rossiia* (Leningrad: Izdatel'stvo Leningradskogo universiteta, 1991), 124, 126.

3. Alexander Amfiteatrov, "Kon' blednyi," in *Mutnye dni,* vol. 15 of his *Sobranie sochinenii* (St. Petersburg: Prosveshchenie, 1912), 12.

4. The People's Will was formed after the schism of the revolutionary group Land and Freedom (Zemlia i volia) in 1879 with the express purpose of carrying out systematic acts of terrorism directed against tsarist officials. Their ultimate target was Tsar Alexander II himself, and after a succession of failed attempts, they achieved their goal on March 1, 1881. The five conspirators were swiftly caught up in the police dragnet and executed on April 3, 1881. Subsequently, through the concerted action of police chief Sudeikin and his agent, Sergei Degaev, the remnants of the organization were destroyed. The classic histories of the revolutionary movement and the People's Will are Franco Venturi's *Roots of Revolution: A History of the Populist and Socialist Movements in Nineteenth Century Russia,* trans. Francis Haskell (New York: Knopf, 1960); Adam B. Ulam, *In the Name of the People: Prophets and Conspirators in Pre revolutionary Russia* (New York: Viking, 1977); Richard Wortman, *The Crisis of Russian Populism* (London: Cambridge University Press, 1967); Deborah Hardy, *Land and Freedom: The Origins of Russian Terrorism, 1876–1879* (Westport, Conn.: Greenwood Press, 1987); and Norman Naimark, *Terrorists and Social Democrats: The Russian Revolutionary Movement Under Alexander III* (Cambridge, Mass.: Harvard University Press, 1983).

5. Savinkov's archive is located in the State Archive of the Russian Federation (GARF), and his saved newspapers clippings can be found in f. 5831, op. 2, d. 374.

6. In April 1909 a group of formerly Marxist intellectuals and religious thinkers published a collection of articles entitled *Landmarks* that took the radical and liberal Left to task for privileging external, material, and social change over the individual's moral and spiritual development, and bewailed the direction in which the Left was taking the country. The liberal intelligentsia and the press roundly abused the *Landmarks* authors as reactionaries. On the *Landmarks* controversy, see Christopher Read, *Religion, Revolution, and the Russian Intelligentsia, 1900–1912: The "Vekhi" Debate and Its Intellectual Background* (London: Macmillan, 1979), 141–61, and Marshall S. Schatz and Jane Burbank, introduction to Nikolai Berdiaev, Sergei Bulgakov, Semen Frank, Mikhail Gershenzon, A. S. Izgoev, Bogdan Kistiakovskii, Peter Struve, Marshall S. Shatz, and Judith E. Zimmerman, *Vekhi = Landmarks: A Collection of Articles About the Russian Intelligentsia,* ed. and trans. Marshall S. Schatz and Judith E. Zimmerman (Armonk, N.Y.: M. E. Sharp, 1994), xi–xxiv. Scholars who have situated their discussion of *The Pale Steed* in the context of this polemic include Marina Mogil'ner, "The Russian Radical Mythology (1881–1914): From Myth to History" (PhD. diss., Rutgers University, 2000), 146–76 (also published as *Mifologiia podpol'nogo cheloveka* [Moscow: Novoe literaturnoe obozrenie, 1999]); Aileen Kelly, "Intelligentsia Self-Censorship," in *Toward Another Shore: Russian Thinkers Between Necessity and Chance* (New Haven: Yale University Press, 1998); and Scott W. Palmer, "A Crisis of Faith: Boris Savinkov and the Fighting Organization (1903–1912)," *Scottish Slavonic Review* 18 (1992): 35–53. The most recent article to appear on *The Pale Steed* continues

to view the text through the lens of morality; see Daniel Beer's "The Morality of Terror: Contemporary Responses to Political Violence in Boris Savinkov's *The Pale Steed* (1909) and *What Never Happened* (1912)," *Slavonic and East European Review* 85 (2007): 25–46.

7. Spence, *Boris Savinkov,* 67–69.

8. The unmasking of Azef, the Central Committee's liaison between it and the ruggedly independent Combat Organization, culminated in national and international headlines in late January to early February 1909, but it had been under way in the SR Central Committee throughout the previous year. While the publication of *The Pale Steed* and Azef's unmasking were temporally almost coincidental, and thus would amplify each other's impact on the public imagination, this article makes it clear that *The Pale Steed* was written under a different inspiration—the literary and religious mentorship of the Merezhkovskys, dating back to 1907. Savinkov wrangles explicitly with the problem of *provokatsiia* (police provocation) in his 1912 novel, *To, chego ne bylo* (*That Which Never Happened*). On the Azef affair, see Boris Nicolaevsky's classic study, *Aseff, the Spy, Russian Terrorist and Police Stool* (Garden City, N.Y.: Doubleday, Doran and Co., 1934), recently republished as *Istoriia odnogo predatelia: Terroristy i politicheskaia politsiia* (Moscow: Vysshaia shkola, 1991); and Anna Geifman, *Entangled in Terror: The Azef Affair and the Russian Revolution* (Wilmington, Del.: SR Books, 2000). For a broader discussion of the internal agency of the tsarist secret police and police provocation, see Nurit Schleifman, *Undercover Agents in the Russian Revolutionary Movement: The SR Party, 1902–1917* (Basingstoke, Hampshire, Eng.: Macmillan, 1988), and Jonathan Daly, *Autocracy Under Siege: Security Police and Opposition in Russia, 1866–1905* (Dekalb: Northern Illinois University Press, 1998).

9. See Gippius's introduction to Savinkov's posthumously published poetry in Boris Savinkov, *Stikhotvoreniia* (Brussels, 1930), ix. Only recently has the Russian philologist E. I. Goncharova published a small part of the correspondence between Savinkov and the Trio (Zinaida Gippius, Dmitry Merezhkovsky, and Dmitry Filosofov) from Savinkov's personal archive at GARF, illuminating the religious-philosophical background of *The Pale Steed.* See E. I. Goncharova, "Pis'ma Z. Gippius k B. Savinkovu: 1908–1909 gody," *Russkaia literatura* 3 (2001): 126–62, and idem, "'Religioznaia obshchestvennost' i terror: Pis'ma D. Merezhkovskogo i Z. Gippius k Borisu Savinkovu (1908–1909)," *Russkaia literatura* 4 (2003): 140–61.

10. "By the time he had reached adolescence, Boris had been exposed to a rather wide range of literature, including the Russian masters (Dostoevsky, Gogol, and Pushkin were his favorites) as well as the works of Lord Byron, Alexandre Dumas, Victor Hugo, Mayne Reid, Sir Walter Scott, and Robert Louis Stevenson." Spence, *Boris Savinkov,* 8.

11. As Monika Greenleaf has explained, for Byronic imitators the attraction of the Byronic *poema* lay "not in creating a cast of three-dimensional, life-like characters in an independent narrative, but to the contrary, in devising a serial, a series of suppletive Byronic heroes incompletely differentiated from their author and his on-going biography." See Monika Greenleaf, "Pushkin's Byronic Apprenticeship: A Problem in Cultural Syncretism," *Russian Review* 53 (1994): 392.

12. *That Which Never Happened* (*To, chego ne bylo,* 1912) is an exception, since it may be characterized as a historical epic of 1905 with a third-person omniscient narrator instead of Savinkov's first-person narrator. Savinkov's fascinating biography

is beyond the scope of this essay, but a brief biographical sketch is in order. Born on January 19 (old style), 1879, Boris Savinkov was a scion of the nobility, the son of a military judge and the grandson of generals. After arrests, imprisonment, and exile in conjunction with his student revolutionary activity, in 1903 Savinkov embarked on a career as a professional terrorist in the elite SR Combat Organization.

After sending many of his comrades to death, however, Boris Savinkov outlived revolutionary terror, without himself ceasing to be a terrorist. The Combat Organization was disbanded in 1910 owing to organizational failure and the moral blow that terror had sustained as a result of the unmasking of a series of provocateurs in the SR party (foremost among them Azef) and the undermining of the heroic mythology, to which Savinkov's *The Pale Steed* had contributed.

The February 1917 revolution, however, opened Russia to contestants for "the morning star," and Savinkov vied at first successfully for center stage. Acting minister of war in Kerensky's government and, after the October coup, a self-anointed "General," Savinkov joined whoever was game (the Whites and then the anarchist "Greens") against the Reds, and energetically lobbied international leaders such as Churchill, Masaryk, Pilsudski, and Mussolini to collaborate in the fight against the Bolsheviks. After the civil war, the Soviet government considered Savinkov its most dangerous enemy, and in August 1924 the counterespionage arm of the GPU lured Savinkov back to the USSR on the pretext that he would take the lead of an anti-Soviet underground terrorist organization, "The Trust," in Moscow. Instead, Savinkov was arrested by the GPU the day after he crossed the Soviet border. When Savinkov, who had hitherto been the emigration's most notorious opponent of Bolshevism, declared fealty to the Soviet government during his trial before the Military Tribunal of the Supreme Court of the USSR on August 27, 1924, the émigré community was stunned by his traitorous complicity in the Bolshevik's propaganda coup. Less than a year later, on May 12, 1925, a brief notice in *Izvestiia* reported that Savinkov had committed suicide, plunging to his death from the fifth-floor window of his luxurious prison cell in the Lubyanka.

13. See Mogilner's chapter on Savinkov's *The Pale Steed* in her dissertation, "The Russian Radical Mythology," 146–76. Contemporaries perceived both Savinkov and his hero George as Nietzschean, and Mogilner adopts this characterization. Shocked readers from the revolutionary underground interpreted George as preaching the transcendence of morality and murder for personal as well as political aims. This is a profound misreading of *The Pale Steed.* See also Edith Clowes, *A Revolution in Moral Consciousness: Nietzsche in Russian Literature 1890–1914* (Dekalb: Northern Illinois University Press, 1988), 94. In her discussion of George's debased Nietzscheanism, Clowes notes that George confuses Nietzsche with Smerdyakov.

14. See also Fyodor Dostoevsky, *The Brothers Karamazov,* trans. Richard Pevear and Larissa Volokhonsky (New York: Farrar, Straus and Giroux, 1990), 67 (hereafter cited as *BK*). Unless otherwise noted, all translations are my own.

15. Margarita Pavlova, "Mucheniki velikogo religioznogo protsessa," in *Tsar' i revoliutsiia,* ed. M. A. Kolerova (Moscow: O.G.I., 1999), 45.

16. See Zinaida Gippius, "Revoliutsiia i nasilie," in Kolerova, *Tsar' i revoliutsiia,* 103–28.

17. For the Merezhkovskys' engagement with religious philosophical issues, see Read, *Religion, Revolution,* 13, 30; Bernice Glatzer Rosenthal, "From Decadence to

Religious Renewal: The Parallel Paths of Merezhkovsky and Ivanov," *Slavonic and East European Arts* 6 (1990): 33–55; and C. H. Bedford, "Dmitry Merezhkovsky, the Third Testament and the Third Humanity," *Slavic and East European Review* 42 (1964): 144–60.

18. See Goncharova, "Pis'ma Z. Gippius," 126.

19. Gippius, "Revoliutsiia i nasilie," 103, 108, 117.

20. In her essay in this volume, Donna Oliver shows how the desire for self-sacrifice, with its origins in the Russian Orthodox tradition of kenoticism, led many young idealists in the 1870s and 1880s to see service to the revolution as a Christian duty.

21. Gippius, "Revoliutsiia i nasilie," 120.

22. Ibid.

23. Ibid., 128. In the original Russian, Gippius's salvo reads, "No chtoby eta nevozmozhnost' stala real'noi, eto neobkhodimo!"

24. Through an accretion of multiperspectival fragments the story of the Giaour's tragic past is told: his beloved, Leila, had been the concubine of the local despot, Hassan. When the affair was discovered, the Giaour fled, while his mistress was meted the traditional punishment for female infidelity: she was sewn up in a sack and drowned. To avenge her death, the grief-stricken Giaour joins a band of Albanian freedom fighters, and under the pretext of "national liberation" murders Hassan. Subsequently he seeks sanctuary in a monastery, and though he bequeaths his substantial fortune to the monastery, he shuns the monks' devotions and haughtily refuses expiation and absolution. Meanwhile he is tormented by a vision of Hassan's severed hand, which lures him to commit suicide. Only at the end of the poem, in the Giaour's deathbed confession to the friar, is the reader vouchsafed more than a tantalizing glimpse of his forbidding mien. Yet his confession is not a plea for absolution but a rejection of heavenly paradise in favor of the earthly paradise of Leila's embrace.

25. See Hans Rothe, "Dostoevskij und Byron," in *Slavisches Spektrum: Festschrift für Maximilian Braun zum 80. Geburtstag,* ed. Reinhard Lauer and Brigitte Schultze (Wiesbaden: Harrassowitz, 1983), 352–69. Rothe notes that the matter of Byron's influence on Dostoevsky has been largely overlooked by the scholarship, and confines himself to tracing mentions of Byron in Dostoevsky's correspondence, novels, and journalism. For the supposed "overcoming of Byron," see Greenleaf, "Pushkin's Byronic Apprenticeship," 382–98. Greenleaf convincingly argues that Pushkin was in fact the author of the myth of his overcoming of Byron, which subsequent scholarship has uncritically repeated, and that he actually preserved and refined a number of Byron's more sophisticated narrative and authorial strategies. See also Dan Terkla, "Byron's Underground Manfred," *The Comparatist: Journal of the Southern Comparative Literature Association* 14 (1990): 5–14; O. N. Osmolovskii, "Dostoevskii i Bairon: K postanovke problemy," *Voprosy russkoi literatury* 29 (1977): 100–107.

26. But Byron's earliest reception in Russia was as a political incendiary, whose savage satire of Russia's most deserving and exalted targets was coveted contraband among the Decembrists and the like-minded. Spinning copy from his salacious escapades and active support of the Greek national liberation movement, Byron imposed his genteelly self-promoting presence on an international audience that was eager to consume his flouting of moral and political norms in serialized form. Such literary gigantism could not be lightly reckoned with, and the meta-literary plot line of Pushkin's great "novel in verse," *Evgenii Onegin,* follows the *poema*'s plot line: Pushkin the

author exposes, trivializes, and overcomes Byron, just as his heroine, Tatiana, exposes and overcomes Onegin.

27. In his notebook sketches he contemplates having the Prince (Stavrogin) "publicly denounced" as "a predator, a wild beast, Byron's Corsair, etc.: that to kill means nothing to him." Fyodor Dostoevsky, *The Notebooks for the Possessed,* ed. Edward Wasiolek, trans. Victor Terras (Chicago: University of Chicago Press, 1968), 207–8.

28. Fyodor Dostoevsky, *The Diary of a Writer,* trans. and annotated by Boris Brasol (Salt Lake City, Utah: Gibbs M. Smith, 1979), 939.

29. Ibid., 943.

30. Dostoevsky's defense of Byron was first conceived at Nekrasov's funeral, in rebuttal to a young heckler's assertion that "Nekrasov stands higher than Pushkin and Lermontov. They are only Byronists." See Leonid Grossman, *Dostoevsky: His Life and Work* (Indianapolis: Bobbs-Merill, 1975), 543.

31. Zinaida Gippius, *Dmitrii Merezhkovskii* (Paris: YMCA Press, 1951), 162.

32. Fyodor Dostoevsky, *Demons,* trans. Richard Pevear and Larissa Volokhonsky (New York: Vintage, 1994), 43.

33. Gippius, *Dmitrii Merezhkovskii,* 162.

34. Ibid., 163.

35. There is no exact date given for the Merezhkovskys' acquaintance with Savinkov. Memoiristic and textual evidence points to January–February 1907. From Gippius's own recollections, it seems clear that she wrote "On Violence" in the wake of her impressions of Savinkov. In her memoir, she recalls her introduction to Savinkov described above, and subsequently notes that "I suggested that I will write 'On Violence' based on some of our recent conversations." Gippius, *Dmitrii Merezhkovskii,* 162.

36. Temira Pachmuss, "Boris Savinkov v zhizni Zinaidy Gippius," *Pamiatniki kultury: Novye otkrytiya: Pis'mennost', Iskusstvo, Arkheologiia: Ezhegodnik* (1997), 106. Pachmuss does not give the date of this entry from Gippius's Warsaw diary, in which Gippius recalls the bizarre circumstances of her break with Savinkov in June 1920.

37. Gippius recorded her recollection in 1911 in a work entitled "About the Cause," which was intended as a history of the Trio's religious-political crusade. Reprinted in Temira Pachmuss, ed., *Between Paris and St. Petersburg: Selected Diaries of Zinaida Gippius* (Urbana: University of Illinois Press, 1975), 145.

38. Fondaminsky (who wrote under the pseudonym Bunakov) was Jewish, but he was amenable to the rabidly anti-Semitic couple because he was "completely unlike any other Jew, a most Christian person." Ibid.

39. See Mogil'ner, "The Russian Radical Mythology," 156. Victor Chernov, the leading SR theoretician, made this association public in his official party response to *The Pale Steed.*

40. Merezhkovskii, "Kon' blednyi," 129.

41. Boris Viktorovich Savinkov, *Izbrannoe* (Moscow: Novosti, 1990), 313. Mogil'ner notes that revolutionaries had transformed this biblical expression into a stock phrase. This common usage does not contradict my argument that Savinkov is consciously referring to Dostoevsky's Grand Inquisitor; in fact, it was Dostoevsky who first challenged this usage precisely by means of the Grand Inquisitor.

42. Dostoevsky, *BK,* 257.

43. Savinkov, *Izbrannoe,* 313. Smerdyakov exhibits just such presumption when he cynically argues that God (if he existed) would forgive his apostasy in the face of torture: "And so, why should I come out looking so specially to blame, if, seeing no

profit or reward either here or there, I at least keep my skin on? And therefore, trusting greatly in the mercy of God, I live in hopes that I'll be completely forgiven sir." Dostoevsky, *BK,* 131.

44. Dostoevsky, *BK,* 52.

45. Savinkov, *Izbrannoe,* 320.

46. Ibid., 356.

47. Goncharova, "Pis'ma Z. Gippius," 130.

48. Dostoevsky, *BK,* 245.

49. Goncharova, "Pis'ma Z. Gippius," 130.

50. Ibid., 131. Savinkov is superimposing Nietzsche's terms on Dostoevsky. See Edith Clowes's discussion of Ropshin's "misreading" of Nietzsche. Clowes, *Nietzsche,* 91.

51. Spence, *Boris Savinkov,* 36.

52. See Viktor Chernov, "Savinkov v riadakh P.S-R," *Volia Rossii* 14–15 (September 1924): 159, and his letter to his wife dated February 15, 1909, reprinted in Vera Glebovna Uspenskaia, "'Moi trud ne prinesët mne nichego, krome gorya': Iz perepiski B. V. Savinkova," *Istochnik* 4 (1995): 13.

53. Goncharova, "Pis'ma Z. Gippius," 164. In addition, Gippius chided Savinkov for being as enamored of George's paramour, Elena, as George himself was.

54. And also of what could be said to constitute Savinkov's scruples. In his *Memoir of a Terrorist,* Savinkov portrays himself as firmly and vocally opposed to the killing of innocent victims—the Grand Duchess Elizabeth Fyodorovna and the Grand Duke Paul's children, who accompanied the Grand Duke Sergei in his carriage at the time of Kaliaev's planned assassination. In the *Memoir* version, Kaliaev is less "fastidious" (Albert Camus referred to the members of the Combat Organization as "fastidious assassins") than Savinkov and is willing to kill the entire family if the organization should deem it necessary. See Boris Viktorovich Savinkov, *Vospominaniia terrorista* (Moscow: Moskovskii rabochii, 1990), 116. When Savinkov reprises this scene in *The Pale Steed,* Vanya abhors the taking of innocent lives, whereas George is nonchalantly amoral.

55. From a letter to his wife dated February 15, 1909, in "Moi trud," 16.

56. For an account of Sergei Nechaev's (1847–82) career as a notorious revolutionary and con artist and his role in the genesis of Dostoevsky's novel *Demons,* see the essay by Val Vinokur in this volume.

57. From the Spirit's address to the church in Thyatira in Revelation 2:26–28. "And he that overcometh, and keepeth my works unto the end, to him will I give power over the nations: And he shall rule them with a rod of iron; as the vessels of a potter shall they be broken to shivers: even as I received of my Father. And I will give him the morning star."

58. Revelation 16:4.

59. Savinkov, *Izbrannoe,* 312.

60. A comparison of Verlaine's poem with Byron's "The Giaour" reveals numerous similarities. In his confession to the friar, the Giaour admits, "Yet lurks a wish within my breast / For rest—but not to feel 'tis rest— // Soon shall my fate that wish fulfill; / And I shall sleep without the dream / Of what was, and would be still, // Dark as to thee my deeds may seem— / My memory now is but the tomb // Of joys long dead—my hope—their doom." Byron, *Three Oriental Tales,* 210.

61. Revelation 9:6.

62. Savinkov, *Izbrannoe,* 313.

63. Ibid., 341.

64. My analysis is indebted to Girard's theory of mimetic desire and notes the following typical elements: the necessity of the rival as the obstacle to stimulate desire, the rival as the double of the desiring subject; the symmetrical, duel-like structure of the violent contest, and the ultimate lack of satisfaction. See René Girard, *Deceit, Desire, and the Novel* (Baltimore: Johns Hopkins University Press, 1976).

65. Savinkov, *Izbrannoe,* 370.

66. A copy of *The Pale Steed* with Tolstoy's annotations is preserved in Tolstoy's library at Yasnaya Polyana. See O. V. Rozinskaia, "Dva lika, dve sud'by," *Vestnik Moskovskogo universiteta, Ser. 9, Filologiia* 54 (1999). Viktor Chernov recalled his bemusement at Savinkov's penchant for expressing pacifist Tolstoyan sentiments in private and bombastically blowing the battle bugle in his war journalism. See Chernov, "Savinkov v riadakh," 161.

67. Savinkov, *Izbrannoe,* 374.

68. "*Balagan*" is the Russian term for puppet booth theater, similar to the European Punch and Judy show. Interest in *balagan,* along with other forms of commedia dell'arte, revived among the modernists at the beginning of the twentieth century. See J. Douglas Clayton, *Pierrot in Petrograd: The Commedia Dell'Arte/Balagan in Twentieth Century Russian Theater and Drama* (Montreal: McGill-Queen's University Press, 1994).

69. Savinkov, *Izbrannoe,* 371–72.

70. Ibid., 374.

71. Ibid., 372.

72. For this precise wording, see Gippius's preface to Savinkov's *Kniga stikhov,* xi. Marina Mogilner also discusses the value that readers attributed to the "reality" of Savinkov's depiction of revolutionary terrorism. See Mogil'ner, "The Russian Radical Mythology," 146–76.

73. Savinkov's use of the metaphor of *balagan* to describe the revolutionary struggle, and particularly the image of the revolutionary terrorists as puppets, may reflect the disillusionment that Savinkov experienced as the result of his superior Azef's unmasking as a police spy.

Andrei Bely's *Petersburg* and the Dynamics of Political Response

Timothy Langen

Near the middle of *Petersburg* and at the peak of its narrative tension, after Nikolai Apollonovich Ableukhov has read a letter demanding that he assassinate his father (the reactionary Senator Apollon Apollonovich Ableukhov) using a bomb already in his possession, and after he has rather inexplicably started the bomb's timing mechanism, he confronts his friend, the radical intellectual Alexander Ivanovich Dudkin. It is Dudkin who gave him the bomb in the form of a sardine can with a windup clock, wrapped in a kerchief, but without telling him what it was. Nikolai Apollonovich informs Dudkin that he will have nothing to do with the plot, but Dudkin has no idea what he is talking about. He knows nothing of the letter and assumes that the bomb has been routed to the Ableukhov house merely for safekeeping (who would search a senator's home for a bomb?). The conversation proceeds through maddening degrees of mutual noncomprehension between the sleep-deprived Ableukhov and the feverish Dudkin until the latter finally comes to understand the outrageous intrigue in which he has been implicated. "I'm confident," he tells Nikolai Apollonovich, "that I can disentangle the knots of these vile machinations."[1]

The knots, alas, prove too tangled, and Dudkin loses his mind and murders Lippanchenko, the man who gave *him* the bomb. The episode serves as a parable for the hazards of explanation[2] in *Petersburg,* a tangled novel that seems to accommodate a great number of explanations without quite succumbing to any of them. This resistance to explanation (or at least to decisive explanation) is itself explicable in several ways: in terms of the generally modernist idiom in which Bely wrote, in terms of his peculiar philosophical skepticism, and in terms of the magical, incantatory, and precognitive powers he ascribed to language.

Political novels, though, are supposed to explain. By the time Bely wrote *Petersburg,* Russia had more than half a century's worth of socially and politically engaged literature—devoted to a variety of topics, and written from disparate points of view, but all committed to the explanation and judgment of various modes of social thought and action. The novel proved an enormously powerful means of exploring what a nihilist might believe and what the effects of those beliefs might be on his life, or what the motivations behind revolutionary violence are, or what sort of life a liberal might lead. They posed questions like "Who is to blame?" and "What is to be done?"[3] and tried in various ways to answer those questions. Characters and narrators expound copiously, motivations and consequences are traced to distant points, and no matter how dark the theme, the reader rarely despairs of understanding. Given the decades of political violence that Russia suffered in the late nineteenth and early twentieth centuries, Bely would seem to have had fresh material perfectly suited to that sort of novel.

However, *Petersburg* departs from the tradition. Its main plot concerns a political assassination, and its main characters are nearly all revolutionaries, representatives of the state, or double agents. Yet Bely does not give a coherent account of the sociopolitical views of even one of his characters (or allow them to give such an account).[4] He tells us next to nothing of the views of the "party" that demands the assassination. He gives the merest hint of Nikolai Apollonovich's state of mind when, two and a half months earlier, he proposed killing his father. That hint, moreover, suggests that the proposal had more to do with lovesick despair and personal animus than with any political theory or conviction. The plot proceeds either unbeknownst to or directly athwart the will of its nearest participants. Saturated with politics, this novel seems to make a point of explaining none of it. This essay examines some of the reasons for the lack of explicit sociopolitical theorizing in so overtly political a novel (and by an author who was not averse to theorizing), and also explores the sense in which *Petersburg* can be a means for thinking about what is, after all, the main vehicle of its plot: revolutionary terrorism.

Political Perplexities

In the middle of September 1908, just past the middle of his own life's journey, Andrei Bely brought his friend Nikolai Valentinov to Petrovsko-

Razumovskoe, near Moscow. He wanted to contemplate Dostoevsky's novel *Demons,* and in particular one notorious event that had inspired it: a conspiratorial assassination that had occurred there thirty-nine years earlier. The conspirators, and especially their leader, Sergei Nechaev, had developed a set of principles according to which anything—*anything*—that helped the political cause was ipso facto good, and anything that hindered it was bad. The cause was equally simple: the wholesale destruction of a corrupt, unjust sociopolitical order, with the confident assumption that something better would arise to replace it (just what that something was, or how to build it, was a question for the future). These principles had the undeniable attraction of clarity, though they did require, if followed consistently, the rejection of all moral bonds attached to any principle or personal affection whatsoever other than the overriding goal of revolution.[5] Not one to shrink from extremes, Nechaev energetically severed those bonds when he and four other members of his cell killed a fifth, Ivan Ivanovich Ivanov, who had been wavering in his commitment. Thereafter the conspirators would be strangers to the ordinary world of laws, ethics, and friendship. They would be pure revolutionaries. Bely wanted to contemplate this enormity where it had occurred, right there at Petrovsko-Razumovskoe.

His contemplation was largely sympathetic. For a few years following the 1905 revolution, Bely had embraced or tried to embrace radical politics, which for him meant a combination of Marxist social democracy and religious anarchy. As was already his habit, he brought these concepts to the highest level of abstraction, where distinctions between politics and culture, or self and other, or even this and that policy, tended to dissolve into a comprehensive dialectic of immanence and transcendence. At this remove, he was perhaps as extreme and reductive as Nechaev. Like Nechaev, though, he also wanted his principles to have real consequences in the observable world. He usually accomplished this by turning them into poems and other literary works, but he was starting to think something more tangible and political was called for. In this regard, the slogans and accomplishments of the 1905 revolution were unsatisfying. In the October Manifesto of that year, Tsar Nikolai II had granted civil liberties and established a parliament with legislative powers, the so-called Duma. However, these concessions in matters of principle were quickly neutralized in practice, first by the more restrictive Fundamental Laws of 1906 and thereafter by the tsar's prerogative, exercised twice, to dissolve the Duma when it displeased him. Russia remained untransfigured, and the manifestly ineffectual deliberations of the Duma did little to encourage faith in the transformative power of pure ideas. A *real* change was needed, and it seemed that men like Nechaev had understood that. Bely had brought with him to Petrovsko-Razumovskoe a copy of *Demons,* in which revolutionary fervor is treated as a kind of pathological syndrome or even a demonic possession.[6] Well, Dostoevsky didn't get the point, and Bely was going to set things straight and write his own novel about revolution, set in 1905.[7] Valentinov, himself a Socialist Revolutionary (SR), found his friend's notions distressingly extreme.

Bely did write the novel, but not before his thought doubled back on itself. Soon after the excursion with Valentinov he went "from revolution to reaction,"[8] and in 1909 he wrote "The Truth About the Russian Intelligentsia."[9] This was a positive review of *Signposts* (*Vekhi*), a collection of articles excoriating the Russian revolutionary intelligentsia not merely for a few wrongheaded ideas but for its entire outlook and way of being. The revolutionary intelligentsia, according to the *Signposts* authors, showed insufficient regard for tradition, spiritual growth, personal responsibility, and the rule of law. They had warped a healthy passion for justice into a blind faith in destruction. Bely now agreed.

He had recently been spending a good deal of time with Mikhail Gershenzon, the editor of *Signposts,* and Valentinov later asserted that Bely was excessively suggestible and had been unduly influenced by Gershenzon's antiradical views.[10] Be that as it may, Bely did not stop changing his mind. He later identified the years 1912–15 as a time of motion "from reaction to revolution," while 1916–19 saw another move "from revolution to reaction."[11] Bely shifted his views more than once during the writing and revision of this novel, and it is therefore unrewarding to try to deduce a singular political orientation of *Petersburg* from his extratextual writings.

If Bely was not a consistent political thinker, he was nonetheless a consistent symbolist—or so he insisted in *Why I Became a Symbolist and Why I Never Stopped Being One in All the Phases of My Development.*[12] For Bely, this had centrally to do with the dynamic of immanence and transcendence, which was often expressed as *byt* (mundane daily life) versus *bytie* (deep or high or essential or transcendent existence). The poet's urge is upward, toward *bytie,* but he is trapped in, or at least surrounded by, the world of *byt.* And that mundane world is dominated, as one critic puts it, by "calculation and regulation—on the one hand, and anarchy and terrorism—on the other."[13] This much suggests that for Bely, the relevant axis is not right-left but up-down. Certainly it is not only the extreme left and extreme right that are bankrupt in *Petersburg;* the middle is, as well. Indeed, Bely later attributed his initial difficulties in getting the novel published to an unflattering portrait in it of a "liberal professor" that bore too close a resemblance to Peter Struve, the man who first rejected it for publication.[14] Struve, whose main biography in English is subtitled, in its two volumes, "Liberal on the Left" and "Liberal on the Right,"[15] was also one of the contributors to *Signposts.* His position—or rather the shifty position of *Petersburg*'s wishy-washy liberals, who "had in their fright begun snuggling up" (*Petersburg,* 105) to the more vigorous conservatives—is no more appealing than any other political position (except, perhaps, in an important negative sense: the political moderates do not execute anyone or attempt murder in this novel).[16]

It may appear, then, that as a component of mundane *byt,* politics is debased and uninteresting to Bely. However, that is not correct. It is a central tenet of symbolism, or at least Bely's brand of it, that *byt* is, or can and should be, infused with *bytie.* Anyone who has read *Petersburg* will have noticed the abundance in it of things sticky and stinky, cold and hard, bloated and ungainly. This is the world of *byt,* which must be sensed before it can be transfigured. Indeed, *Petersburg* dwells on the level of sensation, much as it forswears the explanatory habits that characterize the political novels of Turgenev, Dostoevsky, and Tolstoy. The problem with politics is not that it is debased but that it promises an order, regeneration, or a decency that it cannot deliver. It trusts its own theories, procedures, and explanations too fully. Explanation presupposes at least some distinction between the inquiring subject and the object under investigation, but *Petersburg* repeatedly forces every mind back to the blurry world of the stuff it is contemplating. This blurring of distinctions may have its origin in the broad symbolist urge to reconcile dichotomies (including, ultimately, to move from *byt* to *bytie*), or simply in Bely's literary technique, or in his personality. Whatever its origin, though, Bely's habit of destabilizing categories also constitutes a mode of political thinking, and one with special relevance to the dynamics of revolutionary violence and terrorism in Russia at the beginning of the twentieth century.

Provocation and Asymmetrical Reciprocity

If we take *Petersburg* as (among other things) a genuine political novel, albeit of an unfamiliar type, we may observe that the essential dynamic of terrorism in this novel is not fanaticism. The novel presents no causes to which one would devote one's life, let alone any lives devoted to any such cause. Second Lieutenant Sergei Sergeevich Likhutin is perhaps fanatically devoted to the honor of his military rank and uniform—but it is the humbling of that honor which enables his personal growth and the reconciliation of his marriage. In any case, he is neither a terrorist nor the target of one. The characters involved most directly in the terrorist plot are either searching for the right belief (Nikolai Apollonovich and Alexander Dudkin) or without any ostensible ideological commitments whatsoever (Lippanchenko and Morkovin).

Nor is the essential dynamic of terrorism in *Petersburg* provided by hatred. Hatred does exist, for without it Nikolai Apollonovich might never have proposed assassinating his father. Historians of Russian political culture sometimes attribute revolutionary violence to the radical intelligentsia's visceral hatred of the regime.[17] Such personal motivations are highly difficult to trace and may vary from person to person, and even within a single mind there may be both conflicting and compounding urges. In *Petersburg,* no terrorist act is carried through from conception to execution in cold blood. Resentments are diffuse and free-floating, not consolidated and directed. Watching his father try to find the words to talk about his estranged wife (that is, Nikolai Apollonovich's mother), Nikolai Apollonovich "felt a surge—can you imagine of what? Of love! For the old despot who was condemned to be blown to bits" (*Petersburg,* 162). Nikolai Apollonovich hates *and* loves his father.

The essential dynamic of terrorism in *Petersburg* is provocation. In the strictest sense, an agent provocateur is a secret government agent who poses as a member of an oppositional group and causes the members of that group to commit a crime they would not otherwise commit.[18] The most notorious example in Russia was Evno Azev, head of the Combat Organization of the SR Party, who in 1909 was exposed as a double agent who was really working for the secret police. He had arranged several political assassinations, including, spectacularly, that of Minister of the Interior Viacheslav von Plehve in 1904. The Russian secret police had used agents provocateurs for some time as a way of manipulating the groups trying by various means to oppose them. In the case of Azev, his actions became so extreme that they probably did not serve either side particularly well, but only served to agitate both. Azev became a symbol of political intrigue and provocation, and he was one model for Lippanchenko.[19]

In such cases, there are really *two* things to worry about: your friends may actually be your enemies (even if they are not trying to get you to commit a crime), and your actions may be controlled or provoked by someone other than yourself (even if you know who is provoking you and why). Both of these paranoia-inducing possibilities were "provocations" in a larger sense, and both operate extensively in *Petersburg.* Bely's literary habit of blurring distinctions among categories (subject/object, immanent/transcendent) thus corresponds to what is, at least in *Petersburg,* the central fact of political action: you can never be sure whether you're playing into your enemy's hands—indeed, you can never be sure it's not your enemy who is playing you. After Nikolai Apollonovich has read the letter demanding that he fulfill his promise to kill his father at the party, he is confronted by Morkovin, who is a member of both "the Party" and the secret police. Morkovin is trying to make sure that he will carry out the assassination.

> "And what if I refuse?"
> "I will arrest you."
> "Me? Arrest me?"
> "Don't forget that I am . . ."
> "A conspirator?"
> "An official of the secret police!"
> "But what would the Party say to you?"
> "The Party would vindicate me. Using my position in the secret police, I would take vengeance on you on behalf of the Party." (*Petersburg,* 148)

Nikolai Apollonovich is in a bind, and Morkovin narrows his options precisely by being able to play both sides: "Choose," he demands of Nikolai Apollonovich, "arrest, suicide, or murder" (*Petersburg,* 148).

The range of Nikolai Apollonovich's autonomy or agency is, it seems, highly restricted, and in this setting it seems the only agents are agents provocateurs. But even they may eventually lose, as Azev did, and as Lippanchenko does. The real political actor in *Petersburg* is provocation itself. Early in the novel, before Dudkin is even named (he is just "the stranger"), he sits in a tavern with the bomb destined for the Ableukhov home.

> Cutting across columns of conversations, he caught fragments, and sentences took form.
> "Do you know?" was heard from somewhere on the right. And died away.
> And then surfaced:
> "They're planning . . ."
> "To throw . . ."
> A whisper from behind:
> "At who?"
> And then an indistinct couple said:
> "Abl . . ."
> They passed by:
> "At Ableukhov?!"
> The couple completed the sentence somewhere far away:
> "Abl-ution is not the sol-u-tion for what . . ."
> And the couple hiccupped.
> And the stranger stopped, shaken by all he had heard:
> "They're planning . . ."
> "To throw . . . ?"
> whispering began all around:

> "Probable . . . proof . . ."
>
> The stranger heard not "prob" but "prov," and finished it himself: "Prov-ocation?!"
>
> Provocation began its revelry all along the Nevsky. Provocation had changed the meaning of the words that had been heard.
>
> He had simply, on his own, added the preposition "at." With the addition of the letters "a" and "t" an innocent verbal scrap had changed into a scrap with horrible contents. And, most important: the preposition had been added by the stranger.
>
> Provocation, accordingly, had its seat within him. (*Petersburg,* 16)

In this passage, provocation is not just the planned manipulation of one group or individual by another but rather the very susceptibility of individuals and groups to outside suggestion. Provocation has infiltrated Dudkin just as the secret police infiltrated the SRs.

It was typical for Bely to carry things to this pitch of abstraction, and probably also a big part of the reason why he could move so quickly from revolution to reaction and back. The categories he really cared about were much more expansive than political poles could delimit. But again, his literary habits affected his representation of political actions, including political violence. For not only provocation but terror itself expands into a kind of atmosphere that transcends the ability of any individual to control it.

Indeed, terror is even more mobile than most of Bely's categories. It pertains to nearly every aspect of *Petersburg,* and nearly every character seems to experience it. It seems less a tactic for which one might blame one party or another than a background category that overlaps nearly all others, a quality that saturates the status quo. And even as a tactic, terrorism's goal is not the death of any individual or even the achievement of a specific military object but the creation of an atmosphere in which social compacts cease to function.[20]

Writing in 1904 after the assassination of Minister of the Interior von Plehve, Struve blamed it on the government:

> Russian autocracy, in the person of its last two emperors and their ministers, has stubbornly cut off the country from all avenues of legal and gradual political development. . . . The terrible thing for the government is not the physical liquidation of the Sipiagins and von Plehves, but the public atmosphere of resentment and indignation which these bearers of authority create and which breeds in the ranks of Russian society one avenger after another. . . . [Von Plehve] thought that it was possible to have an autocracy which introduced the police

> into everything—an autocracy which transformed legislation, administration, scholarship, church, school, and family into police [organs]—that such an autocracy could dictate to a great nation the laws of its historical development. And the police of von Plehve were not even able to avert a bomb. What a pitiful fool.[21]

Struve cannot yet know that the assassination was an inside job, but that knowledge would hardly have blunted his indignation. Here is a government dedicated to the repression of its citizens, with varied and powerful means of control at its disposal and the inclination to use them, and it cannot prevent such a simple, predictable act.

The "atmosphere" as Struve describes it is characterized not only by provocation (government breeding new avengers, in this case inadvertently) but also by asymmetry. The powerful government is opposed by people who are limited in their options (no "legal and gradual" paths) but who are nonetheless able to resist effectively. Rather than a classic war in which two armies confront one another, strength against strength, Russia in the early twentieth century presents a struggle between two radically dissimilar sides, in which each uses its strengths against the other's weakness—a dynamic that will be familiar to anyone who follows world events today.

Petersburg relies heavily on asymmetry as a compositional principle. "Were one to compare the wizened and utterly unprepossessing little figure of my elder statesman with the immeasurable immensity of the mechanisms managed by him," the narrator remarks, "one might perhaps lapse into naive astonishment for quite some time" (*Petersburg,* 5). The physical puniness and the institutional power of Apollon Apollonovich operate as a kind of counterpoint in this novel, at first in stark contrast but gradually merging in a downward arc, until he goes the way of all flesh. Even at the beginning, though, he is frightened of the city's industrial population and he craves isolation. Dudkin, the radical intellectual, is also isolated, and he is (unlike Apollon Apollonovich) impoverished, and the state is as ominous to him as the crowd is to Apollon Apollonovich. Lippanchenko is physically huge and tactically astute, but he succumbs to the scissors wielded by a Dudkin gone mad. Every strength hides a weakness, and those weaknesses are in themselves a provocation to further violence.

Bely finds other ways to manipulate asymmetries in this novel; the phenomenon itself, and not just its political ramifications, seemed to interest him. Second Lieutenant Sergei Likhutin's attempted suicide, for example, is an asymmetrical response to his wife's defiance. He does not want her to attend Tsukatov's ball, and she goes anyway. He has none of her social skills or connections, nor any chance of wounding her in precisely the same way she has wounded him. Indeed, he is not even thinking of wounding her, exactly, when he prepares to kill himself. He is just certain that he must do *something*, and the only option that presents itself to his increasingly unstable mind—the option of suicide—is way out of proportion to the slight he has received. So too Nikolai Apollonovich's proposal to kill his father, also motivated partly by despair, also out of proportion to the offense. Indeed, the proposal itself seems prompted less by any single event than by a concatenation of considerations—an atmosphere—hovering around the senator.

This dynamic operates in the novel's ontology as well. Earlier I said that *Petersburg* does not so much analyze as immerse itself in the peculiar logic of its situation. Consider the following passage, at the end of the novel's first chapter. The narrator is giving a tally of some of the main characters:

> Cerebral play is only a mask. Under way beneath this mask is the invasion of the brain by forces unknown to us. And granting that Apollon Apollonovich is spun from our brain, nonetheless he will manage to inspire fear with another, a stupendous state of being which attacks at night. Apollon Apollonovich is endowed with the attributes of this state of being. All his cerebral play is endowed with the attributes of this state of being.
>
> Once his brain has playfully engendered the mysterious stranger, that stranger exists, really exists. He will not vanish from the Petersburg prospects as long as the senator with such thoughts exists, because thought exists too.
>
> So let our stranger be a real stranger! And let the two shadows of my stranger be real shadows!
>
> Those dark shadows will, oh yes, they will, follow on the heels of the stranger, just as the stranger himself is closely following the senator. The aged senator will, oh yes, he will, pursue you too, dear reader, in his black carriage. And henceforth you will never ever forget him!

On one level, this passage recapitulates elements of the novel's political plot: it reminds us of the target of assassination (Apollon Apollonovich), the radical intellectual ("the stranger," Dudkin), and the spy ("shadow") who will be following Dudkin. But important elements of mood or atmosphere are also summed up here. The "invasion of the brain" provokes a kind of paranoia that we may be the unwitting instruments of other wills. And the asymmetrical relationship between creator and created being (narrator and Apollon Apollonovich, or Apollon Apollonovich and the stranger and shadows) acquires a kind of reciprocity. Apollon Apollonovich can act on the reader (and possibly even the narrator), the stranger can act on Apollon Apollonovich, and the stranger's shadow can act on him. We have a hierarchy of being, and yet one in which the various levels can act on one another.

All of this is not to suggest that *Petersburg* is a conscious political allegory. Rather, it is to say that literary form is a way of thinking applicable to many orders of discourse, including the political. The literary form of *Petersburg*, which privileges the sudden, the eccentric, the unexpected convergence, and even the conundrum, may seem utterly alien to the rational discourse of politics. Yet these syncopated cognitive rhythms may have the surprising potential to correct some of the imbalances of that discourse.

Culture, Communication, and Collapse

Some corrective was surely needed, for, as Bely was working on the novel, the world seemed on the brink of collapse. Long before the actual start of World War I, a sense of impending doom had infiltrated the minds and writings of many Russians and other Europeans.[22] This is the environment in which terrorism, and more generally asymmetrical destruction, would seem to operate most effectively. A healthy polity, like a healthy body, can absorb a fair degree of punishment without lapsing into crisis, while one teetering on the brink of the abyss may need only a slight push to speed it to its doom. This, at least, was the logic of Russian revolutionary and anarchist groups, who carried out acts of terrorism in the faith that the hopelessly anachronistic, brittle Russian autocracy would not long withstand them.[23]

Very little in *Petersburg* is durable. From the little pencils that Apollon Apollonovich breaks when agitated to the entirety of European civilization, everything seems on the verge of catastrophe. Sofia Petrovna's attending the ball against her husband's wishes is sufficient to push him to attempt suicide. Nikolai Apollonovich need only utter a foolish word in a moment of desperation, and a bomb is delivered to him. And the reader is constantly reminded of Apollon Apollonovich's increasing frailty—this despite the physical exercises the senator performs daily for the preservation of his health. It is a losing proposition.

Apollon Apollonovich is well aware of his vulnerability, and not only to old age but also to the political terrorism of his times. Riding to work, he contemplates the row of houses on the prospect. "This row differed from the line of life: for many a wearer of diamond-studded decorations, as for so many other dignitaries, the middle of life's road had proven to be the termination of life's journey" (*Petersburg,* 10). In this passage, a long, healthy life is implied as the normative condition (Apollon Apollonovich's colleagues *should* have been in the middle of their days), to which the present condition (they were killed) is sharply contrasted. But the passage subtly evokes another normative order as well: the spiritual hierarchy in Dante's *Divine Comedy.* Dante enjoyed great prestige among the Russian symbolists,[24] and Bely's reference to "the middle of life's road" is an unmistakable echo of Dante's opening line in the *Inferno.* But the allusion is comprehensible only as a contrastive device. Dante's world is one of order and commensurability, even symmetry (punishments fit crimes; the virtuous are rewarded, the evil punished), and the narrative direction is upward, from hell to heaven. *Petersburg,* however, depicts a descent toward chaos; its world is one of disproportion and fragment.

It is also a world of potential, as though all these shards awaited only the right act of vision or violence to reconfigure them into something beautiful or awful. Political revolution is one potential here, but Bely gives little hint what a transfigured polity might look like. As for the revolutionary Dudkin, he informs Nikolai Apollonovich early in the novel that he has been reading mystical and religious texts, including, as he reports, the Apocalypse (56). *Petersburg* is, in fact, loaded with references to the apocalypse, which offers one key to the novel's symbolic order.[25] Apocalypse is a sort of *ne plus ultra,* a total transformation of *byt* to *bytie,* and thus perhaps a beacon against which the symbolist artist checks his work.

But apocalypse attained is by definition a showstopper, after which *Petersburg*'s themes of love, hate, revolution, reaction, reason, and madness would lose recognizable form. Apocalypse must remain on the novel's horizon: looming, even sensible in some way, but never fully realized. Like Dante, Bely may allude to a divine dispensation (though far less explicitly), but he too must return to this world. And like Dante, he uses the motif of personal love as a figure for the sort of earthly transcendence that *is* possible before the end times. Conservatives, liberals, and radicals may not join hands in this novel, and humankind may not yet be reunited with God, but estranged husbands and wives do reconcile—in two different families, the Ableukhovs and the Likhutins.

These familial reconciliations actually do occur in the novel, and so they are unlike the religious and political transformations that are hinted at but not depicted. But the reconciliations are still miraculous, and we are not privy to the communication that enacts them. On both occasions the narrator announces this fact, explaining that the conversations will remain "between them" (*Petersburg,* 137), and "an impenetrable mystery" (*Petersburg,* 272). Creative or transformation communication, it seems, cannot be depicted in this novel.

Pathological communication, on the other hand, is everywhere, and it seems to result from an imbalance of sending over receiving. "Whenever

[Apollon Apollonovich and Nikolai Apollonovich] came into contact with one another," the narrator explains, "they gave the appearance of two air vents turned face to face, and the result was a most unpleasant draft" (*Petersburg,* 71). The key fact here, simple as it is, is that father and son are not listening to each other. The typical response, certainly in this novel and perhaps also in our world, is for the speaker to turn up the volume. The addressee then resorts to earplugs, in the form of either physical isolation (witness Apollon Apollonovich's careful regulation of his public accessibility, or Sofia Petrovna's habit of locking herself in her room to keep her husband out), or strenuous daydreaming, or explicit rebuff (as when Apollon Apollonovich refuses to speak with the liberal professor at the ball). The speaker shouts, the addressee flees or barricades himself, and in this context terrorism is simply (to adapt von Clausewitz) the extension of speech by other means. Without the notion that there is someone who might at least receive a sufficiently loud "message" and be terrorized by it, the rationale for terrorism collapses. And so, to hasten that collapse, the leaders of countries insist on principle that messages so delivered will *not* be received, and that taking the demands of terrorists seriously would only encourage more terrorism. Instead, one is told that it is we who have to send our enemies a message. Judged by moral standards or by local, pragmatic ones, this position may or may not be correct—likely it is correct in some cases and not in others. But a purely formal, abstract view will notice a ratchet effect: messages get louder as hearing gets harder.

This imbalance between sending and receiving causes both to become automated and uncreative, and perpetuates the atmosphere of provocation. At its extreme, this syndrome leaves the realm of communication altogether and leads to the motif of extermination that is so prevalent in this novel. Apollon Apollonovich reflects that "the islands," home to much of the city's industrial population, "must be crushed!" (*Petersburg,* 11). *That* is what one naturally does in response to terrorism. It is not necessarily what one does to end wars, where treaties may be negotiated with considerable give-and-take. Such a treaty had been achieved with the Japanese just before the start of *Petersburg*'s plot,[26] and that is a normal thing (though Apollon Apollonovich disapproves of this particular one). But when the "coarse" workers begin to strike they are less like enemy soldiers and more like the bedbugs in Dudkin's garret and the cockroaches that Lippanchenko crushes so assiduously. You do not reason or negotiate with them; you visit Armageddon upon them. This is perhaps the dark side, or even (just conceivably) a conscious parody, of the theme of apocalypse—at least as it pertains to the attempts of *mortals* to establish a new dispensation by means of force. In this novel you can't even get rid of cockroaches that way.

Writing, Reading, Thinking, and Listening

Given an atmosphere of sociopolitical fragility, asymmetrical retaliation, and pathological communication, what are the responsibilities of the writer? Surely one of the most important is to resensitize the apparatus of perception and to deautomate thought. In a review for the *New Yorker,* one year after the terrorist attacks of September 11, 2001, Louis Menand deplored the lack of such writing:

> The initial response of most cultural and political critics to the attacks of September 11—a completely unanticipated atrocity carried out by an organization that few people in the West had ever heard of and whose intentions are still not entirely comprehensible—was: It just proves what I've always said. The attacks were treated as geopolitics for dummies, confirming conclusions that sensible observers had reached long before. September 11 showed that the United States is hated by many good people around the world because it is an imperial bully; the United States is hated by many bad people around the world because it is a beacon of freedom and opportunity; Islam is a civilization irredeemably hostile to Western values; Islam is a civilization assimilating Western values; globalization has gone too far; globalization has not gone far enough; Arafat is a terrorist; Zionism is racism; movies are too violent; and postmodernism is dead. The surprising thing about most of the published reflections on September 11 is how devoid of surprise they are. They are so devoid of surprise as to be almost devoid of thought.[27]

The challenge is to say something new in response to surprising events, and few writers meet that challenge.

This was one of Bely's preoccupations even when he was not responding to an objective crisis. In "The Magic of Words" he describes what he calls "putrid words," words that at one time embodied a fresh insight but which (we might now say) have exceeded their shelf life.[28] Those words stultify thought and stifle creative effort. Bely writes about poetry as the highest form of verbal creativity, but—if Menand is correct—one needs a bit of creativity to write intelligently about sociopolitical events as well. As Menand demonstrates, our own explanatory repertoire is highly prepackaged and uncreative, perhaps even more than was the case in Bely's time. And yet even then the interpretive ingredients were pretty well packed, and they are remarkably familiar a century later.

One package: globalization: imperialistic ambitions (already!) confronted by the people being imperialized, the breakdown of familiar and usually rural forms of social organization; anachronistic government principles and policies leading to a brittle harshness. An urban populace systematically exploited at work, alienated from meaningful social contact at home, and politically impotent. A whole group (or even class) of people excluded from the possibility of a humane life and also from any humane way of improving that life. What do you expect?

Another package: deracinated intellectuals who have step-by-step lost any sense of responsibility for their words and actions, any sense of compromise, any sense of human frailty; intellectuals who convince themselves and those who happen to be suffering at the moment that suffering is neither divinely ordained nor pragmatically necessary, but rather the gratuitous invention of class (or religious or national or racial) conspirators. The corresponding (irresponsible and unrealistic, but morbidly attractive) notion that the present order need only be smashed, and something far better will surely follow. The loss, at the same time, of traditional religion and morality, which might constrain these base instincts and violent utopian schemes. What do you expect?

The genius of *Petersburg,* read as a political novel, is that it coordinates incompatible—or at least competing—interpretations of the social, economic, intellectual, and political world. Struve "on the left" made many of the points in the first explanatory package above, and later, "on the right," he made points from the second package—but not at the same time. Both packages will operate effectively on *Petersburg,* though, and a reader who wishes to comprehend it as a whole must attend to their interaction and mutual interference.

Apollon Apollonovich is a highly effective government official concerned with improving the quality of life in Russia, and a man who hates and fears Russia. He is a powerful monster and a frail old man capable of love.

Nearly every major character acts (wittingly or no) for and against the revolution and the reaction.

Dudkin is sincere, impoverished, dissolute, intelligent, cowardly, courageous, and unbalanced.

The plot is deliberate and not.

Likhutin's honor is noble and obtuse, his actions are restrained and impetuous.

Revolutionary violence arises from poverty, government oppression, provocation, illness, miscommunication, generalized agitation,

> unrealistic expectations, dark motives, and an atmosphere that no one really controls. It can be justified. It cannot be justified. It should be welcomed and embraced. It should be averted at all costs.

A nuanced treatment of early twentieth-century terrorism might entertain many of those sorts of points (minus the specific characters), but the task of explanation would eventually require the subordination of some factors to others, in the interests of presenting a unified picture. In *Petersburg,* though, the principle governing the representation of sociopolitical life really does seem to be: enlist and then disrupt all sequences that exclude what they cannot make neat, all explanations that subdue unruly facts, all judgments that reduce complex phenomena to a sterile "good" or "bad." The solution in this novel is not some sort of explanatory happy medium any more than the ineffectual liberal professor represents a workable political position. Rather, it is to exercise a different kind of thought, in which the mental habits of prepackaged explanation are suspended (to the extent possible) and bits of experience, intuition, and reason collide, combine, and disintegrate.

In the mode of thinking embodied in *Petersburg,* surprise trumps explanation, every order is asymmetrical and unstable, and the tiniest detail might hold the potential for transcendence; consequently, attention and receptiveness matter more than logic and decisiveness. This creative open-mindedness is what allows the Likhutins and the Ableukhovs to reconcile. It may be what has allowed individual Palestinians and Israelis to make music together in Jerusalem, or Catholics and Protestants in Belfast, or whites and blacks in Johannesburg. By itself, open-mindedness is clearly not adequate to the world, which regularly demands explanation, judgment, decision, and action. But when those functions hypertrophy and the joint forces of intellect and will threaten to subjugate the world—as with Apollon Apollonovich and Lippanchenko, and Nechaev and von Plehve—then perhaps the best thing for a novel to do is not to tell us who is to blame or what is to be done. Perhaps, like *Petersburg,* it should teach us to listen.

Notes

1. Andrei Bely, *Petersburg,* trans. Robert A. Maguire and John E. Malmstad (Bloomington: Indiana University Press, 1978), 178. Subsequent page references are given in parentheses in the text. The novel was first published in serial form in 1913–14, and then as a book in 1916. Bely revised it (with substantial excisions) for publication in Berlin in 1922. The translators Maguire and Malmstad take this latter (1922) edition as their base text. For critical studies of this novel in English, readers may wish to consult some of the following works: Vladimir E. Alexandrov, *Andrei Belyi: The Major*

Symbolist Fiction (Cambridge, Mass.: Harvard University Press, 1985); Carol Anschuetz, "Bely's *Petersburg* and the End of the Russian Novel," in *The Russian Novel from Pushkin to Pasternak,* ed. John Garrard (New Haven: Yale University Press, 1983), 125–53; David M. Bethea, *The Shape of Apocalypse in Modern Russian Fiction* (Princeton: Princeton University Press, 1989); Samuel D. Cioran, *The Apocalyptic Symbolism of Andrej Belyj* (The Hague: Mouton, 1973); John D. Elsworth, *Andrey Bely: A Critical Study of the Novels* (Cambridge: Cambridge University Press, 1983); Gerald Janecek, ed., *Andrey Bely: A Critical Review* (Lexington: University Press of Kentucky, 1978); Roger Keys, *The Reluctant Modernist: Andrei Belyi and the Development of Russian Fiction 1902–1914* (Oxford: Clarendon Press, 1996); Timothy Langen, *The Stony Dance: Unity and Gesture in Andrey Bely's* Petersburg (Evanston, Ill.: Northwestern University Press, 2005); Magnus Ljunggren, *The Dream of Rebirth: A Study of Andrej Belyj's Novel "Petersburg,"* Stockholm Studies in Russian Literature 15 (Stockholm: Almqvist and Wiksell International, 1982); John E. Malmstad, ed., *Andrey Bely: Spirit of Symbolism* (Ithaca, N.Y.: Cornell University Press, 1987); Robert Mann, *Andrei Bely's "Petersburg" and the Cult of Dionysus* (Lawrence, Kans.: Coronado, 1986); James West, "Kant, Kant, Kant: The NeoKantian Creative Consciousness in Bely's *Petersburg*," in *The European Foundations of Russian Modernism,* ed. Peter I. Barta (Lewiston, N.Y.: Edwin Mellen Press, 1991); Aleksandr Woronzoff, *Andrej Belyj's "Petersburg," James Joyce's "Ulysses," and the Symbolist Movement* (Berne: Peter Lang, 1982).

2. I am indebted to Gary Saul Morson for this concept. See his "Gogol's Parables of Explanation: Nonsense and Prosaics," in *Essays on Gogol: Logos and the Russian Word,* ed. Susanne Fusso and Priscilla Meyer (Evanston, Ill.: Northwestern University Press, 1992), 200–239.

3. The titles of novels by Aleksandr Herzen and Nikolai Chernyshevsky, respectively.

4. We come the closest to a reasonable knowledge of Senator Ableukhov's views, but even in this case our information is hardly as complete as what we might expect in a novel by Turgenev, Dostoevsky, or Tolstoy.

5. Bakunin and Nechaev, "The Catechism of the Revolutionary, 1868," in *Imperial Russia: A Source Book, 1700–1917,* ed. Basil Dmytryshyn (Gulf Breeze, Fla.: Academic International Press, 1999), 350–54.

6. For a more complete treatment of Dostoevsky's use of Nechaev in his novel *Demons,* see Val Vinokur's contribution to this volume.

7. This incident is recounted in N. Valentinov, *Two Years with the Symbolists,* ed. Gleb Struve (Stanford: Hoover Institution on War, Revolution, and Peace, 1969), 174–80. It is also treated in A. V. Lavrov, *Andrei Belyi v 1900-e gody* (Moscow: Novoe literaturnoe obozrenie, 1995), 269–70. Lavrov gives a good deal of useful information about Bely's views at this time.

8. "Andrej Belyj: Lettre autobiographique à Ivanov-Razumnik," ed. Georges Nivat, *Cahiers du Monde Russe et Sovietique* 15, nos. 1–2 (1974): 45–82, 47.

9. "Pravda o russkoi intelligentsii: po povodu sbornika *Vekhi,*" *Vesy* 5 (1909): 65–68.

10. Valentinov, *Two Years,* 201–22. For a challenge to Valentinov's version of the Bely-Gershenzon relationship, see Arthur Levin, "Andrey Bely, M. O. Gershenzon and *Vekhi:* A Rejoinder to N. Valentinov," in Janecek, *Bely: A Critical Review,* 169–80.

11. "Belyj: Lettre autobiographique à Ivanov-Razumnik," 45–82, 47.

12. Andrei Belyi, *Pochemu ia stal simvolistom i pochemu ia ne perestal im byt' vo vsekh fazakh moego ideinogo i khudozhestvennogo razvitiia* (Ann Arbor, Mich.: Ardis, 1982).

13. L. Dolgopolov, *Andrei Belyi i ego roman "Peterburg"* (Leningrad: Sovetskii pisatel', 1988), 259.

14. Andrei Belyi, "Vospominaniia, tom III, chast' II (1910–1912)," in *Literaturnoe nasledstvo* 27–28 (1937), 409–56, 455.

15. Richard Pipes, *Struve: Liberal on the Left, 1870–1905* (Cambridge, Mass.: Harvard University Press, 1970), and *Struve: Liberal on the Right, 1905–1944* (Cambridge, Mass.: Harvard University Press, 1980).

16. See Vinokur in this volume on "middle" positions in Russian political and literary discourse, and on the general unavailability of satisfying political orientations.

17. In his contribution to this volume, Martin A. Miller suggests that the corrosive experiences and petty humiliations of political exile may also have contributed to the willingness of many revolutionaries to use violence against the government.

18. For a fascinating early example, see Richard Pipes, *The Degaev Affair: Terror and Treason in Tsarist Russia* (New Haven: Yale University Press, 2003).

19. See Lynn Ellen Patyk in this volume on the Azef case and the life and career of Boris Savinkov, the head of the Combat Organization of the SRs and mastermind of the assassinations of von Plehve and the Grand Duke Sergei Alexandrovich.

20. For more on the purposes of terrorism, see Vinokur in this volume.

21. *Osvobozhdenie* (Stuttgart), III, no. 52 (July 19–August 1, 1904), 33. This translation is taken from Richard Pipes, *The Russian Revolution* (New York: Knopf, 1991), 15.

22. One particularly important source for Bely and other Russian symbolist writers was Vladimir Soloviev, and especially his poem "Panmongolism."

23. It is in some ways the logic of our times as well: when Americans were instructed soon after September 11, 2001, to be vigilant but keep on shopping, the idea was to demonstrate the vigor of our way of life, which would not be easily perturbed by wanton acts of violence. Whether massive economic consumption as such should be considered healthy is beyond the scope of this essay. The consumption did, however, prove robust.

24. On this topic, see Lena Szilard, "Andrei Belyi and His Beatrice," in *The Silver Age in Russian Literature: Selected Papers from the Fourth World Congress for Soviet and East European Studies,* ed. John Elsworth (New York: St. Martin's Press, 1992), 171–80.

25. This topic has received a good deal of scholarly attention. Interested readers might start with Cioran, *The Apocalyptic Symbolism;* Bernice Glatzer Rosenthal, "Revolution as Apocalypse," in Janecek, *Bely: A Critical Review,* 181–92; and Bethea, *The Shape of Apocalypse,* especially chapter 2, which is devoted to *Petersburg.*

26. That is, the Treaty of Portsmouth, which ended the Russo-Japanese War of 1904–5.

27. Louis Menand, "Faith, Hope, and Clarity: September 11 and the American Soul," *New Yorker,* September 16, 2002, 98–104.

28. Andrey Bely, "The Magic of Words," in *Selected Essays of Andrey Bely,* ed. Steven Cassedy (Berkeley and Los Angeles: University of California Press, 1985), 93–110.

Exile's Vengeance: Trotsky and the Morality of Terrorism

Martin A. Miller

Moral arguments justifying and condemning the use of tactical violence to achieve desired political ends have been advanced and discussed for more than two centuries. In the modern era of European history, Maximilien Robespierre and his ideological theoretician Louis-Antoine de Saint-Just were among the first to formulate the notion of justifiable state violence in 1793 during the French Revolution's Reign of Terror. Karl Heinzen's 1849 essay "Murder," published in the German radical paper *Die Evolution,* and Sergei Nechaev's 1869 essay "Catechism of a Revolutionary" are among the earliest attempts at a moral justification of terrorism from below. Very few individuals, however, have presented arguments both for and against terrorism on ethical grounds. One reason is that so few have had the opportunity to have experienced both the radical, illegal underground in a high-intensity period of political violence and, later, the heights of state power. One of these rare figures was Lev Davidovich Trotsky, whose life encompassed the roles of both outlaw and Leviathan and who composed both a comprehensive critique of terrorism and an influential justification of it at different moments in his career. His work therefore represents an important pathway to understanding the links between state and antistate political violence, which are usually considered entirely separate subjects.[1] This essay seeks to analyze his opposing and contradictory conceptualizations of political violence and to explain their moral basis in historical context.

***

In 1909, Lev Trotsky (né Bronstein) was a committed Marxist revolutionary living a peripatetic existence in political exile from tsarist Russia and deeply engaged in the bitter ideological divisions that defined and divided the European social democratic movement. One of the most charged issues facing Russian revolutionaries at the time, regardless of party affiliation, was the question of whether or not to accept terrorist tactics as a means of sabotaging the autocratic system. The battle lines on the radical left over supporting or criticizing terrorist actions had already been drawn in earlier ideological wars between the followers of Karl Marx and anarchists loyal to Mikhail Bakunin. Marx and his collaborator Friedrich Engels had earlier corresponded with each other frequently about the futility of political violence carried out by elite squads or individuals representing larger movements. Of the effort by the Irish Fenians to bomb the Clerkenwell prison in London to free political prisoners, Marx called it "a secret, melodramatic sort of conspiracy."[2] Engels wrote back to him that this "stupid affair in Clerkenwell was obviously the work of a few specialized fanatics" in "the arson business" who think they "can liberate Ireland by setting fire to a tailor's shop in London."[3] Later, after the assassination of Tsar Alexander II by members of the People's Will (Narodnaia volia) in St. Petersburg and the killing of Lord Cavendish, the chief British official responsible for control of Ireland, in the Phoenix Park bombing, Engels referred to these events as characterized by "infantile behavior" and "sheer folly, [and] a piece of pure Bakuninist histrionic, senseless '*propagande par le fait.*'"[4] In another letter he noted that "the anarchists commit suicide every year, and this will continue until anarchism is subjected to serious persecution" in France, Switzerland, and Spain, where they were numerous.[5] A decade later he continued to attack the anarchists' tactics of political violence, believing they "were on the verge of extinction" as a result of their unproductive *attentats*. "The chasm between us and the anarchists," he concluded, "is gaping."[6]

Lenin carried this discourse further, arguing as early as the summer of 1902 that "the noisy preaching of terrorism" by the Socialist Revolutionary (SR) Party "as a means of political struggle was doing the most serious harm to the [revolutionary] movement of the masses," and "serve[d] only to sow harmful illusions."[7] Despite further criticism of SR violence, his attitude toward terrorism was nevertheless far less consistent than the positions Marx and Engels had taken. For example, in the spring of 1906, amid the dying flames of the 1905 revolution, Lenin wrote that the Bolsheviks recognized "that [their] party must regard the fighting guerrilla operations of the groups affiliated with it as being in principle permissible and even advisable in the present situation."[8] In a weak attempt to avoid the obvious contradiction he was presenting, he emphasized that he was seeking to make a distinction between political violence on behalf of the peasantry carried out by the SRs and battle operations involving a widespread movement of militant insurrectionaries "that must be conducted under the control of the [Bolshevik] party."[9] Lenin seemed to be admitting that some forms of violence were acceptable while others were not, without providing any clear ethical principles or political criteria apart from asserting Bolshevik exceptionalism.

Within the next few years, acts of terrorism directed against the tsarist officialdom, mainly by SR and anarchist militants, reached a crescendo and began to decline. The casualty figures in the thousands still appear as astonishing as they did a century ago. Although the available statistics vary depending on which files are included and what definitions are used, we find estimates for the period between 1901 and 1916 as high as 17,000 terrorist acts overall, with 9,000 casualties for 1905–7 alone.[10] However, unlike the political violence taking place in France at the same time, which engulfed ordinary citizens in acts of terrorism, the great majority of the victims in Russia were targeted precisely because they were either representatives or symbols of the tsarist regime.[11]

Trotsky entered the revolutionary discourse on Russian terrorism with his 1909 article, "The Collapse of Terrorism," which was published in the Polish Marxist journal, *Przeglad Socjal-demokratyczny* (*The Social Democratic Review*).[12] It has received very little attention in the biographical literature, from Isaac Deutscher to Dmitry Volkogonov. Indeed, Trotsky himself does not mention it in his autobiography, *My Life,* and it does not appear in the major anthologies of his writings, although he did include it in the personally approved Russian edition of his collected works issued by the Soviet state publishing house in the early 1920s, where it has remained virtually buried. Nevertheless, the argument of the article, which Trotsky considered rooted in an ethical framework, stands as a seminal contribution to the history of antiterrorist theory.

The article was written soon after the stunning revelations that Evno Azev, a leading member of the Combat Organization of the SR Party, was simultaneously a paid agent of the state secret police.[13] The Azev affair permitted Trotsky, along with many others deeply involved in the revolutionary struggle against the autocracy, to expand the framework of his denunciation of terrorism. Indeed, most of the evidence for his critique of political violence at this time was rooted in the sensational assassinations carried out by the SR Party's terrorist wing in the years before, during, and immediately after the 1905 revolution. To mention only the most prominent victims, these acts included the killing of the Grand Duke Sergei Alexandrovich, Minister of the Interior Viacheslav von Plehve, and Prime Minister Peter Stolypin.

Trotsky begins his argument with the historical recognition that "liberation by means of the knife" has been utilized by individuals and groups dissatisfied with the unjust policies of regimes and their leaders as long as there have been tyrants in power. In Russia, he finds that this strategy has taken on a particularly important role in large measure as the consequence of a Europeanized "bureaucratic hierarchy of absolutism," which has created "its own revolutionary bureaucracy, an original product of the Russian intelligentsia." As the tsarist government sought to compete with Western states, it was compelled to reproduce the economic, military, and technological aspects of its European rivals. This tendency was replicated in the formation of the "bureaucratic terrorism" of the People's Will, under the direction of an intelligentsia faction inspired by political violence as a means to abolish tsarism. For Trotsky, however, this only recreated the age-old politics of terror with a new collective leadership, leading to the mechanical and useless process of murdering one despot and having him replaced with another—"satrap after satrap, minister after minister, monarch after monarch, Ivan after Ivan," a trajectory that separated the revolutionary movement ever further from the core elements of the social order.

Because of the wholesale adoption of these European-driven influences, the educated elites of Russia, both the state and its radical opponents in the intelligentsia, developed concepts and tactics that left them in antagonistic relations with the broad masses of society. In Trotsky's words, the intelligentsia found itself "spiritually revolutionized before the economic development of the country could give birth to revolutionary classes on which it could have counted on for support." Under these desperate circumstances, the intelligentsia had no alternative but to intensify its increasing dependence on "the explosive strength of nitroglycerine." Without a realistic strategy apart from the reliance on political violence, the People's Will quickly "reached its zenith, then rapidly fizzled out to nothing, having burnt in its own fire the supply of military force which the intelligentsia, so weak in numbers, could have mustered."

Trotsky continues by arguing that the more recent "second wave of terrorists are already emerging as imitators" of the first era of "capitalist *Sturm und Drang*" that had created the People's Will. Just as the earlier group had operated without roots of support in the larger society of workers and peasants, the SR terrorists functioned as an elite acting apart from any potential mass participation in the revolutionary cause. Terrorism, Trotsky states, requires an intensive concentration of energy on "the great moment" of violence, a reverence for "the significance of personal heroism," and a single-minded commitment to "the hermetic secrecy of conspiracy." The result is the diffusion of a myopic illusion, namely, that there are only two points of conflict to conceptualize, "the government and the fighting organization." As a result, the terrorists seek to balance the battlefield they have theorized by obtaining an equality of weapons: from "pitchforks and boathooks" to guns and bombs. What the terrorists do not realize is that even if they could achieve the downfall of the police by violent means, without societal involvement in the process of transformation, the outcome would only be "the unavoidable signal for the political downfall of their party," not its moment of victory. In the absence of participation and support from the workers and peasants, power would soon dissolve back into the hands of the forces of reaction.

Despite claims by Andrei Zheliabov at his trial in 1881 and later SR terrorists that they were acting in "self-defense" against tyrannical authority, Trotsky locates "the psychological source of terrorism" in the desire for revenge. When injured or damaged by the brutal policies of the authorities, it is understandable that individuals can easily be persuaded that satisfaction lies in a violent response. This is what drove Vera Zasulich to shoot General Trepov in St. Petersburg, an event that inspired a rash of imitations leading to the assassination of Tsar Alexander II. "What started as an instinctive feeling of revenge," argues Trotsky, "developed into an entire system from 1879 to 1881." However, he continues, these outbursts cannot succeed in altering the causes of the injustices that motivate the need for settling scores by recourse to pistols and explosives.

"After the smoke of the explosion drifts away, panic subsides and the murdered minister's successor arrives; once again, life settles into its old routine. The wheels of capitalist exploitation turn round as before, only police repression becomes more brutal and shameless; as a result, in place of burned-out hopes and artificially aroused awareness, we have disillusionment and apathy." Worse, the aftermath of "propaganda by the deed" produces in society a deeply felt sense of defeat as the "hopes for a great avenger and liberator who will do their work for them" does not materialize. At the same time, the state is often emboldened and strengthened by the violence from below and resorts to even greater acts of repression, as was the case with Alexander III after his father's assassination. Meanwhile, many members of the social order either are distracted by the frisson of violence or find themselves drawn into passive support of the very regime that acts against their interests by restricting their liberty even further. For social democrats, Trotsky concludes, this strategy of terrorist acts is to be condemned and fought against. "We must learn to see the monstrous evidence of the class structure in all crimes against the individual, in every attempt to maim or stifle a human being, body and soul, so that we may direct all our strength toward a collective struggle against this class structure." Only in recognizing this will "the burning desire for revenge achieve its greatest moral satisfaction." Thus, because the tactics of political violence have been exhausted, he proclaimed, "terrorism in Russia is dead."

Trotsky's emphasis on the psychological dynamic of revenge was perhaps more significant in understanding his own situation than it was in understanding the motives behind the violent tactics of the People's Will and the SRs. Trotsky's identity at this time was shaped in large measure by his status as an exile. The tsarist regime had imprisoned him and then expelled him, declaring him essentially an outlaw and assuming he would sink into utter insignificance, wandering from one country of asylum to another, unable to pose a threat to Russia's security by arousing its workers and intellectuals to opposition. To replace this loss, Trotsky joined the expanding émigré community in Western Europe and devoted his life to avenging the humiliation and repression he had suffered at the hands of the autocracy in St. Petersburg.[14] After bitter years of party fights, clandestine meetings, poverty, and social marginalization, unexpectedly and against all odds, he and many other revolutionary exiles suddenly received their chance for revenge in 1917.

A decade later, at which time the circumstances of Trotsky's life had completely changed, so also had his position on terrorism. When he returned to the problem of terrorism, he was no longer a revolutionary exile editing limited-circulation Marxist newspapers and formulating position papers analyzing the incompatibility of the forces of industrial capitalism and the legitimate authority of the autocratic regime in Russia.[15] He had played a key role in the events of the October Revolution that brought the Bolsheviks to power, had negotiated with the Germans at Lenin's request (despite his personal disagreement) the unilateral withdrawal of Russia from the Great War, had commanded the strategy of the newly created Red Army to victory in the Russian Civil War, and had established the policies of war communism to solidify that military triumph in Bolshevik Russia.[16] Trotsky's photograph hung from public buildings, his writings appeared frequently in the new communist press, and large crowds hung on his words when he gave speeches at ceremonial or commemorative events in Red Square. In the hierarchical *nomenklatura* of the time, he was truly second only to Lenin himself in significance.

When Trotsky wrote "The Collapse of Terrorism," he could not have imagined, even in a fantasy, the enormously powerful position he would occupy in 1920. He was no longer competing with parties willing to use terrorist tactics to bring down the tsarist regime. He was now in power and had a new identity to forge, a revolution to defend, and a regime to legitimize. The challenges to those tasks, following the successful conclusion to the civil war, had also changed. One of the most serious was the question of terror. The Bolsheviks had been criticized from a variety of quarters for their excessive reliance on brutal methods of enforcing their authority. Beyond the expected disagreements from "bourgeois" governments in the West, many former members of the tsarist radical underground and fellow political exiles had also turned against Bolshevik power.[17]

However, Trotsky did not feel it necessary to confront directly the issue of revolutionary state terror in any depth until he read a long essay from the pen of a former comrade in the international Marxist movement who had himself achieved a position of great prestige even without ever gaining actual political power. Karl Kautsky, the titular head of the German Social Democratic Party, was a direct link to Marx and Engels, both of whom he had known personally. As one of the founding editors of the influential Marxist organ *Die Neue Zeit* (*New Times*), his writings were widely read and held by many socialists in high regard both in and outside Germany.[18]

The Bolshevik seizure of power and proclamation of the world's first Marxist government in 1917 did not produce unanimous applause within the socialist movement. The prominent Marxist theorist Rosa Luxemburg had already engaged Lenin in debate over what she perceived as the authoritarian nature of Bolshevik leadership policies and practices.[19] Barely six months after the Bolshevik insurrection that brought down the Provisional Government in October 1917, Kautsky published a critical pamphlet, *The Dictatorship of the Proletariat,* to which Lenin responded almost immediately in an essay with the insulting title, *The Proletarian Revolution and the Renegade Kautsky.* As the elder statesman of a movement in which he was gradually losing his place of significance, Kautsky was stung, and went on the attack once more in 1920 with a treatise he called *Terrorism and Communism.* Joining what was now a full-scale public debate without the former modes of comradely deference, Trotsky wrote a long piece intentionally using Kautsky's identical title in which he bitterly attacked his antagonist. Whereas Kautsky had argued that terrorism and communism were mutually contradictory concepts and realities, Trotsky in his riposte formulated a ringing defense of the necessity of conflating the two, written in a style of total confidence in his ideas that in turn reflected the authoritative position he occupied in the Bolshevik government.

The debate between Trotsky and Kautsky concerned many issues of contemporary urgency, including the reasons for seizing power rather than waiting for either the development of a mass movement or a process of elections with a working-class majority to accomplish the same goal of realizing a socialist polity, and the justification of setting up "a dictatorship of the proletariat" under Bolshevik control. Kautsky's critique was both disturbing and important to Leninists because it boldly established a moderate position within the Marxist ideological spectrum, capable of attracting young recruits to the cause of socialism, on the general problem of how economies transitioned from capitalism to socialism and the significance of achieving socialism through parliamentary means. Trotsky argued that Russian economic conditions, less developed than those in most Western European countries, necessitated an insurrectionary seizure of power, and he counted on the emergence of similar revolutionary events in Europe in the near future to demonstrate the global demise of the class divisions of the capitalist system. Instead of supporting the Bolshevik cause, Kautsky, in the opinion of both Lenin and Trotsky, had turned into a "renegade" by joining the opposition to revolution. Particularly unforgivable in Trotsky's view was Kautsky's decision to participate in the postwar Weimar government by joining Friedrich Ebert's Independent Socialist Party cabinet.[20]

On the issue of terrorism, a central theme of the debate, Trotsky aspired to a level of ideological consistency that completely contradicted the position he had staked out so carefully in "The Collapse of Terrorism" and that he now abandoned without mentioning. Kautsky's main point in his essay was that the Bolsheviks, once they acquired power, had betrayed Marxism by introducing dictatorial methods of state terrorism, methods not unlike the reactionary politics of the tsarist autocracy they had replaced. He saw no justification in a socialist regime for the denunciation of "enemies of the state," some of whom were arrested and being brought before revolutionary tribunals. Trotsky's answer was that revolutions require such severity. "The iron dictatorship of the Jacobins" during the French Revolution failed not because of its methods but because it could not overcome its internal and external enemies who fought to restore the old regime. The Paris Commune of 1871 also fell because it too could not withstand the assaults against it. The "proletarian dictatorship in Russia" was facing even more difficult circumstances, surrounded by military invasion on all fronts and by "countless internal enemies" who sought to bring down the revolution and return the monarchy to power. History's lessons, according to Trotsky, were that there is "no other way of breaking the class will of the enemy except [through] the systematic and energetic use of violence.... The more ferocious and dangerous is the resistance of the class enemies who have been overthrown, the more inevitably does the system of repression take the form of a system of terror."

Thus, "Soviet terrorism" is for Trotsky equated with "revolutionary terrorism" in situations where violence must be employed for purposes of survival and eventual success. The term he uses with evident pride is "Red Terror" to describe the tactics necessary to engage the enemy in what is for him an extension of the civil war—the counterrevolutionary class war.[21] There is no alternative "in a moment of the greatest peril, foreign attacks, and internal plots and insurrections" other than "to have recourse to severe measures of State Terror" (*TC*, 57). The revolutionaries leading the fight on behalf of the working masses can only attain their end of guaranteeing the consolidation of socialism by utilizing "all methods at its disposal; if necessary, by an armed rising; if required, by terrorism." He further argues that "intimidation is a powerful weapon of policy, both internationally and internally." To succeed, the revolution must break the will of its enemies by both creating fear and carrying out violence (*TC*, 58).

The only moral condemnation of the state terror of a revolutionary class conceivable in Trotsky's mind is the position of a total pacifist who rejects violence in every form. But this is not admissible for the Bolsheviks. Addressing Kautsky directly, Trotsky writes, "The gendarmerie of tsarism throttled the workers who were fighting for the socialist order. Our Extraordinary Commissions shoot landlords, capitalists, and generals who are striving to restore the capitalist order. Do you grasp this distinction? For us Communists, it is quite sufficient" (*TC*, 59). He had clearly not forgotten his own description of the reigning motive for terror—revenge—upon which he established his opposition to terrorism ten years before in "The Collapse of Terrorism."

Is there an ethical foundation to Trotsky's argument here? Baruch Knei-Paz, who has written one of the most comprehensive studies of Trotsky's ideas, believes that the defense of Red Terror was "an extreme form of utilitarianism." By this he means that Trotsky could not permit anything to stand in the way of realizing the consolidation of the revolution. Any threat, real or perceived, had to be combated with all the force necessary for victory. The goal determined the means. The Red Terror was therefore morally justifiable because violence was employed for the purpose of realizing a classless society under socialism. Workers required recourse to terror in order to secure their power against the forces of the old regime. The White Terror, by contrast, was not justifiable because it served a reactionary regime run in the interests of elites against the majority of society. The strategy, Knei-Paz notes, is reminiscent of Rousseau's ruthless ethical formulation that in certain political situations, men have to be forced to be free.[22]

George Kline has investigated another pathway into this problem. Trotsky's acceptance of the morality of violence is rooted in his Marxist "obsessive future orientation," in which he justifies "the devaluing and instrumentalizing of present existents, from whole cultures and social classes to small groups and individuals." In simpler terms, most of what constitutes the culture of the present is, in this view, regarded as having intrinsic value only in terms of how it serves the goals of the desired future order. Thus, whatever is categorizable as an agent of the capitalist economy and its bourgeois political structure assumes the value of an obstructor to the future socialist society and must be struck down by "the sword of revolutionary terror." According to this logic, Kline continues, Trotsky saw no limit from a moral standpoint to the use of violence to advance toward that radiant future society. Any discussion of the sanctity of human life, as Kautsky attempted to propose, is hypocritical when conducted in the framework of a political order that brutalized its citizens, whether monarchical or democratic. Since state violence was pervasive in history, the only defensible position from the perspective of communist ethics was to argue that terror was an absolute necessity. Trotsky distinguished his principle from the state terror of the past in one other regard: he predicted that violence would decline in proportion to the maturation of socialism.[23]

An equally important matter that has not been addressed adequately in the literature concerns the reasons behind the extraordinary shift in Trotsky's views on terrorism from the position he took in the 1909 essay to the one he argued in 1920. Much attention has been appropriately placed on explicating the ideological meaning of his writings and his place vis-à-vis the Marxist factions competing with one another for influence both in Russian Marxist circles and in West European Social Democratic parties. In the process, however, the larger context of his life as an exile and its significance has been neglected.

Exiles have been part of the landscape of Western civilization since the dawn of recorded history. Exile itself has long been a form of punishment for regimes to exclude members of their societies whom they perceive as politically threatening. To live in exile is to be deprived of one's cultural moorings and requires a process of adaptation and acceptance of loss that ultimately contributes to the redefinition of self that must take place in the absence of the homeland. Few writers have made the pain of this displacement more palpable than Edward Said in his poignant essay, "Reflections on Exile."[24]

Russian political exiles began to make their appearance in the capitals of Western Europe soon after the Decembrist uprising of 1825.[25] Although Alexander Herzen and Lenin may be among the best known of these exiles, they represent only the most visible layer of the thousands of comrades who gathered in increasing numbers in the decades leading up to and following the First World War in Geneva, Paris, Berlin, and London, where neighborhoods sprouted in which only Russian could be heard in the local bookstores and cafés and at party meetings. By the time Trotsky arrived abroad in 1907 after escaping a prison sentence, he found a substantial community of embittered exiles, all of whom had dedicated their lives to undermining from afar the tsarist regime that prevented them from returning home. The very phenomenon of exile was understood as a temporary status, a zone where identity was characterized not by efforts at assimilation but by a consensus of exclusion, which was in itself an extension of the outlaw identity that the Russian authorities had initially assigned them. The task at hand for Trotsky and most of the exiles in his circle was to overcome the alienation, separation, and loss of cultural identity they found themselves confronting by choosing a career in the radical underground. Their ideological pronouncements and endless debates were assertions and affirmations of a new identity as heroic warriors without a country, attached to ideas instead of place, to political comrades instead of families. Above all, they sought to avoid the descent into a meaningless existence in foreign obscurity and what might be called social death. To escape this horrifying fate, the source of the original exclusion, the tsarist state, had to be assaulted in words and deeds. The mission required nothing less than a total construction of a new order, complete with ethical principles contrary to those that had justified their exclusion, and controls against the possibility of ever again being expelled. The outlaw would be legitimized as the Leviathan, using all available means, including violence, to secure that situation.

Within a decade, Trotsky's life had irrevocably changed once again. He had paid attention to the "lessons of history" from the Terror of the French Revolution and the failure of the Paris Commune. He had devoted much time to establishing strategies against his enemies abroad and in opposition political parties and factions at home. However, he neglected one critical enemy, who would ultimately destroy him. After a savage struggle with Joseph Stalin over control of the Soviet governing apparatus, which intensified after Lenin's death in January 1924, Trotsky was again exiled from his homeland, this time permanently.

He was refused entry into country after country (including the United States) until the authorities in Mexico City permitted him to immigrate in 1930. There he spent the final decade of his life writing his magisterial history of the Russian Revolution and issuing critiques of Stalin's distortions of Lenin's revolutionary legacy. He was well aware of the irony of his position. Having been the theorist of state terror while in power, he was now turning into a critic of the Bolshevik police state he had helped create. He was also well aware that his anti-Stalinist writings threatened his very existence; the assassination squads sent to kill him under orders from Moscow were both rumored and real. He sought, and found, a grand arena, rare for exiles, from which to conduct his counterattack.

In the spring of 1937, after officially receiving political asylum in Mexico, Trotsky arranged for the creation of an international commission of inquiry in order to publicly reply to the charges of "crimes against the Soviet state" of which he had been convicted in absentia in Moscow during the infamous purge trials the year before. A number of significant figures accepted the invitation to participate, including the distinguished philosopher John Dewey, who agreed to chair the proceedings.

Trotsky was so convinced of his eventual exoneration that he issued a statement on February 9, 1937, that "if this commission decides that I am guilty in the slightest degree of the crimes which Stalin imputes to me, I pledge in advance to place myself voluntarily in the hands of the executioners of the GPU."[26] The hearings took place during the next months in Mexico City, and when the final report was issued, on September 21, 1937, the commission had found that the eighteen charges brought against Trotsky in Moscow were insufficiently proven to indicate any measure of guilt. While this conclusion obviously pleased Trotsky, the embarrassment it caused Stalin was the final stimulus for his decision to have Trotsky assassinated.

Buried in the long report of the transcript of these hearings, published in 1937 as *The Case of Leon Trotsky,* was Trotsky's most extensive discussion of the subject of terrorism since his article on the Red Terror in *Terrorism and Communism* almost two decades earlier. In his effort to discredit the allegations of anti-Soviet activities leveled against him, Trotsky turned his attention to the issue of political violence in the context of a socialist state. He reviewed his earliest years as a revolutionary Marxist in the tsarist era, when, as he put it, "the problem of terror was a life and death matter in the political as well as the personal meaning of the term" (*CLT,* 490). On the one hand, he knew terrorists personally from that time, having spent time with them in prison and exile, listening patiently and sympathetically to their explanations and justifications; on the other, this was a period when he agreed with the Marxist position on terrorism taken by all factions, including "Plekhanov, the founder of Russian Marxism; Lenin, the leader of Bolshevism; and Martov, the most eminent representative of Menshevism." Though they found consensus on little else, they were consistent in their opposition to the use of terrorist tactics as practiced by the SRs. Trotsky then reviewed his 1909 article, "The Collapse of Terrorism," from which he provided extensive quotations to demonstrate his agreement with this orientation. He concluded from this look back that "terrorism has always remained for me nothing but a blind alley" (*CLT,* 491).

As for the contemporary situation, Trotsky argued that "the Stalinist bureaucracy has created a revolting leader-cult," endowing leaders with divine attributes. This "'hero' cult," he wrote, "is also the religion of terrorism, only with a minus sign" (*CLT,* 493).[27] As he claimed to have shown in that first article, the SRs in the earlier era of terrorism had worshipped a similar charismatic image of false heroism, leaving the masses in passive isolation. The charges of terrorism leveled against him by Stalin and his supporters in Moscow, Trotsky claimed, were completely baseless. This was not "class vengeance," which was the only kind of political violence Trotsky admitted to finding morally justified. Rather, "the real terrorists" in the Soviet Union were the agents of the secret police, the GPU, who had conspired to assassinate Sergei Kirov, to orchestrate acts of disruption and destruction at factories, and then to blame these acts on Trotsky and his alleged followers (*CLT,* 497). The alleged hit list of Soviet leaders, which included Stalin, Kirov, Voroshilov, Kaganovich, and Ordzhonikidze (but not Molotov, Trotsky exclaims in feigned shock), was in reality the product of that same bureaucratic security service acting under orders from Stalin and his "totalitarian regime" (*CLT,* 500–501, 509). This unacceptable departure from the socialist goals set by Lenin "will be overthrown by the toiling masses," Trotsky predicts, either with or without violence (*CLT,* 514).

Trotsky took one more opportunity to write directly on the problem of terrorism. In 1938, he composed an essay called "Their Morals and Ours," in which he attempted to distinguish between his Bolshevik morality and Stalin's betrayal of the Marxist-Leninist principles on which it was, in his view, based. In this article Trotsky took "full responsibility for the Decree of 1919," which permitted the taking and killing of hostages designated as enemies of the Bolshevik regime. He defended this act as a consequence of the life-and-death struggle of the Russian Civil War, which, he now confessed, "can be called, not without foundation, disgusting barbarism."[28] Violence of this type is justifiable if victory is to be gained because of what he termed "the dialectical interdependence of end and means." Specifically, he continued, returning to an earlier argument, "a means can be justified only by its end. . . . Is everything therefore permissible? No." Only that which really leads to the "abolition of the power of man over man" is morally defensible. Thus, violence is permissible only if it serves the cause of proletarian liberation. "Revolutionary morality rejects servility in relation to the bourgeoisie."[29]

In the end, Trotsky's argument is not convincing. He was never able to establish a separate code of ethics to clearly distinguish his own revolutionary morality from what he saw as Stalin's "bureaucratic terrorism." He failed to provide objective criteria to permit a philosophical distinction other than the relativism of historical circumstances and the agency of personal interpretation. Trotsky convinced himself that the battle lines drawn during the civil war continued in its aftermath. These continuing threats to the permanence of Bolshevik power entitled him to justify all acts of violence in the name of the "proletarian dictatorship" outlined originally by Marx. Hence, he sees the utter necessity for the Red Terror. However, he does not answer the crucial question: what was the ethical difference between his acceptable state violence and Stalin's party purges, trials, and executions fifteen years later? He was trapped between, on the one hand, denying the moral absolutism of the sanctity of human life, and on the other, the recognition that a declared end can justify the means to get there, regardless of how destructive the violence. This was hardly an attempt to formulate the trajectory toward the realization of the virtuous society, the common good, or the rights of citizens. He fails to assign moral obligations to any social constituency except the working class, whose freedom, he argues, can only be achieved by ending social inequality, and that can only take place under the direction of his (and not Stalin's) interpretation of Marx's analysis of capitalism.

As the discussion above makes clear, Trotsky's contradictory positions on the subject of terrorism over the course of his political career were driven by the circumstances of the historical moments in which he wrote. He was an intellectual ideologist whose futile search for theoretical consistency was ultimately overwhelmed by the force of the roles he adopted in these moments. When he wrote "The Collapse of Terrorism," he was in the process of formulating a position on political violence that was necessary because of the importance of the tactic at the time. No fledgling Marxist could avoid taking sides on the problem, since the violence of the SR campaign of terrorism had reached epidemic proportions in Russia at that time. Trotsky's solution was to follow the lead of his ideological mentors, from Marx to Lenin, by defining the contemporary political violence as "individual" acts perpetrated by elite squads of political fanatics committed to the illusion that such idealized heroism would bring down the regime. Trotsky subscribed to another faith, namely, that without the active participation of the channeled rage of the politically repressed and economically exploited masses, such tactics of violence against officialdom would only lead to a strengthening of the brutality of tsarism. The anticipated revolution, in other words, would recede farther from the realm of possibility and the regime would retaliate more violently, sanctioning ever greater police powers and further deprivations of liberty. Despite Trotsky's reliance for guidance on the discourse of Marxism, his 1909 essay remains one of the most cogent arguments expressing the futility of utilizing political violence to undermine, delegitimize, or overthrow a despotic regime, so long as it was carried out in the form of political assassinations conducted by individuals outside the class struggle and without the involvement of a mass insurrection of workers and peasants. At the same time, he did not recognize his own rage as that of an excluded exile, a rage he had projected on the proletariat in his theory. He wanted the workers to mobilize and achieve "class consciousness," but he also desired his own role in the struggle to bring down the forces responsible for his status as an outlaw expelled from his country.

By contrast, Trotsky wrote the essay justifying the Red Terror at a time when he had been catapulted to the heights of power in the newly established socialist state in Russia. His return from exile was a consequence of the general amnesty issued by the newly installed Provisional Government in March 1917, after the Romanov dynasty had been overthrown. This extraordinary act permitted all political prisoners to be liberated from the labor camps of Siberia and all radical opponents of the old regime to return from abroad as legally constituted citizens of the nascent Russian Republic. Far from expressing gratitude for this unexpected turn in their lives, the exiles who returned to the Finland Station in Petrograd devoted themselves primarily to realizing the conceptions of revolution that had driven them into the lawless underground parties in the first place.[30] The October insurrection in which the Bolsheviks took command of the center of government in an overnight military operation produced an astonishing result: it brought to power a whole cadre of revolutionaries who had spent most of their adult years out of Russia. They had lived their lives abroad, rootless and victimized, their mentality shaped more by intense party debates over ideological tactics, revolutionary strategy, and complex theoretical discourses than by the quotidian realities of Russia. They returned with pent-up rage and powerful utopian fantasies that they were to put into practice as the new figures of authority and legitimacy.[31] This, then, was not only the world's first socialist state but the first modern government dominated by former political exiles.

The place to turn to understand Trotsky's thinking at this moment in time is his military oeuvre. Even after the successful conclusion of the civil war, Trotsky continued to operate in a military mind-set. The civil war may have ended, but class warfare under socialism had only begun. His role as its leader included expanding and justifying the tactics of violence into all areas of Soviet society to maintain victory. Like a soldier who cannot accept demobilization, Trotsky was unable to renounce the importance of a battle first established while he was in exile. He spoke and wrote of permanent revolution, but he lived as though he were in permanent war.[32]

The volte-face executed by Trotsky between 1909 and 1920 is breathtaking. At this point, Trotsky turned to the situation facing the Parisian members of the Committee of Public Safety in 1793, when state terrorism was proclaimed as a national necessity for the preservation of the revolution and the security of the citizenry. The assumption here is that the state possesses a monopoly on violence and should make full use of this authority against all groups defined as a threat to national security. The notion of justified state terrorism is completely absent in his earlier essay. He did not even mention the end of the *Communist Manifesto,* where Marx discussed the barest outline of what he meant by the "dictatorship of the proletariat" following the advent of socialism in a futuristic postrevolutionary era. However, in *Terrorism and Communism,* he identified himself with the embattled members of the Paris Commune, where terrorism was justified under specific conditions, as Trotsky perceived them, of enemy assault on the revolutionary government of the newly empowered masses.

Finally, in exile, out of power, and under judicial attack by Stalin, Trotsky found his first essay a convenient explanation to argue that he had always been against terrorism since his first days as a revolutionary Marxist. Now it was Stalin and his bureaucracy who represented the real face of terrorism. This time Trotsky indulged in a selective memory process when, in a transparent effort to present himself as a lifelong opponent of terrorism, he deliberately neglected to quote from *Terrorism and Communism.* Here the need to defend himself overpowered his honesty in dealing with his own past. He seems never to have fully comprehended the extent to which his changing positions on terrorism were defined by his perceptions of the political authority—tsarism first and, later, Stalinism—against which he had rebelled. This rebellion was fashioned out of the conditions of his early underground experiences as an outlaw-revolutionary and the burning anger he harbored all his life for being imprisoned and forced into exile. "We spent decades in underground conditions, carried on our struggle, fought on the barricades, overturned the old regime, and cast aside all in-between groups such as the SRs and Mensheviks and . . . took power into our hands."[33]

It was precisely those conditions in the underground that fostered the violent rage that motivated Trotsky's seemingly contradictory perspectives on political violence. The bitterness remained in response to his experiences as an exile in Europe, where, although political activities illegal in Russia might be protected by law, he was always aware of being socially and politically marginalized.[34]

For some of these politically committed opponents who have been humiliated, marginalized, and excluded, terrorism can become an appealing weapon of choice. Indeed, even in the passages of the 1909 essay where Trotsky rejects the violent tactics of the individual assassins represented by the SR terrorists, he is already forming his own alternative form of violence, namely, the proletarian-inspired upheaval that can act out its role as avenger of the masses. His personal vengeance against the tsarist regime was projected into a narrative of class vengeance using Marxist ideology as the justification for the coming to power of the repressed peasantry and workers. Terrorism is about contesting for authority and legitimacy, but it also involves a cry for inclusion and redress for the insults of marginalization, motivated by rage and the desire for retribution and reprisals. Having lived so much of his life as an opponent, the one thing Trotsky shared with his Stalinist enemies was his violent intolerance of an opposition.

Notes

The author thanks the members of the Triangle Intellectual History Seminar at the National Humanities Center and Anthony Anemone for their valuable criticism of earlier drafts of this essay.

1. For this analysis, see Martin A. Miller, "Ordinary Terrorism in Historical Perspective," *Journal for the Study of Radicalism* 2, no. 1 (2008): 125–54.

2. Karl Marx and Frederick Engels, *Collected Works* (New York: International Publishers, 1987), 42:501–2. Marx to Engels, December 14, 1867. Hereafter cited as *CW.*

3. Engels to Marx, December 19, 1867, in Marx and Engels, *CW,* 42:505–6. In this letter, Engels's scorn for this form of violence is evident as he added, "Especially in America there has been a lot of bluster amongst this explosive and incendiary fraternity, and then along comes some individual jackasses [who] instigate this kind of nonsense."

4. Engels to Eduard Bernstein, June 26, 1882, in Marx and Engels, *CW,* 46:288.

5. Engels to Johann Philipp Becker, December 16, 1882, in Marx and Engels, *CW,* 46:405.

6. Engels to Pablo Iglesias, March 26, 1894, Karl Marx and Friedrich Engels, *Werke* (Berlin: Dietz Verlag, 1968), 39:229.

7. V. I. Lenin, *Polnoe sobranie sochinenii* (Moscow: Gosizdatpolitlit, 1959), 6:375–76. Hereafter cited as *PSS.*

8. V. I. Lenin, "A Tactical Platform for the Unity Congress" (March 1906), quoted in *The Terrorism Reader,* ed. Walter Laqueur and Yonah Alexander (New York: Meridian Press, 1987), 216.

9. Lenin, *PSS,* 12:229. On Bolshevik duplicity in addressing the admissibility of terror, see Anna Geifman, *Thou Shalt Kill: Revolutionary Terrorism in Russia, 1894–1917* (Princeton: Princeton University Press, 1993), 84–122, 247.

10. Norman M. Naimark, "Terrorism and the Fall of Imperial Russia," *Terrorism and Political Violence,* Summer 1990, 171–92. Naimark lists 2,563 government personnel killed and 2,954 wounded between 1905 and 1908, in addition to "several thousand civilians who were killed and wounded." More recently, lower numbers are cited in A. I. Ushakov, *Politicheskaia politsiia i politicheskii terrorizm v Rossii* (Moscow:

AIRO-XX, 2001), 19. For the overall estimates, see Geifman, *Thou Shalt Kill,* 21, 264.

11. For a comparison of the two movements, see my "Terrorism: The Great Game," in *Playing Politics with Terrorism,* ed. George Kassimeris (London: Hurst, 2007), 15–35.

12. The second part did not appear until 1911, when it was published in the November issue of *Der Kampf.* The articles were republished in L. D. Trotsky, *Sochineniia* (Moscow: Gosudarstevennoe izdatel'stvo, 1926), 4:345–69. All subsequent quotations are from this text, with the page numbers indicated parenthetically.

13. See Anna Geifman, *Entangled in Terror: The Azef Affair and the Russian Revolution* (Wilmington, Del.: SR Books, 2000).

14. Although he wrote about these years of prison and exile with some degree of levity in his memoir, his anger is only thinly veiled. See *My Life* (New York: Pathfinder Press, 1970), 187–285. See also the account of this period in N. S. Vasetskii, *Trotskii: Opyt politicheskoi biografii* (Moscow: Respublika, 1992), 51–74.

15. The best collection of these writings can be found in his *Sochineniia,* vols. 4, 6, 8, and 9.

16. See the recently issued collection of previously unpublished archival documents on Trotsky's role at this time at the helm of state with Lenin: Valerii Krasnov and Vladimir Daines, eds., *Neizvestnyi Trotskii. Krasnyi Bonapart. Dokumenty, Mneniia, Razmyshleniia* (Moscow: Olma-Press, 2000), 409–80.

17. See in particular Kropotkin's personal protests to Lenin in 1919, as described in Martin A. Miller, *Kropotkin* (Chicago: University of Chicago Press, 1976), 241–42. His protesting letters are reproduced in P. A. Kropotkin, *Selected Writings on Anarchism and Revolution,* ed. Martin A. Miller (Cambridge, Mass.: MIT Press, 1970), 323–39.

18. Kautsky's published books and essays number well over 150 items. After assisting Engels as his private secretary, Kautsky established his reputation with *The Erfurt Program* (1891), *The Agrarian Question* (1899), and his critiques of Eduard Bernstein's evolutionary Marxism on the right and Lenin's Bolshevism on the left of the international social democratic movement.

19. Rosa Luxemburg had written a criticism of Lenin's theory of the party's centralized control over a revolutionary vanguard of workers in 1904 in *Die Neue Zeit* ("Organizatsionsfragen der Russischen Sozialdemokraten") and continued to argue her differences with Lenin after the 1917 revolution.

20. On Kautsky's ideas and career, see John H. Kautsky, *Karl Kautsky: Marxism, Revolution and Democracy* (New Brunswick, N.J.: Transaction Press, 1994).

21. Leon Trotsky, *Terrorism and Communism,* trans. Max Shachtman (Ann Arbor: University of Michigan Press, 1961 [Russian, 1920]), 55. Henceforth cited as *TC.* All further quotations in the text are from this work, with page numbers noted in parentheses.

22. Baruch Knei-Paz, *The Social and Political Thought of Leon Trotsky* (Oxford: Clarendon Press, 1978), 248–51.

23. George Kline, "The Defense of Terrorism: Trotsky and His Major Critics," in *The Trotsky Reappraisal,* ed. Terry Brotherstone and Paul Dukes (Edinburgh: Edinburgh University Press, 1992), 156–65.

24. Edward Said, "Reflections on Exile," in *Altogether, Elsewhere: Writers on Exile,* ed. Marc Robinson (New York: Harcourt, Brace, 1994), 137–49. See also *The Bitter*

Air of Exile: Russian Writers in the West, 1922–1972, ed. Simon Karlinsky and Alfred Appel (Berkeley and Los Angeles: University of California Press, 1977).

25. Martin A. Miller, *The Russian Revolutionary Émigrés, 1825–1870* (Baltimore: Johns Hopkins University Press, 1986).

26. That is, the Soviet secret police. *The Case of Leon Trotsky: Report of Hearings on the Charges Made Against Him in the Moscow Trials* by the Preliminary Commission of Inquiry, John Dewey, Chairman (New York: Merit Publishers, 1968), x. This is a reprint of the original volume, which was published in 1937. Hereafter cited as *CLT.* All further quotations in the text are from this work, with page numbers noted in parentheses.

27. Trotsky is referring to the charges being made in Moscow that he was behind a plot to assassinate a number of ranking Bolshevik Party members, which has never been demonstrated with valid evidence. In addition, Trotsky was well aware of Stalin's obsession with Ivan the Terrible, which dated back to Robert Vipper's biography of Ivan, first published in 1922. Stalin later commissioned its republication. Vipper was of the opinion that "the government of Ivan Grozny permitted the free exchange of opinion," that Ivan succeeded in vanquishing his internal enemies, and that he introduced beneficial "social and administrative reforms." See the excerpt in Thomas Riha, *Readings in Russian Civilization* (Chicago: University of Chicago Press, 1974), 98–109.

28. Leon Trotsky, *Their Morals and Ours* (New York: Pathfinder Press, 1969), 28–29. The decree can be found in Krasnov and Daines, *Neizvestnyi Trotskii,* 152. Trotsky did not mention that he had issued similar edicts even earlier. On August 4, 1918, he wrote, "Root out the counter-revolutionaries without mercy, lock up suspicious characters in concentration camps. . . . Shirkers will be shot, regardless of past service." Quoted in Dmitry Volkogonov, *Trotsky: The Eternal Revolutionary* (New York: Free Press, 1996), 213.

29. Trotsky, *Their Morals and Ours,* 36–37. On this theme, see Maurice Merleau-Ponty's interesting analysis in his *Humanism and Terror* (Boston: Beacon Press, 2001), 71–98.

30. There are many accounts of this transitional period, but one of the best remains Edmond Wilson's classic narrative, *To the Finland Station,* originally published in 1940 and still in print.

31. This subject is one waiting for a specialized study. By checking the biographies of the Bolshevik leadership in the immediate aftermath of the Bolshevik seizure of power, one finds that for the great majority, long years of prison and exile abroad dominated the pre-1917 years. See K. A. Zaleskii, *Imperiia Stalina: Biograficheskii entsiklopedicheskii slovar'* (Moscow: Veche, 2000), and P. Kallinkov, ed., *Russkii biografichekii slovar'* (Moscow: Terra, 1998–2001). In 1916, Trotsky was still struggling as an exile against what he called the "bourgeois state." He was ordered to leave France in October, and found himself under arrest upon arrival on Spanish soil. Finally leaving for Russia by ship, he revealed his anger at Europe and his relief to at last be returning to Russia in a letter to Alfred Roesner: "For a long time I watched through the mist as that old scoundrel, Europe, slipped further away." Quoted in Volkogonov, *Trotsky,* 63.

32. See the collection of essays that clearly demonstrate this orientation in Leon Trotsky, *Military Writings* (New York: Merit Publishers, 1969).

33. Letter from Trotsky dated January 10, 1919, in Trotsky, *Military Writings,* 148.

34. The frustrated rage of the Russian exiles, even when they were in relatively comfortable positions abroad, can be found in their writings from the very beginnings of the emigration in Europe. See Miller, *The Russian Revolutionary Emigrés.* For the later decades, see the revealing letters compiled by Michael Confino, *Anarchistes en exile: Correspondence inédite de Pierre Kropotkine à Marie Goldsmith, 1897–1917* (Paris: Institute d'études slaves, 1995). Further examples can be found in Michael Glenny and Norman Stone, *The Other Russia: The Experience of Exile* (New York: Viking, 1990); Karlinsky and Appel, *The Bitter Air;* and Lesley Chamberlain, *Lenin's Private War: The Voyage of the Philosophy Steamer and the Exile of the Intelligentsia* (New York: St. Martin's Press, 2006).

The Afterlife of Terrorists: Commemorating the People's Will in Early Soviet Russia

James Frank Goodwin

> From the threshold of one hall [of the Museum of Revolution], he suddenly caught clear sight of two large portraits of Zheliabov and Perovskaia at the top of the opposite wall. Their faces were open, fearless, their looks indomitable; and to all who entered they called out, "Kill the tyrant!" Struck in the throat by the gaze of each *Narodovolets*, as if by two arrows, Stalin staggered back. Wheezing and coughing, he pointed his shaking finger at the portraits. They were taken down immediately. In Leningrad, too, the first relic of the Revolution, the wreckage of Alexander's carriage, was also removed from its museum.
>
> —ALEXANDER SOLZHENITSYN, *IN THE FIRST CIRCLE*

The phenomenon of Russian revolutionary terrorism has received extensive treatment in recent studies, but scholars have devoted comparatively little space to the image of Russian terrorists during the early Soviet period. Despite the Bolsheviks' traditional opposition to methods of revolutionary terrorism, analyzed by Martin A. Miller in his essay in this volume, there arose within Soviet society a strong impulse to commemorate the martyrs of the revolutionary movement, especially the pioneering "terrorists" of the 1870s. Although the revolution's legacy of terrorism remained predominantly negative, insofar as terrorist methods invariably failed to weaken the autocratic state (as Marxists have often noted), nonetheless, memory of the terrorist episode in early Russian populism offered a significant benefit to Soviet Russian culture. Regardless of terrorism's eventual "collapse," dramatic accounts of its best-organized and most memorable manifestation, the Executive Committee of the People's Will (Narodnaia volia), provided Soviet readers with exemplary models of self-sacrifice, revolutionary heroism, and passionate hatred of the old monarchy. Unlike the terrorist fighters of the Socialist Revolutionary Party, moreover, the daring assassins of Tsar Alexander II ("executed" on March 1, 1881) remained uncompromised by a history of opposition to Bolshevism. To the builders and supporters of a new Soviet society, *narodovol'chestvo* epitomized precisely the kind of militant determination and unwavering commitment to revolution their own success demanded.[1]

Yet even as the new Soviet state formally recognized the honorable motives of its terrorist forerunners, official encouragement of commemoration also facilitated a certain revival of interest in the ideas, personalities, and achievements of *narodovol'chestvo.* The remarkable literary productivity of the populist movement's surviving veterans suggests that the legacy of terrorism in the Russian revolutionary experience carried a greater potential for popular appeal in Soviet society than originally anticipated. Early Soviet Russia did not merely pay tribute to *narodovol'chestvo,* but in effect permitted its former participants to celebrate it more openly and extensively than ever before. From the standpoint of a truly proletarian dictatorship, of course, popular interest in *narodovol'chestvo* and its fallen leaders could pose little threat to a society armed with knowledge of populism's historical failures, but the concentration of power in a single leader after 1928 inevitably exposed the objective impossibility of coexistence between an autocratically directed state and a popular legacy of tyrannicide. By 1935 the inherently oppositionist threat posed by *narodovol'chestvo* finally outweighed its commemorative value for Russian society under Stalin.

The outlook for the resurrection of the People's Will seemed promising when the Bolsheviks came to power. Notwithstanding their populist idealization of the peasant commune and other ideological errors, Lenin's admiration for the selfless heroism, organizational skill, and fighting spirit of the *narodovol'tsy* obviously favored the survival of their legacy.[2] The official call to honor leading representatives of the People's Will in works of "monumental propaganda" during the first year of Soviet power marked an important step toward their formal commemoration. Andrei Zheliabov (1851–81), Sofia Perovskaia (1853–81), Nikolai Kibalchich (1853–81), and Stepan Khalturin (1856–82),[3] martyrs of the terrorist struggle and conspiracy to kill Alexander II, all received an honored place among the thirty-one "revolutionists and social activists" to whom the Arts Section of Narkompros (the People's Commissariat for Enlightenment) proposed monuments for the first anniversary of the October Revolution. Although not all of the projects were realized, a ceremonial presentation of a sculptural monument to Perovskaia took place at Petrograd's Nikolai (Moscow) Station on December 29, 1918. Attended by leading Narkompros representatives Anatoly Lunacharsky and Nikolai Punin, together with veteran narodovolets Nikolai Morozov (1854–1946), the event reminded observers of the terrorist contribution to the Russian Revolution.[4] The same period saw the renaming of central streets in Petrograd after Zheliabov, Perovskaia, and Khalturin.

The survival of a productive group of populist elders during the 1920s proved equally significant for the heritage of *narodovol'chestvo.* Leading veterans from the People's Will numbered among the small percentage of nineteenth-century revolutionists who survived prison and exile before the fall of the monarchy. They found institutional identity within the Society of Former Political Prisoners and Exiles (*Obshchestvo byvshikh politkatorzhan i ssyl'no-poselentsev*), established in Moscow in March 1921, four years after the amnesties of the February Revolution conclusively rehabilitated political convicts of the tsarist era.[5] While the younger veterans of twentieth-century parties naturally dominated the society's ranks, by 1925 at least sixty veteran populists comprised a visible contingent among the three thousand members of the society. Of the almost nine hundred members who registered with the society following its first All-Union Congress in 1924, forty-four individuals still identified themselves with populist organizations of the 1870s, predominantly the People's Will.[6] All members of the society shared the common experience of incarceration and exile under the tsars, but the criterion of punitive repression undoubtedly privileged the People's Will, since its members generally endured the longest periods in Russian prisons or banishment to isolated settlements. Leading narodovoltsy Mikhail Frolenko (1848–1938), Nikolai Morozov, and Mikhail Ashenbrenner (1842–1926) deserved special honor as longtime survivors of the Peter-Paul and Shlisselburg prisons, where they each spent twenty or more years, while Anna Yakimova-Dikovskaia (1856–1942) and Anna Pribyleva-Korba (1849–1939) lived out extensive sentences of deportation in Kara and other distant areas of eastern Siberia. No less significantly, several elders also enjoyed a unique authority in the society as veteran representatives of the People's Will's Executive Committee, the principal source of organized terrorist activity in the movement. Having endorsed the Executive Committee's declaration of war on the autocracy, Frolenko, Yakimova, Morozov, Pribyleva-Korba, and Sofia Ivanova-Boreisho (1856–1927), together with independent veteran Vera Figner (1852–1952),[7] all witnessed populism's fatal transition from propaganda to organized terrorism and worked closely with its leading martyrs, Zheliabov, Perovskaia, Khalturin, and Alexander Mikhailov (1855–84). Frolenko and Yakimova personally helped implement the Executive Committee's attempts on the tsar.[8]

The veteran narodovoltsy made their greatest contribution to the populist heritage through their writings, which together formed a substantial literary monument to the terrorists' achievement. From 1923 to 1931, their memoirs of the populist movement and biographical portraits of its activists regularly filled the pages of *Katorga i ssylka* (*Hard Labor and Exile*), the society's official thick journal, while also supporting two large series of books and pamphlets through the society's publishing house.[9] In addition to describing life under conditions of hard labor and exile, the society's publications devoted substantial space to the evolution of the People's Will, including the development of the ideas and events that led to its unlikely assassination of the tsar.[10] The birth of the Executive Committee in 1879, only months after Alexander Soloviev's solo attempt on the tsar the previous April, represented a culminating moment for the movement, after which the more radical populists began to reject the unsuccessful methods of agitation in the villages and to accept the demand for a ruthless armed struggle against the monarchy and its agents.[11] It was precisely in this transition, however, that Bolshevik publicists perceived the fatal shortcoming of revolutionary populism, which broke with the masses and adopted the regressive and futile methods of individual terrorism. In light of the ideological stigma that threatened the survival of its heritage, explicating the People's Will's conception of violence, the party's adoption of a terrorist program, and the specific circumstances that encouraged it all became common aims of the surviving fighters.

Remarks by Figner, Yakimova, Frolenko, and others on the origins and role of terrorism demonstrate some of the strategies by which the veterans exonerated both themselves and their comrades for Soviet-era readers. By drawing a stark contrast between the chronic inertia of Alexander II's regime, on the one hand, and society's urgent need for liberty and justice, on the other, the well-known memoirs of Vera Figner seek to illuminate the progressive forces at work within the terrorist movement. The radicals' drift toward terrorism did not indicate a loss of faith in popular enlightenment, Figner explained, for their program of agitation in the villages remained very much alive; rather, the morbid condition of social initiative, all but dead from the pressure of the state's "unendurable" despotism, demanded violent resuscitation by means of "dagger, revolver and dynamite." Thus the pioneers of organized terrorism began to wage an active struggle against the government, convinced that only a direct attack on the tsar would "unleash the living forces in the people." For the revolutionist, commitment to the terrorist struggle carried the high risk of one's own death, which all members were required to accept in accordance with the organizational statutes. Demands of this nature were great, Figner insisted, but their austerity "elevated the individual and removed him from all banality," so that "one felt more alive" and aware that "an ideal lives and should live within one." Assessing the movement's evolution toward the assassination, Figner described a predominantly constructive experience, regardless of the negative consequences of "demoralization" and "corruption" that affected both individual and society. Despite the Executive Committee's regrettable creation of a "cult of dynamite" and a "halo for the terrorist," Figner nevertheless continued to associate its struggle with "solidarity," "brotherhood," and selfless "heroism."[12]

The individual experiences of Figner's surviving comrades on the Executive Committee generally supported her version of the terrorists' rationale. Closely involved in the construction of bombs and munitions for the committee, Anna Yakimova aimed in her recollections to dispel the common perception that a thirst for "revenge" motivated the regicide. Much like Figner, Yakimova argued that only the violent destruction of the autocrat promised the political freedom necessary for the people's development and "the revelation of its will." She also applied a similar metaphor of stagnation to describe Russia's situation during the final years of Alexander II's reign. Through active political struggle, "agitation by the fact," and "disorganization," the People's Will hoped both "to awaken the slumbering kingdom" and simultaneously "to destroy that fatalism, the absolute submission to fate" that had paralyzed propagandists of the word. By stimulating popular belief in the success of the struggle, the party might introduce new forces and thereby inject new life into the struggle. Reiterating one of Figner's main points, Yakimova argued that the People's Will never limited itself to terrorism alone, but routinely conducted active organizational and literary-propagandistic activity among workers, students, and the military.[13]

Support for the Executive Committee's intentions came from two other former members as well. Mikhail Frolenko, a leading militant of the committee's southern contingent, reminded readers of the radicals' sensitivity to popular moods along the road to terrorism. Recalling the "dark cloud" that smothered everyone around him, Frolenko argued that public dissatisfaction with the tsar, particularly in southern centers such as Odessa, finally pushed the question of his assassination to the forefront of the movement's agenda. The committee resolved, however, to attempt an assassination only on behalf of an entire organization, for fear that their purely political act might otherwise degenerate into a "typical murder."[14] One of the committee's agents and signalers on March 1, Anna Pribyleva-Korba, placed great emphasis on the lofty "moral attributes" that guided her fellow fighters, the "flower of the intelligentsia of the late 1870s." To her mind, each and every member of the Executive Committee of the People's Will possessed "enormous, effective energy, great strength of will, and unlimited steadfastness." Neither ambition nor a desire for glory guided them, only a "profound and inexhaustible love" for each other and the workers of Russia. Altruists by nature, Korba insisted, committee members picked up weapons and became terrorists only to defend the interests of the people.[15]

The aim to rehabilitate by means of commemoration also inspired a genre of popular literary portraits of leading narodovoltsy and other populists. Series such the *Inexpensive Library of the Journal Hard Labor and Exile* and *Members of the Executive Committee of the People's Will* continued a longstanding populist tradition of paying tribute to outstanding personalities and their role in the movement.[16] Two of the legendary figures, Perovskaia and Zheliabov, perhaps best exemplified the redeeming characteristics of valor, commitment, and humanity which their surviving associates sought to honor. They were also two of the committee's principal "terrorists" insofar as they both took an active part in all the attempts on the tsar, Perovskaia playing a key organizing role in the final, successful one. To a large extent the iconography of Perovskaia drew on her prerevolutionary profile by the radical Sergei Kravchinsky (Stepniak), whose book *Underground Russia* memorialized Perovskaia's noble character, her independence, "absolutely fearless" nature, and complete freedom from "fruitless reveries." Thanks to her independent outlook and wholehearted devotion to her cause, Kravchinsky recalled, Perovskaia excelled as one of the movement's outstanding initiators at an early stage. Only after joining the People's Will in its fight against the tsar, however, did Perovskaia discover the "magnificence" of her gifts and sense of "duty, discipline and diligence."[17] Figner corroborated Kravchinsky's observations in her own memoirs, noting that Perovskaia brought into the movement "pure soul" and feeling, which her reason, upon joining the People's Will, finally conquered. Ever "vigilant and prepared" in her activities, Figner insisted, Perovskaia's simplicity concealed "a strong will and steadfast character." With great appreciation for Perovskaia's heroic initiative in orchestrating the bomb attacks on March 1, Figner carried its significance a step further: without Perovskaia's "composure, deliberation, and direction" that day, the tsar would not have fallen.[18] Finally, in a popular sketch of 1930, one of Perovskaia's closest companions from the "going to the people" movement, Alexandra Kornilova-Moroz (1853–1938?), described Perovskaia's great courage upon joining the People's Will, for which she resolved to perish rather than flee abroad with her fellow "propagandists" in the Black Repartition (Chernyi peredel) Party. Kornilova also called attention to Perovskaia's stoic, unbending behavior during her trial, where she declared "immorality and cruelty" to be unthinkable charges from anyone familiar with "our life and the conditions under which we were forced to act."[19]

Commemoration of Zheliabov emphasized his extraordinary success as an agitator, first in persuading the committee to take decisive action against the tsar, then in attracting reliable workers and students to the committee's fighting detachments, including two of the bomb throwers and martyrs of March 1, Ignaty Grinevitsky (1856–81) and Timofei Mikhailov (1859–81). His popular biography by Lev Tikhomirov (1852–1923), another leading Executive Committee member, remained a standard tribute long after Tikhomirov unexpectedly renounced his revolutionary past. As a former "propagandist" like Perovskaia, Zheliabov first had to vanquish within himself a deep sense of partisan independence before he could embrace terrorism, centralization, and conspiracy. Once he committed to the committee and its program, however, Zheliabov became its greatest organizer. An "extraordinary orator," Tikhomirov recalled, Zheliabov consistently agitated for decisive action in whatever form it assumed, including "punishment" of the tsar. An uplifting, contagious love of life best explained the power of Zheliabov's character in Tikhomirov's account. Never "falling in spirit," even on the eve of 1881, with close friends disappearing and the complete annihilation of their ranks looming ahead, Zheliabov managed to generate confidence through his "cheerfulness" and "indestructible faith in the success of the cause."[20] Mikhail Frolenko's recollections further enlarged the monumental significance of Zheliabov's buoyant personality, which reflected the rich inner life of the terrorists, as well as their lack of despondency. In his efforts to draw Zheliabov into the Executive Committee in 1879, Frolenko established contact with him in Odessa, where he discovered a "garrulous, lively person" who loved to sing and tell stories of his work among students in the south. One merely needed to see and hear Zheliabov's manner of speaking in order to recognize "his purely rebellious nature." Noting Zheliabov's natural proclivity for optimism in revolutionary struggle, Frolenko confirmed the impact of Zheliabov's "positive" outlook on his comrades. When one listened to Zheliabov, he claimed, what one previously thought "to be small, insignificant, and grey" turned out to be "bigger, more important, and brighter."[21]

Emphasis on the valiant motives of Perovskaia, Zheliabov, and their fellow terrorists served to mitigate their lingering association with the regressive tactics of "individual terrorism." At the same time, the authenticity implicit in their eyewitness accounts allowed veteran memoirists to pass authoritative judgment on inaccurate pictures of the movement by non-veterans. Thus, in an austere review of *The Year 1881,* a theatrical production at the Revolutionary Workers' Theater, Anna Yakimova sharply criticized its creators for distorting the true atmosphere in which the March 1 plot unfolded. In Yakimova's assessment, the play's depiction of resistance to the terrorist program on the part of Nikolai Rysakov (1861–81), a student and the first bomb thrower on March 1, gave the impression that the Executive Committee "dragged the first passer-by into a terrorist plot," whereas in reality Rysakov rushed at the opportunity and never showed a sign of remorse for terrorism until his arrest. The authors were incorrect to add "nonsense about personal feelings" to a speech by Perovskaia, whose thoughts were utterly free of personal concerns when committee business was at hand. It was also misleading, Yakimova insisted, to present Zheliabov as a "poser" at whom Perovskaia and others gazed "spellbound" when, in fact, the narodovoltsy never regarded one another in such a manner. These and other distortions of fact and chronology merely demonstrated the scriptwriter's unfamiliarity with the psychology and lifestyle of the old revolutionists, as well as the conditions of life under which they were forced to act.[22] In the eyes of Yakimova, the Executive Committee was neither indiscriminate in its attitude toward new recruits nor entranced by personalities in its own ranks. The creative urge to dramatize the terrorists' struggle failed to justify a violation of representational accuracy.

Throughout the 1920s the veteran narodovoltsy apparently managed to build their literary monument to the terrorist struggle without significant interference from the state, which continued to characterize the People's Will as an admirable though fatally misguided forerunner from the pre-Marxist era. Their place in the pantheon of revolutionary heroes was confirmed in at least two substantial histories of the Communist Party of the mid-1920s, whose authors expressed great respect for the revolutionary efforts of *narodovol'chestvo,* even while emphasizing the inevitability of its political failure.[23] Yet the same uncompromising principles and passionate commitment that inspired their terrorist mission in 1881 also posed a certain threat to the narodovoltsy elders and their commemorative enterprise. The defiant opposition expressed in 1922 by Figner, Frolenko, Pribyleva-Korba, Yakimova, and others to the Bolsheviks' trial of ten leading SRs may have played a role in temporarily ameliorating the defendants' sentence,[24] but at the cost of exposing the elders' willingness to utilize their prestige to denounce communist injustice. Despite receiving some formal recognition from the state, throughout the 1920s the narodovoltsy undoubtedly retained the stigma of a political tendency that accepted the need for armed struggle against state tyranny.

The logical impossibility of continuing to commemorate a violently populist legacy began to emerge clearly in 1929, when the fiftieth anniversary of the formation of the People's Will provoked a vociferous debate in the Communist Party over its heritage. In his 1929 article, "The Historical Significance of the People's Will," the veteran Bolshevik and editor in chief of *Katorga i ssylka,* Ivan Teodorovich (1875–1937), initiated an extensive discussion on the terrorist stream of populism that brought more publicity to it than any other previous or subsequent publication. Declaring the study of populism far from complete, Teodorovich's article attempted to refute a prevailing notion, perpetuated by historian Mikhail Pokrovsky and his school, that the People's Will isolated itself from the masses, allied itself with the bourgeoisie, and sought by means of terrorism to achieve mere constitutional reforms. Teodorovich argued that the goals of the terrorists were not simply "libertarian," as the Pokrovsky line assumed, but both popular and genuinely revolutionary, insofar as they never lost sight of the peasantry's key role in Russia's development. The terrorists essentially anticipated Lenin, moreover, in their aim to impart conscious leadership to a spontaneous movement by the peasantry and thereby to merge intelligentsia and masses into a "revolutionary creation." Through Teodorovich's approach, even the terrorist tactics of the narodovoltsy received a certain justification, for as one proclamation demonstrated, their "incorrect, exaggerated assessment of terrorism" followed from the ultimately progressive aim of "awaking the popular masses." The sources Teodorovich used for support proved no less controversial than the approach itself. Along with the terrorists' own agitational literature, in his tribute Teodorovich also cited favorable statements about the narodovoltsy by Marx and Lenin. In a letter of late 1880, for example, Marx spoke triumphantly of "our success" among the "terrorist" Executive Committee members in Russia and drew a sharp, ironic contrast between the terrorists' readiness to "risk life and limb" and the decision of their opponents—Plekhanov and other "propagandists" in the Black Repartition—"to spread propaganda in Russia" by "moving to Geneva!" Teodorovich also criticized Plekhanov and other Russian Marxists more directly for disregarding Marx's belief in one of populism's main assumptions, "the *possibility* of noncapitalist development in backward countries" (emphasis in original).[25] Thus the "utopian" program for socialist revolution of the People's Will reflected the objective conditions of Russia's situation, Teodorovich claimed, rather than a loss of faith in the masses or capitulation to liberal, petit bourgeois instincts.

The exchanges between Teodorovich and his opponents took place over the course of six months between the summer of 1929 and the spring of 1930. Sharp replies to Teodorovich, along with his counterresponses, appeared in *Pravda, Izvestiia,* the journals *Bolshevik, Proletarskaia revoliutsiia*

(*Proletarian Revolution*), *Katorga i ssylka,* and others, while Teodorovich defended himself at meetings of the Society of Marxist Historians and the Society of Former Political Prisoners. Apart from the many specific objections to his readings of Marx, Lenin, and the writings of the narodovoltsy themselves, most significant were the charges by historian Isaak Tatarov that Teodorovich sought to "resurrect populism" and "revive neopopulist views." Accused of seeking to "reassess," "idealize," and "modernize" *narodovol'chestvo* by exaggerating its proximity to Leninism, particularly through the idea of a proletarian alliance with the peasantry, Teodorovich stepped up his attacks on Pokrovsky and Pokrovsky's followers with a barrage of quotations from Lenin in support of his claims. In the wake of debates before the Society of Marxist Historians, however, the Culture and Propaganda division of the Communist Party's Central Committee intervened with a set of *Theses for the Fiftieth Anniversary of the People's Will.* The *Theses* reiterated the heroic merits of the terrorists but officially condemned Teodorovich's analysis for, among other things, its "attempt to embellish" *narodovol'chestvo* [*popytka priukrashivaniia*] and thereby encourage "the old populist theory of the peasantry's independent, 'haphazard' [*samotekom*] path to socialism."[26] The Communist Party line on Teodorovich was spelled out more forcefully in *Pravda,* which declared the "neo-populist" position of Teodorovich and his supporters to be "mistaken and politically harmful."[27]

If the issue of terrorism's value for the revolutionary movement still occupied only a secondary place in the discussion of Teodorovich and his thesis, it soon returned to the foreground when his opponents extended their criticism to the journal *Katorga i ssylka,* on whose pages Teodorovich most often propagated his views.[28] Questioning the journal's decision to devote so much space to Teodorovich and his incorrect reading of Lenin, an editorial in *Proletarskaia revoliutsiia* also reprimanded *Katorga i ssylka* for "describing individual terrorist acts" and for "glorifying" or "admiring hero-terrorists" without attempting to illuminate their real historical significance. Thus, "instead of a critical assimilation of the past," memoirs of terrorist acts merely offer "an inadmissible and harmful idealization of a bankrupt tactic."[29] Stepping forward on behalf of *Katorga i ssylka* and the Society of Former Political Prisoners, Emelian Yaroslavsky admitted that the society's journal suffered from certain defects and agreed that the subject of individual terrorism required more commentary in light of Lenin's views; but he defended *Katorga i ssylka* from the specific attacks in *Proletarskaia revoliutsiia,* reminding readers that the society could not compel its many non-Marxist veterans of the revolutionary movement to "speak in a Marxist tongue."[30] Despite Yaroslavsky's authority in the Communist Party, the veteran publicist Mikhail Olminsky supported criticism of *Katorga i ssylka* and remarked that one recent article in particular suggested "a concealed appeal to methods of terrorism."[31] Several months later, the Central Council of the society and the editorial board of *Katorga i ssylka* issued a joint response to the *Proletarskaia revoliutsiia* editorial in which they admitted to general errors and shortcomings but defiantly dismissed most of the specific charges leveled against them, especially the "serious political accusation" of "idealizing terrorism." Insisting they had always regarded terrorist tactics as inapplicable to the proletarian cause, the authors rejected the need "to struggle rabidly and furiously" against the terrorism of the past, as their critics suggested, for to deny terrorist tactics in their history meant "to repudiate the subjective and personal merits" of those who employed it.[32] The authors' self-defense thus successfully exposed the contradiction inherent in their critics' advice for proper commemoration: neither the Society of Former Political Prisoners nor its journal could easily celebrate the struggles and "subjective revolutionism of many terrorists" (Lenin's words) while simultaneously condemning their most characteristic and defining acts.

Convinced of the Leninist Orthodoxy of his interpretation, Teodorovich continued to reiterate his position, but his article in the same 1931 issue of *Katorga i ssylka*—apparently his final contribution to the debate—also reflects greater resignation to official moods.[33] If he defended the popular essence and benevolent spirit of Alexander II's assassins, calling for commemoration of their great "enthusiasm," their "faith in the people" and "love for the people," Teodorovich also linked the terrorists' vision directly to the Communist Party's "great process of collectivization," in which the proletarian, "applying the former [populist] hatred of the landowner," is "now capably directing that hatred toward the *bourgeoisie* and peasant-exploiters [*kulachestvo*] . . . in order to uproot capitalism in the countryside."[34] Discourse on populist terrorism thus began to reflect more directly the political demands of the moment. The practical relevance of the debate had been made explicit in the Central Committee's *Theses for the Fiftieth Anniversary of the People's Will,* which declared the anniversary to be "not only of purely historical interest" but also of "current political significance," in light of the Communist Party's preoccupation with the issue of proletarian-peasant relations.[35] At least one scholar of Soviet historiography has emphasized the close connection between the discussion of prerevolutionary populism and internal conflicts over agrarian policy between 1928 and 1930.[36] The violent repercussions of Stalin's call in late 1929 to liquidate the *kulaks* as a class, however, may represent the most important circumstance that tempered admiration for the People's Will. By the winter of 1930, when the war against the kulaks reached its peak, the anathema against "idealizing terrorism" followed consistently from the state's efforts to expose kulak "terrorism" in the countryside.[37]

The publication of Stalin's "Letter to the Journal *Proletarian Revolution*" in late October 1931 abruptly ended public disputes over issues pertaining to revolutionary events and their "Leninist" interpretation. Ostensibly an attack on historian Anatoly Slutsky for questioning Lenin's assessment of German Social Democrats in the Second International, Stalin's "Letter" ultimately directed his "protest" to the editors of *Proletarskaia revoliutsiia* for turning Slutsky's "slanderous" and "falsifying" critique of Lenin's Bolshevism into "an object of discussion."[38] The extent to which the debate over *narodovol'chstvo* may have prompted Stalin's "Letter" can only be surmised, but apparently no further arguments about the significance of the People's Will or its terrorist program appeared in the official press. Instead, those like Yaroslavsky, whose careers survived the subsequent campaign against "rotten liberalism," began to work out a less equivocal "Marxist-Leninist" line on populism.[39] Fortunately for the legacy of *narodovol'chestvo,* by that time the commemorators of populist terrorism had already managed to produce a truly astonishing volume of literature on the movement for the anniversary. Between 1930 and 1931 the publishing house of the Society of Former Political Prisoners alone issued seven large collections of memoirs and documents prepared especially by the society's own "Circle of Narodovoltsy," including an album-sized reprinting of all the original issues of the People's Will periodicals and agitational leaflets from 1879 to 1881. The society also printed a series of short, popular biographies of the Executive Committee leaders. According to the editors of *Katorga i ssylka,* narodovoltsy veterans contributed more than two thousand pages to society publications over the course of a single year (1930).[40] In the wake of Stalin's "Letter," however, such a conspicuous exhibition of commemorative literature about terrorists could not continue without proper guidance for readers. By 1933, the fiftieth anniversary of Marx's death, a collection of materials on the March 1 conspiracy cautioned its readers against attempts to "overestimate the past," for the work of the People's Will, while undeniably "heroic," represented a stage in Russia's revolutionary movement which the proletarian struggle "had long ago passed and surpassed."[41]

The murder of Sergei Kirov on December 1, 1934, marked the beginning of the end of Soviet commemorations of populist terrorism. Reportedly comparing himself with Zheliabov,[42] Kirov's assassin offered grounds for recalling the violent sedition latent in the heritage of *narodovol'chestvo.* Soon thereafter, the secretary of the Communist Party's Central Committee, Andrei Zhdanov, made public Stalin's warning that "if we raise our people on the People's Will, then we will raise terrorists."[43] A resolution by the Central Committee "On Propaganda Work," passed on June 14, 1935, stated unequivocally that Marxism developed in the struggle against populism and more precisely *narodovol'chestvo,* "the worst enemy of Marxism," with its ideas and methods of "individual terrorism" that "exclude organization of a mass party."[44] Within two weeks of the resolution the Politburo approved the final liquidation of the Society of Former Political Prisoners. The simultaneous closure of its museum and publishing house, the true "face of the Society, around which its consciousness revolves," in the words of one senior member, removed any further possibility of unauthorized publications on the revolutionary movement.[45] By 1937, allusions to the People's Will strictly followed the Communist Party's assessment. The article on *narodnichestvo* in the first *Great Soviet Encyclopedia* ignores the merits of the Executive Committee while emphasizing that its "theoretical sources and tactical formulations" cultivated "enemies of the Party and Soviet power" like the assassins of Kirov.[46] Similarly, the *Short Course* on Communist Party history of 1938 branded the terrorist acts of the People's Will "harmful for the revolution" and indicative of a lack of faith in the masses.[47]

Remarkably, no less than five former members of the Executive Committee—Vera Figner, Mikhail Frolenko, Anna Yakimova, Nikolai Morozov, and Anna Pribyleva-Korba—lived long enough to witness the dismantling of their collective monument to the terrorist achievement. While their literary testament restored memory of the lofty aims that inspired their turn to terrorism, it also accelerated its own suppression, for the engaging legacy of the People's Will demonstrated greater vitality than the official disclaimers that framed it. Ironically, its virtual annihilation in the mid-1930s came at the hands of an autocratic regime about to unleash a campaign of state terror, not on behalf of its people, but against them.

Notes

1. Throughout this article I translate the Russian word "narodnichestvo" as "populism," the term traditionally used to describe the broader current of nineteenth-century Russian revolutionary thought that culminated in the terrorist achievement of the People's Will party in 1881. Although comprising different tendencies and political affiliations, *narodnichestvo* remained a meaningful term to describe the generally non-Marxist faith in Russia's ability to reach a more just and egalitarian society without the experience of Western capitalism and the social inequality it fostered. The meaning of the Russian word "narodovol'chestvo," by contrast, is far more specific, referring almost exclusively to the ideology represented by the People's Will and its Executive Committee, which aimed to accelerate the downfall of autocracy by means of regicide. Because it is virtually untranslatable, throughout the article I have left the term

"narodovol'chestvo" in its original, transliterated form. According to Vera Figner in her widely published memoirs of the populist movement, the "terrorists" of the late 1870s to 1880s—those members of the Land and Freedom (Zemlia i volia) party and then the People's Will (Narodnaia volia) who endorsed methods of armed struggle—were more frequently described simply as "radicals."

2. Well known, for example, is Lenin's vision, expressed in *What Is to Be Done? Burning Questions of Our Movement* (1902), of a new organizational structure capable of producing "Social-Democratic Zheliabovs" who would "rouse the whole people to settle accounts with the shame and curse of Russia." See V. I. Lenin, *Selected Works in Three Volumes* (Moscow: Progress Publishers, 1977), 1:225.

3. Hereafter dates of former members of Nardonaia volia are given when they are first mentioned in the text.

4. The proposed list of subjects was published in the newspaper *Izvestiia* on August 2, 1918. See: *V. I. Lenin i izobrazitel'noe iskusstvo: Dokumenty, Pis'ma, Vospominaniia,* ed. V. V. Shleev (Moscow: Izobrazitel'noe iskusstvo, 1977), 270, 345. Like many of the first projects for monumental propaganda, Grizelli's sculpture of Perovskaia failed to satisfy the prevailing taste and was eventually removed. A report on the celebration appeared in the newspaper *Art of the Commune* (*Iskusstvo kommuny*) on January 6, 1919. For the text of the report and a photograph of participants standing before the monument at Nikolai (Moscow) Station, see *Serdtsem slushaia revoliutsiiu: Iskusstvo pervykh let Oktiabria,* ed. M. Iu. German (Leningrad: Avrora, 1980), 14–15. Monuments to Zheliabov remained in the planning stages for several more years. Natan Altman completed his famous bronze relief of Khalturin in 1920.

5. L. Starr, "Pervye shagi," in *Desiat' let, 1921–1931: Sbornik statei i vospominanii k desiatiletnemu iubileiu Obshchestva politkatorzhan,* ed. L. Starr, V. Pleskov, and G. Kramarov (Moscow: Obshchestvo politkatorzhan, 1931), 16. Starr notes that the local branches of the society in other cities functioned "completely independently" of Moscow during the early years.

6. For detailed statistics on the society's membership numbers and personal data in 1925, see "O Vsesoiuznom S'ezde Obshchestva politkatorzhan," *Katorga i ssylka* 16 (1925): 267–73. An assessment of the society's activity following its five-year jubilee announced that sixty-one narodovoltsy had joined. See "Iz zhizni Obshchestva: Pervoe piatiletie (1921 g.–12 marta 1926 g.)," *Katorga i ssylka* 23 (1926): 283.

7. Figner did not officially join the society until 1932, although she apparently participated in the work of the society's "Kruzhok narodovol'tsev" (Narodovoltsy Circle) and in many of the society's publications throughout the 1920s. Speculation about her opposition to the society is offered in "Vera Figner i Obshchestvo politkatorzhan i ssyl'noposelentsev: Soobshchenie I. Garelina," *Pamiat'. Istoricheskii sbornik* 3 (Paris, 1980): 393–402.

8. Figner, Frolenko, and Yakimova-Dikovskaia appear to have been the most active of the former "terrorists" in the society. By contrast, Morozov's name appears less frequently in society productions and publications.

9. Declaring the "literary question" one of its chief concerns, from its beginning the society's founders set out to establish a series of collections on the subject of penal servitude, but by its sixth issue, in 1924, *Hard Labor and Exile* (*Katorga i ssylka*), the series had evolved into a regularly issued "historical revolutionary anthology" of more than three hundred pages. See V. Pleskov, "'Prestuplenie—bez nakazaniia,'" in *Desiat' let, 1921–1931,* 37; and B. Koz'min, "Istoriko-revoliutsionnuiu knigu—v massy

(Literaturno-izdatel'skaia deiatel'nost' Obshchestva)," in *Desiat' let, 1921–1931,* 82–84, 86. Other venues for publicity of *narodovol'chestvo* included the State Publishing House (Gosizdat), the Leningrad journal *The Past* (*Byloe*), and the Granat Brothers' *Encyclopedic Dictionary,* which presented forty-four populist autobiographies in its fortieth volume of 1927.

10. A 1929 bibliography of publications on Narodnaia volia lists more than 1,200 works, by far the majority of them published in Soviet Russia after 1917: M. Drei, *Opyt ukazatelia literatury po istorii partii 'Narodnoi voli'* (Moscow: Obshchestvo politkatorzhan, 1929).

11. Franco Venturi, *Roots of Revolution: A History of the Populist and Socialist Movements in Nineteenth Century Russia,* introduction by Isaiah Berlin, trans. Francis Haskell (New York: Grosset and Dunlap, 1960), 632. In her analysis of the movement's drift toward terror, Vera Figner described the radical populists' realization that they could no longer sustain propagandistic work on the periphery and "must continue," like Soloviev, to strike at the center. See Vera Figner, *Zapechatlennyi trud: Vospominaniia,* 2 vols. (Moscow: Mysl', 1964), 1:171–72. This 1964 edition reproduces the text of the 1933 edition. Figner's memoirs first appeared in 1921 and 1922 through the Zadruga publishing house, then in three more full editions (two as part of her collected works) through the publishing house of the Society of Former Political Prisoners (1928, 1932, 1933), and in an abridged edition (1934). They retained an unusual immediacy for memoirs of that period, since she could rely on written reflections she had composed in Shlisselburg in 1883, only a short time after the downfall of the original Executive Committee. Her notes were discovered in the tsarist police archives and returned to her in 1917. In his summary of Figner's life, Richard Stites notes a contradiction between her "evocation of violence" and instances in which "she fully admits its corrupting role." See Vera Figner, *Memoirs of a Revolutionist,* authorized translation from the Russian. Reprint of 1927 edition published by International Publishers, with new introduction by Richard Stites (DeKalb: Northern Illinois University Press, 1991), xix. This translation of Figner's memoirs is abridged.

12. Figner, *Zapechatlennyi trud,* 1:171–73, 178–79, 207–8, 221, 284–86.

13. A. V. Iakimova, "Iz dalekogo proshlogo (Iz vospominanii o pokusheniiakh na Aleksandra II)," *Katorga i ssylka* 8 (1924): 9–10.

14. M. Frolenko, "Nachalo 'Narodovol'chestva'," *Katorga i ssylka* 24 (1926): 20, 22, 24.

15. A. P. Pribyleva-Korba, "Ispolnitel'nyi komitet, 1879–1881 gg.," *Katorga i ssylka* 24 (1926): 27.

16. A list of titles in these and other series published by the society is included in *Izdatel'stvo Vsesoiuznogo obshchestva politkatorzhan i ssyl'no-poselentsev: Katalog izdanii, 1921–1931* (Moscow: Obshchestvo politkatorzhan, 1931).

17. S. M. Stepniak-Kravchinskii, *Podpol'naia Rossiia: Prilozhenie no. 3 i 4 k zhurnalu 'Vokrug sveta'* (Leningrad: Krasnaia gazeta, 1929), 109–11, 117, 124–25, 129. For an account of Kravchinsky's life and works, see Peter Scotto's essay in this volume. A large portion of the text on Perovskaia in a commemorative pamphlet of 1917 is also taken directly from Kravchinsky's profile. See *Geroi russkoi revoliutsii, no. 2* (Petrograd: Natsional'naia biblioteka, 1917).

18. Figner, *Zapechatlennyi trud,* 1:274–76.

19. A. I. Kornilova-Moroz, *Sof'ia L'vovna Perovskaia: Chlen ispolnitel'nogo komiteta 'Narodnaia volia'* (Moscow: Obshchestvo politkatorzhan, 1930), 33–34, 44.

20. *Andrei Ivanovich Zheliabov: Chlen ispolnitel'nogo komiteta partii 'Narodnaia volia': Materialy dlia biografii,* predisl. V. N. Figner (Moscow: Obshchestvo politkatorzhan, 1930), 16, 31, 36–37, 42, 44–46. In her preface to this pamphlet, Vera Figner confirmed that Tikhomirov was the author.

21. M. F. Frolenko, "Lipetskii i Voronezhskii s'ezdy," in *Sobranie sochinenii,* 2 vols., ed. I. Teodorovich, 2nd ed. (Moscow: Obshchestvo politkatorzhan, 1932), 1:12–13, 18–19. In his autobiography of 1925, surviving narodovolets Alexander Pribylev also noted the powerful effect Zheliabov had on his listeners: "Avtobiografiia A. V. Pribyleva," in *Deiateli SSSR i revoliutsionnogo dvizheniia Rossii: Entsiklopedicheskii slovar' Granat* (Moscow: Sovetskaia entsiklopediia, 1989), 193.

22. A. V. Iakimova, "Po povodu p'esy '1881 god'," *Katorga i ssylka* 15 (1925): 274–76.

23. V. I. Nevskii, *Ocherki po istorii Rossiiskoi kommunisticheskoi partii,* 2nd ed. (Leningrad: Priboi, 1925), 113–14; *Istoriia VKP(b),* ed. Em. Iaroslavskii, G. Kramol'nikov, N. El'vov, and O. Rimskii, 4 vols. (Moscow: Gosizdat, 1926), 1:49–50. Nevskii described Narodnaia volia's rapid degeneration from a "glorious, powerful and formidable" party into one of ordinary "liberalism," while Yaroslavsky underscored its inability to understand the significance of the working class.

24. See, for example, the analysis of the trial and the reaction of the veteran *Narodovol'tsy* in Mark Iunge, "Ugroza likvidatsiia OPK v 1922," in *Vsesoiuznoe obshchestvo politkatorzhan i ssyl'noposelentsev: Obrazovanie, razvitie, likvidatsiia, 1921–1935. Byvshie chleny obshchestva vo vremia Bol'shogo terrora: Materialy mezhdunar. nauch. konferentsii (26–28 okt. 2001),* ed. Ia. Leont'ev, M. Iunge (Moscow: Obshchestvo Memorial, Izdatel'stvo Zven'ia, 2004), 47–49. See also Sergei Krasil'nikov, Konstantin Morozov, and Igor' Chubykin, "Starye revoliutsionery i protsess nad sotsialistami-revoliutsionerami letom 1922," in *Vsesoiuznoe obshchestvo politkatorzhan i ssyl'noposelentsev, 1921–1935,* 67–74.

25. I. A. Teodorovich, "Istoricheskoe znachenie partii Narodnoi voli," *Katorga i ssylka* 57–58 (1929): 7–13, 20–21, 34. According to Teodorovich, by 1882 Marx believed that the peasant commune in Russia could in fact serve as a starting point for socialist development under certain conditions.

26. I. A. Teodorovich, *Istoricheskoe znachenie partii Narodnoi voli: Sbornik 1, s prilozh. tezisov kul'tpropa TsK VPK(b) k 50-letiiu partii 'Narodnoi voli'* (Moscow: Obshchestvo politkatorzhan, 1930), 150–51, 169, 184, 244, 279. V. Malakhovskii, I. Tatarov, P. Gorin, D. Kin, Ts. Fridliand, M. Savel'ev, and Em. Gazganov were among the historians who spoke out against Teodorovich's conception.

27. Reprinted in *Diskussiia o 'Narodnoi vole': Stenogrammy dokladov V. I. Nevskogo, I. A. Teodorovicha, I. L. Tatarova i prenii po dokladam, s prilozheniem tezisov Kul'tpropa TsK VKP(b) o piatidesiatiletii 'Narodnoi voli'* (Moscow: Komakademiia, 1930), 191–207. This collection also includes the speeches before the Society of Marxist Historians on the subject of Teodorovich's article.

28. Thus the same article in *Pravda* claimed that Teodorovich's original article aimed "to express the standpoint of the editorial board of *Katorga i ssylka,* the organ of the Society of Former Political Prisoners." *Diskussiia o 'Narodnoi vole,'* 1.

29. S. Bur, "Po zhurnalam: 'Katorga i ssylka,' 1929 no. 8–9, 10, 11, 12 i 1930, no. 1, 2, 3, 4, 5," *Proletarskaia revoliutsiia* 9 (1930): 170–72.

30. Em. Iaroslavskii, "Pis'mo v redaktsiiu: Kakim dolzhen byt' i kakov est' zhurnal 'Katorga i ssylka'," *Proletarskaia revoliutsiia* 11 (1930): 185, 187.

31. M. S. Ol'minskii, "Otvet t. Iaroslavskomu," *Proletarskaia revoliutsiia* 11 (1930): 188. The editors of *Proletarskaia revoliutsiia* expressed their agreement with Olminsky on the same page. The article that troubled Olminsky, written by Sergei Nikonov, appears in *Katorga i ssylka* 12 (1929): 57–64. Nikonov vehemently protested the accusations in "Pis'mo v redatskiiu," *Katorga i ssylka* 3 (1931): 253–55.

32. "Nash otvet," *Katorga i ssylka* 3 (1931): 8–9, 12–13.

33. Teodorovich's reputation in the Communist Party was also damaged, apparently, by his defense of the "agrarian scholar" Nikolai Kondratiev and others during the criminal investigation of the Peasant Labor Party in 1930. See: I. Rozental', "Teodorovich Ivan Adol'fovich," in *Politicheskie partii Rossii, konets XIX–pervaia tret' XX veka. Entsiklopediia* (Moscow: Rosspen, 1996), 604–5.

34. I. A. Teodorovich, "1 marta 1881 goda," *Katorga i ssylka* 3 (1931): 66, 72. Teodorovich also published this article under the same title as a separate pamphlet through the society's publishing house in 1931.

35. Teodorovich, *Istoricheskoe znachenie,* 253.

36. John Barber, "The Bolsheviks' Predecessors," in *Soviet Historians in Crisis, 1928–1932* (New York: Holmes and Meier, 1981), 80–99. Barber argues, for example, that the exchanges over Narodnaia volia were not only a debate about "historical accuracy" but also "a reflection of the deep division among the Communist Party leadership in the aftermath of the grain-collection crisis of early 1928." For another informative study of the debate over populism and other issues in the context of struggles between Marxist historians such as Pokrovsky and Yaroslavsky, see George M. Enteen, "Marxist Historians During the Cultural Revolution: A Case Study of Professional In-fighting," in *Cultural Revolution in Russia, 1928–1931,* ed. Sheila Fitzpatrick (Bloomington: Indiana University Press, 1978), 154–68.

37. As Lynne Viola explains in her study of collectivization, reported acts of violence by "kulak terrorists" were not all "kulak" in social origin, a fact that defied official interpretation. See Lynne Viola, *Peasant Rebels Under Stalin: Collectivization and the Culture of Peasant Resistance* (New York: Oxford University Press, 1996), 113–14.

38. I. V. Stalin, "O nekotorykh voprosakh istorii bol'shevizma. Pis'mo v redaktsiiu zhurnala 'Proletarskaia Revoliutsiia,'" *Proletarskaia revoliutsiia* 6 (1931): 7, 8, 10. More specifically, Stalin rejected the suggestions that Lenin failed to seek a break with German Social Democratic opportunists before the war and that Lenin and the Bolsheviks failed to give sufficient support to the Left German Social Democrats. For a detailed, post-Stalin assessment of the letter, its background, and the many errors in Stalin's accusations, see V. A. Dunaevskii, "Bol'sheviki i germanskie levye na mezhdunarodnoi arene (Nekotorye aspekty temy v osveshchenii sovetskoi istoriografii kontsa 20-kh–nachala 30-kh godov)," in *Evropa v novoe i noveishee vremia: Sbornik statei pamiati akademika N. M. Lukina* (Moscow: Nauka, 1966), 491–513.

39. See, for example: Em. Iaroslavskii, "Marks i revoliutsionnoe narodnichestvo," *Istorik-marksist* 1 (1933): 33–66.

40. *Izdatel'stvo Vsesoiuznogo obshchestva politkatorzhan i ssyl'no-poselentsev: Katalog izdanii, 1921–1931* (Moscow: Obshchestvo politkatorzhan, 1931), 191–99; *Literatura partii 'Narodnoi voli': 'Narodnaia volia', 'Listok Narodnoi voli', 'Rabochaia gazeta'. Dokumenty,* ed. A. V. Iakimovoi-Dikovskoi, M. F. Frolenko, M. I. Drei, I. I. Popova, N. I. Rakitnikova, and V. V. Leonovicha-Angarskogo (Moscow: Obshchestvo politkatorzhan, 1930); "Nash otvet," *Katorga i ssylka* 3 (1931): 12.

41. "Ot redaktsii," in *1 marta 1881 g.* (Moscow: Obshchesto politkatorzhan, 1933), 1–2.

42. V. Z. Rogovin, *Stalinskii neonep* (Moscow, 1994), 79; Roy Medvedev, *Let History Judge: The Origins and Consequences of Stalinism,* rev. ed., ed. and trans. George Shriver (New York: Columbia University Press, 1989), 337. Nikolaev also reportedly compared himself to Radishchev.

43. M. G. Sedov, "Sovetskaia literatura o teoretikakh narodnichestva," in *Istoriia i istoriki. Istoriografiia SSSR: Sbornik statei* (Moscow: Nauka, 1965), 257. Zhdanov quoted this remark by Stalin at a meeting of the Communist Party's City Committee in Leningrad on February 25, 1935.

44. "O propagandistskoi rabote v blizhaishee vremia," *Pravda,* June 14, 1935.

45. M. Iunge, "Zakrytie OPK: Dokumenty iz fonda Ezhova," in *Vsesoiuznoe obshchestvo politkatorzhan i ssyl'noposelentsev, 1921–1935,* 335, 340.

46. I. Menitskii, "Narodnaia volia," *Bol'shaia sovetskaia entsiklopediia* (Moscow: Sovetskaia entsiklopediia, 1939), 41:168–86; Em. Iaroslavskii, *Razgrom narodnichestva* (Moscow: Partizdat TsK VKP(b), 1937), 3.

47. *Istoriia Vsesoiuznoi kommunisticheskoi partii (bol'shevikov): Kratkii kurs* (Moscow: Gosudarstvennoe izdatel'stvo politicheskoi literaturi, 1938), 12–13.

"Everyone Here Was Carrying Out Orders": Songs of War and Terror in Chechnya

Anna Brodsky

"Fighting international terror" has become a convenient catchphrase for many politicians, including Vladimir Putin, who has consistently presented Russia's war in Chechnya under the banner of fighting terrorism.[1] Putin started the Second Chechen War as Russia's response to brazen acts of Chechen terrorism in the fall of 1999, including the bombing of an apartment building in Moscow that claimed the lives of some three hundred people and an incursion by Chechen fighters into Dagestan. Although the circumstances surrounding that explosion were and remain mysterious, the government promoted the second Chechen campaign as an "antiterrorist operation."[2] The war that had begun as a struggle with a breakaway former Soviet republic was now described as a purely defensive war against "international terrorist gangs" and "armies of killers,"[3] the latest front in the global war on terrorism.

The antiterrorist rhetoric gained momentum in 2001 after the September 11 attacks in the United States and President Bush's announcement of a global war on terror. Putin now claimed that his goal was "to eradicate, eliminate, and liquidate terrorism."[4] The Russian government could now reaffirm its own war slogans, silence Western opposition to the war, and promote an alliance between Russia and the United States. Playing the antiterrorist card seems to have worked. Western politicians have, to a great extent, accepted Putin's rhetoric and turned a blind eye to the kind of war the Russian government has been waging in Chechnya. "The antiterrorist operation," in fact, became a total war, with the mass destruction of towns and cities, cleansing operations, mass disappearances, and the near total destruction of Chechnya's infrastructure. By the year 2006, the war had resulted in three hundred thousand Chechens dead, tens of thousands scattered through Russia and Europe, and thousands of Russian soldiers dead. This disparity between rhetoric and reality suggests just how amorphous and without definition the "war on terror" has become. From the politicians' point of view, the ability of a global war on terror to justify all kinds of military actions is, without a doubt, one of its great attractions. And yet, Russia's own war on terror has exacted a terrible cost in terms of military morale and has coarsened the fabric of Russian society.

In this essay, I look at representations of the Chechen war in Russian popular soldier songs and cinema. Such sources are especially important for gauging Russian responses to the conflict because the war is almost a taboo subject in the government-controlled press. Part of the considerable interest of these popular arts is the light they can shed on the way the war on terrorism is perceived by those charged with actually fighting it. These arts reflect a disturbing gap between the terrible realities of the Chechen war (e.g., civilian casualties, torture, rape, summary executions) and the way soldiers perceive it. In the absence of a credible sustaining vision, the soldiers seem to regard the war as a kind of masculine ritual, an ordeal mainly if not solely designed to bind them together. At the same time, the soldiers think of themselves as innocent victims, even when they candidly admit to committing war atrocities. As Stephen Hutchings points out in his chapter on television coverage of the terrorist attack on School No. 1 in Beslan in this volume, "the image of the archetypal Russia as victimized subject" is essential in the present-day construction of Russian identity. The sense of national victimization, according to Hutchings, pervades the Russian news media. It is also found in Russian films, for example, in Valery Todorovsky's 2004 film *My Stepbrother Frankenstein,*[5] and in Fyodor Bondarchuk's 2005 film *The Ninth Company* (*Deviataia rota*). Indeed, a besetting sense of futility and victimization seems to pervade much of contemporary Russian culture.[6]

Soldiers' songs from the Chechen war give an important historical dimension to Russians' current and pervasive sense of victimization and their refusal to accept responsibility for the violence they unleash. For these songs descend from a long tradition of Russian soldier songs, above all World War II songs, which played a particularly important role in rousing and maintaining morale.[7] Those songs were sentimental, filled with references to loving families and faithful sweethearts, and determinedly high-minded:

lyrics described the girl back home pledging her undying love on one condition, the soldier's brave conduct in battle against the enemy.[8] The songs left no doubt about the heroic stature of the struggle against a brutal foreign aggressor. These sentiments may have been cheap, but they were potent. They roused people's sense of an urgent moral issue at stake, and satisfied, at a primitive but powerful level, people's need to believe in the justice of their cause.[9] The songs gave the soldiers a vivid conception of an unjust enemy[10] and assured them of a populace back home that supported them and loved them. They also conveyed the idea that life beyond the military was what ultimately gave meaning and sustenance to military life.

When juxtaposed to this tradition, soldier songs from the Chechen war suggest a very different and troubling image of today's Russian soldier. Contemporary soldiers' songs convey no sense of the justice of the war, no clear conception of an enemy, and little or no proprietary sense linking the soldier to his struggle. The war seems to take place in a moral vacuum and to consist of violence without a cause or an object. Many soldier songs from the Chechen war seem to agree that the soldiers don't need this war.[11] These songs are produced by a wide variety of sources. Some are written and performed by patriotic groups like the Blue Berets or Liube, while others are sung by individual performers or small groups of ex-soldiers. These songs can be heard on the radio; random assortments appear on tapes and discs. Quite a few songs are posted on Internet sites, which attract many ex-soldiers interested in exchanging songs or looking for recordings of specific songs dealing with the conflict.[12]

The soldiers' confusion about the violence they unleash is suggested by their inability to admit the slightest responsibility in these songs. Instead, they appear as innocent bystanders, victimized by their own government's bad faith. The songs repeatedly express distrust and disappointment in the government. For example, the Blue Berets' song "Russia" describes the country as a victim of violent leaders—Razin, Lenin, and Stalin. Razin taught Russia to be violent, Lenin tamed her, and Stalin subdued her with barbed wire. Russia herself is only misguided. This callow but simple-hearted and victimized Russia keeps laughing while her soldiers are dying: "You cannot live a day without a war, as if war was nothing but a toy. You guffaw while soldiers die. Razin taught you, Lenin tamed you, Stalin tied you up in labor camps with barbed wire."[13] Some songs blame the politicians in the Kremlin for exploiting the soldiers for political gain while remaining cynically indifference to their lives: "In May we took Bamut without any losses. And you were truly great and fought like a lion. Then Yeltsin came to call us to the elections. He handed us bunches of medals to make us vote for him."[14] And yet, despite frequent criticisms of the Kremlin's ruthlessness and political exploitation of the soldiers, the songs fail to mention any resistance to orders or show any inclination to disobey. On the contrary, while the politicians are indifferent and deceitful, the soldiers fulfill the orders as best they can. For example: "Do not judge us, do not pity us. Everyone here was carrying out orders."[15]

The Russian soldiers' painful sense of isolation also finds expression in lyrics about troubled relations with families back home. Soldiers' alienation from their families is an entirely new motif in the genre of Russian war songs. For instance, one soldier sings that even his mother will not understand his life in Chechnya. His actions must remain hidden, and the only time he can reveal the truth is when his mouth is pried open at night by bad dreams: "Even my mother won't understand this last war. Only at night, delirium might pry open my mouth."[16] When mothers appear in the songs, they do not urge their sons to go bravely into battle, as they did in the songs of World War II. The only thing they ask is for their sons to come back safely. They appear solely as mourners, who weep over their dead sons.[17] A common motif is a lament by a mother who will never again see her son.[18] The songs frequently describe prematurely aged and grieving mothers at cemeteries where they visit the graves of their beloved sons: "If you just glance at what lies on the granite slab by the tomb-stone, your heart will grow heavy. Some one left there a hand written note: 'Happy birthday, my son.' This was the mother who was here. She aged so early, and the Chechen war left grey streaks on her temples. The carnation she left looked like an unhealed wound against the piercing whiteness of her letter."[19]

While mothers grieve, wives are not necessarily expected to be loyal to their soldier husbands and lovers. The relatively upbeat song "Aty-Baty,"[20] whose melody is reminiscent of Soviet marching band tunes, tells a story about a professional soldier whose beautiful wife leaves him while he is fighting in Chechnya. The song claims that the wife is innocent of all wrongdoing. The problem is that family life and the life of a soldier are incompatible. The soldier opts for life in the military without much regret. In another song, a soldier's wife contemptuously tells her ex-soldier husband that he and his kind didn't fight for any noble cause but were bought for a bottle of vodka and a stick of salami: "Even my wife keeps telling me that they bought us a bottle of vodka and a stick of salami."[21] The soldiers' isolation from their families and loved ones increases their sense of victimization and underlies the lack of any conviction in the justice of their cause. The soldiers do without the sentimentality of the songs from World War II, but their uprootedness from any sustaining context is disturbing and contributes to the resentment and cynicism of these songs.

A strikingly uniform feature of these songs is the surprising absence of references to the Chechens.[22] When the songs mention the enemy, his image is usually metaphoric and elusive. Indeed, the enemy's invisibility is his most important trait. The songs refer to the enemy as "ghosts" ("*dukhi*"), "wolves," or "invisible snipers." The dramatic contrast to World War II songs again suggests some profound anomie and alienation. The existence of a clearly defined adversary ensures that the war effort has some point, but the sense pervading many of these songs is that the war in Chechnya has no purpose. Shared convictions about the injustice of the enemy also ensure that the war does not outrage the soldiers' moral feelings: the violence seems only just. Without a foe, however, the violence is unredeemed and bewildering. The existence of an enemy serves as a limiting principle for violence, which is justified only insofar as it tends to defeat the enemy. The soldier songs coming from Chechnya, however, taken together with reports of numerous atrocities committed by Russian soldiers, suggest they really do not see much, if any, limit to the violence allowed.[23]

There is yet another aspect to the startling absence of reference to the Chechens in these songs. The soldiers' resentful sense of victimization not only seems to block compassion for the Chechens but may even fuel their brutality. In the past century, the rhetoric of German victimization was used by the Nazis to justify war and even genocide. In contemporary Russia, too, according to Serguei Oushakine, the rhetoric of national trauma pervades ultranationalist, xenophobic, and anti-Semitic writings.[24] Many social scientists have suggested that the development of empathy toward members of an opposing group is a key factor in putting an end to atrocities and mass violence.[25] Empathy is "a normative ideal" that is necessary if warring groups are ever to live in peace and heal their wounds.

In sum, the soldiers express little or no devotion to their country or the sense that they are protecting the loved ones back home, nor does the Chechen foe seem to loom very large. The soldiers' only commitment seems to be to one another. Indeed, the war experience has come to take on the dimensions of a ritual. The war becomes a mere backdrop to the virile rites of solidarity through endurance. The song "War Is War" both proclaims the deceit of the government ("again the politicians cheat us while we fulfilled orders") and extols the bonding of the soldiers. The message of such a song is clear: the soldiers take no interest in the political purpose of the conflict. The message the song seems to convey is that a soldier need only learn the meaning of true camaraderie and protect his fellow combatants. The song "At War" ("*A na voine*") by A. Gazaliev extols friendship above all other laws: "At war, there is no higher law than friendship. We stand pressing our shoulders together. We stand pressing our back together. This is our military fraternity, and our mutual defense."[26] Soldier songs advocate an intensely intimate form of bonding: not only do the soldiers stand together ("pressing shoulders together")—a cliché of military solidarity—but they stand back to back as well. For example, "Tell Me, Officer" ("*Ty skazhi komandir*") by Vitaly Leonov describes a soldier weeping over the loss of his friend: "Where are you, my friend? What happened to you? Why aren't you among those who came back from the battle? Tears are choking my throat. . . . Did you remember that I asked you to stay close to me all the time?"[27] The soldier wants to go back alone to the battleground to look for his friend's body and feels that it is no one's business but his own. This theme of intense love between soldiers is reminiscent of the love warriors felt for each other in Homer's *Iliad* and recalls, in the Russian context, Gogol's homosocial Cossacks.[28] In this day and age, it can hardly come as a surprise that the traditional theme of friendship between soldiers in wartime has an erotic intensity. Passionate same-sex attachments are characteristic of isolated male warrior societies where all the needs, including the need for intimacy, are satisfied without women. In the particular context of the war against Chechnya, however, the male bonding takes on a special meaning. For it seems that the army has become a hermetically sealed universe unto itself: in it, the soldier finds both his family and his love. A song by A. Dmitrishin, "His Majesty, the Soldier" ("*Ego velichestvo patsan*"), is a good example of the army's insularity: "The Chechen war is black. It is not governed by the state and it has no limits, and this is why the soul deprived of faith is full of despair. But he is not guilty of anything. He is in the trenches because he is under oath. His battalion commander is his mother and father, and his bravery will shine through."[29]

This ardent, insular, and intense solidarity between soldiers who have served in Afghanistan and Chechnya derives much of its force from the hazing rituals that Russian soldiers are forced to endure. These rituals are worth exploring since they affect the way we understand the songs' celebration of solidarity between comrades at arms. And they suggest what an exclusive and dangerous camaraderie it is. Hazing starts the moment a soldier begins his two-year service and lasts for the first twelve months. This system is known as "*dedovshchina*" and is based on a strict principle of seniority: second-year servicemen abuse the new conscripts and effectively turn them into slaves. *Dedovshchina* differs from conventional military training, which is intended to break down individuality and blend conscripts into a group. During the hazing period, however, the new conscripts are frequently deprived of food, beaten (sometimes severely), and forced to do menial service. Sexual abuse is not unknown. The officers either contribute to the hazing or turn a blind eye to it.[30] At the end of the first year, the conscripts become recognized "elders" ("*dedy*") and the cycle begins again: it is now the turn of the new "elders" to abuse others.[31]

Dedovshchina resembles an initiation rite, of a kind familiar in military societies throughout the world.[32] In the absence of a sturdy legal system and reliable law enforcement, however, hazing can be lethal.[33] Every year scores of young soldiers die from abuse or suffer serious physical and psychological injury.[34] According to James Waller, bonding based on "a culture of cruelty" such as *dedovshchina* "carries with it a repression of conscience where outside values are excluded and locally generated values dominate."[35] Whatever the soldiers do in Chechnya they do as a group that rejects the very notion of individuality and, consequently, individual responsibility.[36] A brutal and exaggerated initiation rite induces a brutal and exaggerated sense of comradeship that is not only intense but blind, and ultimately is unscrupulous. This is the kind of bond that Russian soldiers today find so meaningful and that they celebrate in their songs.

The soldiers' sense of the war as a perennial male ritual unrelated to politics and history recently found expression in the mainstream film *The Ninth Company,* by Fyodor Bondarchuk.[37] Although the film depicts events in Russia's war in Afghanistan, at least one critic wrote that the film, if only covertly, deals with the war in Chechnya and the fate of the "Russian boys" sent there to fight.[38] A certain equivalence between the two wars is evident. Both wars entailed a Russian incursion against an Islamic foe. More generally, it is hard to regard a film about an earlier war as devoid of reference to a contemporary conflict. Bondarchuk's film describes the fate of seven soldiers who fight in a war that lacks any evident purpose. In the film, the irrelevance of the war's political goal is particularly glaring: the soldiers are fighting for the Soviet Union at a time when it is already on the brink of dissolution, a point one of the soldiers emphasizes. In the film, the young men initially undergo hazing, which turns out to be a powerful "bonding" device. The brutal sergeant, for example, only wishes the young conscripts well and wants to turn them into "real men" and "real soldiers" capable of surviving the challenges of war. Their bonding culminates in the shared sexual experience: they all have sex with the same willing young woman.

In the second part of the film the young men are in Afghanistan, where they are assigned to guard a mountaintop. Through most of the film, the enemy is barely present. In the last scene, however, the Afghanis appear noiselessly from all directions, looking like ghosts, their exotic rags flying in the wind. The fighters' ghostly appearance is a visual pun on the military slang word "*dukhi*" (ghosts) reserved for Afghan and, later, Chechen rebels. In the final battle, the seven young men fulfill their military duty the best they can and die as true heroes. Their heroic deaths, however, serve no purpose. The men, as we find out, were defending a place of no importance for the withdrawal of Soviet troops. In fact, the army commanders had forgotten about them in the haste of retreat. The film has the same ambivalence as the soldiers' songs: although the war serves no political or moral purpose, the soldiers must nonetheless sacrifice their lives.[39]

Not surprisingly, some thought that the film had an antiwar message, since the young men's lives were cut short senselessly. Some critics even expressed hope that this film would prevent another senseless war like the one in Chechnya, or Abkhazia.[40] Others, however, saw the film as a patriotic glorification of a soldier's duty and valor, just the kind of film needed to foster fighting spirit in young Russian men.[41] In other words, the film seemed to excite perfectly contradictory responses. One critic, however, did see danger in the film's ambivalence. Dmitry Bykov saw the film's cult of heroism as a way of training viewers to be obedient to state authority. The war's obvious lack of purpose, he maintained, preempts viewers' questions about the reason for soldiers' sacrifice and trains them to admire useless bravery, accept futile deaths, and admire the aesthetics of war for war's sake:

> In all the interviews before the film came out, Bondarchuk and his actors kept repeating: "The film is about boys becoming men." One may wonder about this interpretation. OK, they became men at the cost of terrible humiliations and hardships. And then they were betrayed and killed, though it is not exactly clear who killed them: those who forgot to send reinforcement, or those who withdrew the troops from Afghanistan? So, it is important to become a man, and it is not important what happens to you afterwards. This is a handsome and noble idea but it absolves the Motherland of any responsibility. What we see, then, is patriotism without the Motherland and bravery without a purpose. The question "what for?" must be abolished altogether. There is no purpose here. Everything is done in order to achieve some high ideal of manhood. It is manhood for the sake of manhood. To become a man and then be killed is in itself the highest goal and the highest embodiment of beauty.[42]

Bykov objects to the idea of fostering manliness through abusive *dedovshchina* and senseless wars. More to the point, he objects that these rituals become a reason unto themselves, and that they distract soldiers and the viewing audience from seriously addressing the real issues posed by war.

However, despite Bykov's trenchant analysis, even he overlooks an important element of the film—the fate of the Afghani civilians. Neither

Bykov nor any other critic, so far as I can tell, commented on the shocking scene where the soldiers of the Ninth Unit blow up an entire Afghan village with all of its inhabitants. Even though we do not see the destruction of the village in detail (it is filmed as if from a distance), the scene represents nothing short of a massacre. Yet the soldiers, the nice guys of the film, do it without any regret, and the viewers are drawn to accept the military men's point of view. The director tries to slip in a "moral" justification for this war crime: the soldiers raze the village after a small boy from the settlement kills one of the Russians. But this can hardly excuse the wanton destruction of an entire town and ignores the fact that no reason or excuse exists for the Russian presence in Afghanistan in the first place—a point that the film constantly makes. The fact that even liberal critics have failed to comment on this scene suggests that Russian audiences have grown inured to mass civilian deaths in the course of the ten-year Chechen war.

To be fair, there are here and there signs of a new willingness to address the war seriously and to face up to Russian atrocities. For example, a song by Sergei Kopytin describes a Russian atrocity in 2000 at Ageshty, an actual event in which federal troops fired on the town for no reason.[43] Kopytin describes how the soldiers got drunk and started firing. Not only did the soldiers go unpunished but, as the song tells us, they were even rewarded for what they did: "An order came from the commanding officers to reward us with decorations. What do you want: we are at war, we now must fight." While addressing the soldiers' misery in the Afghan heat, the main focus of the song is the fate of the people on the other side of the conflict and the injustice done to them.

Another song by A. Marshal entitled "Mountain Man" ("*Gorets*") describes the fate of an old man whose house is destroyed and whose daughter and granddaughters are killed by shell-fire.[44] The song expresses sympathy for the old man's sorrow and even his desire for revenge: "The old man stood on the road and lifted his rifle. His hands held the rifle awkwardly." The songwriter however, stops short of placing the blame for the death of the old man's family on the fellow Russians. The old man's house, he claims, was destroyed by accident: "At night a random shell exploded next to his house."

A recent film by Pavel Kostomarov and Antuan Kattin, *Peaceful Life* (*Mirnaia zhizn'*, 2004), also depicts the suffering of the Chechen people. The film is a documentary about the life of two Chechen refugees, father and son, who work in a desolate Russian village fixing a cow barn. The two men fail to win the respect of their drunken supervisor or the other men on the job. One of their coworkers, who is going to be a soldier in Chechnya, tells the father and son that they will be dead in a year's time. After the job is finished, the father and son are not paid for their labor. The film suggests that the Russians regard their intolerance and cruelty as the norm, and expresses a sense of hopelessness.

Political terror is and no doubt will long continue to be the source of countless evils. But one facet in particular is that terrorism, and the war on terror, can be very easily manipulated by states to whip up public support as they pursue their own agendas. War has traditionally mobilized populations, but only because the people knew who the enemy was and were convinced that their cause was just. The war on terror—at least when manipulated as cynically as the Putin government has done—blurs the moral certainty that has sustained nations at war in the past. It leaves the soldiers and civilians back home with little more than a sense of victimization, resentment, and a dangerously hermetic sense of camaraderie. Popular entertainments, including films and soldiers' songs, offer a particularly vivid expression of the military and cultural malaise in a time when the Russian government claims to be a partner in the global war on terrorism.

Notes

1. The conflict that began in 1999 was the second phase of a war that initially began in 1994. For accounts of the First Chechen War, see Vanora Bennett, *Crying Wolf. The Return of War to Chechnya* (Oxford: Pan Books, 2001); Carlotta Gall and Thomas de Waal, *Chechnya: Calamity in the Caucasus* (New York: New York University Press, 1998).

2. Dmitri V. Trenin and Aleksei V. Malashenko (with Anatol Lieven), *Russia's Restless Frontier: The Chechnya Factor in Post-Soviet Russia* (Washington, D.C.: Carnegie Endowment for International Peace, 2004), 119.

3. Ibid, 119.

4. Ibid, 124. See also Jim Nichol, "Chechnya Conflict: Recent Developments," in *Chechnya Revisited,* ed. Yu. K. Nikolaev (New York: Nova Science Publishers, 2003), 21.

5. For a detailed analysis of Todorovsky's film, see the contribution by Brian James Baer to this volume.

6. This sense of victimization extends, paradoxically, even to the Russian legal system, which has resisted bringing those responsible for war crimes to justice out of a sense that soldiers who commit atrocities are also victims of war. In a series of notorious cases, Russian juries have exonerated Russian soldiers charged with the brutal murder of unarmed Chechen civilians. For details of these trials, see "Prestupleniia na voine," http://www.voinenet.ru (accessed May 15, 2009); Anna Politkovskaya, "Ostraia iuridicheskaia nedostatochnost'," *Novaia gazeta,* December 19, 2002, and "Budanov poluchil to, chto zasluzhil," *Novaia gazeta,* July 28, 2003; Anna Lebedeva, "Delo Ul'mana zhivet," *Novaia gazeta,* April 7, 2005; and Oleg Orlov, "Podsuden li kapitan Ul'man?" *Novaia gazeta,* April 29, 2006. For the best account of the everyday atrocities that have occurred in Chechnya in recent years, see Anna Politkovskaya, *A Dirty War: A Russian Reporter in Chechnya* (London: Harvill, 2001), and *A Small Corner of Hell: Dispatches from Chechnya* (Chicago: University of Chicago Press, 2003).

7. Robert A. Rothstein, "Homeland, Home Town, and Battlefield: The Popular Song," in *Culture and Entertainment in Wartime Russia,* ed. Richard Stites (Bloomington: Indiana University Press, 1995), 77–107.

8. The song is "*Esli budesh' ranen,*" lyrics by I. Utkin, music by S. Kats, 1941. In other songs, young women promised to reward their men's courage in war with love, fidelity, and marriage when they come back from the front lines. "Bud' smelym, bud' khrabrym v zhestokom boiu, za russkuiu zemliu srazhaisia. I pomni pro Don, pro nevestu svoiu. S pobedoiu k nam vozvrashchaisia." (Be brave and courageous in battle, fight for the Russian land. And don't forget the river Don and your bride. Return to us victorious.) Unless otherwise noted, all translations are mine.

9. The vital role of war songs is not, of course, confined to Russia. For a description of French soldier songs in World War I, see Regina M. Sweeney, *Singing Our Way to Victory: French Cultural Politics and Music During the Great War* (Middletown, Conn.: Wesleyan University Press, 2001), 45.

10. J. R. Smyth, writing on posttraumatic stress disorders, throws light on the soldiers' need for a vividly imagined enemy. Smyth argues that reactions to wartime stress focus on causality. "It is the question of where to lay blame that is critical. Fundamentally, each view compels an underlying moral judgment, and is not merely a neutral investigation of causality." See J. R Smyth, *A Review of 120 Years of Psychological Literature on Reactions to Combat from the Civil War Through the Vietnam War: 1860–1980* (unpublished manuscript, Duke University, 1981), cited in Sarah A. Haley, "Some of My Best Friends Are Dead: Treatment of the PTSD Patient and His Family," in *Post-Traumatic Stress Disorder and the War Veteran Patient,* ed. William E. Kelly (New York: Brunner/Mazel, 1985), 54.

11. One song, "Bro" ("*Bratan*"), by the group Blue Berets (Golubye berety) claims that although this war is "ours," we really don't need it: "Our needless war" (*Eto nenuzhnaia nasha voina*). Recording available at http://www.rsva.ru/music/memory/song91.mp3 (accessed June 10, 2009).

12. Unless otherwise noted, the lyrics quoted in the article can be found at "*Rossiiskii Soiuz veterenov Afganistana: Soldatskie pesni,*" http://www.rsva.ru/music/index.shtml (accessed May 14, 2009).

13. From the album *Ranenyi gorod* by the Blue Berets. For the texts, see http://avtomat2000.com/ranen.html (accessed May 14, 2009).

14. Raian Farukshin, "Vitek," http://avtomat2000.com/rf.html (accessed May 14, 2009).

15. "Ne sudite nas, ne zhaleite nas. Kazhdyi, kto zdes' byl, vypolnial prikaz." Oleg Akulov, "Nad Argunom," from the collection *Chechnya v ogne 2,* Kul'turnyi tsentr. Soldaty Rossii, http://soldats.narod.ru (accessed May 14, 2009).

16. "O poslednei voine, dazhe mat' ne poimet. Tol'ko noch'iu vo sne zuby bred razomknet." Vasilii Dvortsov, "Skobelevskii motiv," http://artofwar.ru/r/rassypuha/text_0260-1.shtml (accessed June 10, 2009).

17. For example, A. Kliminiuk' in "Again the Clouds Have Gathered over Chechnya" ("*Opiat' navisli tuchi nad Chechnei*") sings about "the tears of inconsolable mothers."

18. A. Dmitrishin, "His Majesty, the Soldier" ("*Ego velichestvo patsan*").

19. B. I. Ivanov, "*Na granitnoi plite,*" from the collection *Na Kavkaze delo bylo,* Soldatskaia studiia, http://www.avtomat2000.com/kavkaz2.html (accessed May 14, 2009).

20. For a recording of this song, go to http://www.rsva.ru/music/friend/song57.mp3 (accessed June 10, 2009).

21. "Da mne zhena i ta tverdit, chto nas kupili za 'Iubileiku' i za palku kolbasy." From "War Is War" ("*Voina voinoi*"), by V. Zavodchikov.

22. Of the approximately two hundred songs about Chechnya I have seen, only four or five have referred to Chechen fighters.

23. Pertinent here is the fact that the heroic stature of the Great Patriotic War has come under severe attack in post-Soviet Russia. Its reputation has been badly tarnished by revelations about the Molotov-Ribbentrop pact, the government's culpable failure to prepare for war, and the brutality of the military, including the use of *zagran otriady* (troops that shot those who fell behind or tried to surrender) and *shtrafbaty* (the punitive battalions sent on suicide missions). As Nina Tumarkina in *The Living and the Dead: The Rise and Fall of the Cult of World War II in Russia* (New York: Basic Books, 1994), 202, points out, by the early nineties, "the cult of the Great Patriotic War had been replaced by a rich amalgam of passion, regret, nostalgia, rage, and remembrance."

24. Serguei Oushakine, "Vitality Rediscovered: Theorizing Post-Soviet Ethnicity in Russian Social Sciences," *Studies in East European Thought* 9, no. 3 (September 2007), http://www.springerlink.com/content/dq1u258525334227/ (accessed June 4, 2009).

25. Gezine Schwan, "The Role of Education in German-Polish Reconciliation," in *Truth, Justice, and Reconciliation: Proceedings* (Stockholm: Stockholm International Forum, 2002), 180. Jodi Halpern and Harvey M. Weinstein, "Empathy and Rehumanization After Mass violence," in *My Neighbor, My Enemy: Justice and Community in the Aftermath of Mass Atrocity,* ed. Eric Styover and Harvey M. Weinstein (Cambridge: Cambridge University Press, 2004), 303–19.

26. "A na voine, kak na voine, prevyshe druzhby net zakona, plecho k plechu, spina k spine, i eto bratstvo na voine i krugovaia oborona." For a recording, go to http://www.rsva.ru/music/unit/song136.mp3 (accessed June 10, 2009).

27. "Gde ty, druzhan ty moi, chto zhe striaslos' s toboi? Pochemu tebia net sredi tekh, kto vernulsia iz boia? Kom k gorlu podkatil. . . . Ia zhe tebia prosil, chtob ty vse vremia derzhalsia vmeste so mnoi." For a recording, go to http://www.rsva.ru/music/favorites/song23.mp3 (accessed June 10, 2009).

28. On the subject of homoeroticism in Gogol's works, see Simon Karlinsky, *The Sexual Labyrinths of Nikolai Gogol* (Cambridge, Mass.: Harvard University Press, 1976).

29. "Cherna Chechenskaia voina, bez gosudarstva i bez mery, i ot togo, ne znaia very, dusha otchaian'ia polna. No on ni v chem ne vinovat. V okopy leg on pod prisiagoi. Emu otets i mat' kombat, i on nazlo blesnet otvagoi." The entire text can be found at http://avtomat2000.com/av.html (accessed June 10, 2009).

30. On recent deaths from hazing in the Russian army, see Aleksandr Gol'ts, "Vsia Korolevskaia rat'," *Novaia gazeta,* December 3, 2005.

31. On the history of *dedovshchina,* see Igor Obraztsov, "The Reasons for *Dedovshchina* and Ways to Prevent It: A Retrospective Analysis," in *Dedovshchina in the Post-Soviet Military: Hazing of Russian Army Conscripts in a Comparative Perspective,* ed. Françoise Daucé and Elisabeth Sieca-Kozlowski (Stuttgart: Ibidem-Verlag, 2005), 105–9.

32. See Donna Winslow, "Rites of Passage and Group Bonding in the Canadian

Airborne," in *The Hazing Reader,* ed. Hank Nuwer (Bloomington: Indiana University Press, 2004), 147–83. The Nuwer collection also describes instances of hazing in the armed forces of the United States and the Czech Republic.

33. On the methods of torture and hazing in the Russian army, see the Human Rights Watch report, "The Wrongs of Passage: Inhuman and Degrading Treatment of New Recruits in the Russian Armed Forces," available at http://www.hrw.org/en/reports/2004/10/19/wrongs-passage-0 (accessed May 14, 2009).

34. One horrific case of near lethal hazing involving a soldier by the name of Andrei Sychov attracted national and even international attention. See Igor Reif, "Dedovskie metody," *Novaia gazeta,* March 20, 2006.

35. James Waller, *Becoming Evil: How Ordinary People Commit Genocide and Mass Killing* (Oxford: Oxford University Press, 2002), 208.

36. E. Aronson and J. Mills, "The Effect of Severity of Initiation on Liking for a Group," *Journal of Abnormal and Social Psychology* 59 (1969): 177–81.

37. *Deviataia rota* was a box office success in Russia and received the Nika Award for best film of the year. One of the film's admirers was Russian president Putin; see "Krivoe dulo slave ne pomekha," http://9rota.lacory.ru/viewtopic.php?t=576&sid=4107f115f4280d61583cf1d0f48c3d22 (accessed May 14, 2009).

38. Dmitrii Bykov, "R-r-rota!" *Ogonek* 39, 2005, http://www.ogoniok.com/4913/35/ (accessed May 14, 2009).

39. Anastasia Krivoshanova pointed out that the film sends a confusing message. Anastasia Krivoshanova, "Deviataia rota," *Skepsis* 3–4, 2005, http://www.scepsis.ru/library/id_197. html (accessed May 14, 2009).

40. Natal'ia Osipova, "Deviataia rota," *Kino-Ru,* November 13, 2005, http://www.kino.ru/review.php?id=2599 (accessed May 14, 2009).

41. Sergei Minaev, "Vremia geroev," *Vzgliad,* October 18, 2005, http://www.vz.ru/columns/2005/10/18/10172.html (accessed May 14, 2009).

42. Bykov, "R-r-rota!"

43. Aleksei Gerasimov, "Ageshty rastreliany iz 'Alazani,'" *Kommersant,* July 21, 2000, http://www.kommersant.ru/doc.aspx?DocsID=153612 (accessed May 14, 2009).

44. A recording is available at http://www.rsva.ru/music/legent/song84.mp3 (accessed June 10, 2009).

Narrating Terror: The Face and Place of Violence in Valery Todorovsky's *My Stepbrother Frankenstein*

Brian James Baer

> The media certainly does not create the terrorist, but like a skilful make-up artist, can assuredly make of him either a Saint or a Frankenstein's monster.
>
> —H. H. A. COOPER

> Valery Todorovsky has made a crucial film for our time. Future generations will see it and understand the reasons behind the crisis of our regulated and comfortable civilization—the catastrophes that befell mankind after 9/11.
>
> —VALERY KICHIN

For those acquainted with modern military history, the phrase coined by the Bush administration, "global war on terror," has a distinctly oxymoronic ring, insofar as war and terror for most of the twentieth century formed a mutually defining opposition, delineating very real differences in terms of the conduct of operations and the treatment of combatants. Nevertheless, in the aftermath of the Beslan atrocity of September 2004, the Russian government, as Stephen Hutchings shows in his essay in this volume, has followed the United States' lead in redefining the insurgents in Chechnya as terrorists in a global jihad. This redefinition has helped to disassociate the violence from any "legitimate" political aspirations of the Chechen people and reinscribe it within the "illegitimate" context of global Islamic extremism.[1]

The distinction between war and terrorism is one that governments have long sought to enforce in order to maintain what Max Weber described as the state's "monopoly on the legitimate use of violence." However, as Alex Houen points out, "there is still no internationally accepted definition of terrorism," and Joseph Zuleika and William A. Douglass note the "play with meaning and confusion of contexts inherent in the word 'terrorism.'"[2] The refusal of terrorists to respect the "proper" *place* (designated war zones) and the "proper" *face* of violence (lawful combatants) challenges the best efforts of governments to define and discursively to contain such violence. Therefore, Houen maintains, "producing a narrative or theory that outlines an etiology of terrorism and accounts for its effects is obviously a form of counter-terror itself."[3]

In this volume, Birgit Beumers analyzes what we might call, following Houen, counterterrorist narratives that arose in the aftermath of the terrorist attack during a performance of the popular musical *Nord-Ost* at a Moscow theater in 2002. By recounting the tragedy in terms of clear-cut good and evil and by abjuring commentary on the government's deadly handling of the affair (approximately 130 civilians died as a result of a botched attempt by Russian Special Forces to free the hostages), these narratives embed terror, Beumers asserts, "in structures of play that seemingly remove its unpredictability and make it appear controlled." Valery Todorovsky's 2004 film, *My Stepbrother Frankenstein* (*Moi svodnyi brat Frankenshtein*), however, stands out starkly against the backdrop of such counterterrorist narratives by eschewing black-and-white moral categories and by dramatizing the utter failure of traditional narratives to contain terrorist violence.

Situating the problem of terror within the context of a family drama, the film dramatizes the effects of terrorism, described by Houen as "blowing a hole in the very fabric of everydayness."[4] The film tells the story of a middle-class Moscow intelligentsia family that is plunged into a world of paranoia, panic, and death by the sudden appearance of a physically and mentally impaired Chechen war veteran, Pavlik Zakharov (played by Daniil Spivakovsky), who claims to be the illegitimate son of the father, Yulik (Leonid Yarmolnik). The wife, Rita (Elena Yakovleva), a real estate agent, initially takes pity on the young man but grows increasingly frightened of him and the threat he poses to her two children, Egor (Artem Shalimov) and Anya (Marianna Ilina). Yulik, on the other hand, at first wants nothing to do with Pavlik, but later comes to appreciate his traditional masculine qualities of courage, loyalty, and sacrifice. The film ends when Pavlik, who has grown increasingly paranoid throughout the course of the film, "abducts" the family with the purpose of protecting them from the "spooks" (*dukhi*) he sees all around him. Each of the characters that comes into contact with Pavlik in the course of the film applies a traditional narrative to make sense of him and his experiences, but in every case the narrative proves inadequate to contain Pavlik's violence and paranoia, underscoring terrorism's power to unsettle, confuse, and simply ignore the distinctions people make between legitimate and illegitimate forms of violence.

While Western critics have described the film as tracing "the after-effects of war," Russian critics immediately recognized the film to be about terrorism precisely because of the way its violence intrudes on everydayness.[5] Valery Kichin, in a review of the film, compares Pavlik's arrival in Yulik's home to a civilian catastrophe, an airplane crash, resembling in many ways a terrorist attack: "This film resembles that Tupolev-154 that daily carried a hundred fifty civilian passengers into the sky and didn't return. The stewardesses had probably already served the coffee, and people were reading the glossy Aeroflot magazine about the good life. But a second later a thin sheet of fuselage burst open an abyss, war and peace, reminding the country that only two centimeters separates us from hell."[6] Similarly, Leonid Yarmolnik, the actor who plays the father, digresses in an interview from a discussion of war to a discussion of terror:

> When there is an explosion in the subway or underground walkways and they don't show us who did it, we have an abstract desire to seize hold of some kind of fetish and to call that evil. We're afraid to let our children out, we're afraid to come home late, we worry about our wives and mothers. . . . When there was an explosion near the Hotel National, not far from the journalism faculty of Moscow State, my daughter could have been there. It's simply monstrous [*chudovishchno*]! You panic when you understand that at that time in the subway, driving between the Avtozavodskaia and Paveletskaia stations, there were people in the subway cars going to work or to school, reading, laughing, or just napping. . . . It's unthinkable! And you feel resentment, hatred, and helplessness—you just want to scream.[7]

Here Yarmolnik compares Pavlik's sudden appearance in Yulik's life not to conventional warfare but to a terrorist attack in the Moscow subway. For Yarmolnik, Pavlik embodies less the ravages of war than the insidious threat of terrorism, which respects neither the proper place nor the proper face of violence.

Containing Terror I: The Place of Violence

Todorovsky's film stands out against other filmic representations of the conflict in Chechnya, such as Sergei Bodrov's *Prisoner of the Mountain*

(*Kavkazskii plennik,* 1996), Alexander Rogozhin's *Checkpoint* (*Blokpost,* 1998), Aleksei Balabanov's *War* (*Voina,* 2002), and Nikolai Stambula's *Forced March* (*Marsh-brosok,* 2003). These films, even when exposing the moral ambiguities and uncontrollable violence of war, tend to romanticize—or at least to confirm—the cultural, geographic, and even linguistic particularity of Chechnya, those features that form the basis of modern national identity. In so doing, intentionally or not, they portray the conflict in Chechnya as a war of national independence. Indeed, all the film depictions of the conflict in Chechnya mentioned above take place outside Russia proper.[8] Todorovsky's film, on the other hand, takes place in Moscow and does not feature a single terrorist or ethnic Chechen among its main characters. Todorovsky, in other words, refuses to contain the violence of the Chechen conflict either geographically or ethnically.

One of the defining features of terrorism is that it does not respect traditional combat zones. In fact, terrorism aims to transform all of civil society—the so-called home front—into a potential field of violence, implicating civilian populations in political struggles and avoiding direct confrontation with recognized military forces. This dislocation of the place of violence is dramatized in *My Stepbrother Frankenstein* through an elaborate spatial metaphor of containment that runs throughout the film and breaks down the opposition of inside and outside. By situating terror in the very bosom of civilian domestic life, this film unsettles traditional associations of inside with safety and outside with vulnerability.

The film opens in the kitchen of the family home. Yulik has just shown Rita a letter from a woman he had an affair with over twenty years ago. Rita slaps him. The camera then shows Anya, eavesdropping, and follows her as she goes to her older brother's bedroom. The children have already read the letter, and Anya asks Egor if their parents are going to get a divorce. The letter has brought unexpected strife into the family home. Gradually, the film moves into ever more public spaces. In the next scene, Yulik is in his friend Edik's office. Edik (Sergei Gasarov) is a doctor, and while a group of young children are given a diagnostic test, Edik and Yulik sit in the back office, drinking vodka, as Yulik relates his predicament. The next scene takes place in an empty apartment that Rita is showing to prospective buyers. Here we have a private dwelling now on the market, open to the public. Rita tells her clients that the most important thing about a place is its "aura," and leaves them alone to get a feeling for it. This offhanded comment about the home's aura foreshadows Pavlik's paranoid obsession with *dukhi,* or "spooks," "ghosts"—and also soldiers' slang for Chechen fighters[9]—which he hears in the attic of Rita and Yulik's apartment house. Following that scene, Yulik, a physicist turned fiction writer, is in the editorial offices of his publisher when he learns that his son from that long-ago affair is coming to Moscow. After that, Yulik is shown in the train station, the most public space in the film, waiting for his son to arrive. When Pavlik finally steps off the train, strangely dressed and with a patch over his right eye, Yulik cannot bring himself to claim him. He leaves the station without greeting his son.

This initial play with space culminates in the scene that follows, in which the family is shown together at the kitchen table, enjoying a very tense dinner. Rita, clearly upset, scolds her son for wearing his sunglasses inside. She eventually leaves the table and goes outside to where Pavlik is sitting on a bench with a suitcase, patiently waiting in front of the family's apartment house. She invites him inside. The confusion of inside and outside, public and private is now complete, when the stranger who is Yulik's son—can one's son be a stranger?—is invited to come off the street into the family home.

Subsequent scenes reinforce this confusion. For example, when Rita is showing the empty apartment to another couple—had the first couple picked up a negative aura?—she repeatedly mentions that the walls have been reinforced with steel and concrete: "Throughout the apartment house, on all the other floors, the walls are made of wood, but here they're steel and concrete." (She had also mentioned this to the first couple, and over the phone to another potential buyer.) The husband then asks what the advantage of such reinforcement is: "So that means if the whole house catches fire, we'll be safe, right?" Before Rita can answer, Yulik retorts, "If everyone burns, you'll burn, too." Yulik's remark underscores the fact that, despite the best precautions, it is impossible to insulate the family from outside threats. The scene ends when, after the showing, Rita asks where Pavlik is. Learning that he's in their home, and knowing the other children will have returned from school, Rita panics: "Who knows what he might do." Their own home, it turns out, like the luxury apartment built of concrete and steel, is no longer a safe haven from violence.

The play with space continues when Rita travels outside Moscow to visit Yulik's mother at her dacha to ask for money to help pay for an operation on Pavlik's eye. If in the Russian cultural imagination the dacha, like the kitchen, is the ultimate safe haven, a sanctuary of private life, and the babushka the ultimate guardian of that private life, the viewer's expectations are quickly dashed. Yulik's mother is a bitch. She immediately scolds Rita for not having come last week to help her move back to the city. When Rita tells her of Yulik's illegitimate son, the grandmother feigns delight, much to Rita's chagrin: "How wonderful. . . . He's the spitting image of Yulik [*odno litso*]. Wonderful." When Rita asks for money, the grandmother wonders why Yulik himself didn't come. She then tells Rita, "You're not good [*vrednye*] for him. If Yulik hadn't married you, he would have achieved great things in science." These harsh remarks, delivered by the grandmother in a conversational tone with a smile on her face in the idyllic setting of the dacha—they are outside having tea—expose animosity and discord behind the façade of the happy family. The inner core of the family turns out to be rotten. Pavlik, however, is oblivious to the grandmother's comments, which are in any case directed at Rita. He likes the dacha because it is protected from the outside world, and he comments rather ominously, "This is a nice place you have here. Quiet. You could hide [*skhoronit'sia*] something here if you had to." Ironically, this place that is good for hiding things—a foreshadowing of Pavlik's later use of the dacha as a refuge from the spooks and police—is where the fissure running through the family is laid bare.

Pavlik's increasing paranoia leads to ever more intrusions of the outside world, specifically the violence of the Chechen conflict, into the family home. Pavlik hears voices in the attic and thinks he's hearing Chechen guerrillas, or *dukhi,* "spooks." He convinces Yulik to go with him to the attic, where the *dukhi* turn out to be bums. Yulik, however, is so caught up in the paranoid hysteria of the moment that he jumps on a bum who is trying to escape and begins to beat him. Pavlik has to pull him off the man. Indeed, Pavlik's paranoia is so extreme—and contagious—that there is no longer any safe haven for the family. When guests at a party at Yulik and Rita's propose a toast to the hosts, Pavlik warns them not to drink: someone may have poisoned the alcohol. Once again Pavlik's suspicions infect one of the most protected sanctuaries of Russian private life; the guests represent the tiny circle of Yulik and Rita's closest friends. The party ends with Yulik threatening to beat up his best friend, Edik, for having told him that Pavlik is ill and poses a real threat to their safety. To the extent that terrorist violence is aimed ultimately not at annihilating the citizens of the developed world but rather at infecting their comfortable, protected lives with fear, uncertainty, and suspicion, Pavlik can be said to embody that terrorism.

Soon after the party, it becomes clear to a reluctant Yulik that he must remove Pavlik from the family home. He tells him to pack his things and get in the car: "We're leaving." "Where to, Dad?" Pavlik asks. "To a safe place." "That's right," Pavlik says. "We should have gone a long time ago. They'll come and we won't be here." Yulik then takes Pavlik to the countryside and leaves him on a deserted country road. Pavlik remarks, "I don't like it here, Dad. It's open space." The freedom traditionally associated with open space is now, in Pavlik's eyes, seen as vulnerability, just as the protection associated with inside spaces has been transformed into a kind of imprisonment. In any case, Yulik's attempt to banish Pavlik and the paranoia he has brought into their lives fails. Pavlik winds up in jail for beating up a non-Russian, and Yulik bails him out. On the way out of the jail, a policeman takes Yulik aside and tells him Pavlik is a hero for doing what he's done: "Your son's done a good thing. They need to be beaten, but beaten lawfully." The remark is disturbing, and Yulik does not reply, for what could it mean "to beat someone lawfully"? It recalls Weber's notion that the state possesses a monopoly on "legitimate" forms of violence. It also points to the breakdown in civil rights—in civilian protections—in those nations targeted by terrorists, one of the more troubling effects of terrorist violence, a disturbing analogy to the terrorists' own refusal to recognize civilians as protected from political violence.

Although Yulik springs Pavlik from one place of confinement, the jail, he later takes him to another, a mental hospital, where, at the urging of his family and friends, he plans to have him committed. But while they sit waiting in the dark hallway of the overcrowded institution, their attention is drawn to a mother and son. The son, clearly another traumatized veteran of the war in Chechnya, is in an autistic state, rocking and groaning, his gaze fixed on the floor. The distraught mother is trying to communicate with him. Pavlik addresses the man: "Lieutenant, don't be afraid." The soldier stops rocking and groaning; the mother is elated. At that moment Yulik realizes that Pavlik has experienced something he cannot begin to imagine, and refuses to commit him.

Todorovsky's ambivalent relationship to containment as a solution to terrorism is brought home in the final sequence of the film, when Pavlik takes the family at gunpoint out to the grandmother's dacha in order to protect them from the encroaching spooks. From the outside, Pavlik appears to have been transformed into a terrorist. When he gives Yulik and Rita instructions on where to meet him and the children, he tells them threateningly, "Do everything as I have told you." He then informs them that he has a weapon. When they are finally together in the back of a taxivan, Pavlik sits with his arm around Anya as if she were his hostage. When Yulik asks where they're going, Pavlik replies, "To a quiet place. We'll wait there a while." He then shows them the pistol in his belt.

Exactly how Pavlik acquired the pistol he uses to "kidnap" the family is unclear, although earlier in the film a pistol had been mentioned by the colonel of Pavlik's army regiment, whom Yulik and Pavlik run into outside the police station. Yulik invites the colonel, Timur Kurbatov (Sergei Garmash), back to the house. Pavlik drinks too much and falls asleep, after which Timur recounts to Rita and Yulik the traumatic and heroic events of Pavlik's service in Chechnya: among other things, he saved the colonel's life and watched his best friend die before his very eyes. At one point the colonel says of Pavlik, "He's stubborn. He still can't forget that I promised to give him a pistol." Rita, agitated at the thought of Pavlik with a firearm, asks if he's brought it with him. "What are you thinking?" the colonel says. "I understand very well that a pistol is necessary in war, not in civilian life, among your relatives and friends." However, the next day Timur and Pavlik are discovered scaling the narrow ledge outside the top floor of the apartment building, spying on a "suspicious-looking man." The colonel is then asked to leave, and as he goes, Yulik says to him, "I didn't expect this of you, Timur. I didn't expect this." It seems Pavlik had succeeded in convincing the colonel that a simple separation of war and civilian life was impossible, that violence was no less a threat in Moscow than it had been in Chechnya. Had the colonel then decided to give Pavlik the pistol he'd once promised him?

If Pavlik, like a terrorist, effectively confuses civilian life and war, the director abjures the counterterrorist consolation of reinstating a clear separation between the two. After the family escapes from the dacha and Pavlik is shot by the special forces brought by the police to the scene, the camera initially focuses on the family—Yulik, Rita, Egor, and Anya—huddled together, wrapped in blankets. The camera then pulls back and moves away from the family to focus on the police, who are laughing and discussing the "success" of their mission. The family is now out of the frame, and the camera remains fixed on the police while the credits roll. Rather than the return of private life to the family, the film's ending suggests that private life as they once knew it has been lost forever, and their stunned silence testifies to the ultimate failure of narrative to contain the paranoia and violence embodied by Pavlik.

Containing Terror II: The Face of Violence

Whereas most recent films about the conflict in Chechnya depict the experience of Russians in a "foreign" land, among a "foreign" people, thereby suggesting an ethnic interpretation of "us" and "them," *My Stepbrother Frankenstein* embodies terrorist violence in the form of a provincial Russian, exposing the fissures in contemporary Russia's own identity. For example, when Yulik tells Rita that the love affair that resulted in Pavlik happened "twenty years ago," he suggests a link between their comfortable post-Soviet present and the Soviet past. When Pavlik later sings the once popular song "Malinovka" that Yulik used to sing to his mother, it represents not only Yulik's younger days but also nostalgia for a simpler time in Russia's past, one that seems a million miles away from the cosmopolitan, globalized culture of today's Moscow elite (Egor has a copy of Andy Warhol's silk-screened image of Marilyn Monroe on the wall of his bedroom). Moreover, Pavlik's arrival in Moscow from the deep provinces points up the historic divide in Russian culture between the center and the periphery that has only been exacerbated since the fall of the Soviet Union. In this way, Todorovsky stages the confrontation of post-Soviet Russia with itself—and in doing so confuses the very concepts of "us" and "them," legitimate and illegitimate typically reinforced in counterterrorist narratives.

To the extent that terrorism tends to be about the other, "i.e., one's country, one's class, one's creed, one's president, oneself can hardly be a terrorist,"[10] Pavlik is a troubling figure. Although ethnically Russian, he highlights an otherness at the heart of Russian culture itself, rather like the homegrown terrorists Timothy McVeigh and Ted Kaczynski in the United States, who have been thoroughly eclipsed in public discourse on terrorism by the image of the radical Islamist. As the illegitimate son of Yulik, Pavlik is a member of the family, but he does not quite belong. And while, at least according to the grandmother, he looks exactly like his father, he is a simple provincial who couldn't have less in common with Yulik, a Russian *intelligent,* living in the heart of Moscow. Moreover, since military service is even more of a class marker in Russia than it is in the United States, Pavlik's physical and psychic scars mark him in terms of class, suggesting his separation from the world of his father's second family and friends.

The class issues surrounding military service in Russia are exposed in a short exchange between Pavlik and Egor. Pavlik enters Egor's bedroom and says, "You'll be in the army soon." Egor asks, "Why soon?" In the unlikely event that Egor does serve in the army, it would be after his graduation from the university; someone of his class would never serve, as it seems Pavlik did, directly out of high school. Egor adds, "Not everyone is inclined to serve in the army," as if it were a matter of choice. Pavlik then asks, "Could you walk up to someone and smash them in the face [*v mordu sdvinut'*]?" After a short pause, Pavlik reassures him: "You don't need to serve. Your brother's already served for you." So different are Egor and Pavlik that the word "brother" here takes on figurative overtones and conjures the metaphor of the national family and of Christian fraternity: Pavlik has sacrificed himself for his Russian "brother."

Scholars such as Bernard Lewis have argued that the phenomenon of modern terrorism is produced from the clash of traditional cultures with modern social and economic realities.[11] The sense of dislocation and alienation that this engenders leads to what Lewis calls a violent "backlash" in defense of traditional religious and social values that are perceived to be "under attack" from the hegemonic culture of the West. In this sense, too, Pavlik is linked to terrorism. He is a walking exemplar of traditional patriarchal values.[12] Most notably, Pavlik addresses Yulik as *batia,* an outmoded form of address still used in some Russian dialects. Moreover, he always defers to Yulik, and when Egor disobeys his father, Pavlik steps in: "What's wrong with you? Dad said to go to sleep. That means go to sleep." Pavlik's loyalty to his new family—and in particular to his new father—is total.

The confusion of "us" and "them" embodied by Pavlik is a major theme in *My Stepbrother Frankenstein* and is elaborated in a number of different ways, but most spectacularly in the story told by Pavlik at Yulik and Rita's party. Earlier at the party, one of Rita's friends serves Pavlik some food, and while they're alone at the table says to Pavlik, with great sincerity, "Well, Pavlik, we all respect you very much. We're simply proud of you and wish you the very best. Really, with all my heart." Rita's friend treats Pavlik like a traditional war hero, invoking the sentiments of respect and pride. However, later on, after Pavlik warns them that their drinks may have been poisoned, the guests ask him who might have done this. Pavlik launches into a story from his time in Chechnya: "I personally wiped out four spooks. And then one came at me—a big one. Bearded. He stank. He screamed: 'Take that, Russian pigs.' Vasya put four bullets into him for sure. And then they ran to the village. Me and Vaska followed them in an APC [armored personnel carrier]. The locals started running around, shouting: 'Don't. We're on your side. What are you doing? We're on your side.' But we wiped them out." Rita's friend who had told Pavlik how proud she was of what he'd done in Chechnya now asks, flabbergasted, "Who? The civilians?" "Who could tell them apart?" Pavlik answers. "It was dark. Scary. We turned on our headlights. We got twenty of them for sure." And then, as if to drive home the complete confusion of war and private life, Pavlik adds, "After that they gave Vaska leave. He went to get married, while I spent the next three days cleaning the blood off the wheels. That's the story." The stunned guests sit there in silence. The distinction between soldier and terrorist breaks down when Pavlik and Vasya kill civilians and enemy combatants alike, and the distinction between private life and military service seems untenable: immediately after the massacre, Vaska leaves to get married.

The experience of guerrilla war teaches Pavlik the deadly consequences of an inability to distinguish between us and them and instills in him the paranoid delusion that the enemy is everywhere, that anyone could be a spook. Protection requires constant vigilance. Not long after he arrives in Moscow he tells Rita, "Don't be afraid of me, Rita. You should be afraid of something else." Rita retorts, "Why do I need to be afraid. There's nothing I need to be afraid of." Pavel brings the conversation to an uncertain conclusion with the remark, "Alright. God willing, everything will turn out." It isn't clear who or what this "something else" refers to until Pavlik begins to hear spooks in the attic and sees them all around. In a similar vein, when speaking with Egor about serving in the military, Pavlik asks his half brother whether he would be capable of hitting someone in the face. "Who?" Egor queries. "Anyone [*khot' komu*]," Pavlik replies, underscoring the notion that violence has been dislocated, separated from a specific, clearly distinguishable object and made indiscriminate.

In fact, Pavlik's "enemies" are not limited to ethnic Caucasians. While the man selling watermelons at the market, whom Pavlik will later assault, is from the Caucasus, not all the "spooks" Pavlik sees are dark-skinned. When he picks up Anya from school and takes her with him to the jewelry store to look at diamonds—he wants a fake eye made out of a diamond—he takes note of the salesperson, who is watching the odd pair very closely. He says to Anya, "You see, he's nervous, and we're calm. That means we're strong. And he's afraid of us. A spook." Later, when he's at the baths with Yulik, he assaults the man who takes the birch twigs they'd bought, hitting him several times on the head with a large bucket used for rinsing. As they hurriedly exit the baths, Yulik asks Pavlik, "Is he alive?" to which Pavlik responds, "Who? The spook?" and the scene ends there.

Todorovsky skillfully exploits the ambiguity of the word *dukh* to underscore the dubious ontological status granted the enemy by Pavlik's paranoid imagination. They are there but not there, all around but invisible, reflecting the "slippery/phantom quality" that terrorism has acquired.[13] When Pavlik calls the jewelry store salesman a *dukh,* Anya, confused by the remark, queries, "Whose [*chei*]?" to which Pavlik responds, "No one's [*nichei*]."

Containing Terror III: Narrating Violence

Because Pavlik is Russian and a soldier, all the characters in the film make an effort to find a narrative that will "legitimate" him: good son, courageous soldier, loyal friend. Not surprisingly, Pavlik's father, Yulik, makes the most concerted effort to find a narrative that will make sense of Pavlik, one that will contain his bizarre and increasingly violent behavior. The problem of narration is raised in the very title of the film, which invokes Mary Shelley's monster. That reference constructs Yulik as Pavlik's creator: he is his biological father and, like Dr. Frankenstein, a scientist; he is also like Mary Shelley in that he now writes science fiction. The burden, it would then appear, is on him to find an appropriate narrative for his creation, and he is indeed the character most determined to find a way to redeem his illegitimate progeny. By the end of the film, however, none of the narratives he invokes works, a failure foreshadowed early in the film when Rita berates Yulik as a failed writer: "You can't even write an article for a journal for three kopecks."

Frankenstein is certainly the most overt intertextual reference in the film. Like the fictional monster, Pavlik has been virtually "resurrected" from the dead. At the hospital, the doctor tells Yulik that, with such a wound, it's a miracle Pavlik survived. Later, the link to Mary Shelley's monster is made more directly. Egor, who is most disturbed by Pavlik's presence in the home, shows a video of the 1931 James Whale film *Frankenstein* to two girlfriends. Pavlik enters the room, and it becomes obvious that Egor has planned the viewing to make fun of Pavlik as a kind of monster. Egor later asks his father to throw Pavlik out of the house, then hires two men to assault him.

While the links to Frankenstein are drawn rather overtly, even this narrative fails to contain Pavlik and his experience of violence. For example, when Egor plays the video for his friends, not only does Pavlik fail to see the connection to himself, but one of Egor's friends grows uncomfortable with the joke, understanding perhaps that if Pavlik is Frankenstein, they are the townspeople with pitchforks, and so forces Egor to turn the movie off. Later, Pavlik's discussion with Timur is filmed in black and white and on grainy film stock, like the Frankenstein film watched by Egor and his friends. In this way Todorovsky sets off the Frankenstein narrative in formal terms, suggesting the impossibility of integrating that experience of violence into his new family's Moscow life: filmed in glossy color, that Moscow life belongs to a completely different genre.

With his own masculinity challenged by the post-Soviet marketplace, Yulik first inscribes Pavlik within a traditional narrative of masculine heroism, but that attempt ends in disaster. Although Yulik is at first the most reluctant to let Pavlik into his life, he soon bonds with his son at the baths. There, in a very touching scene, Yulik washes Pavlik's back, and they beat each other with birch twigs. The scene ends with Pavlik assaulting and nearly killing a man who tries to take their birch twigs.

Nevertheless, Yulik, a Moscow *intelligent,* is flattered by Pavlik's respect for him as the family patriarch and, impressed by Pavlik's unhesitating defense of him and his family, soon begins to adopt a more traditional masculine stance himself. When he and Pavlik return from the baths, there is a party going on in full swing at the apartment. After Pavlik tells his disturbing story of his encounter with the Chechen civilians, the party breaks up. Near the elevator, Yulik's best friend, Edik, tells Yulik to take Pavlik to a hospital. Yulik is offended and nearly starts a fistfight. Edik, astonished, says to his wife: "He was going to punch me in the face." Immediately following that, back in the apartment, Yulik slaps Rita in the face when she begins to scold him for doing nothing about Pavlik. His attempt to defend Pavlik ends with a most unheroic gesture. In fact, every episode in this narrative of masculine heroism ends with an act of senseless violence: their trip to the bathhouse ends with Pavlik rendering another customer unconscious; their search for "spooks" in the attack ends with Yulik assaulting a homeless man;

and his defense of Pavlik nearly ends with Yulik physically assaulting his best friend and then slapping his wife. Rather than bringing order, Yulik's assertion of patriarchal power generates increasingly random violence.

Later, in the hospital, when Yulik witnesses Pavlik calm the traumatized soldier, he is moved. He now sees Pavlik not as a masculine hero but as a kind of "holy fool," a traditional Russian motif of the simpleton endowed with great spiritual insight. However, in the end, none of the narrative motives invoked by Yulik succeeds in containing Pavlik's violence, and the family ultimately finds itself literally captured within Pavlik's own paranoid narrative. In the final scene, when the camera shoots the family, now huddled outside in blankets, from above, the indistinguishable words—one hears only the indistinct conversations of the policeman—and the distant shot underscore the absence of a narrative that could contain Pavlik, whose body now lies dead in the family dacha. There is no comforting moral to this story.

Conclusion

One of the ways in which governments have dealt with the threat of terrorism has been to designate terrorism as illegitimate and to paint the terrorist as a monster. As Zulaika and Douglass comment in *Terror and Taboo,*

> At a primal level, terrorism is set apart from any other form of struggle. The terrorist becomes the paradigm of inhuman bestiality, the quintessential proscribed or tabooed figure of our times. In contrast, despite its toll in millions of lives, the discourse concerning conventional warfare neither taboos the soldier nor defines and defiles war as an incomprehensible aberration. There are even military conventions that distinguish between licit and illicit warfare. War, then, does not pose the perplexities of a Lockerbie, which is perceived of as entirely arbitrary.[14]

What makes *My Stepbrother Frankenstein* such a provocative metaphor for terrorist violence is that it refuses to offer a comforting counterterrorist narrative, one that would make sense of the arbitrariness of terrorist violence. Like the diamond Pavlik wants placed in his empty eye socket, the film draws attention to the wounds inflicted by violence and the failure of aesthetics to redeem injury: wouldn't the diamond make the wound appear more horrible still?

If, as Zulaika and Douglass propose, terrorism news is typically presented "within a hierarchy of values in which 'we' are at the top and the practitioners of terrorism at the bottom," *My Stepbrother Frankenstein* offers a different perspective.[15] Rather than portraying the terrorist as ethnic other, Todorovsky focuses on the otherness at the heart of Russian culture itself, reflected in, for example, the stark class differences of post-Soviet society, something typically obscured in the dominant terrorism discourse. Moreover, Todorovsky resists the temptation to portray his terrorist as either one of "us" or one of "them," or—to paraphrase Cooper—as either a saint or a Frankenstein's monster.[16] Pavlik is both a saintly Dostoevskian simpleton à la Prince Myshkin, willing to sacrifice himself for his family, and a deformed and dangerous monster unable to distinguish between friend and foe.[17] He is both a victim and a perpetrator of the indiscriminate violence governments would label "terrorist."

By making Pavlik the face of violence and the Moscow home of an intelligentsia family the place of violence, Todorovsky stages the "play with meaning and confusion of contexts inherent in the word 'terrorism.'" In doing so, he suggests rather ominously that traditional distinctions between terrorism and war may now be obsolete, as both terrorist attacks and official military responses to terrorist threats have transformed the civilian landscape into a war zone and civilians into casualties. Moreover, by showing how Pavlik comes to embody and reproduce the very terror that had so disfigured him, the film suggests that what we do to protect ourselves from terrorism may come to look very much like terrorism itself. In the final analysis, no narrative may be capable of containing that violence.

Notes

The epigraphs to this essay are from, respectively, H. H. A. Cooper, "Terrorism and the Media," in *Terrorism: Interdisciplinary Perspectives,* ed. Yonah Alexander and Seymour Finger (New York: John Jay, 1997), 154, and Valerii Kichin, "Moi svodnyi brat Frankenshtein—geroi nashego vremeni," *Rossiiskaia gazeta,* October 22, 2004, http://www.yarsk.ru/press/?1=100000154 (accessed March 6, 2006).

1. As Mark Baker reported for Radio Free Europe/Radio Liberty on September 7, 2004, in an article titled "On Beslan, Putin Looks Beyond Chechnya, Sees International Terror": "Russia has been fighting a brutal war in Chechnya the past five years. Over the same period, Chechen militants have carried out multiple acts of terrorism on Russian soil. Yet to hear Russian President Vladimir Putin in recent days, the Russia-Chechnya conflict seemingly had little to do with the school hostage crisis in Beslan. In spite of claims by the hostage takers they were acting for an independent Chechnya, Putin—instead—pinned the blame on 'international terrorists.' RFE/RL reports Putin may be hoping to legitimize the Chechen war as part of the wider global struggle against terrorism—and at the same time discrediting Chechens' aspirations for independence" (www.rferl.org/featuresarticle/2004/09 [accessed March 20, 2006]). While Valery Andreyev, head of the local branch of the FSB (the Rus-

sian intelligence service), announced initially that ten of the thirty-two hostage-takers were from Arab countries—and that one was black—it later turned out there were only three "international terrorists," all Algerian-born British citizens (http://www.res.ethz.ch/news/sw/detailscfm?ID=9844&nav1=1&nav2=2&nav3=2 [accessed March 20, 2006]). The vast majority were from Chechnya and neighboring Ingushetia. In his article "Chechnya: 'War on Terror' Legends Debunked," Thomas de Waal concludes that, "despite what Putin might say, despite some links with international jihadists, this conflict remains very much Russia's home-grown problem: its horrors have been bred locally." *Index on Censorship,* November 18, 2004, http://idl.stanford.edu/103/chechnya/IDL103 _Additional _Reading _7.pdf (accessed March 11, 2006).

2. Alex Houen, *Terrorism and Modern Literature, from Joseph Conrad to Ciaran Carson* (Oxford: Oxford University Press, 2002), 7; Joseph Zulaika and William A. Douglass, *Terror and Taboo* (London: Routledge, 1996), 16.

3. Houen, *Terrorism,* 11.

4. Ibid., 14.

5. None of the short English-language reviews of the film makes any mention of the word "terror." For the American reviewers, this is a film about war and its effects. See, for example, the reviews at www.citypages.com/movies/detail.asp?MID=6605, www.vibewire.net/3/node/3557, or http://efilmcritic.com/review.php?movie=10828 (accessed May 5, 2009).

6. Kichin, "Moi svodnyi brat Frankenshtein," http://www.yarsk.ru/press/?i=100000154 (accessed May 5, 2009).

7. Leonid Yarmolnik, interview, "Ot oshchushcheniia bespomoshchnosti prosto vyt' khochetsia," http://www.runet.de/interview.php?CatId=2&NId=70 (accessed May 12, 2006).

8. A notable exception to this would be Vladimir Khotinenko's film *Musul'man* (*The Muslim,* 2000), which features a Russian Afghan War veteran who converts to Islam before returning home to Russia. He is by far the most positively portrayed character in the film.

9. *Dukhi,* "spooks," is a term derived from *dushmany,* used first in Afghanistan and then in Chechnya to refer to armed resistance fighters. Although derived from *dushman,* the original meaning of *dukh* is "spook," "ghost," or "spirit" (*Tolkovyi slovar' iazyka sovdepii,* ed. V. M. Mokienko and T. G. Nikitina [St. Petersburg: Folio-press, 1998], 184).

10. Zulaika and Douglass, *Terror,* 13.

11. See in particular Bernard Lewis, *What Went Wrong? The Clash Between Islam and Modernity in the Middle East* (New York: HarperCollins, 2002).

12. It is noteworthy that in such films as *War* and *Prisoner of the Mountain,* it is the Chechens who exemplify those values. In *War,* for example, the Chechen warlord who holds the characters hostage proudly boasts that he knows his family back seven generations. In *Prisoner of the Mountain,* the old Chechen man who holds the two Russian soldiers hostage in hopes of exchanging them for his son, who is being held by the Russians, dresses in traditional Chechen dress and lives a very traditional life in the mountains.

13. Zulaika and Douglass, *Terror,* 14.

14. Ibid., 6.

15. Ibid., 13.

16. That ambivalence is captured in the plot summary of the Frankenstein movie offered to Pavlik by one of Egor's girlfriends: "He's a monster, but he's good [*dobryi*]. And nobody likes him." To which Pavlik, oblivious of the connection between him and the monster, responds, "Who could ever love him?"

17. The fact that Pavlik appears in many ways to be a Dostoevskian idiot is perhaps not accidental. Todorovsky produced the celebrated 2003 television serial *The Idiot*, based on the novel by Dostoevsky.

Stage(d) Terrorism

Birgit Beumers

> It's so simple to kill an idea, assassinate the sense in things. . . . The meaning of life, the big idea, . . . it's in people, it's in all of us, and no one's guarding us!
>
> —PRESNYAKOV BROTHERS

On November 8, 2002, the play *Terrorism* by the Presnyakov Brothers,[1] the leaders of Russia's New Drama movement,[2] opened at the Moscow Art Theater, the country's most prestigious theater, founded in 1898 by Konstantin Stanislavsky. Barely two weeks before the premiere, however, terrorism had struck Moscow's theater scene in a different and much more real way: for the first time in history a theater became the site of a terrorist attack when Chechen terrorists under the command of Movsar Baraev seized the Dubrovka Theater Center during a performance of the musical *Nord-Ost.* The siege of several days ended when Russian Special Forces pumped an anesthetizing gas into the theater, entered the theater, and killed all forty-two terrorists. Tragically, 130 of the approximately eight hundred hostages died through the effects of the gas.[3]

The attack was by no means the first terrorist act in Moscow,[4] but for Russia it became a disaster on the scale of 9/11 for the United States, as the journalist Andrei Kamakin has argued: "Destroying the World Trade Center in New York, the terrorists aimed at the heart of world economy; taking hostage the peaceful spectators of *Nord-Ost,* international terrorism hit the heart of all mankind."[5] Kamakin here emphasizes less the cost in human lives and property damage than the assault on human dignity caused by acts of terror, a point echoed in the words of the character from the Presnyakov Brothers' play cited in the epigraph to this essay. It is, as Brian Baer argues in "Narrating Terror" in this volume, the intrusion of violence into the previously protected sphere of everyday life that characterizes terrorism.

In this essay I explore the significance of the terrorist attack during a performance of the musical *Nord-Ost* and discuss the choice of target as well as some public responses, before considering how the reaction to the siege, and to Chechen terrorism in general, has been dealt with in fictional terms and turned into a subject for theater, film, and musical productions. I argue that fictionalization through mass media makes terrorism part of everyday life. As terrorism is enacted—in films, on stage, and in song—it becomes embedded in structures of play that seemingly remove its unpredictability and make it appear controlled. Yet terrorist acts are unpredictable; they represent randomness in a world we would like to see ordered. Thus, the reenactment of such events within firm rules of the game—allowing both repetition and variation—offers, as Johan Huizinga argues in his study of the structures of play, *Homo Ludens,* a way of perfecting life through rigid temporal, spatial, and generic structures: "[play] creates order, *is* order. Into an imperfect world and into the confusion of life it brings a temporary, limited perfection."[6]

Nord-Ost and Terrorism on Stage

On October 19, 2001, the first Russian musical, *Nord-Ost,* premiered in Moscow.[7] For the first time, a show—theatrical or musical—opened in a specially designated venue rather than in one of the numerous repertoire theaters, where it would have taken its turn with other productions. The "stationary" stage for *Nord-Ost* was also a first step toward aligning musical production with the standards of New York's Broadway and London's West End theaters. The venue was the former House of Culture of Moscow's Ball-Bearing Factory, renamed the Dubrovka Theater Center, which could seat 1,150 spectators and is located in the east of Moscow's center. *Nord-Ost* played to an almost full house every night of the first year of its run, a success that cannot be explained solely by a popular cast; indeed, the troupe was relatively young, and its members gained popularity through the musical rather than being recruited as stars. Instead of a star bill, the creative team relied on the reputation of the musicians Georgy Vasilev and Aleksandr Tsekalo, a popular duo also known as "Ivasi," and a well-known Russian, or rather Soviet, plot: Veniamin Kaverin's epic *Two Captains,* which had been awarded the Stalin Prize in 1946. The novel's plot stretches over thirty years, from 1913 to 1943, including the crucial and formative years of the Soviet state, from the revolution to the civil war, through the Stalin era to World War II. The Soviet past offered suitable scope for the exposure of heroism, and the choice of this text was no doubt intended to appeal to a now lost sense of national identity and pride.

The heroic epic deals with themes that expose the corruption of prerevolutionary Russia in order to underscore the contrast with Soviet Russia as a country that gave the opportunity to every man, even a poor, dumb boy, to become a hero. The story begins in 1913 with news of the failure of Captain Tatarinov's Arctic expedition. Several years later the boy, Sanya Grigorev, witnesses the murder of a postman who is carrying a letter from Tatarinov in which the latter implicates his brother Nikolai in the expedition's failure. Although he had nothing to do with it, Sanya's father is arrested for the murder. Prerevolutionary society, in other words, is ruled by envy (Nikolai's envy of his brother's achievements and his secret love for his sister-in-law, Maria) and injustice (the arrest of the innocent Grigorev). Soviet Russia allows the underprivileged but honest boy Sanya to become a pilot and to accomplish Tatarinov's mission of exploring the Arctic. Sanya discovers Tatarinov's vessel when he has to make an emergency landing, and he finds Tatarinov's diary preserved by the indigenous people of the Arkhangelsk region. Kaverin's epic ends on the high moral code of right and wrong upheld by the two captains of sea and air, Tatarinov and Grigorev.

Despite the obvious ideological thrust of the adventure story, the libretto develops the melodramatic line, which is particularly suited for exploitation in a mass entertainment form such as the musical. The melodrama involves two love triangles: first, the relationship among Maria, Tatarinov, and Nikolai, and second, the relationship among Sanya's school friend Romashov, Katya, and Sanya. After being widowed, Maria Tatarinova moves together with her daughter Katya from the northern seaport back to Moscow. There she eventually accepts Nikolai's proposal, but soon after the marriage she learns about Tatarinov's letter and, feeling that she has betrayed her husband's memory, commits suicide. Meanwhile, Sanya has entered the boarding school run by Nikolai, where he and Katya meet and fall in love. But Romashov is a rival in this love. During the Leningrad blockade Romashov lies to win Katya's heart, but, in a neat parallel to Maria Tatarinova's devotion to her husband, Katya remains loyal to Sanya. True love triumphs when Katya joins Sanya in the Arctic region near her father's vessel.

Kaverin's novel provided ideal lines, political and personal, for the development of a libretto that combines melodrama with Soviet heroism. It allowed the composers to diversify the plot with a range of national dances and military choreography, folk tunes and Soviet mass songs of everyday life (*byt*), and the heroic achievements of Soviet life in the 1930s, while completely ignoring the terror and fear of the period. The height of the Great Purges coincided with the country's territorial conquests undertaken by heroic pilots and explorers of the Arctic such as Valery Chkalov and Georgy Ushakov.[8] In this sense, the story that lies at the heart of *Nord-Ost* plays out, enacts, and repeats a heroic national past, thus recreating the myth of the Soviet nation and its great achievements within the conventions of socialist realism.

Building on an indigenous Soviet story, a plot known to every Russian parent and grandparent, the producers of *Nord-Ost* set out to create the first genuine Russian musical. To this end they deployed an effective PR team and a Western-style marketing strategy that included a Web site with an online ticket booking system, information on the musical's score, a performance archive, information on the cast and the production team, press releases and reviews, downloadable desktop pictures, and mobile phone tunes. A separate site devoted to the children's troupe (www.nordostiki.ru) provided information on the children in the show, the "nordost-ies," who were not listed in the program booklet. The campaign also included banners for *Nord-Ost* in the metro, radio and television ads, posters in the streets, and information on the back of metro tickets throughout the summer of 2001. The slogan for the production was repeated on every wall and surface and broadcast from every media source until by the end of the summer all Muscovites knew that "Every evening exactly at 9:45 a full-size bomber plane lands on the stage."

Nord-Ost underpinned Russia's pride in Soviet history and culture, but it also portrayed the new Russia's consumer- and entertainment-oriented society. It became a symbol of Russia as a country with a past and tradition, albeit Soviet. The critic Valery Kichin not only compared *Nord-Ost* to Glinka's *Ivan Susanin,* asserting that if Glinka had composed the first Russian opera, then *Nord-Ost* was the first Russian musical,[9] he also commented astutely that "it is not accidental that the terrorists targeted *Nord-Ost.* Their hatred fell on the sense of national pride inherent in the production."[10] The choice of *Nord-Ost* as the target of an attack by Chechen terrorists dealt a blow to Russia's ambition to develop a mass and consumer culture, its alignment with Western modes of cultural production, and a nation-building project based on the superficial myth of Soviet achievements of the 1930s.

Suddenly, with the terrorist attack of October 23–26, 2002, *Nord-Ost* turned into a symbol of Russia's weakness and failure, so much that the state wished to brush over the hostage crisis in the eyes of the public. The absence of a memorial to the victims who died as a result of the Russian Special Forces' botched attempt to liberate the hostages suggests an unwillingness to remember an event that has come to symbolize Russia's shame. Victims of terrorism are remembered in other places, as happened after the Pushkin Square subway passage bombing, but on this occasion victims of the fight against terrorism seemed to shame the country. Similarly, the absence from the official Web site (www.nordost.ru) after the siege of any information about the events of October 23–26 was striking: the list of victims appeared on another "important" site (www.vazhno.ru), as if the production team wanted to dissociate the musical from the siege. The producers' unwillingness to memorialize the victims is further manifest in the omission of any mention of the victims from the new program booklet printed for the revival, and in the failure to mention the victims during the last performance in May 2003. *Nord-Ost* tried hard to remain just a show. The Moscow government supported the musical's revival and was complicit in its attempt to forget the events of October 2002, partly, no doubt, to quiet allegations of the military's mishandling of the storming of the theater. Nevertheless, the show that was Russia's pride had, once and for all, shamed Russia, and no revival could refresh its entertainment value. Despite a new program design and a completely renovated theater, nothing could deflect from the horror that overshadowed the show, and particularly the venue. Audiences did not flock to the revived production, which opened on February 8, 2003, and the musical closed on May 10, 2003, after which a shortened version of *Nord-Ost* started a grand tour of the Russian provinces. This reaction is comparable to the media responses to the Beslan school siege, as Stephen Hutchings describes in this volume: brushing over the atrocities and focusing instead on the heroicizing (or rather iconization) of the child victims and the grieving mothers.

The first performative "enactment" of the terrorist attack on the Dubrovka Theater came immediately after the siege and consisted in authentic and fictionalized accounts of the event, partly in an attempt to purge from memory the horror of the events and partly in response to the reading masses' attraction to accounts of tragedies and horrific events. Thus, the historian Viktor Stepakov compiled a detailed report of the events, on which he hinged a general history of Chechen violence, and the renowned crime fiction writer Eduard Topol collated a range of interviews, interspersed with news reports, as well as the correspondence between the U.S. citizen Sandy Alan Booker and his fiancée, Svetlana Gubareva, from Karaganda (Kazakhstan).[11] The journalist Tatiana Popova, who was among the hostages, provided a reliable account, complementing her personal recollections with notes from news agencies and online publications to offer a full picture of the events as they developed, inside and outside the building. Popova maintains that the terrorists had no plans to end the siege peacefully but seemed determined to destroy the building in an act of martyrdom, and that the hostage crisis was part of a grander scheme. She notes, for example, that Chechen leaders denounced the terrorist attack on the Dubrovka Theater

Center, and that the terrorists inside the theater placed calls to the Arab Emirates and Turkey but not to Chechnya. Here Popova helps build the myth that Chechen terrorism is part of a larger network with al Qaeda connections, as would also be claimed in the reporting on Beslan (see the essay by Stephen Hutchings in this volume). Popova stresses that Moscow's Chechens and Muslims offered themselves in exchange for the Russian hostages, and that Kadyrov's condemnation of the attack and his refusal to negotiate with the terrorists indicated the desire of the Chechen government to dissociate itself from the attack. Rather than blaming the FSB for the deaths of so many hostages, Popova offers a detailed account of an insider, combined with thorough journalistic research, and provides a unique insight into individual tragedies. Her account makes clear that, in a paradoxical role reversal, the audience of *Nord-Ost* was transformed from spectators into the subjects of a spectacle that was observed by millions of viewers.

Terrorism on Stage and on Screen

Less than two weeks after the siege, Moscow's prestigious Art Theater had to tighten security measures as it premiered the play *Terrorism* by the Presnyakov Brothers.[12] *Terrorism,* like most plays by the Presnyakov Brothers,[13] aims at exploring the sources of violence, aggression, and terror. "Not just in one, but in several plays of the Presnyakovs violence emerges as a widely accessible medicine against psychological paralysis and a quite effective substitution for one's identity—even if only temporary."[14] The critic Pavel Rudnev reiterates this point: "The Presnyakov Brothers have written a play about how terrorism has become the norm of everyday behavior, it literally subordinates itself to the rhythm of our life. The heroes (like all of us) need terror like the air to breathe, and terror can whip up people who are indifferent to suffering and death, including their own."[15] *Terrorism* condenses manifestations of terror and violence into a series of episodes, thereby creating the illusion that events that at first appear unrelated are actually interconnected.

Terrorism consists of six such episodes. The first scene features several stranded passengers at an airport: some baggage has been left on the runway, which has to be checked for explosives before flights can take off again. One passenger decides to return home, a place he considers safe—an illusion that will shortly be dismantled. The second scene shows a man and a woman in bed. It emerges later that she is the wife of the passenger who returns to the illusion of a safe home; she is with her lover, who ties her up at her request, but then falls asleep, turning what began as a game into reality.

Indeed, real violence (her being tied to the bed involuntarily) is shown to be much more exciting than playing with violence (her being tied to the bed voluntarily for a sadomasochistic sex game). The third scene is set in an office and only remotely related to other events. An office assistant has hanged herself in the lounge, and as colleagues discuss the suicide, the workers' fear of each other and of the office manager is articulated. The episode is related to the first two scenes through the mention of the "boss"—who is the passenger from the first scene, away from work on a business trip.

In the fourth episode two old women are sitting on a bench in a courtyard. Through their conversation we learn that one of them is guarding her grandson and the other is planning to poison her son-in-law, who, she fears, may be plotting to kill her in order to inherit her flat. The Presnyakovs' world is ridden with suspicion and mistrust. Violence can erupt at any moment from beneath the surface of a seemingly peaceful life: the grandson plays with a laser pointer, a sobbing man passes by. This man is the passenger from the first episode who has returned from the airport and discovered his wife in bed with her lover. The fifth scene is set in the shower room of a police station. In the ensuing dialogue, more plot lines come together. Some police officers bully a colleague, discharging on him their aggression, accumulated during a day of violence and terror. They gloat over images of horrible violence, forcing their colleague to look at the torn body of the victim of a gas explosion, a woman who had been tied to her bed; this is, of course, the passenger's wife, tied to her bed by her lover. Anguish, aggression, and terror turn man into a cold-blooded murderer and killer. It turns out that, in a fit of mischief, the grandchild guarded by one of the old women pressed the doorbell, thus triggering a gas explosion after the passenger and deceived husband, who is also the man sobbing in the yard, had opened the gas tap—presumably to poison his wife and her lover. Bit by bit, the interwoven net of violence coalesces into a pattern. The fragmented and episodic structure of the Presnyakovs' play embodies chaos while indicating subterranean links and hidden connections between the seemingly chaotic range of characters and actions. Thus, they allow the spectator to assemble the episodes and create a kind of harmony. Such a harmony is possible because the authors, satisfying their own underlying longing to organize chaos, provide pointers for coherence and structure in the seemingly incoherent plot. In the final scene the deceived husband is again on board an aircraft, which he believes is about to crash. He tries to call his wife but is unable to get a connection. Moreover, it appears that the flight has not even taken off. The authors have thoroughly misled the spectator into believing that he or she can reassemble the plot. However, the final episode demolishes the audience's confident belief that it has solved the riddle and made a connection between things. In fact, the spectator may be able to connect events but cannot know whether they have already taken place or are about to take place (is the passenger trying to stop an event, the gas explosion, that already happened in scene 4?). Finally, the repeated motif of the left baggage on the airfield, which had led to the airport closure at the beginning and is responsible for the delay in takeoff at the end, creates a circular structure as well as a temporal non sequitur. As a result, the passenger's actions appear to be of no consequence: whether he returns home or not, outside the airport or on board the plane, violence is omnipotent and omnipresent; in either case the apartment will explode. Violence repeats itself: it is perpetrated through the overarching structure that traps the passenger in a charmed circle from which he is unable to escape, and in the all-pervasive scenes of violence in the office, at the police station, and elsewhere where violence is repeated and applied to others.

Terrorism does not follow chronology, nor is it organized around one central event. Instead, it explores the interconnection of aggression and the sources of violence in a society where people do not care for each other but display only suspicion: the boss and the office workers, the wife and her lover, the granny and her daughter and son-in-law all mistrust each other. Terror resides inside the human being and fear is invoked only by external events. It is our own fear of betrayal, isolation, exposure, and weakness that makes us not victims but aggressors, who justify our acts by claiming self-defense. As the passenger concludes at the end of the play, we are more likely to destroy our own human nature than to be physically killed through acts of terrorism. This would be terrorism's greatest victory—the destruction of the human quality in man: "Deluding ourselves that somebody out there is going to kill us, when actually it turns out we kill ourselves. . . ."[16] If terror turns the world into one ruled by suspicion and mistrust, it destroys the most important human feature—trust—and thus scores a victory in annihilating the building block of human interaction. Thus, terror aligns the new Russia with its Soviet (Stalin-era) past, when society was governed by suspicion and fear. In this respect, a new enemy, or "other"—Chechen, Muslim, al Qaeda—replaces internal (KGB) and external (the United States in the cold war) enemies of the past, as Hutchings points out. This new enemy brings Russia out of its previous isolation by uniting it with the global war on terrorism.

Since *Terrorism* opened at the Moscow Art Theater on November 8, 2002, in the aftermath of *Nord-Ost,* it is not surprising that reality and performance were somewhat blurred: the metal detectors at the entrance were real, while the security guards along the stage, with laser guns and orders that confined the viewers to their seats, were part of the performance.

Lipovetsky has argued that *Terrorism* blurs the distinction between external and internal violence, as well as the borderline between the real and the enacted: "*Terrorism* is a work about general, mutual aggression that penetrates public and private space, office and personal life, disrupts the linear flow of time, and inverts cause and effect. . . . Violence weaves together all the plot lines of the play into one whole, where cause and effect can no longer be differentiated from one another."[17] In his production at the Moscow Art Theater, Kirill Serebrennikov[18] linked the episodes through three instances of a mother aggressively disciplining her nine-year-old boy. In this way, Serebrennikov suggested that the origin of terrorism resides in childhood. The mother remembers being beaten and subjected to aggressive behavior from her father when a child. By instilling her own sense of rejection in her child, she also transforms herself from victim into aggressor. As Marina Davydova concluded in her review of the production, "Evil gives rise to evil, violence generates violence. The victim becomes the executioner, the executioner becomes a victim. Our little life enters into this vicious circle."[19]

Serebrennikov explored the fact that the characters in the Presnyakov Brothers' play have no names but rather are labeled "man," "woman," "passenger," and so forth. He exploited this anonymity and cast his thirteen actors in multiple roles, so that an actor playing a violent and aggressive character in one scene might have played a meek character in another scene. Moreover, Serebrennikov overlapped attributes of gender, age, and ethnicity by dressing Russian characters with Tatar or Muslim accessories. Where the Moscow Art Theater was famous for its psychological realism and method acting, which requires a close identification of the actor with the character, Serebrennikov took a diametrically opposed approach and deployed "typage" in Eisenstein's sense: "A typage tendency may be rooted in theater; growing out of the theater into film, it presents possibilities for excellent stylistic growth, in a broad sense—as an indicator of definite affinities to real life through the camera."[20]

Through paced choreography, for example, in the office scene with the secretaries hopping around the boss, Serebrennikov underlined the ritualistic aspect in the everyday. The performance was set on a catwalk, on which the "acts" of violence were demonstrated, again dwelling on the ritual, repetitive aspect that underlies every scene: in Serebrennikov's staging, violence and aggression formed a never-ending cycle. The set design included a bomb timer placed over the stage, set to time out at the end of the show, after two hours and twenty minutes. Serebrennikov positioned the game clearly in time and space. He interpreted the manifestation of violence as a performance, but one in which the actors did not identify with the characters and the characters had no psychological depth. Violence, in this interpretation, is performed, enacted, or narrated, but not lived through. Therefore, the fear it might provoke is not real but emulated, displayed, or demonstrated. Thus, fear and violence are reduced to a verbal or narrative rather than physical level. By refraining from illustrating the violence described in the play, Serebrennikov was able to emphasize the illusionary and playful quality of the text, where words do not carry meaning but function merely as a cover-up for the absence of meaning and as a background rhythm for paced movements, as some critics have astutely observed: "The action reminds, above all, of an intricate dance, only instead of music there are words."[21] The musical quality of the text in Serebrennikov's production deprived the word of its function to convey meaning; instead, physical movements did this. Serebrennikov took the Presnyakovs' play about cause and effect beyond the logocentric to the visual level.

Serebrennikov's concern with choreographed movement instead of action, with rhythm instead of content, illuminates the key that made his production—and also film versions—of this and other plays by the Presnyakov Brothers so successful: the reliance on patterns of movement and voice, on art forms such as ballet and song that adhere to rigid forms of performance reminiscent of a ritual. Serebrennikov deployed ritual forms, patterns, or rules of the game, unveiling the myth that cradles the viewer in the confidence of his or her own ability to assemble the episodes according to known patterns. But terror has no pattern or logic; it is unpredictable. In the end, the Presnyakov Brothers undermine their own and the audience's assumed position of superiority and certainty: does the passenger's final phone call mean that none of the violence between the first and the last episode really happened?

We Turn the Nightmare into a Fairy Tale . . .

If *Terrorism* explored the roots of violence and terror through the ritual of stage performance in order to demonstrate our ultimate inability to understand terrorism or overcome our fear, then other recent Russian cultural products have deliberately drawn on terrorism to make it part of an "official," or public, cultural discourse. The most interesting example of this process of cradling the masses in the belief of security and safety at a time of increasing terrorist attacks may be Evgeny Lavrentev's feature film *Countdown* (*Lichnyi nomer,* 2004), in which Russia's recent experience of terrorism is rewritten with a happy ending—unlike the much more disturbing representations of the Chechen campaigns in such films as *My Stepbrother Frankenstein* (*Moi svodnyi brat Frankenshtein,* dir. Valery Todorovsky, 2004) discussed by Brian Baer in this volume, or more recently Alexander Veledinsky's *Alive* (*Zhivoi*, 2006) and Alexander Sokurov's *Alexandra* (2007), which depict the effect of the horror of the Chechen war on soldiers and citizens.

Countdown deals with two terrorist events simultaneously: the 1999 bombings of two Moscow apartment buildings and the 2002 *Nord-Ost* siege. It does so in a manner that fully supports the state, which, not surprisingly, subsidized the film's production. The complex and often preposterous plot produces a national hero in the figure of an FSB[22] officer, implicates the oligarch Boris Berezovsky[23] in terrorist activity, clears the FSB of the common accusation of staging the 1999 Moscow apartment bombings, and successfully resolves the hostage crisis comparable to the one that disrupted *Nord-Ost*.

Countdown tells the story of Agent Smolin, who is compelled by his Chechen captors to confess that he and his team, on behalf of the FSB, planted the bombs in the apartment buildings in 1999. Behind the scenes, oligarch Pokrovsky's assistant Boikos records Smolin's "confession" in order to use it against the Russian government. Smolin escapes from his captivity during a Russian air raid but is soon captured by the Russian army, which accuses him of collaborating with the enemy. However, Smolin manages to flee again during a visit of the U.S. journalist Catherine Stone. In exile in his Gibraltar villa, Pokrovsky is infuriated by Smolin's escape, as it diminishes the value of the tape with Smolin's confession. In collaboration with some Arabs, Pokrovsky has financed an attack on the Moscow circus to force the government into allowing his return to Moscow, where, he suggests, he can end the siege—which, in fact, he has financed. In the meantime, at the Arab camp, Ansar Allah, the "master" (a bin Laden look-alike), gives Khasan the order to proceed with the circus siege, but for a different reason: it will serve as a cover-up for the theft of plutonium for a dirty bomb to be exploded over Rome during an upcoming G8 summit. The circus is seized and a bomb is placed in the center of the arena, in the same way that the explosives in the *Nord-Ost* siege had been placed at strategic positions in the auditorium. Smolin's daughter Ira is among the hostages, and it is to fetch her that Smolin enters the building through the sewage system, in yet another reference to the *Nord-Ost* siege, during which the gas was pumped into the theater not through the air ducts but the sewage pipes. Putting the private before the political, Smolin first rescues his daughter and a dozen other children before pursuing the Arab terrorists. The Arab faction of the terror command has, apparently, set up the Chechen members of the group, whom it leaves behind in the circus when it sets off to collect the plutonium and hijack a plane. Once on board the aircraft, the bomb is connected to an altimeter that will explode the plane if it drops below 3,000 meters. After an American controller deactivates the device, Smolin kills all the terrorists on board, takes control of the plane, and lands it safely on a derelict airfield in Belarus.[24] His plan to end the circus siege now foiled, Pokrovsky is forced to abandon his plan to return to Russia.

Despite its depiction of Russian antiterrorist forces as loyal, committed, motivated, and, most important, competent, *Countdown* actually draws on a number of real events and characters: Smolin is an idealized version of a real military intelligence officer kidnapped by Chechen terrorists,[25] the plot of the circus siege is clearly derived from the *Nord-Ost* siege, and the oligarch Pokrovsky's involvement in this siege is designed to discredit Boris Berezovsky, the oligarch who dared to oppose Putin. The film is structured around the stark opposition between "good" and "bad" characters, representing pro- and antigovernment positions, respectively: FSB officer Smolin is a hero, the oligarch Pokrovsky is a devil.

But *Countdown* is also an attempt to create a new image of Russia and a Russian hero, and to revive the myth of a strong and powerful empire. The slogan for *Countdown* reads, "It only remains to be victorious."[26] While the multi-million-dollar budget was intended to create a new Russian hero, to show the military in a positive light, and to expose the threat from the oligarchs, the film did not gross as much as the blockbuster of 2004, *Night Watch*.[27] Interestingly, the film shows the Chechens not as evil but as the victims of an Arab conspiracy of global scale. The borderline between good and evil is thus brought into a new global alignment: rather than Russia fighting Chechnya, the film is quite explicit about the struggle between the civilized world and Arab terrorism. *Countdown* illustrates how the Kremlin would like to see Russia and its heroes depicted in the cinema: Russia is a powerful country, an integral part of Europe, willing to risk the threat of nuclear disaster on its own territory in order to save the "old world." Smolin sets new standards of behavior for the hero of Russian blockbusters: he may act on his own accord and without orders from his commanding general, because he knows his priorities and the difference between right and wrong. Such heroes enrich the country—and the FSB—with their moral standards, which are formed by personality rather than military drills.

A state-subsidized and, in the Russian context, politically correct film, *Countdown* clears the FSB of allegations that it was behind the Moscow apartment block bombings of 1999. By making the Chechen terrorists part of a global conspiracy of Arabs versus non-Arabs, *Countdown* also places the Russian campaign against Chechnya in a broader context and makes the Chechens victims of a larger controversy. By showing Chechen rebels being manipulated by power-hungry oligarchs, the film justifies both the government's fight against terrorism in a global context and its crackdown on independent business oligarchs like Berezovsky and Khodarkovsky. In the figure of oligarch Pokrovsky, *Countdown* portrays Berezovsky as a man involved in terrorism and willing to sacrifice innocent people for the sake of his political aims and ambition. In turning the horrors of real terrorism into a fairy tale of Russian statehood, *Countdown* inverts the Stalinist slogan of the 1930s that socialism turns fairy tales into reality. In *Countdown*, post-Soviet Russia transforms the horror of real terror into a fairy tale of security. The utopianism of the Soviet era has been replaced by a culture that provides an escape from reality in its pseudo-engagement with violence and war, albeit in fictional accounts. *Countdown* is "an uplifting picture . . . like any work of folklore where the fool, at closer inspection, turns out to be quite clever, and the lazy-bones is really a hero. Folklore does not lie—is simply knows that people are different depending on the circumstances."[28] However, the fairy tale of the Russian superhero who can—in a manner reminiscent of the legendary dragon fighters of the Russian *bylina*[29]—handle any number of terrorists single-handedly is painted in coarser strokes and brighter colors than the fairy tales told by Stalinist musicals: "In *Kuban Cossacks* the work was done with a fine brush, but *Countdown* has been painted with a broom."[30] This connection to Soviet mythmaking accounts for the mass appeal of the hero figure: if Russian film heroes of the late 1990s like Balabanov's Danila Bagrov (*Brother*, 1997) lived by their own rules, deciding for themselves how to act in a corrupt world in which the government and the police were no better than criminals, then in the new millennium it is the state and its agents who take the law in their hands. *Countdown* emphasizes the strength of the state in a Hollywood manner, thus embarking on a mythmaking operation in grand American style.

However, there is one curiosity here: this Russian myth is articulated without the computer-generated special effects that are so prominent in American blockbusters.[31] Once again, Russia tries to be better and greater than America: if in Hollywood blockbusters special effects are needed to assist the hero in his mission, the makers of *Countdown* destroyed two bomber planes, four aircrafts, and several tanks and jeeps, as well as a real Iliushin 76, during the shooting of the film. Turning reality into a fairy tale apparently relies on an authentic feel in order to make the fairy tale more believable: relying on special effects would have emphasized the fictional quality of the actions depicted on-screen.[32]

Independent Versus Commercial

If feature films allow the manipulation of reality through narrative and image, then documentary films rely much more on authentic footage. Documentary films also tend not to achieve blockbuster status (unless they are made by Michael Moore) and are usually aimed at select audiences or festivals. A documentary filmmaker thus relies less on spectator numbers and, working on a smaller budget, can afford a certain degree of independence from state funding.

Andrei Nekrasov's *Disbelief* (*Nedoverie,* 2004) is a documentary based on the Moscow apartment bombings of 1999. In September 1999, shortly after former FSB chief Vladimir Putin was appointed prime minister, two explosions shattered several Moscow apartment buildings. At about the same time, explosions occurred in other Russian cities as well, notably Volgodonsk and Buinaksk (Dagestan).[33] At the time, most of the independent media, especially NTV, conjectured that the Moscow bombs had been planted by the FSB to justify the second Chechen campaign, which had begun in autumn 1999. A successful war would, so the theory went, allow Russia to assert its power and enable Putin to demonstrate his leadership qualities. An edition of the satirical program *Puppets* (*Kukly*) on NTV in October 1999 that parodied FSB agents planting the devices was taken off the air before a scheduled rebroadcast the next day. Still, the media assembled clues that suggested FSB involvement in the explosions: for example, an FSB officer by the name of Vladimir Romanovich appears to have rented the basements in both bombed apartment blocks and later died in a mysterious car crash on Cyprus. Nekrasov's film includes footage with the lawyer for several of the victims' relatives, Mikhail Trepashkin, who was arrested after obtaining a court injunction that would have allowed him to examine the files on the official investigation of the bombings.[34] Nekrasov's film, however, centers on Tatiana Morozova, the daughter of one of the victims, who now lives in the United States. Nekrasov follows Tatiana on her journey back to Russia, to Moscow and to her native village in the Urals, where she tries to find her roots now that her home has been destroyed. Nekrasov's documentary is not neutral and does not seek to establish the underlying causes of terrorism, but explores the consequences of terror and hints at the Russian government's use of terror methods to manipulate popular opinion. While *Countdown* reinforces the state's role as guardian of security, Nekrasov's *Disbelief* undermines the citizens' trust in the state and exposes the state's potential involvement in plots that serve its own political agendas, not unlike the behavior of the fictional oligarch Pokrovsky in *Countdown.* The documentary thus inverts the role of the good and bad characters, turning the state into the perpetrator of evil and the investigators of truth—lawyers, the independent media, and documentary filmmakers—into the "brave heroes."

If the documentary film represents a piece of investigative journalism, then at the other end of the spectrum stands the commercial exploitation of terrorism.[35] Ivan Shapovalov, one of Russia's top music producers who launched the pop duo T.a.t.U. with a campaign that played on the supposed lesbianism of the two young, underage singers, tried to present a new project with the singer n.A.T.o, the sixteen-year-old Natalia Shevliakova from Cheliabinsk, whom he had discovered on the Internet. n.A.T.o produced an album with love songs based on Arabic tunes and sung in Turkic tongues. The main song, "Choriavon,"[36] tells of local men who leave the village for a hunt and are tragically killed by an avalanche.[37] This song is followed by a series of love songs that cover themes ranging from falling in love, through caring and fearing for the beloved, to separation and lost love. The songs are romantic, at best melodramatic. But n.A.T.o's big Moscow launch in a concert scheduled for September 9, 2004, in the House of Unions (where Stalin held his major congresses) had to be canceled—perhaps not so much because of its proximity to the 9/11 anniversary as because of the Beslan siege and the explosion of two passenger planes at the end of August. Furthermore, the tickets for the show had been designed as plane tickets; the singer was to appear in a *shahid* outfit, carrying microphone transmitters on a belt as if they were explosives and wearing a chador, while images of terror broadcast on Al-Jazeera were projected onto a screen. Bodyguards in camouflage were to fire paintballs at the audience. The soft lyrics of the songs and the absence of any political agenda suggest that this was a pure PR campaign that backfired. Indeed, the video clip in which n.A.T.o blew herself up was removed from the Internet site (www.natomusic.com), no album was ever launched in Russia, and the canceled concert ultimately took place in a small restaurant of the Tinkoff brewery in January 2005. n.A.T.o attempted to shock through references to terrorism as an artifice, making terror part of mass culture and using fear as a publicity gag: "n.A.T.o is merely a female singer with a headscarf and a veil. If our society is afraid of a woman in a black headscarf that means only one thing: the society is sick and needs to seek treatment."[38]

There would appear to be a substantial difference between fear as explored in the films and play discussed above and Shapovalov's PR campaign devised as a provocation of society's fears of *shahid,* and by extension all Muslim women. There is much more to n.A.T.o than a black veil to which Shapovalov refers above—namely, the entire PR campaign. Shapovalov created a show with a *shahid,* a woman prepared to blow herself up in an act of martyrdom. It is less the social fear that he comments on than his own anger at a society that refuses to follow his approach and emulate violence. Yet the ritual performance of a *shahid* is an act that does not lend itself to reenactment or ritualization. Shapovalov's project reveals the limitation of play as a means of ordering the chaos of terror, allowing repetition and using predictable forms that create an illusion of safety. The reaction of audiences, however, reveals their disappointment that the imitation did not go far enough: "I'd imagined this would be way more radical. . . . Machine guns, the whole silent guard routine—you're really not going to shock anyone with that kind of thing these days."[39] The failure of the n.A.T.o project illustrates that in the unpredictable scenario of a pop concert the audience had no rules to rely on; terrorism is here not "staged" and ritualized but used as a backdrop to increase sales and media interests. As such, it is deployed for commercial ends in an attempt to tantalize the audience with the thrill of terror.

The Show of Terrorism

Fictional versions of terrorism tend to delude the public into believing, ultimately, that the state's structures protect them and state institutions combat terrorism efficiently. Reliving terrorist acts may be part of a mass psychotherapy, but reworking such acts, often with a "happy ending," can also anesthetize society in the belief that it is safe from danger. By making terrorism part of fictional discourses, artists "normalize" the topic itself: they make it appear manageable and harmless, which is both dangerous for the consumer-spectator and undermines the fear-instilling model on which terror builds. The fictionalized versions discussed to this point are, as it were, "spectacles," demonstrations of acts of terrorism within a set of rules and genre conventions that make it "safe." In these demonstrations the element of play (enactment) is used to imagine a reality that is like the actual world, but where the course of events differs from the real world and where a "happy ending" is possible. Through their enactment, events can be manipulated and the imperfect real world can be ordered. In his seminal study on the functions of play in culture, Huizinga argues that play presents an event in an organized manner, following rules of the game. While terrorism impinges on public safety, it is also absorbed into cultural discourse as enactments rework the past and analyze the causes that allow the transposition of a freak event into a fixed pattern by emulating, enacting, and repeating it. "[Play] assumes fixed form as a cultural phenomenon. Once played, it endures as a new-found creation of the mind, a treasure to be retained by the memory. It is transmitted, it becomes tradition. It can be repeated at any time . . . or at fixed intervals like the mystery. In this faculty of repetition lies one of the most essential qualities of play."[40] Play pretends that a segment of infinite and chaotic reality is ordered for the limited period of the performance in the rigid structure of a ritual. Thus, by staging terror, authors, directors, filmmakers, and producers allow the audience to pretend that together they can master a phenomenon that cannot, in real terms, be controlled. The reworking of terrorism through cultural production thus offers a way of creating a myth in which reality becomes manageable and controllable and the present is immortalized and remembered in a glorified form.

While some artists explore the roots of terrorism, others exploit it, and yet others create myths that envelope the population in a false sense of security. Both producers and consumers have different needs. For some it is the debate on aggression arising from fear that matters, for others it is the faith in the system, and for still others it is important to understand that the world is corrupt. The Presnyakovs see violence and fear as an omnipotent threat to human dignity, while for Lavrentev, terrorism is a plot of nefarious "evil-doers." Nekrasov views terrorism as part of political and governmental strategies designed to keep people afraid, so that the rulers may stay in control; Shapovalov simply exploits terrorism commercially. While cinema tries to reassure audiences of the state's ability to protect its citizens (*Countdown*) or to undermine the state's claim to do this efficiently (*Disbelief*), the performing arts reflect on the effect of terrorism on human values (*Terrorism*) or transform anxieties about terrorism into a commercial project (n.A.T.o). Staging terrorism in film, theater, or musical performances creates the illusion of a controllable phenomenon and desensitizes audiences by making fear and violence part of everyday discourse.

Genre conventions of the blockbuster demand a happy end: the government and the security services must catch the terrorist and save the hostages. But if blockbusters make the fictional space safe for audiences, they leave the real world as unsafe as ever. Further, while watching horror and violence on-screen, we are desensitized to the violence both in the screen world and in the world around us. As the passenger in *Terrorism* quoted in the epigraph says, terror destroys something inside man, and the loss of that human concern for others is our greatest loss. The stage turns real terror into the representation of terror. In the scenic representation the audience is seemingly in control of the crisis because of the ritual form: terror becomes part of normalcy. As Debord suggests, "Everything that was directly lived has moved away into a representation."[41] By being performed, horrifying events are emotionally, temporally, and spatially distanced; they become performable, repeatable, and controllable events, and as such part of theatrical conventions and repertoires.

Notes

1. Oleg (b. 1969) and Vladimir (b. 1974) Presnyakov (as transliterated in English-language publications) come from Sverdlovsk (Ekaterinburg). They created their own theater at the Ural State University, where they studied philology. Their plays have been widely translated and staged internationally, notably at the Royal Court Theatre,

London. For a full discussion, see Mark Lipovetskii, "Teatr nasiliia v obshchestve spektaklia," *Novoe literaturnoe obozrenie* 73 (2005): 244–78. See also Birgit Beumers and Mark Lipovetsky, *Performing Violence: Literary and Theatrical Experiments of New Russian Drama* (Bristol and Chicago: Intellect, 2009).

2. The movement was named after the "New Drama" festival initiated in 2002 by Eduard Boyakov, formerly director of the National Theater Festival "Golden Mask" and currently director of the Praktika Theater. The second edition, in September 2003, was held in conjunction with the Moscow Arts Theater and teatr.doc; since 2006 it has moved to the auspices of the Praktika Theater.

3. For an account of how special forces ended the siege, see http://news.bbc.co.uk/1/hi/world/europe/2363601.stm (accessed August 14, 2006).

4. For a timeline of recent Chechen history, see http://news.bbc.co.uk/1/hi/world/europe/country_profiles/2357267.stm (accessed August 14, 2006). Terrorist attacks included those on the Okhotny Riad Shopping Mall, Moscow, August 31, 1999; the apartment building bombing in Buinaksk, Dagestan, September 4, 1999; the apartment building bombing in Pechatniki, Moscow, September 8, 1999; the explosion in an apartment building on Kashirskoe Shosse, Moscow, September 13, 1999; the truck explosion of an apartment building in Volgodonsk, September 16, 1999; the planting of fake explosives in Riazan, September 22, 1999; the pedestrian subway bombing beneath Pushkin Square, Moscow, August 8, 2000; the siege at Dubrovka Theater Center, Moscow, October 23–26, 2002; suicide bombings during a rock concert at Tushino, Moscow, July 6, 2003; a suicide bombing outside the National Hotel, Moscow, December 9, 2003; an explosion in the metro near Avtozavodskaia Station, Moscow, February 6, 2004; suicide bombings that destroyed two planes from Moscow (Domodedovo) on their way to Volgograd and Sochi, August 24, 2004; Riga railway station, Moscow, August 31, 2004; and the hostage crisis at the Beslan school, September 1–3, 2004.

5. Andrei Kamakin, "Posle 23 oktiabria," *Itogi* 43, October 29, 2002, http://www.itogi.ru/paper2002.nsf/Inside/Itogi_2002_43.html (accessed August 14, 2006).

6. Johan Huizinga, *Homo Ludens: A Study of the Play Element in Culture* (London: Routledge and Kegan Paul, 1949), 29.

7. For a full discussion of the musical, see Birgit Beumers, "Pop Post-Sots: Mass Musicals in Russia," *Slavic and East European Journal* 48, no. 3 (Fall 2004): 378–95.

8. On the role of aviation, see Emma Widdis, *Visions of a New Land* (New Haven: Yale University Press, 2003), 128–35, and Scott Palmer, *Dictatorship of the Air: Aviation Culture and the Fate of Modern Russia* (Cambridge: Cambridge University Press, 2006); on the exploration of the Arctic, see John McCannon, "Tabula Rasa in the North: The Soviet Arctic and Mythic Landscapes in Stalinist Popular Culture," in *The Landscape of Stalinism,* ed. Evgeny Dobrenko and Eric Naiman (Seattle: University of Washington Press, 2003), 241–60.

9. Valerii Kichin, "Rubikon pereiden," *Izvestiia,* October 8, 2001.

10. Valerii Kichin, "Il-76 do Rima ne doletit," *Rossiiskaia gazeta,* December 6, 2004.

11. Viktor Stepakov, *Bitva za "Nord-Ost"* (Moscow: Eksmo, 2003); Tat'iana Popova, *"Nord-Ost" glazami zalozhnitsy* (Moscow: Vargius, 2002); Eduard Topol', *Roman o liubvi i terrore* (Moscow: AST, 2004). See also Gubareva's Web site, http://freerepublic.com/~svni/ (accessed August 14, 2006).

12. I refer in the following to the versions of the play included in Brat'ia Presnia-

kovy, *The Best: P'esy* (Moscow: Eksmo, 2005), and Presnyakov Brothers, *Terrorism,* trans. Sasha Dugdale (London: Nick Hern Books, 2003). The production at the Moscow Art Theater, discussed below, diverges from this version in the choice of scenes, and adds one episode.

13. As examples, *Floor Covering* (*Polovoe pokrytie,* 2000), *Europa-Asia* (2001), and *Playing the Victim* (*Izobrazhaia zhertvu,* 2002).

14. Lipovetskii, "Teatr nasiliia," 258.

15. Pavel Rudnev, "Terror na stsene," *Nezavisimaia gazeta,* November 1, 2002.

16. Presnyakov Brothers, *Terrorism,* 58.

17. Lipovetskii, "Teatr nasiliia," 260.

18. Kirill Serebrennikov was born in 1969 in Rostov-on-Don, where he studied theater. He moved to Moscow in the late 1990s and made the television serials *Rostov-Papa* and *Diary of a Murder* (*Dnevnik ubiitsy*). His Moscow stage debut was with Vasily Sigarev's *Plasticine* (*Plastilin*) in a small experimental theater. He specializes in producing contemporary plays and made his debut at the prestigious Moscow Art Theater with the Presnyakov Brothers' *Terrorism.* This was followed by a production of the Presnyakovs' play *Playing the Victim* (*Izobrazhaia zhertvu*), which Serebrennikov subsequently adapted for the screen. This film won the main prize at the Kinotavr Open Russian Film Festival in 2006 and the main award at the first Rome Film Festival in October 2006; see Oleg Sulkin, review of *Playing the Victim, KinoKultura* 14 (2006) http://www.kinokultura.com/2006/14r-izozhertvu.shtml (accessed December 15, 2006).

19. Marina Davydova, "Provereno. Miny est'," *Izvestiia,* November 10, 2002.

20. Sergei Eisenstein, *Film Form* (San Diego: Harvest, 1977), 9.

21. Marina Zaionts, "Terroristy, na vykhod!" *Itogi* 46, November 19, 2002, http://www.itogi.ru/paper2002.nsf/Article/Itogi_2002_11_19_12_4608.html (accessed August 14, 2006).

22. The FSB (Federal Security Service) is the Russian intelligence service, which in 1991 succeeded the USSR's Committee for State Security (KGB).

23. Boris Berezovsky (b. 1946) founded the automobile company LogoVaz in 1989, and later acquired a substantial number of shares in the television station ORT when it was partly privatized in 1995. In 1996 he joined the Presidential Security Council. He owned shares in several print media, such as the papers *Kommersant* and *Nezavisimaia gazeta.* In 2001 he moved to London, where he was granted political asylum.

24. The film's nod in the direction of Belarusian president Lukashenko as Russia's loyal political ally was particularly interesting, coming as it did in late autumn 2004, when Ukraine was going through the Orange Revolution and moving away from the Russian Federation and toward Europe.

25. For an account of the kidnapping of GRU Lieutenant Aleksei Galkin, see http://2002.novayagazeta.ru/nomer/2002/89n/n89n-s23.shtml (accessed August 14, 2006).

26. "Ostaetsia tol'ko pobezhdat'," www.kinopoisk.ru/level/1/film/81202/ (accessed August 14, 2006).

27. *Night Watch,* the first Russian blockbuster, was released in July 2004 and grossed over $16 million. *Countdown,* released in December 2004, grossed $4.5 million.

28. Kichin, "Il-76."

29. Such as Alesha Popovich, Dobrynya Nikitich, and Ilya Muromets, all of whom feature prominently in contemporary Russian feature-length animation projects.

30. Andrei Shchigolev, "Drugoe kino," *Iskusstvo kino* 4 (2005): 53.

31. See the review of *Countdown* by David MacFadyen, "Countdown," *KinoKultura* 10 (2005), http://www.kinokultura.com/reviews/R10-05lichnyinomer.html (accessed August 14, 2006).

32. Nevertheless, fewer viewers saw *Countdown* than saw blockbusters that relied on special effects, such as *Night Watch* and *Turkish Gambit* (2005).

33. An explosion in Ryazan was apparently averted thanks to citizens' vigilance, although the FSB later denied that the sacks discovered contained any explosives.

34. Convicted and sentenced to four years in prison camp, Trepashkin was released in November 2007. For an American investigative journalist's account that supports the involvement of the FSB in the bombings, see David Satter, *Darkness at Dawn: The Rise of the Russian Criminal State* (New Haven: Yale University Press, 2003).

35. Compare to the late 1980s, when holidays in mock concentration camps offered participants an experience of the "real" Holocaust.

36. "Choriavon" was released as a single in Germany, where n.A.T.o gave a few concerts in 2005.

37. The song's story is reminiscent of the tragedy in the Karmadon Gorge, Ossetia, where on September 20, 2002, a glacier slid into the valley, killing more than one hundred local people and the film crew of Sergei Bodrov Jr.

38. Shapovalov, quoted by Bogdan Stepovoi, "Ex-producer of 'TATU' to promote a 'Shakhid,'" September 10, 2004, http://english.pravda.ru/printed.html?news_id=14160 (accessed August 14, 2006).

39. Jens Mühling, "A t.a.T.U. for Terrorists?" *Der Spiegel,* January 21, 2005, http://www.Spiegel.de/international/0,1518,337939,00.html (accessed August 14, 2006).

40. Huizinga, *Homo Ludens,* 28.

41. Guy Debord, *Society of the Spectacle* (Detroit: Black and Red, 1983), no. 1, no pagination.

Russia's 9/11: Performativity and Discursive Instability in Television Coverage of the Beslan Atrocity

Stephen Hutchings

When New York's Twin Towers fell, news broadcasts struggled to convey the enormity of this strike at the symbolic heart of the world's sole superpower. Since 9/11, however, concrete features have been ascribed to the faces of the perpetrators of the Evil, stories of bravery have emerged from the rubble of the World Trade Center, and 9/11 has been inscribed into the narrative of post–cold war American nationhood, just as it has enabled al Qaeda to fill the chasm left by the dissolution of the evil Soviet empire. Tales of martyrdom among the passengers of the jet that was downed in Pennsylvania, the bravery of firefighters who returned repeatedly to the collapsing towers, and the final mobile phone calls to loved ones from those aboard the two jets that crashed into the towers all now feature prominently in 9/11 folklore.

Since 2001, the 9/11 "brand" has also been exported to other nations. The Madrid bombings preceding the Spanish elections of 2004 have been dubbed "Spain's 9/11," just as the Beslan school siege became known as "Russia's 9/11," and the events in Britain of July 2005 are now referred to ubiquitously as "7/7."[1] Paradoxically, an event designed to shake the world's superpower from its consumerist fantasies has itself taken the form of a consumer format. But it is a format with national specificities. In Russia's case the Beslan outrage coincided with a new curtailment of media freedom: one of NTV's flagship talk shows, *Freedom of Speech* (*Svoboda slova*), hosted by the prominent liberal journalist Savik Shuster, was, in a development not directly related to Beslan, canceled in the very same month. Shortly before this, Leonid Parfenov's equally controversial current affairs magazine program, *Lately* (*Namedni*), suffered a similar fate. Some commentators will point to post-9/11 and post-7/7 curtailments of free speech in the United States and the United Kingdom, but in Russia the imposed constraints not only were much harsher, they were in effect well before the emergence of any hint that the country was about to suffer a terrorist outrage of this order. Russia also deviates from other "warriors on terror" in that its nation-building project must navigate between a partially rehabilitated Soviet past and an ambivalently viewed, Western-dominated present, and in the intensity with which recent terrorist outrages have shaped that navigation. Writing before Beslan, Ivan Zassoursky suggests that the 1999 Moscow apartment bomb blasts, which he refers to as the Russian equivalent of 9/11, "started the process of the almost instant reconstruction of the Russian mentality."[2] Unusual too is Russia's television culture, emerging from (and now retracting back into) a controlled environment of mutually reinforcing, state-sponsored voices emphasizing the inevitable, the ritualistic, and the positive.[3] Still developing a set of generic conventions for the representation of anomalous, unanticipated catastrophes, and despite a sequence of recent disasters exposing media incompetence and inexperience (e.g., the Chernobyl nuclear power plant leak, the *Kursk* submarine disaster, the *Nord-Ost* theater siege, the apartment bombs—all precursors of Beslan), Russian news broadcasts confronted in the 2004 school siege a milestone in this process.

My exploration of how the approach to the problem adopted by Russian news links with and ultimately complicates the national identity construction task it has been assigned should be read in parallel with the essays of Birgit Beumers and Anna Brodsky, who, referring to different manifestations of Russia's "war on terror" against Chechen rebels, likewise broach that war's myth-generating and nation-building capacities in the context of a specifically Russian cultural discourse on terrorism. My own angle on that specificity focuses on certain challenges posed to a media system by its need to collude with a government regime that, authoritarian public image notwithstanding, is beset by profound ideological instability. My analysis is based on six editions of *Vremia* (*Time*), the main evening news program of Channel 1, now effectively (along with the RTR channel) Putin's official mouthpiece. The sequence spans the event and its immediate aftermath (the siege itself lasted from September 1 to 3, with September 6 and 7 declared national days of mourning). Since my focus is on the ideological, post-atrocity processing of meanings derived from Beslan rather than on the spontaneous representation of the atrocity itself, I draw mostly from the

9 P.M. *Vremia* bulletins of September 4, 5, and 6. The dates of the broadcasts referred to in my analysis are given parenthetically in the text. All translations from the Russian news scripts are mine.

My argument proceeds thematically, engaging first the key imagery and mythology to emerge from Beslan, then aspects of the news discourse supporting the mythology, to show that both seemingly performed the (re)integration of a fragmented nation. I then identify within the representational strategies underpinning this process a tension between the requirement that the events be assimilated to familiar models and the need to render them in their shocking, chronotopic alterity. This distinction, I believe, maps onto the contrast drawn by Birgit Beumers between the "chaotic movement" embodied by terrorist acts and the need to "embed them within rigid structures of play." I conclude with two brief but hopefully instructive post-Beslan epilogues. One draws parallels between the Russian media's culture of terrorism and that of the BBC following the 7/7 London bombings. The other reinforces the paradox according to which the more tightly controlled a nation's media, the more unstable is the media's war-on-terrorism discourse.

Terror and the Iconography of Nation Building

Russia's worst terrorist crisis began when gunmen took schoolchildren and adults hostage on September 1, 2004, at School No. 1 in the Russian town of Beslan in North Ossetia. At 9.30 A.M., the morning of the first day of the autumn semester, a group of around thirty armed men and women, arriving in a GAZel van and a GAZ-66 military lorry, stormed the middle school, whose pupils were ages seven to eighteen years. Most of the attackers wore black ski masks, and a few were seen carrying explosive belts. After an exchange of gunfire with police in which five officers and one terrorist were killed, the attackers seized the school building, taking more than 1,300 pupils, parents, and teachers hostage and traumatizing them with the prospect of blowing up the school with the numerous bombs they had earlier wired throughout the building. Their demands seemed to involve the immediate withdrawal of Russian troops from Chechnya. On September 3, the third day of the standoff, shooting broke out between the hostage-takers and Russian security forces.[4] The reasons for the shooting and the bloodbath that followed are to this day unclear, but it seems likely that unprovoked, precipitous action by the FSB troops surrounding the school may have played a role.[5] According to official government data, 344 civilians were killed, 186 of them children. Hundreds more were wounded. The terrorist attacks were masterminded by Chechen terrorist leader Shamil Basaev and his Ingushetia-based deputy, Magomet Evloev. President Putin ordered a two-day national mourning period for September 6 and 7. The second of these days saw 135,000 people join an antiterrorism demonstration in Moscow's Red Square. The identities of the hostage-takers is one of the many contentious issues surrounding the siege, but according to official Russian sources, the attackers were an international group consisting of Arabs, Tatars, Kazakhs, Chechens, Uzbeks, and one local Beslan resident. (As Beumers's account of post-*Nord-Ost* reporting confirms, the propensity of the Russian media to internationalize terrorist incidents on Russian soil by linking them to the Arab world rather than to Chechnya is well established.)

September 1 marks the day when children throughout Russia return to school after the summer holidays, bearing gifts for their teachers in a time-honored ritual occupying a sacrosanct place in the Russian calendar, a ritual, moreover, unifying communist past with postcommunist present. If 9/11 was an assault on sacred American space (the Twin Towers of the World Trade Center symbolized the United States' position at the core of global capitalism), then Beslan was a calculated affront to hallowed post-Soviet temporality. The terrorist mission and the Russian media response thus furnished mirror images of one another as Channel 1 acted to annul the traumatic insult to Russia's collective memory by saturating its coverage with melodramatically effective pictures of the very category of Russian citizens (children) whose sacred day had been defiled.

Indeed, Channel 1 lost no time in exploiting the memories of a Soviet Union unified around shared rituals. Reports on reactions to the tragedy on September 4 broadcast from across the former USSR formed part of an implicit effort to reunify the space of the former superpower.[6] Putin picked up this thread in his speech to the nation broadcast on the morning after the siege, referring wistfully to a "gigantic country which had proved unsuited to the modern world," but whose "core" (*iadro*) had been conserved and strengthened through the post-Soviet Russian Federation (September 4, 2004). Beslan provided an opportunity to reconstruct (post-)Soviet space. It also served to rearticulate a set of values associated with Soviet times. In this sense, it confirms Birgit Beumers's earlier assertion that terrorism, particularly in its Russian variant, tends to be "absorbed into cultural discourse through a reworking of the past." It also provides indirect support for the argument mounted in Anna Brodsky's essay, which posits a convergence between the separatist terrorism of the present period and the state violence of the Stalin era.

Throughout carefully edited coverage of the siege's immediate aftermath, images of mothers in head scarves weeping for their children, familiar from Soviet World War II iconography, were accompanied by the emotional, sometimes even pseudo-religious, words of the newsreader, Ekaterina Andreeva, declaring, in a striking break with the journalistic conventions associated with newsreading, "We weep with you" (*My plachem s vami*), and, in a trope of established socialist realist lineage, claiming Beslan's children as the "loved ones" (*rodnymi*) of the entire country (September 5, 2004).[7] Thus, when Putin addressed the Beslan parents the next day, telling them that "the whole country suffers, grieves and prays with you" (*vsia strana stradaet, skorbit i molitsia s vami*), his words appeared to emerge organically from the journalistic discourse by which they were framed, masking and "naturalizing" his control over an ideologically subservient media (September 6, 2004).

Another abiding image, used in a recurring continuity montage, was that of distraught parents displaying photo-portraits of their lost children (September 5 and 6, 2004). This image became an icon of post-Soviet culture thanks to the popular missing persons TV show *Wait for Me* (*Zhdi menia*), itself founded on the conceit of an eternally fragmented national family forever in the process of being made whole.[8] The family trope was deployed in a highly individualized manner. The September 5 *Vremia* evening broadcast, for example, headlined with the tale of one injured girl, now "smiling again for the first time." It concluded with images of children in their hospital beds surrounded by their teddy bears, elaborating an "imaginary community," to cite Benedict Anderson's richly productive term, intimately sharing the despair and hopes of each parent in turn (September 5, 2004).[9] The visual rhetoric, with its pathos-inducing close-ups of abandoned toys strewn across the disaster scene, was as emotive as the accompanying commentary. The *Vremia* bulletin of September 6 opened with images of siege victims, each separated from the next by the sound of a gunshot. The same bulletin concluded with a montage of images of children recovering in hospitals, accompanied by the sound of a heartbeat growing in volume to the point where it merged with that of every viewer, who now also shared the perspective of the wounded child-victim (September 6, 2004). The switching of subject positions achieved a binding of subject (protective parent) to object (vulnerable child) and of imagined community of anonymous viewers to individualized victims. The heartbeat metaphor would have been familiar to most Russian viewers, since it was used during Yeltsin's 1996 reelection campaign, when the ORT channel (now Channel 1) ran a highly effective advertisement incorporating an electronic countdown to election day accompanied by the sound of a heart beating and a slogan implying that the infant "heartbeat" of Russian democracy was at stake. Thus, the heartbeat metaphor acquired in Beslan a metonymic dimension (the heartbeat of real Russian children, maimed by terrorism, was now under threat), which in turn enhanced its performative effect; the onus was on actual doctors and nurses, and by implication all Russians, to preserve the heartbeat of these real children and thereby maintain the nation's breath of life.[10]

Vremia made much of the transportation of injured children to Moscow hospitals. The reassuring scenes of children in their hospital beds surrounded by bustling medical teams portrayed the children's arrival in Moscow as a homecoming from the traumas of the front line, aligning center (the capital) and periphery (the North Ossetian town of Beslan) in an intimate embrace (September 4, 2004). At the same time, Moscow was itself simultaneously depicted as the locus of renewed danger. On September 1, Beslan reports were succeeded immediately by a follow-up report on an earlier Moscow metro bomb in which the Islamic group responsible was linked to al Qaeda. The report also included security advice to Muscovites on using the metro and an interview with Sergei Ivanov (the minister for foreign affairs), who referred to a hidden enemy in a war in which the front line is everywhere (September 1, 2004). This constant oscillation in Moscow's status from (secure) center to (endangered) front line reminded viewers of the previous spate of terrorist bombings on the Moscow metro and the apartment bombings of autumn 1999 in Moscow, Volgodonsk, and Buinaksk, which provided the immediate pretext for the Second Chechen War. It thus established Beslan as part of a logical sequence of events and, far from resulting in a sense of inconsistency, consolidated its mediatory, nation-binding function. Moscow was now both the vulnerable "child" of an entire nation at risk and the paternalistic "protector" of that nation.

Tales of heroism were quick to emerge after September 3. Particularly prevalent were narratives of official FSB heroes. In a defiantly nostalgic but now increasingly common reinvocation of the self-sacrificing dedication of the secret police, *Vremia* dedicated an entire report to the fate of an FSB soldier whose face had been deeply disfigured by the injuries he had suffered but who nonetheless declared his intent to return to active service as soon as he had recovered (September 4, 2004).[11] Such narratives were complemented by tales of martyrdom on the part of ordinary people, including the grandfather who perished at the school rescuing other people's grandchildren (September 5, 2004), tales which drew sustenance from the tide of World War II mythology then rising in anticipation of the sixtieth anniversary of the victory over fascism. Equally reminiscent of old World War II films and documentaries was the demonization of the hostage-takers. Andreeva's characterization of the terrorists as "scum" (*podonki*) in the September 6 broadcast and her question, "Who are they, these beasts [*zveri*] who shot children in the back?" recall Stalinist depictions of the Nazis (September 6, 2004). Actual events again conspired with the intertextual myths cited in the nation-building project with which they coincided to forge a single master narrative of Russian identity that transcended the divide between present and past, fact and fiction, objective account and propaganda mission and that generated, seemingly spontaneously, an image of the archetypal Russian as a victimized but resilient subject.

Russia's refusal to be bowed by Beslan was emphasized in reports on choreographed occasions depicting Putin bombarding his staff with questions, engaging in practical actions rather than verbal rhetoric (September 4, 2004).[12] In his address to the nation, he spoke of the need for a "mobilization of the country" (*mobilizatsiia strany*), describing the terrorist action as a "challenge to the whole of Russia" (*vyzov vsei Rossii*) (September 6, 2004).

Vremia struck a balance between this unified national perspective and the need to internationalize Beslan. The first day's report was framed by reports on terrorist activities in Chechnya and Afghanistan and a Hamas bus bomb in Israel before the broadcast moved to domestic issues, in a reversal of the usual *Vremia* running order (September 1, 2004).[13] The post-siege analysis featured reports on the identity of the terrorists, referring pointedly to "10 immigrants from Arab countries" (*10 vykhodtsev iz arabskikh stran*), along with one Negro, Chechens, Daghestanis, and a local resident (September 4, 2004). This analysis was complemented by reports on condemnations from CIS leaders and sympathetic Western governments, though, in a tactic reminiscent of Soviet tendencies, none of the accompanying calls for a peaceful resolution to the Chechen crisis was mentioned (September 4, 2004). Russia was thus located at the interface between two geosemiotic spaces with opposing values, the first extending from Russia's borders through Chechnya to Afghanistan and Egypt (the terrorist "breeding grounds") and the second extending from Moscow through the former Soviet republics to Europe and the United States (the "terror-fighting" nations). Such a location simultaneously confers on Russia intranational coherence and credibility as an international force. Beslan, then, can be said to have enabled Channel 1 to "perform" Russia's intranational coherence through a horizontal (re)integration of former Soviet space with the peripheral, contemporary space of Beslan, the space of the center (Moscow), and the space of the civilized world beyond.

The Vertical Integration of Discourse Levels

The horizontal integration was complemented by a vertical integration resulting from a conflation of normally discrete discourse levels. In his account of media discourse, Norman Fairclough distinguishes "sequential intertextuality" (the combination of different genre and discourse types in linear sequence) from "embedded intertextuality" (the incorporation or embedding of one genre or discourse type within another).[14] Later, referring specifically to the news reporting of disasters, he lists the main categories subject to intertextual linking as the discourse of state leaders, that of the victims, bureaucratic-technical discourse (e.g., references to the legal issues involved in the investigation following the disaster), scientific-technical discourse (e.g., descriptions of crime detection technology), and the discourse of the ordinary witness.[15] The news script, while providing the horizontal link between discourse types in an intertextual sequence (e.g., interviews with the victim, then with witnesses; an account of the technical aspects of the disaster; the speech of the state leader), also embeds within itself elements from each of these discourses. But, given the news script's primary function—that of mediating the values of the official realm as they are delivered to the ordinary viewer—the structure of the embedding process must ensure the preeminence of what Fairclough generalizes as "discourses of public life" (e.g., discourses spoken by the impersonal, anonymous voices of officialdom) over what he calls, invoking Habermas, "lifeworld discourses" (e.g., discourses articulated from the individualized subject positions of ordinary people).[16] This can be achieved via mechanisms that ensure the framing of "lifeworld" discourses by public life discourses. In other words, the "objective neutrality" of the news script is a function of the clarity with which "subjective" (lifeworld) discourses are held in check and framed by public life discourses. Fairclough expresses this elsewhere by reference to the related distinction (originating with Goffman) between *author* (the source of a discursive account), *animator* (the person speaking the words), and *principal* (the person whose position they represent). Thus, a newsreader might *animate* words of reassurance whose *author* is a senior soldier, but of which the government is the hidden *principal.* By placing the words in quotation marks, and in the absence of a terrorist counterstatement or a clear indication of the government's agenda, the impression is created of an objective account, authenticated by reference to a neutral, technocratic discourse.

Beslan precipitated a breakdown in the principles of embedding and the implicit rules by which author, animator, and principal are articulated in "objective" news reporting. When, immediately following the siege, Andreeva embedded within her news script the emotive rhetoric of condemnation (rhetoric later adopted by Putin), she abandoned any attempt to frame lifeworld discourses by public discourse, or to order the voices of author, animator, and principal according to any preexisting hierarchy. For by reassuring the people of Beslan that "we weep with you" (*my plachem s vami*), and then, in reference to the pouring rain in Beslan, that "nature wept with the people" (*priroda plakala vmeste s narodom*), she integrated author, animator, and principal into a single outpouring of nationalist rhetoric. Similarly, when referring to the hostage-takers as "terrorists [who] called themselves suicide bombers [*smertniki*], but when it came to fighting . . . hid behind children," Andreeva aligned her own status as animator and author entirely with the vernacular discourse of the hypothetical outraged citizen who served as the statement's principal.[17] And in announcing that the terrorists had been "annihilated" (*unichtozheny*) and "liquidated" (*likvidirovany*), that they had not escaped "righteous punishment" (*vozmezdiia*), she synthesized a brutal Russian military idiom and the pseudo-religious language of moral indignation within a minimally marked journalistic discourse (September 6, 2004). This, to be clear, is quite different from the mere loss of objectivity often suffered by newsreaders and journalists when such horrific events occur on Western soil—following the 7/7 events in the United Kingdom, for example. In such cases, the position of the principal (official government sources) may come to dominate that of the author (the BBC), but the words of the animator (the newsreader) are nonetheless phrased in a professional lexicon that maintains the formal boundaries separating journalist from government (or journalist from eyewitness). The generic integrity of the bulletin as "objective news" broadcast is thus maintained in a way that it was not in the case of Beslan.

During the unfolding of the Beslan atrocity, *Vremia* displayed a correspondingly anomalous approach to the horizontal, sequential relationship between newsreader and on-site journalist. Channel 1 inverted the norm by which the anchor frames the more subjective voice of the live reporter with the more measured discourse of the newsroom. On-site reporters, to be sure, were only marginally less partisan than news anchors; the conclusion drawn in one report was that, because of the "sacrilege" (*koshchunstvo*) against Islam constituted by the Beslan atrocity, "terror had lost" (*terror proigral*) (September 4, 2004). But it fell to Andreeva to then pronounce the final anathema: "It is impossible to find any justification for such scum" (*Nevozmozhno naiti opravdanie takim podonkam*), finally exhorting viewers, "Do not be indifferent!" (*Ne bud'te ravnodushnymi*) (September 4, 2004). Her embedding discourse was thus contaminated by the subjective core of the complex of discourses it was intended to embed, as the process of vertical integration flattened all discourses into the single, undifferentiated voice of wounded nationhood. The temporary weakening of journalistic codes of objectivity is far from unique to Russian media responses to terrorist atrocity, but the post-Beslan descent into extreme, patriotic emotionalism was of an order unparalleled elsewhere. More important, however, and in a further departure from post-terror reporting in the West, such hysterical excess points to the insecurity of the state-controlled media's position in Russian society rather than the secure enchainment of the media to their governmental masters

The Terror Chronotope

The integration process coexisted with the need to convey the full scale of the disintegration it reversed and upon which it was predicated, and the sense of unprecedented horror the outrage provoked. When it first broke, the newsreader referred to its "epicenter" (*epitsentr*), announcing that the channel was ready to go live to the scene at any point (September 1, 2004). Three days later, on September 4, the *Vremia* format was suspended as the program switched to an extended, heavily edited account of the previous day's events. (On September 3, *Vremia* had been stunned into virtual silence by the tragic dénouement, curtailing its lunchtime edition, which went on air soon after the carnage had occurred for ten minutes, before ceding the air waves to an adaptation of Lawrence's *Women in Love,* its pretense at live spontaneity virtually abandoned.)[18]

As Patricia Mellencamp has observed in her account of television coverage of catastrophe, "television is shock and therapy; it both produces *and* discharges anxiety."[19] Indeed, operating in parallel with representations of the siege as connoting sheer alienating difference was a contrary tendency to reorient them toward the familiar sphere of the self.[20] Within minutes of the first report, it was referred to by the now standard abbreviation for "terrorist act," *terakt* (September 1, 2004). The second day featured the ritualistic litany of foreign condemnations, technical maps of the school depicting in precise diagrammatical form the location of hostages and hostage-takers (a ploy tested in coverage of the Moscow theater siege two years earlier), expert commentaries, speculative analyses of the terrorists' identity and the siege-breakers' strategies, and witnesses' retrospective accounts (September 2, 2004). All these devices indicated a preestablished set of procedures, of which only one had to be deployed for the entire model, or "visual script," to quote Fairclough, to be invoked.[21] When the critical moment was reached, and in accordance with the visual script for terrorist crises, the rhetoric of "breaking news" with which the event had been announced was reinvoked (although following *Vremia*'s embarrassing time delay) and the television screen was awash with chaotic imagery, accompanied by breathless commentary (September 4, 2004). In the aftermath of the crisis the litany of official statements and foreign condemnations gave way to the leader's address to the nation; as the days proceeded, retrospective accounts of the crisis and its aftermath and analyses of its consequences and significance provided a transition into the post-crisis coverage as the news bulletins gradually returned to normal.

If the *terakt* required a dual mode of representation—as both category-defying shock and premodeled media script—then the source of the terror was represented as pure alterity. The hostage-takers generally remained hidden and objectified as the abstract embodiment of evil; at one point, a journalist asked pointedly if the terrorists were "really worthy of the name of human beings" (September 5, 2004). This was in contrast to the ever bolder and ever more acute particularizations of the people's suffering: the close-ups of toys in hospitals, the badly injured boy reassuring doctors of his masculine steadfastness, the grandmother who told of children forced to drink and wash in their own urine (September 4, 5, and 6, 2004).[22] Images of the terrorists, but for the fly-ridden corpses triumphantly displayed at the end of the siege (September 4, 2004) and the degraded figure of one live captive (September 5 and 6, 2004), were restricted to archive footage of armed men praying to Allah (September 2, 2004).[23]

The deletion of individual agency in respect to the source of the terror found linguistic incarnation in the persistent use of impersonal third-person constructions in which, however, the vague, impersonal origins of the terrorists were mirrored in the equally impersonal, official sources working invisibly to capture them.[24] Apprehender and apprehended formed part of a single representational system in which each was dependent on its opposite and both were cast into a single "terror chronotope," a place cut off from the everyday familiar spaces and regularized rituals of news reporting, suspended in an indefinite crisis time devoid of the normal rhythms of cause and effect.[25]

While terror in its essence remained disembodied and unrepresentable, the abstraction of the shady group responsible for the *terakt* was displaced onto the embodied spectacle of the lone captive quivering in humiliation, accompanied by the newsreader's voice-over referring to him in the most derogatory term available—"bandit" (*bandit*)—and announcing with barely disguised contempt that the man "offered a prayer to Allah" with every denial he uttered (September 5, 2004). The image of the abased hostage-taker recalled the constantly rebroadcast Western images of a humiliated, disheveled Saddam Hussein following his capture by the Americans. So recently inflated into a demonic figure of awe, Saddam was now depicted being forcibly subjected to a dental inspection as though he were a reluctant child. As Slavoj Zizek comments in this context, "Enemy recognition is always a performative procedure, which constructs the enemy's true face. Once he is revealed, the omnipotent scary monster turns into a blotch waiting to be erased."[26]

Shreen Hunter has gone so far as to argue that the demonized Islamic other now occupies the role of the treacherous Jew in Russian racist tracts, whose perpetual gesturing both beyond Russia's borders and to its core is replicated in the paranoid dualism of antiterrorist discourse: a September 3 *Vremia* report identifying the Beslan hostage-takers as Arabs and Caucasians linked to bin Laden and Maskhadov then referred to shady Islamist cells (*iacheiki*) at work within Russia's borders (September 3, 2004).[27] These images of international Islamic extremism annulled the moderate Muslim expressions of indignation broadcast on September 1, when a leading Russian imam was heard to curse the kidnappers as "defilers of Islam" (September 1, 2004).[28]

As the ready availability to Channel 1 of moderate Muslim opinion indicates, Russia has not lacked experience in handling the representation of disaster, from the Chernobyl disaster in 1986 to the *Nord-Ost* theater siege in 2002. However, two key principles of the managed media event were not adhered to during the Beslan school siege. First, the switch to what Daniel Dayan and Elihu Katz call a "syntactics of interruption" involving "the most dramatic kinds of punctuation available to broadcasters" was clumsy and incomplete.[29] The regular programming schedule was minimally changed; even the lengthy advertising breaks characteristic of Russian television continued to be aired throughout the crisis, one of the many criticisms made by the *Izvestiia* journalist, Irina Petrovskaia, before the sacking of the paper's editor.[30] Second, post-Beslan coverage did not undergo the long "working through" phase by which, according to John Ellis, "television provides increasing stability to . . . images of disorder . . . by parading issues, questions or worries for a time, within slots that are regular."[31] Within a week of September 3, Channel 1 was more or less back to normal, and by November, bulletins rarely mentioned the siege. There have been few paratextual treatments of the tragedy.[32] Because the extremism of the news discourse failed to be matched by the length of coverage sustained beyond the crisis, the imagined community of outraged patriots became harder to sustain.

Beslan and Generic Transgression

The lack of correlation between the tenor of news broadcasts during and immediately following the Beslan siege itself and that of subsequent broadcasts underscored the degree to which coverage of the crisis transgressed generic boundaries. The extreme rhetorical excesses and emotive photomontages referred to earlier in the essay subverted the very status of the broadcast as news, because the reporting of the atrocity and the emotions it generated were subsumed into the atrocity itself. The abandonment of any pretense at Western-style neutrality betrayed a breach of the frame separating journalist and news team from the event they were reporting, a frame that engaged dialogically with both the Western news model to whose external forms *Vremia* pays lip service and the Soviet propaganda model cited intertextually in the program's retained Soviet-era title and signature tune. Such an approach accorded with the frame-breaking gestures persistently, and often self-consciously, exhibited by post-Soviet news and current affairs programs. The 1991 coup's outcome, for example, was determined by a struggle at the heart of *Vremia,* culminating in reporters taking to the barricades in open support of popular opposition to the putschists. At the height of the 1993 constitutional crisis, news teams broadcast live an assault on their own television tower, displaying flagrant hostility toward the forces opposing Yeltsin. In the 1996 presidential election campaign, NTV took the fateful and overtly acknowledged decision to skew its coverage in favor of Yeltsin, in the long-term interest of sustaining Russian democracy. More recently, in 2001, NTV's political talk show program, *Glas naroda* (*The Voice of the People*), debated a crisis likely to culminate in its own demise (the sudden, government-led takeover of the channel in the interests of stifling the very freedom of expression represented by *Glas naroda;* sure enough, the show was discontinued shortly afterward). Such programs have persistently and self-consciously, if with divergent political purposes, inhabited the boundary between representation and represented, objective fact and impassioned engagement.[33]

In the case of Beslan (as with the 1993 assault on the Russian White House and the 1996 election coverage), the transgression of generic boundaries served the naked interests of the government. However, the effect was in a key sense identical to that achieved in instances of oppositional transgression. For here, too, the transgression indicated a lack of stability in the status of the news broadcast as a *mediator* of state ideology, as a means of grounding the "truth and wisdom" of government policy in the commonsense apparatus and language of "objective reporting." It signaled, in other words, an absence of hegemony in the Gramscian sense.[34] Instead of, as in "mature" democracies, mediating between the interests of the state and the values of the populace at large, post-Soviet Russian news is liable to "break free" from its roots in the official sphere to embrace the oppositional values and interests of a wider populace and "turn against its masters." More often, of course, as we have seen with Beslan, the absence of a convincing and coherent hegemonic strategy on Russian state television is reflected in its tendency to superimpose the language and values of the state in unmediated form on the vernacular culture of the viewing public.[35]

Conclusion

The frame-breaking excesses through which *Vremia* enacted its participation in its own object of representation confirm performativity as the common thread running throughout the aspects of Beslan coverage that we have considered: the iconography of a nation "dismembered" by terrorist outrage and performatively reconstituted, the active reintegration of normally discrete discourse levels, the performance of Russian identity.

Two other high-profile media engagements, however, offer epilogues from which we might initially draw rather different inferences. First, the BBC's treatment of the immediate aftermath of the July 2005 bombings displayed some uncanny resemblances to Channel 1's post-Beslan coverage (which predated 7/7 by almost a year). The Russian emphasis on moderate Islamic condemnations, like that of Channel 1, was intense. And the BBC initially relegated to the margins attempts to link the incident with British involvement in Iraq, or with Islamophobia (a contributor to the first late-evening *Newsnight* broadcast following 7/7 who dared to make these connections was cut short). Given its earlier willingness to locate the causes of Beslan in Chechnya, the BBC thus unwittingly mirrored the strict and unashamedly partisan parameter setting it had earlier identified in Russian coverage of Beslan. Conversely, *Vremia*'s own reports on 7/7 projected onto Britain faults for which it was earlier assailed. For example, in highlighting the BBC's decision to excise scenes from the aftermath of 7/7 considered too distressing, *Vremia* merely echoed earlier criticisms of state-led Russian television for its censorious overreaction to the perceived excesses of NTV coverage of the *Nord-Ost* siege (July 10, 2005). And the special *Vremia* report on protests from British journalists concerning police reticence in releasing fatality numbers replicated a complaint identical to that made by the BBC during Beslan about Russian government/media collusion (July 11, 2005).

The apparent convergence of otherwise quite distinct media discourses (one that of a mature democracy with a relatively autonomous Fourth Estate, the other that of a "managed democracy" in which the first term has now virtually eclipsed the second) that this hall of mirrors effect indicates would seem to caution against overplaying the exclusivity of Channel 1's hysterical patriotism, pointing to the emergence of a global "war on terror" media culture based on an accumulation of televised outrages beamed across the world to audiences ever more accustomed to the generic features of the *terakt* format. But the very mirroring effect that *Vremia*'s account of 7/7 illustrates is also indicative of the manner in which all countries, particularly those in which government and media are bound in close collusion, exploit global terrorism events to bolster their own domestic agendas. This should alert us to the corresponding danger of understating the very real differences dividing public service stations such as the BBC from government mouthpieces such as Channel 1, differences we have already seen reflected in the distinction between a mere reduction in objectivity (BBC) and a complete collapse of the generic norms for news reporting (*Vremia*).

What we also saw, however, was that *Vremia*'s Pavlovian obedience, aversion to alternative opinion, and crude propagandizing are indicative not of a complete convergence of government and media but, on the contrary, of a disjunction born of Channel 1's inability to internalize the political positions it is called on to disseminate. When those positions are themselves riddled with ideological contradictions, the consequences for the reporting of issues surrounding the war on terrorism are considerable. This leads to our second example. For, spurred by Putin's post-tragedy speech, Beslan fueled a wave of Soviet-style patriotic sentiment whose strong anti-Chechen, anti-Muslim element contributed to an alarming anti-immigrant, xenophobic backlash at the grassroots level and an accompanying increase in hate crimes, typified by the interethnic, Russian-Chechen disturbances in the Karelian town of Kondopoga in 2006. This effect in turn has recently precipitated a number of backtracking measures, including a presidential summit on extremism in Russian society in 2006. Putin now mouths the phrase "our many-national, multifaith society" (*nashe mnogonarodnoe, mnogokonfessional'noe obshchestvo*) like a mantra, even as multiculturalism has fallen out of fashion in the United Kingdom and elsewhere in Europe. The xenophobic backlash has also been responsible for a distinct change of tone within the government-controlled media. NTV, for example, now boasts a weekly program devoted to Muslim affairs, fronted by a headscarf-wearing Muslim woman. Reports on the terrorist activity that continues to plague the Northern Caucasus are meticulously purged of any reference to Islam and treated as criminal activity. And coverage of interfaith tensions in Western Europe take a distinctly pro-Islamic, politically correct line, as a report on a Dutch minister's anti-headscarf campaign indicates (November 25, 2006). Like the words of the moderate Muslim interviewee, the presenter appropriates, then ridicules, the voice of his opponent, the Conservative Christian Party proposing the ban. When he reminds us that Holland is called "the most liberal country in Europe," then refers to it as "the most immigrant-tolerant people" (*samyi terpimyi k immigrantam narod*), he too implicitly subjects the self-identification of the Dutch Right to mocking rebuttal: "now regards [immigrants] with suspicion" (*teper' smotrit na nikh s podozreniem*). This performative enactment of multicultural values is in sharp contrast to earlier commentaries on Channel 1's *Odnako* (*However*) program directing virulent criticism at Western multicultural leniency following Chechen terrorist atrocities.[36]

The servile enthusiasm with which Channel 1 imbibed the new tolerance has on occasion led to inadvertent divergences from the elusive government line, as in a report on the Council on Extremism, convened when Putin's grip on the media had strengthened still further (December 12, 2006). During the report a Channel 1 journalist referred with dripping sarcasm to Vladimir Zhirinovsky's presence at a call for vigilance regarding right-wing assaults on foreigners, framing the nationalist leader's comments with a cutting commentary: "Zhirinovsky was astonished, for, until now, he had been considered the country's most extreme politician. Vladimir Vol'fovich thought a little and decided that extremism had nothing to do with him" (*ekstremizm—eto vse-taki ne pro nego*). The audacious sarcasm is articulated from a position at odds with a president calling for the very restrictions on migration recently demanded more colorfully by the now Kremlin-approved Zhirinovsky himself, indicating Channel 1's embarrassing failure to assimilate the government positions it aspires so slavishly to transmit.

By contrast, a report in the very same news bulletin covering celebrations of Russia's Constitution Day concentrates on the actions of the Young Guard, the youth section of the party most loyal to Putin, United Russia (Edinaia Rossiia), broaching the movement's struggle to defeat nationalist extremism, and then its contradictory proposal to replace the phrase "multinational people" with "Russian people" in the country's constitution. Rather than comment on this glaring inconsistency from the politically correct viewpoint of the regime's now official policy of multiculturalism, the presenter opts for a neutral, noncommittal hedging of bets: "clearly it now remains for the State Duma representatives to decide" (*reshat' teper' predstoit, ochevidno, deputatam gosdumy*). Russian news presenters either transparently envelop the regime's guiding voice in a Western-style, pseudo-neutral discourse or articulate it in open, Soviet-style polemic, but never engage in the subtle hegemonic mediation between official and popular culture(s) typical of, say, the BBC. The hedging of bets we see here is rather a function of Channel 1's clumsy struggle to process and make sense of a highly contradictory government stance.

Taken together, our epilogues confirm that the full ramifications of the Beslan tragedy point both outward, toward the wider war on terrorism, and inward, toward the cultural specificities of Russia's own anti-Chechen campaign, but in perhaps unexpected ways. Conventional wisdom dictates that a unified global antiterror campaign, centered in the post-9/11 United States and supported by other Western nations, has been appropriated for cynical nation-building purposes by an authoritarian, non-Western regime desperate to maintain the integrity of an anachronistic imperial state. However, our analysis shows, first, that the so-called global campaign is itself the discursive effect of a decentered process of intercultural mirrorings and exchanges in which each participant articulates a variant of a larger war from which it differentiates itself (the BBC's implicit distinction between understated, post-7/7 British stoicism and American hysteria) yet also cites in the interests of authentication (the term 7/7 is, after all, modeled on 9/11). Second, the invocation of the war on terror for performative, nation-building purposes appears ultimately to work toward a destabilizing rather than unifying effect. This presents particular problems to a state-controlled television channel tasked with imposing ideological conformity on the meanings it broadcasts. The final legacy of the tragedy that was Beslan may yet surprise us.

Notes

1. For example, in a report on the Web site of the United Kingdom's Channel 4, Jonathan Miller describes Beslan as "a byword for horror: Russia's 9/11." See Jonathan Miller, "Another Beslan?" http://www.channel4.com/news/2005/02/week_1/03_basayev.html (accessed February 12, 2005).

2. See Ivan Zassoursky, *Media and Power in Post-Soviet Russia,* trans. Renfrey Clarke (New York: M. E. Sharpe, 2004), 230.

3. News broadcasts under Putin now exhibit uncanny resemblances to their Soviet antecedents, with images of combine harvesters reaping record harvests, "official chronicle" segments detailing the rituals accompanying Kremlin state visits, and obsequious interviews with Kremlin officials. The Soviet concept of news chimed with Marxist-Leninist theories about the long, inevitable march toward world communism and the notion that what is newsworthy is not the anomalous dramas that interrupt progress but the predictable achievement of milestones along the way. Such an approach fits uncomfortably within a consumer economy in which viewers expect news to entertain and surprise.

4. For a detailed eyewitness account of the siege told from the viewpoint of a family caught up in it, see Christopher John Chivers, "The School," *Esquire,* June 2006, 143–60.

5. A December 2005 inquiry into the reasons for the tragedy attributed some of the blame to mistakes made by local authorities. A vigorous yearlong campaign led by the mothers of Beslan victims did much to ensure that the commission reached these conclusions, which, however, fell short of attaching responsibility to the central government.

6. Among the first live reports on reactions to the siege were those from correspondents in Kiev, Kazakhstan, and, most significant, Grozny.

7. For an analysis of the role played by images of the family in Stalinist rhetoric, see Katerina Clark, "Stalinskii mif o 'velikoi sem'e'," in *Sotsrealisticheskii kanon,* ed. Evgenii Dobrenko and Hans Gunther (St. Petersburg: Akademicheskii proekt, 2000), 784–96.

8. The show, among the most popular on Russian television, involves a team help-

ing families across the former Soviet Union to relocate relatives missing, often since the Soviet era, and reuniting them in a display of sentimentality before an audience itself consisting of people looking for loved ones whose photographs they display to the camera.

9. For adumbration of the concept of an "imagined community," see Benedict Anderson, *Imagined Communities: Reflections on the Origin and Spread of Nationalism* (New York: Verso, 1999).

10. Another Yeltsin campaign advertisement involved images of children's drawings and culminated in the suggestive slogan, "Children are our future," implying that the opposition represented the interests of those imprisoned in the past. With Beslan, the abstract image of the child's precarious future is now realized as actual, wounded Russian children.

11. The televisual rehabilitation of the secret police under Putin (himself an ex-KGB officer) has gained pace in the context of the president's efforts to burnish the image of the Russian military forces generally (two examples of this trend are the establishment of Zvezda, a TV channel dedicated to military affairs, and Channel 1's *Special Forces* [*Spetsnaz*], which celebrates the achievements of undercover forces on Russia's borders) and to militarize the national identity project.

12. The portrayal of Putin as a man of action has become part of his televisual iconography. He is often filmed at great length chairing meetings, questioning staff, and striding purposefully through the halls of power.

13. Normally, *Vremia* bulletins begin with national news and progress in concentric geographic rings to regional issues, then out to the former Soviet countries and beyond, but with strictly international items occupying a peripheral position on the news agenda, except in the case of major world events with direct repercussions for Russia. The tendency, true of all national news bulletins, is exaggerated in Russia, where it is not uncommon for bulletins to contain no properly international news at all.

14. See Norman Fairclough, *Media Discourse* (London: Edward Arnold, 1995), 88.

15. Ibid., 99.

16. Ibid., 164.

17. Nomenclature for the hostage-takers oscillated without distinction along a spectrum ranging from *terrorist* through *boevik* (fighter) to *bandit*. By September 3, these terms were being used in contradistinction to the positively loaded term *spasateli* (rescuers).

18. Of all the national news sources, only the newspaper *Izvestiia* gave a full account of events at Beslan, including misjudgments made by the forces attempting to break the siege. The editor was sacked soon afterward as the paper was brought into line with official versions of what happened.

19. Patricia Mellencamp, "TV Time and Catastrophe, or *Beyond the Pleasure Principle* of Television," in *Logics of Television: Essays in Cultural Criticism*, ed. Patricia Mellencamp (Bloomington: Indiana University Press, 1990), 240–67, 246.

20. Mary Ann Doane sees the shock of catastrophe and the banality of mere information conveyed in familiar packages as representing television's two poles: "Information and catastrophe coexist in a curious balance. . . . Television produces both as the two poles structuring the contemporary imagination." See Mary Ann Doane, "Information, Crisis, Catastrophe," in Mellencamp, *Logics of Television*, 222–40, 236.

21. Fairclough, *Media Discourse*, 124.

22. With each successive post-Beslan bulletin, the focus became more local and

individualized, when, based on the post-9/11 coverage, one might have expected a broadening outward to the general circumstances in which the siege took place.

23. No images of the corpses of victims of the siege were shown either during or after the crisis. This is in marked contrast to the *Nord-Ost* theater siege, when NTV was roundly criticized by official sources for the gory detail of its coverage.

24. For example, reports on government positions on the identity of the terrorists were introduced with phrases such as "it is announced that" (*soobshchaetsia, chto*) and "it is presumed that someone higher is behind the terrorists" (*predpolagaetsia, chto kto-to vyshe stoit za terroristami*), the latter phrase illustrating how both the source (*predpolagaetsia*) and the object (*kto-to vyshe*) of the search are deliberately impersonalized. Such linguistic practice confirms Mary Ann Doane's view that catastrophic events, unlike crises, which are accorded subjects, "are . . . subjectless, simply there, they *happen*" (Doane, "Information," 223).

25. Bakhtin defines "chronotope" as "the intrinsic connectedness of temporal and spatial relationships that are artistically expressed in literature," but his concept can be applied across meaning-making activity more generally. See Mikhail Mikhailovich Bakhtin, *The Dialogic Imagination: Four Essays,* ed. Michael Holquist, trans. Caryl Emerson and Michael Holquist (Austin: University of Texas Press, 1981), 84.

26. Slavoj Zizek, *Iraq: The Borrowed Kettle* (London: Verso, 2004), 64.

27. See Shreen Hunter, *Islam in Russia: The Politics of Identity and Security* (London: M. E. Sharpe, 2004).

28. For Russian demonization of Islam in the context of the Chechnya conflict, see John Russell, "Terrorists, Bandits, Spooks and Thieves: Russian Demonization of the Chechens Before and Since 9/11," *Third World Quarterly* 26, no. 1 (2005): 101–16.

29. Daniel Dayan and Elihu Katz, *Media Events* (Cambridge, Mass.: Harvard University Press, 1995).

30. In a blistering full-page assault on all the national television channels, Petrovoskaia lambasted Channel 1 in particular for its minimal coverage on September 3, 2004, and for following its *Vremia* bulletin with an episode of the D. H. Lawrence adaptation, *Women in Love.* See Irina Petrovskaia, "Molchanie gosudarstvennikov," *Izvestiia,* September 4, 2004, 7.

31. John Ellis, "Television as Working-Through," in *Television and Common Knowledge,* ed. Jostein Gripsrud (London: Routledge, 1999), 55–71, 59.

32. This is in contrast to long-term American and British media responses to 9/11 and 7/7, which generated a stream of paratextual documentaries, interviews, and special reports.

33. The turning point during the 1991 coup was the press conference called by the coup leaders, when a bitter struggle within the *Vremia* editorial team resulted eventually in unflattering close-ups of the trembling generals being broadcast live across the nation. For a full account of this remarkable struggle, see Ellen Mickiewicsz, *Changing Channels: Television and the Struggle for Power* (Oxford: Oxford University Press, 1997).

34. For the classic account of hegemony, see Antonio Gramsci, *Selections from the Prison Notebooks of Antonio Gramsci,* ed. and trans. Quentin Hoare and Geoffrey Smith (New York: International Publishers, 1971).

35. The 1993 and 1996 examples are less clear-cut, since they involved an unmediated convergence of "text" and "extra-text," state and populace, in which it was not certain whose interests were best served. (Yeltsin was either "the best chance that the

popular democratic movement had," and therefore worthy of reluctant media support, or a cynical manipulator of media fooled into thinking that he supported democratic reform, or an obstacle to Russian national interests supported by a Western-funded media.) The *Glas naroda* example is complicated by the fact that here television arguably reached out not to a wider populace but to the relatively small group of liberal intellectuals who constituted its viewership.

36. In 2002, the presenter Maksim Sokolov noted sardonically that "the charm of modern European multiculturalism [*multikul'tural'nosti*] consists in the fact that immigrants show not the slightest desire to acquire European culture, customs, and morals and live as a state within a state" (April 3, 2002).

Afterword: Russia, a Revolutionary Life

Nina L. Khrushcheva

Petite bourgeoisie is incompatible with the Russian character—and thank God for it!

—ALEXANDER HERZEN, *RUSSIANS ON RUSSIA*

The petit bourgeois rather than the hero carries history forward.

—ANDREI PLATONOV, NOTEBOOKS: BOOK 14 (1935–36)

Russia has always been a "revolutionary" country. Historically, it moves forward not through evolution, the slow, step-by-step development in which progress occurs over time, but through perpetual revolutions, with their attendant upheavals, crises, and terror. In this sense, as judged by the two epigraphs to this essay, Russia can be considered the realm of the hero, a territory decidedly hostile to the petite bourgeoisie. This kind of revolutionary permanence is a cultural trait that Alexander Herzen encompassed in his immortal maxim, "Disorder will always save Russia."[1] This belief has been a consolation and an inspiration for generations of Russian revolutionaries of all kinds, who have fought, in groups or individually, with or against the state, lawfully or illegally, against their country's traditional inertness, stagnation, and complacency.

Their rebellious efforts, from the abortive uprising of the Decembrists to the assassination campaign of the People's Will, from the Bolshevik Revolution to attempts to reform the Soviet state in the thaw of the 1950s, perestroika of the 1980s, and continuing into the postcommunist world of the 1990s, were intended to create a spark, a rupture, or a break with the past. Nevertheless, despite all these endeavors, neither the late tsarist system nor communism nor postcommunism was able to generate a viable alternative in a society where change, when it occurs, always seems to result in destructive and dysfunctional developments. In each of these cases, the process of replacing the old regime has been twisted and painful beyond expectations and, in the long run, has yielded disappointing results.

Not that the change from monarchy to communism or postcommunism was insignificant: abolishing serfdom in the mid-nineteenth century, creating open access to culture and education in Soviet Russia, and allowing international travel and relative freedom of expression in post-Soviet Russia all represent significant achievements. But this was not the change that generations of tsars, Bolsheviks, reformers, and revolutionaries promised, and today Russia's institutional structures of legal and civil society remain as underdeveloped as during the times of Peter the Great. Because, in the words of Isaiah Berlin, the efforts of those trying to reform Russia, leaders and rebels, were invariably a "mixture of utopian faith and brutal disregard for civilized morality,"[2] particular autocracies may have changed, but autocracy remains the central fact of the Russian state to this day.

Russia's geographic position between the West and the East can provide some tentative answers to the country's political, social, and cultural development. Russia's own philosophers and foreign experts from Peter Chaadaev to Mikhail Epstein and Jeffrey Sachs have marveled over the mystifying nature of this nation, whose enormous landmass spreads over eleven time zones. Discussing the Russian transition from communism to capitalism, Sachs, who served as an adviser to the Russian government in the early 1990s, noted that it was geography that defined behavioral patterns in the former Soviet states. For example, while "countries closest to Western Europe have largely succeeded in economic change and geographic consolidation . . . Russia [has] been caught in by far the deepest and still spiraling crisis."[3] In other words, "proximity to the West induced better policies." Sachs also listed other historical factors linked to geography that have contributed to the difficulty of breaking with the past: the length of time a society spent under socialism, the legacy of autocratic rule, the religious divide between Western and Orthodox Christianity, past experience with multiparty rule. Although none of these factors was entirely deterministic, together they did "condition events."

To draw on Sachs's "geographic" idea, it is the vastness of the Russian land that has long been Russia's handicap: to get anything done rationally and systematically in such an enormous land, there must be effective boundaries and laws. And while Russia has been able to amass an enormous empire, the country has never been able to control its territory or, more seriously, create reasonable living conditions for its people. Russia invented Sputnik, designed the first manned space program, and devised excellent computer systems for, say, KGB monitoring, but it has been absolutely unable to produce decent washing machines. As the contemporary cultural historian Mikhail Epstein has suggested, Russian successes are generally achieved though dilettantism and inspiration, but not methodology: "Our hero was the Jack of all trades: he sews, he mows, he plays the oboe. Each hand does miracles: incredible dress designs, incredible harvests, incredible melodies, while in reality we had convicts in rags and millions starved."[4]

More than a century before Sachs and Epstein, Peter Chaadaev in his *Philosophical Letters* tried to clarify Russianness: "We Russians still look and act like travelers. No one has a defined sphere of engagement; we have no rules for anything; we don't even have a home. Nothing that can tie us up . . . nothing durable, nothing permanent; everything flows by, goes by, without leaving a print either within or outside us."[5] He suggested that "the most important feature of our historic makeup is the absence of free initiative in our social development."[6] A specific character of Russian culture, according to Chaadaev, was that it was "brought from elsewhere and imitative. Russians take on only absolutely ready ideas, and thus do not inherit experiences related to making these ideas work in reality."

Indeed, Russian history has provided ample evidence of our imitative nature: Peter the Great's famous Westernizing reforms manifested themselves in the 1712 creation of St. Petersburg, a grand new capital built in just a decade and with great human sacrifice as Russia's "window onto Europe." The 1917 Bolshevik Revolution represented yet another radical and brutal attempt to rationalize this mystical land, this time by applying Karl Marx's dialectical materialism to a traditional peasant communal country. Finally, post-1991 American-style capitalism was proudly explained by Alfred Kokh, an official close to the privatization chief Anatoly Chubais, as "a period of Social Darwinism during which a process of natural selection must take place."[7]

But these great triumphs—Petersburg's Europeanism, Lenin's socialism, Stalin's industrialization, and Yeltsin's privatization—have been arrogant and revolutionary creations of great "artists" who, in constructing their grandiose realities, insisted that the only way to move their backward and enormous country forward was through fear and force, and quickly. As the thirteenth-century Russian ruler Ivan III once pointed out to a European visitor who reproached him for cruelty, "It is different for you with your enlightened people, with ours this is the only way."[8]

The Grand Prince may indeed have had a point. The attitudes of most Russians toward the West could be best described not by Chaadaev, who like other Westernizers believed that Russians should behave and think like Europeans, but by Slavophiles such as Alexei Khomiakov. Khomiakov believes, for example, that whereas the West is characterized by self-interest and a concern for material goods that outweighs service to the community, it is Russia's strongly collective and traditional culture that sets Russia apart from the West and assures its future glory.[9] The Slavophiles considered the rational individual to be inferior to the community, defined as a universal collective guided by an all-encompassing Orthodox faith that represents a higher spiritual reality (*sobornost'*). The religiosity, capacity for suffering, brotherly love, and cultural unity of the Orthodox community provide a perfect model for the Russian *obshchina-mir* (i.e., peasant commune).[10] To confront this oppressive communal mentality, Westernizers and other rebels and revolutionaries, from the Decembrists to the People's Will, from the Bolsheviks to the Chechen separatists of recent years, often felt they had no choice but to resort to violence to achieve their goals. Caught between the tyrannical top and the complacent bottom, they justified violence by repeating after Ivan III, "With our people this is the only way."

Ironically, in Russia even "individual" terrorism is not an individual matter but, like everything else, is something of a group activity. Like their Russian and Soviet rulers, Russian rebels too are "artists" who "construct their own historical images and whose behavior is consciously symbolic."[11] Their behavior is a grandiose performance—heroic, dramatic, and all too often self-sacrificial—undertaken on behalf of all humanity. This, ultimately, is what unites all Russian rebels, revolutionaries, and terrorists with the imperial state, in its Russian, Soviet, or post-Soviet hypostasis.

Soviet dissident Andrei Sinyavsky (Abram Tertz) in his *Voice from the Chorus* has established a connection between religion, antirationalism, and Russia's artistic character:

> This religion of the Holy Spirit somehow accords with our national characteristics—a natural inclination for anarchy, . . . fluidity, amorphousness, readiness to adopt any mould ("come and rule over us"), our gift—or vice—of thinking and living artistically, combined with an inability to manage the very serious practical side of daily life: "Why bother? Who cares?" we ask. In this sense Russia offers a most favorable soil for the experiments and fantasies of the artist, though his lot as a human being is sometimes very terrible indeed.[12]

In the same work Tertz also commented on the consequences of Russia's spiritual obsessions as well as the extreme nature of Russian thinking, its violent swings back and forth from absolute conservatism (Slavophiles) to absolute radicalism (Westernizers and revolutionaries):

> Because of the Spirit we are sensitive to the influence of all kinds of ideas—so much so that at certain moments we lose our own language and personality and become Germans, Frenchmen, or Jews, and, then,

> recovering our senses, rush from one spiritual servitude to the opposite extreme, freezing in a posture of narrow-minded suspicion and hostility towards everything foreign.
>
> We are conservatives because we are nihilists—the one turns into the other and they are interchangeable in our history. But all this because "the Spirit bloweth where it listeth," and in order not to be blown away by it we turn to stone, protect ourselves with the crust of ritual, the ice of formalism, the letter of the decree or the standard formula. We cling to form because we have not enough of it; we have never had and never can have either hierarchy or structure (we are too spiritual for this), and move freely from nihilism to conservatism and back again.

Surely, the Russian understanding of spirit as the essence of life is yet another imitation: it follows upon the traditions of Byzantium, the original empire of the Holy Spirit. In opposition to the Western structure of suzerain and vassal, in the East there was ruler and serf, that is, an absolute vertical hierarchy (compare Vladimir Putin's "vertical of power"). In such an order the ruler does not provide guarantees or laws, needs no explanations and proofs, but, like God, has the right to punish or pardon his people, whose only responsibility is to submit and obey. In practice it is arbitrary rule, in theory (spiritually) it is the *tsardom* of God on earth.

Harvard historian Richard Pipes recently reconfirmed the Russian desire for a "tsar":

> With few lateral social ties, [Russians] relied on the state to protect them from each other. They wanted their rulers to be both strong and harsh, qualities designated by the Russian word *groznyi*, meaning "awesome" (incorrectly translated as terrible), the epithet applied to Tsar Ivan IV. Experience has taught Russians to associate weak government—and democracy is seen as weak—with anarchy and lawlessness.[13]

Lacking "lateral social ties," with no viable legal institutions, even now, in the twenty-first century, Russians hold on to the grandiose ideal of "awesome" leadership that assures their belonging to a harmonious state order. After Yeltsin's anarchy of postcommunism, when, as some critics complained, "deprived of high ideals, the country disintegrated in just a few years,"[14] Putin's centralization of power for the sake of restoring Russia's "glory, faith, and, above all, its proper place in the world"[15] came as a welcome development for many. Although we still lack free individuals, secure private property, and the panoply of other rights that the West takes for granted, at least our state has given us back our pride! Russia's oil and gas should make the world tremble because Russia "is a great, powerful, divinely ordained state that stretches back a thousand years."

This current state of affairs contradicts a claim Anatoly Chubais made just a decade ago: it would not "take long to implement capitalism in Russia" because "Soviet man like every other man was nothing more than '*Homo Economicus,*' fully engrossed in his economic interests."[16] Yet, as we have seen, "habits die hard and mentalities change slowly."[17] And in Russia, slower than in most places. Although "*Homo Sovieticus,* successor and predecessor of *Homo Russicus,* labored long and willingly, his labor lacked a foundation. . . . There was no firm, lifelong tie with the object and the product of labor. His love [for labor] was general, public and belonged to no one . . . [since] Russians are supposed to be a mystical people who find rational knowledge about the objective world alien."[18] Indeed Russians of all generations have long been plagued with this vision of "public" labor as *podvig,* that is, an exploit, deed, or sacrifice: from eradicating enemies to forging steel to herding sheep, Russians "take up the trade . . . with all [their] heart as if [they are] marrying it."

Leon Trotsky insisted that these everyday heroics are characteristic of "an improved edition of mankind" and are required for "reforging humanity and creating an earthly paradise [which] was the *raison d'etre* of the communist movement."[19] His contemporary and archnemesis, the religious philosopher Nikolai Berdiaev, defined a *specifically* Russian messianic idea of the ethical transformation of society into a purer form of community: "The Russian people . . . has no love for the ordering of this earthly city and struggles toward a city that is to come, towards the new Jerusalem."[20]

A striking similarity among all Russian thinkers, leaders, radicals, and revolutionaries is the belief in some higher harmonious order emulated in the community, in which only *collective values,* not *individual rights,* matter. Even many who have rejected universal *sobornost* in its Orthodox or communist form are still convinced of the grandiosely messianic destiny for the Russian nation: "We are an exception among nations. We exist in order to give a great lesson to the world."[21] To be sure, rarely has a country so recklessly disposed of its citizens to establish cosmic harmony: bleeding to save humanity but refusing to lift a finger to save a lone human being, tsars, revolutionaries, and commissars have likewise sacrificed untold millions of Russians to such dreams.

One can extend this analogy to include even the capitalist reformers of Yeltsin's first post-Soviet government, who also looked with disdain at "small deeds." The postcommunist reformers were not only in the business of "saving" Russia, they were also eager to set an example for the rest of the world: "The aim of privatization was building capitalism. And not just that, the building of capitalism had to happen in just a few *udarnykh* [shock] years, meeting norms of production that the rest of the world spent hundreds of years achieving."[22] To meet these heroic norms, the transition to a market economy in the 1990s took the form of yet another revolution, and the approach was strikingly similar to Lenin's "iron fist" of 1917. And just as people eventually rejected communism because of its broken promises and merciless policies, a large part of the Russian public came to associate the words "democracy" and "reform" with oligarchy and cowboy-style democracy. In a revolutionary fever, Yeltsin's reformers pushed for the privatization of state resources in the absence of a functioning legal system and without the necessary transparency: we are all still living with the results of this debacle. If the image of Boris Yeltsin on top of a tank in 1991 was enough to bring down communism, it was not nearly enough to create a functioning market economy.

Although Russians initially welcomed the demise of socialism and the promise of free access to goods and products, in a few years these advances were taken for granted. Having been taught for centuries that the interests of the state, collectivism, and solidarity are more important than individual profit and competition, the disillusioned public, craving some higher meaning, turned to the wisdom of Alexander Herzen: "Petite bourgeoisie is incompatible with the Russian character—and thank God for it!"[23]

This brief excursion into Russian history and psychology suggests that Russia will not change soon. The late cultural historian Yuri Lotman provided an explanation for the country's movement from one revolutionary extreme to another, from the absolutism of Orthodoxy to dialectical materialism.[24] Citing the unresolved split between the Slavophiles and the Westernizers that still plagues Russia's self-image, Lotman suggested that Russian culture, unlike the cultures of the West, embodies an underlying binary logic of opposition: individuals and groups conceptualize social lives in terms of absolute alternatives, with no neutral ground or compromise. He identified this as a paradox of "tyranny": a "weak state" often functions as "strong" by instilling a controlling government and depriving its people of basic liberties and legal structures, which would allow them to make their own decisions. Although such a state is generally impotent to solve the fundamental problems of modern society, it can be effective in weakening alternative approaches to governance.

According to Lotman, a fateful result of binary thinking is Russia's *revolutionary mentality,* that is, the desire to annihilate the past, which is regarded not as the foundation of organic growth but as a source of error.

Total destruction must precede creation, and so creation can take place only in a void. Means and ends are thus separate, as the desired new world can only be constructed on the ruins of the old, which is perceived as wholly corrupt. Consequently, all Russian revolutions and regimes have felt completely justified in their never-changing motto, "the end justifies the means."

Meanwhile, both the communist and postcommunist claims of a radical break with the Russian or Soviet past can be deceiving: the Russian present always becomes a certain regurgitation of that past, not a true step forward. For example, the indictment of communism is not that it was based on Western rationalism or atheism but that it too quickly succumbed to the Russian traditions of despotism, mysticism, and obscurantism. Despite the Soviets' supposed belief in scientific laws of development and the rationality of their existence, behind Stalin's collectivization of agriculture and the industrial exploits lay not Marxism but the social and moral-psychological tradition of serfdom and the ancient communality of the peasant commune.

Russia's repeated failure to change in evolutionary ways brings to the fore yet another paradox: while tolerating the worst despots in world history, Russians have displayed an almost apocalyptic fear of change, especially change of power. The end of a certain order is often seen by Russian people as the end of order altogether, as this shift tends to bring unexpected and fearful results. In their defense, when things do change in Russia, it is usually for the worse.

Indeed, Russia's liberal promises have been shattered time after time. The assassination of the "Tsar Liberator" Alexander II in 1881 by terrorists of the People's Will organization threw Russia back into conservatism and suspicion toward all modernizing forces. In liberating the Russian people from absolute monarchy, the Bolsheviks subjected them to the dictatorship of the proletariat, which under Stalin's leadership sacrificed tens of millions to its cause. Nikita Khrushchev's de-Stalinization reforms ended with Leonid Brezhnev's stagnation; Yeltsin's attempt at democratization resulted in Putin's authoritarianism. The attack of the Chechen "black widows" and the suicide bombers in the Moscow Dubrovka Theater in 2002 and the Beslan school in 2004 allowed Russian security forces to escalate the war in Chechnya, then to establish a sham "peace" and tighten their grip on power all over the Russian Federation. In the sadly immortal words of Victor Chernomyrdin, Russia's prime minister during the Yeltsin era, "We wanted something better, but it turned out to be more of the same."

Given Russia's fear of change, power here is subject to inertia, which in turn creates a favorable environment for despotism. The leader embodies power and is supported by the population regardless of the policies he implements. This in part explains the phenomenon of the enduring popular devotion to harsh rulers like Peter the Great and Stalin, and it also helps explain Yeltsin's reelection as president in 1996. Despite polls showing almost no popular support for Yeltsin, Russians voted for him, reasoning, "Better the devil we know. . . ." This phenomenon is often subconscious, part of a centuries-old tradition that only time and different—positive—experience may change: "people do more easily what they are used to doing than what they have never done. . . . Habits and expectations, which perversely constrict freedom of choice, can be handed down from generation to generation and survive for centuries by sheer inertia."[25]

With what we know about Russian history, it's difficult to square the high-minded slogans (promises "service to the community, sacred notion of the Motherland, the nation's honor and high morality") with the vicious cycle of despotism, violence, and terror.[26] And yet . . . an unsustainable imperial political culture,[27] an elite class that uses religion as a prop,[28] an economic crisis: what better time to break the pattern and "start an evolution"? "The petit bourgeois," whom Andrei Platonov wanted to carry "history forward,"[29] has long been waiting his turn in Russia. But even if the seeming eternity of Russian revolutions finally does come to an end, our newborn bourgeois may still be unable to enjoy the prosperity experienced by the Western democracies in the past century. While Russia may finally be ready for evolution, the world has changed too: discontent with the status quo is increasing in many countries, acts of terror are more frequent and more geographically widespread. The good news is that today, with extremists gaining strength in so many parts of the world, the country that knows extremist politics better, perhaps, than any other might have something important to share with the rest of the world. In so doing, Russia might finally fulfill Chaadaev's prophesy: "We exist in order to give a great lesson to humanity." Who better to serve the cause of combating terror than a reformed terrorist?

Notes

1. Quoted in *Russkie o russkikh: Mneniia russkikh o samikh sebe* (St. Petersburg: Petro-Rif, 1992), 49. Unless otherwise indicated, all translations from the Russian sources are my own.

2. Isaiah Berlin, "Political Ideas in the Twentieth Century," in *Four Essays on Liberty* (Oxford: Oxford University Press, 1969), 17.

3. This and the following quotations in this paragraph are from Jeffrey D. Sachs, "Eastern Europe Reforms: Why the Outcomes Have Differed So Sharply," *Boston Globe,* September 19, 1999.

4. Mikhail Epstein, "Labor of Lust," *Common Knowledge* 1, no. 3 (Winter 1992): 99.

5. Petr Chaadaev, *Filosofskie pis'ma,* in *Filosofskaia aforistika,* ed. P. S. Taranov (Moscow: Ostozhe, 1996), 553.

6. This and the following quotation are from Petr Chaadaev, *Polnoe sobranie sochinenii i izbrannye pis'ma,* 2 vols. (Moscow: Nauka, 1991), 1:527, 326.

7. Alfred Kokh, interview, *Chas Pik,* October 12, 1992.

8. See Sigmund von Herberstein, *Description of Moscow and Moscovy, 1557,* ed. Bertold Picard, trans. J. B. C. Grudny (London: Dent; New York: Barnes and Noble, 1966).

9. A. S. Khomiakov, "O starom i novom," in *Russkaia ideia,* ed. M. A. Maslin (Moscow: Respublica, 1992), 52–63.

10. See Isaiah Berlin, *Russian Thinkers* (London: Hogarth Press, 1978). *Mir* can also mean "world" or "peace."

11. Lydia Ginzburg, *On Psychological Prose* (Princeton: Princeton University Press, 1991), 16.

12. This and the following quotation are from Abram Tertz (Andrei Sinyavsky), *A Voice from the Chorus,* trans. Kyril Fitzlyon and Max Hayward (New York: Farrar, Straus and Giroux, 1976), 247–48.

13. Richard Pipes, "Flight from Freedom: What Russians Think and Want," *Foreign Affairs,* May–June 2004.

14. Yelena Prudnikova, *Stalin: Vtoroe ubiistvo* (St. Petersburg: Neva, 2003), 9.

15. This and the following quote are from Serge Schmemann, "A Visit with Putin," *International Herald Tribune,* September 16, 2007.

16. Anatoly Chubais, ed., *Privatizatsiia po-rossiiski,* (Moscow: Vagrius, 1999), 29.

17. Stephen Holmes, "Cultural Legacies or State Collapse?" in *Post-Communism: Four Perspectives,* ed. Michael Mandelbaum (New York: Council on Foreign Relations, 1996), 26.

18. This and the following quotation are from Epstein, "Labor of Lust," 92, 102, 99.

19. Quoted in Jochen Hellbeck, *Revolution on My Mind: Writing a Diary Under Stalin* (Cambridge, Mass.: Harvard University Press, 2006), 5–6.

20. Nikolai Berdiaev, *The Russian Idea* (Paris: YMCA Press, 1946), 255.

21. Chaadaev, *Polnoe sobranie,* 1:326.

22. Anatoly Chubais in a television interview on the program *Details,* June 29, 1994.

23. Quoted in Tim McDaniel, *The Agony of the Russian Idea* (Princeton: Princeton University Press, 1996), 39–40.

24. Iuryi Lotman, *Kultura i vzryv* (Moscow: Gnozis, 1992).

25. Holmes, "Cultural Legacies," 26.

26. Boris Vishnevskii, "Liudi bez sviatykh poniatii," *Novaia Gazeta,* June 3, 2009.

27. In the case of a future political collapse, it is not inconceivable that a pragmatic and powerful China might swallow the Far East and Siberia, while the Northern Caucasus and the Volga region might succumb to a Muslim majority. Even "Kaliningrad" reverting to "Königsberg" is not inconceivable.

28. I am thinking here not only of Putin and Medvedev turning religion into a matter of public policy but also of an old acquaintance of mine whose business card mentions his membership on the board of the Cathedral of Christ the Savior.

29. Andrei Platonov, *Zapisnye knizhki: Materialy k biografii,* ed. N. V. Kornienko, M. A. Platonova (Moscow: Nasledie, 2000), 176.

Contributors

Anthony Anemone is an associate professor of Russian and chair of the Department of Foreign Languages at the New School. His essays and reviews on modern Russian literature and cinema have appeared in the *Slavic Review,* the *Slavic and East European Journal,* the *Russian Review, Wiener Slawistischer Almanach, KinoKultura,* and *Studies in Russian and Soviet Cinema.*

Brian James Baer is an associate professor of Russian language, literature, and translation studies at Kent State University. He is the author of *Other Russias: Homosexuality and the Crisis of Post-Soviet Identity* (2009) and the founding editor of the journal *Translation and Interpreting Studies.*

Birgit Beumers is a reader in Russian at the University of Bristol. A specialist on contemporary Russian cinema and theater, she is the author of *Burnt by the Sun* (2000), *Nikita Mikhalkov: Between Nostalgia and Nationalism* (2005), *Pop Culture: Russia!* (2005), and *History of Russian Cinema* (2009) and, with Mark Lipovetsky, of *Performing Violence* (2009). She is the editor of *Russia on Reels: The Russian Idea in Post-Soviet Cinema* (1999) and *24 Frames: Russia and the Soviet Union* (2007), as well as the online journal *KinoKultura* and the print journal *Studies in Russian and Soviet Cinema.* She is currently working on a study of Russian animation.

Sally A. Boniece is a professor of history and coordinator of international studies at Frostburg State University in Maryland. Her work has appeared in *Kritika.* At present she is completing a biography of Maria Spiridonova.

Anna Brodsky is an associate professor of Russian at Washington and Lee University. She has published articles on Vladimir Nabokov, Liudmila Petrushevskaya, and Sasha Sokolov and is now working on the cultural ramifications of the Russo-Chechen conflicts.

James Frank Goodwin is an assistant professor of Russian studies at the University of Florida. He has published articles on Russian anarchism in the journal *Kritika* and in the collection *Times of Trouble: Violence in Russian Literature and Culture* (2007). He recently completed a book on Dostoevsky's *Demons* and the legacy of Bakunin in twentieth-century Russia.

Stephen Hutchings is a professor of Russian and East European studies and deputy head of school and director of research at the School of Modern Languages, Linguistics and Cultures at Manchester University, having previously held a chair at the University of Surrey and an associate professorship at the University of Rochester, New York. He has published four monographs, one edited volume, two coedited volumes, and numerous articles on aspects of Russian film, media, and culture. He has held four large UK Research Council grants and was a national subpanel member in the United Kingdom's 2008 Research Assessment Exercise. He is currently president of the British Association for Slavonic and East European Studies.

Nina L. Khrushcheva is an associate professor of international affairs at the New School in New York City. She is the editor of the Window into Russia series for Project Syndicate: An Association of Newspapers Around the World and the author of *Imagining Nabokov: Russia Between Art and Politics* (2007).

Timothy Langen is an associate professor of Russian and the director of graduate studies in Russian and Slavonic Studies at the University of Missouri. He is the author of *The Stony Dance: Unity and Gesture in Andrey Bely's "Petersburg"* (2005) and coeditor of *Eight Twentieth-Century Russian Plays* (2000), both published by Northwestern University Press.

Martin A. Miller is a professor of Russian history at Duke University. He is the author of *Kropotkin* (1976), *The Russian Revolutionary Émigrés, 1825–1870* (1986), and *Freud and the Bolsheviks: Psychoanalysis in Imperial Russia and the Soviet Union* (1996). He is currently completing a history of the origins of political violence in Russia and France.

Donna Oliver is a professor of Russian at Beloit College. Her research focuses on nineteenth-century Russian literature and literary culture. She has published articles on Dostoevsky and Tolstoy in the *Slavic and East European Journal* and *Tolstoy Studies Journal,* as well as on Eisenstein's work in the theater in *Canadian Slavonic Papers.*

Lynn Ellen Patyk is a visiting assistant professor of Russian studies and history at the University of Florida. Her current work focuses on the literary and cultural history of revolution, terrorism, and human rights in Russia. She is working on a book entitled *Written in Blood: Revolutionary Terrorism and Russian Literary Culture.*

Peter Scotto is an associate professor of Russian language and literature at Mount Holyoke College. His articles on Lermontov, Tsvetaeva, and censorship have appeared in *PMLA* and in *Marina Tsvetaeva: One Hundred Years: Papers from the*

Tsvetaeva Centenary Symposium (1994). He is currently working on an article on Pushkin's prose and is translating the poetry of Alexander Blok.

Ludmilla A. Trigos is an independent scholar who specializes in nineteenth- and twentieth-century Russian literature, cultural mythologies, and violence. She is the author of *The Decembrist Myth in Russian Literature and Culture* (2009) and coedited and contributed to *Under the Sky of My Africa: Alexander Pushkin and Blackness* (Northwestern University Press, 2006). She has taught at Columbia University, Barnard College, Drew University, and New York University.

Val Vinokur is an assistant professor and undergraduate director of literary studies and director of Jewish studies at Eugene Lang College/The New School. His essays, reviews, stories, and poems have appeared in such venues as *Common Knowledge*, the *Boston Review*, *McSweeney's*, the *Russian Review*, *Stanford Slavic Studies*, the *Massachusetts Review*, and the *Journal of Religion and Society*. His book *The Trace of Judaism: Dostoevsky, Babel, Mandelstam, Levinas* was published by Northwestern University Press in 2008. He is a 2008 recipient of a Guggenheim fellowship in the field of translation.